An Everlasting Love

An Everlasting Love

A DEVOTIONAL STUDY OF THE GOSPEL OF JOHN

by John G. Mitchell

with Dick Bohrer

MULTNOMAH PRESS
PORTLAND. OREGON 97266

Scripture references in this volume are from the King James Version of the Bible.

AN EVERLASTING LOVE
© 1982 by Multnomah Press
Portland, Oregon 97266

Printed in the United States of America

First Printing 1982

Library of Congress Catalog Card Number: 82-22285
ISBN 0-88070-005-X

Contents

Foreword

For more than six decades, the author of this exposition of the Gospel of John has been preaching the love and grace of God. During this long period of expository ministry, the author has, like John the Apostle, exalted Christ and warmed his audience with his presentation of the Lord Jesus Christ as the center of our faith and our devotion. It seems fitting that John G. Mitchell, having reached the approximate age of the Apostle when he wrote the Gospel, now presents this intimate insight into the heart of the Savior based on what the Apostle John penned by inspiration of the Holy Spirit.

The Gospel of John has its own peculiar charm among the sixty-six books of the Bible. Its focus is on the Person of Jesus Christ. Its message is that Jesus Christ is the Savior. From the introduction of Jesus Christ as the eternal Word who became flesh to the climax where Peter is questioned about his love for the Savior, the Gospel breathes the love and grace of God and records the exalted revelation of His deity.

What characterizes the writings of the Apostle is precisely what has characterized the expository ministry of the author of this book. Few preachers and faithful expositors of the Word of God have exalted Christ more than John Mitchell. Thousands have been touched by his ministry. This work is a fitting legacy to leave to a new generation of faithful preachers who follow his example.

The Gospel of John is about people, those who were touched by the message of Christ and in whom the Savior's power and grace were manifested. The record of this Gospel is the hall of fame of those who preeminently illustrated what salvation in Christ can accomplish. In this Gospel we meet John the Baptist, Andrew, Simon Peter, Philip, Nathanael, the mother of Jesus, Nicodemus, the woman of Samaria, the nobleman with the sick son, the infirmed man at the pool of Bethesda, and many more. They were people who were saved, healed, and restored.

In his Gospel, John records the first miracle at the wedding in Cana, the great prophecy of the coming of the Holy Spirit, the healing of the blind man, the revelation of Christ as the True Shepherd. As the narrative progresses, we learn about the intimate circle of friends including Mary, Martha, and Lazarus and read the touching story of Mary anointing Christ with her precious spikenard. Only in John's Gospel can we find the Upper Room Discourse with its prophetic foreview of the present dispensation characterized by "ye in Me, and I in you" (John 14:20). Only here in John is the record of the high priestly prayer of Christ (John 17). On the cross He died as no one else had died. He rose as no one else arose. All this was written "that ye might believe that Jesus is the Christ, the Son of God; and that believing ye might have life through His name" (John 20:31).

If this exposition thrills readers with its revelation of Jesus Christ and brings them to trust the Savior and to worship at His nail-pierced feet, then its purpose will have been realized.

John F. Walvoord
President, Dallas Theological Seminary

Preface

"We would see Jesus."

Two men stand before Philip, brushing off the dust from their trip to Jerusalem. Their simple request masks the burning desire which has brought them from their Greek homeland to the Ancient City.

This study answers that request for the reader of John's Gospel. For Dr. John G. Mitchell, Jesus Christ is the center of the book of John.

And who is Jesus Christ?

Jesus Christ is God in human form. He is the heart of the gospel message. He is the One who brings God's everlasting love.

Christ's opponents asked Him Who He thought He was in John chapter 8. His answer was quick. God. "Your father Abraham rejoiced to see My day. I'm El Shaddai. The Almighty One. I'm Abraham's God. I'm Moses' God." He's the Son of God . . . God manifest in the flesh. And He came with explicit purpose.

Jesus Christ came to reveal God. And His everlasting love.

"God so loved the world." This is the crux of John 3:16. Love provided a way for men to be delivered from their sin. Love stepped into the picture and provided a Gift, Jesus, God's only begotten Son, "that whosoever believeth in him should not perish, but have everlasting life." This is the message for the world. But we who believe hear it even more strongly.

Because Jesus Christ came with love for His own.

"Having loved his own which were in the world, he loved them unto the end" (John 13:1). It is the same love—the same divine, infinite, and perfect love which the Father has for the Son, and the Son for the Father—which the Son has for each of His own. "I have declared unto them . . . that the love wherewith thou hast loved me may be in them, and I in them" (John 17:26).

This is Jesus Christ. The Creator God. The Faithful Shepherd. The Gospel of John centers around Him, and Him only. We see the revelation of the Holy God and the love of God in His one Person.

Journey with Dr. Mitchell through the Gospel of John. Much like a trip through the majesties of a beautiful, mountainous countryside, his discussions include trips off the main road to see other parts of the splendor in the scenery. So we enter many more parts of the Bible in addition to John's Gospel. Yet all of this journey brings us close to the beauty of the Lord Jesus Christ. All of his explanations reveal the beauty of God's heart. Because of the careful attention of writer Dick Bohrer to Dr. Mitchell's own unique style and manner of communication, this work preserves the best of the sermons and transcripts from which it was compiled.

Commentaries on John fill shelves of many New Testament libraries. Why another one? Verse by verse studies of the fourth Gospel have given us pages of analysis. Is there need for yet more explanation of its contents? But this one work may be the most important of them all. For its pages are filled with a love for the Savior and a desire to know more about His love for us.

Jeremiah wrote, "The Lord hath appeared of old unto me, saying, I have loved thee with an everlasting love" (31:3). This is the only kind of love God has . . . a perfect, complete, eternal love. This He has shown in Jesus Christ. The One we would see in the Gospel of John.

Editor's Note

For fifteen years this manuscript about the Gospel of John has been on or near my desk. I sensed, each time I worked on it, that I was on holy ground. Many months at a time, I felt I could not work on it because I was not a holy man—holy man enough to do a holy work. It was only when I realized that this book would make unholy men, prone-to-wander-Lord-I-feel-it-men more holy, that I could resume; for it exalts the Lord Jesus Christ Himself, and in so doing, captures hearts.

I also worked diligently to maintain the uniqueness of Dr. Mitchell's material. No transcription, no copy edited version of a man's sermons that doesn't remain faithful to the cadence of his tongue is worth its ink. To remove the vibrations of his voice, that touch of the Tyneside district in England which has marked John G. Mitchell for life, would do violence to any book of his sermons. As a man is known by his words, any edition of his words must remind us on every page of the man who said them.

These sermons were given in 1964-65 when Dr. Mitchell pastored the Central Bible Church in Portland, Oregon. The tapes were transcribed by Miss Jean McNett. Her manuscript of about a thousand pages was virtually error-free. Her little penciled notes in margins, notes of concern for accuracy and clarity, bespoke her own interest in the work and her faithfulness in ministry.

My wife Betty has listened to Dr. Mitchell's more recently recorded radio tapes on the Gospel of John and has taken copious notes which have been unusually helpful in preparing this book.

It has not been difficult to keep the text faithful to Dr. Mitchell's heart as well as to his tongue. God's Word seems to nudge his cup, as it were, and the Living Water that fills him to the brim overflows in love and concern for his listeners. This is not a man who deals in cold truth. The pulsating warmth of his yearning for his Savior and his yearning for men to know Him work at one's heart.

I used to leave the services when Dr. Mitchell spoke longing to become a man of the Book as he is. He is a walking concordance. Give him a Bible word and he'll recite companion verses galore. He brings them from everywhere to play on a biblical theme much like a weaver of nets brings cord upon cord.

He loves God's Word and longs for God's people to become men and women, boys and girls of the Book. He would often admonish those of us who were his students at Multnomah School of the Bible, "Don't you ever read your Bible?"

It is Dr. Mitchell's concern—and my concern—that these pages help readers to "fall in love with the Savior"—to use his own phrase. Anything less than that would make this book mere sounding brass and tinkling cymbal.

Dick Bohrer

Introduction

Who Is Jesus of Nazareth?

Is Jesus of Nazareth the Son of God? Christianity stands or falls on this one question. This was the question that confronted Nathanael at the beginning of Christ's ministry. This is the question that confronts us at the end of the twentieth century.

Is Jesus of Nazareth the Son of God? To Nathanael, the question seemed absurd. The term, "the Son of God," meant nothing less to him than a title of deity. Today many speak glibly of being sons of God, with Jesus being a Son of God like the rest of us, and so the question seems trite. But the force of the question is this: Is Jesus of Nazareth God manifest in the flesh?

"How ridiculous!" Nathanael thought. "Can any good thing come out of *Nazareth*?" (John 1:46). Nazareth was a city known for its sin and moral corruption. The very name became a term of contempt. Can the Messiah come out of Nazareth? Why, the city was never even mentioned by the prophets. Can this Jesus of Nazareth, of despised Nazareth, be the Son of God?

If Jesus Is Not God . . .

If Jesus of Nazareth is not God manifest in the flesh, the implications are disheartening. First, my friends, consider the fact that if Jesus is not God, then we are sinners without a Savior. The very

13

value of the cross is determined by His identity. If Jesus is not God manifest in the flesh, then we have no Savior. If Jesus were only a man, then He died for His own sins. And we are still in our sins. We have no hope.

Furthermore, if Jesus of Nazareth is not God manifest in the flesh, then we are creatures who cannot know our Creator. We are left with no manifestation of God's heart and character.

Creation tells us there is a God, but this natural revelation is limited at best. "The heavens declare the glory of God; and the firmament sheweth his handywork. Day unto day uttereth speech, and night unto night sheweth knowledge" (Psalm 19:1-2). "The invisible things of him from the creation of the world are clearly seen, being understood by the things that are made, even his eternal power and Godhead; so that they are without excuse" (Romans 1:20).

The argument of design declares that we can see God in creation. There must be some Eternal Being who framed the heavens and the earth. The intricate design and precision of creation demands a Designer. (Our whole calendar and time system is based on the order we observe in nature.) Creation tells us there is a God. But it cannot tell us what God is like. If Jesus is not God, we can know nothing about God. We are merely groping in the dark.

One day in Hong Kong I watched a funeral procession. The people were carrying a paper car. They had constructed the automobile out of paper so that the spirit of the dead person would have a vehicle to travel in. Their actions seem foolish, but would we act any differently if we were without Christ? All that we know about God we know because of Christ. If Jesus is not God, then we all are without knowledge of God.

Finally, if Jesus of Nazareth is not God manifest in the flesh, then we are foes of God the Father. We are out of fellowship with God, with no means of approaching Him. Scripture is very clear about this: "No man cometh unto the Father, but by me" (John 14:6). The only way we come back into fellowship with God is through Jesus, His Son. "Our fellowship is with the Father, and with his Son Jesus Christ" (1 John 1:3).

Introduction

But if Jesus is not God the Son, then our fellowship with God is still broken, with no possible means of repair.

God Manifest in the Flesh

Fortunately, the New Testament writers are very explicit about the identity of Jesus Christ. Repeatedly they affirm that Jesus of Nazareth *is* God manifest in the flesh. They were convinced of Christ's deity.

Mark what Nathanael thought of Jesus after he met Him. When Jesus revealed His omniscience to Nathanael, he exclaimed, "Rabbi, thou art the Son of God" (John 1:49). Nathanael's first encounter with Christ not only completely changed his opinion of Christ, but it reversed the course of his life.

Dear Peter likewise declared that Jesus is God manifest in the flesh. In Matthew 16, you remember, the Lord asked the disciples, "What do men say about me?"

"Well, some say you are John the Baptist raised from the dead. Some say you are Elijah. Some say you are Jeremiah. Some say you are one of the prophets."

"Well, what do you think?"

And Peter said, "Thou art the Christ, the Son of the living God."

In John 6, our Lord said, "Except ye eat the flesh of the Son of man and drink his blood, ye have no life in you. Unless you are joined to me, ye have no life. My words, they are spirit and they are life." And the crowds left Him. Christ turned to the twelve and asked, "Will you also go away?"

Peter asked, "Lord, where can we go? Thou alone hast the words of eternal life. And we believe and are sure that Thou art the Christ, the Son of the living God." Peter didn't hesitate. He knew the identity of his Lord.

Listen to Peter in Acts 2. "Ye men of Israel, hear these words; Jesus of Nazareth, a man approved of God among you by miracles and wonders and signs, which God did by him in the midst of you, as ye yourselves also know: Him, being delivered by the determinate counsel and foreknowledge of God, ye have taken, and by wicked hands have crucified and slain: Whom God hath raised up, having loosed the pains of death: because it was not possible that he should be holden of it" (2:22-24).

Go down to verse 32. "This Jesus hath God raised up, whereof we all are witnesses. Therefore being by the right hand of God exalted, and having received of the Father the promise of the Holy Ghost, he hath shed forth this, which ye now see and hear. For David is not ascended into the heavens: but he saith himself, The Lord said unto my Lord, Sit thou on my right hand, Until I make thy foes thy footstool. Therefore let all the house of Israel know assuredly, that God hath made that same Jesus, whom ye have crucified, both Lord and Christ" (2:32-36). The people who heard Peter that day were pierced to the heart, and over 3,000 were added to the church.

All of the Pauline epistles are also based on this one fact: that this Jesus is the Son of God. Philippians 2 describes Jesus Christ as the one, "Who, being in the form of God, thought it not robbery to be equal with God: but made himself of no reputation, and took upon him the form of a servant, and was made in the likeness of men: And being found in fashion as a man, he humbled himself, and became obedient unto death, even the death of the cross. Wherefore God also hath highly exalted him, and given him a name which is above every name: That at the name of Jesus every knee should bow" (2:6-10).

In Colossians, the Lord is "the image of the invisible God" (1:15). It is pleasing to the Godhead that in Jesus all fulness should dwell (1:19). "In him dwelleth all the fulness of the Godhead bodily" (2:9).

The writer of Hebrews exalts Christ as well. "We see Jesus . . . crowned with glory and honour; that he by the grace of God should taste death for every man" (2:9).

The whole New Testament is based on this one fact: Jesus of Nazareth is God manifest in the flesh.

Go on through the Bible. You'll find the fact again and again. The God of glory appeared to Abraham in Ur of the Chaldees and said, "Get out." Abraham obeyed God and went out, not knowing whither he went (join Hebrews 11:8 with Acts 7:2-3). Now Paul identifies the God of glory as Jesus in 1 Corinthians 2:8, where he says that had they, the princes of this world, known it, they would not have crucified the Lord of glory. Jesus Himself said, "Your father Abraham rejoiced to see my day: and he saw it, and was glad" (John 8:56). When Abraham heard the Son of Man, God manifest in the flesh, he obeyed. What do you do?

The Lord came to others. Samuel, when he was disturbed from his sleep, did not know how to account for the voice speaking to him in the night, you remember. He thought Eli, the old man, was calling him. Eli denied calling him and instructed the boy Samuel to "go, lie down: and it shall be, if he call thee, that thou shalt say, Speak, Lord; for thy servant heareth" (1 Samuel 3:9). When the Lord appeared to Samuel the fourth time, there was a ready response: "Speak; for thy servant heareth" (3:10). Saul had a similar response when he met the Lord on the road to Damascus. He cried out, "Lord, what wilt thou have me to do?" (Acts 9:6). Afterward he could say, "Have I not seen Jesus Christ our Lord?" (1 Corinthians 9:1).

Isaiah also had a marvelous encounter with the Lord. He wrote: "In the year that king Uzziah died I saw also the Lord sitting upon a throne, high and lifted up, and his train filled the temple" (Isaiah 6:1). Above the Lord seraphim cried out, "Holy, holy, holy, is the Lord of hosts: the whole earth is full of his glory" (6:3). Isaiah fell on his face and cried out, "I am . . . unclean," and an angel touched him. Then Isaiah heard the voice of the Lord saying, "Whom shall I send, and who will go for us?" And Isaiah said, "Here am I; send me" (6:8). Whom did Isaiah see? We are told in John 12:41 that Isaiah "saw his glory, and spake of Him." When Isaiah saw the Lord Jesus, he said, "Here am I, send me."

The Christian's Response

What has been the response in your heart, my friend? If you are a Christian, you have already affirmed that Jesus of Nazareth is God manifest in the flesh. You have already confessed with your mouth that Jesus is Lord.

But what of the great majority of the world with its billions of souls in spiritual darkness? God has placed us in this generation for a specific purpose. He wants each of us to share with our generation the good news that Jesus is God manifest.

Will you be like Abraham, who obeyed God's call to go "unto a land that I will shew thee?" Abraham went out, not knowing whither he went. He obeyed God. Mark the simplicity and courage of his faith in obedience.

Will you be like dear John, the apostle? He could write, "That which we have seen and heard declare we unto you, that ye also may have fellowship with us: and truly our fellowship is with the Father, and with his Son Jesus Christ" (1 John 1:3).

My friend, may there be in us a real passion for the Son of God, a real heart hunger to be able to say, "Here am I, send me." May we have a real desire to be found with hearts obedient and devoted to the Son of God Himself. This will free us from all pettiness. It will free us from jealousy and envy. To make Him the very object of our heart's affection and devotion will free us from the things that hinder us from being usable in the hands of God.

My fellow believer in Christ, may I plead with you to lay hold of the things of Christ? Oh, that we might have an increased capacity for the truth, and a greater longing to be found usable by Him.

What a wonderful thing it would be if you would dedicate your life to the Lord Jesus Christ and be found usable by Him in reaching our present generation. My, what God could do with you if you were yielded and committed to Jesus of Nazareth. The Gospel through John calls you to such a commitment, a commitment to God manifest in the flesh.

John 1

Christ, The Word

Theme of the Gospel through John

The Gospel of John is a revelation of Jesus Christ as the Son of God. The great question in John is this: "Is Jesus the Son of God?" When you speak of Jesus as the Son of God, you are speaking of Him in His person. This is why, when you come to John 20:31, you find that "these things are written, that ye might believe that Jesus is the Christ, the Son of God; and that believing ye might have life through his name." From the first verse of the Gospel, this theme is built.

Three verses form the primary thesis of John's Gospel. From this foundation he builds his message. All you read in John's Gospel—all the seven miracles the Lord did, all His testimony, all His claims—is nothing more than the proof of these three verses.

> **1:1, 14, 18.** *In the beginning was the Word, and the Word was with God, and the Word was God. And the Word was made flesh and dwelt among us, (and we beheld his glory, the glory as of the only begotten of the Father), full of grace and truth. No man hath seen God at any time; the only begotten Son, which is in the bosom of the Father, he hath declared him.*

In verse 1 you have Jesus in His preincarnation. In the beginning, way back in eternity past, long before history began, Jesus

Christ was God. He did not become the Son of God when He was manifested to men. Rather, being the Son of God, Jesus Christ was manifested to men.

In verses 14 and 18 you have the incarnation of Jesus. Christ is pictured as stepping out of eternity and into human history. The One who was in the form of God became fashioned as a man (Philippians 2:6-8). God tabernacled among men. No man has ever seen God in all of His fullness, but the Son came as a man to reveal the Father. In Christ we see the very heart of God.

John the apostle is not trying to simply write his recollections about the life of Christ. He is not recording vague impressions about his Master. John is deliberately incomplete about many events in the life of Christ in his effort to clearly communicate the intent of his Gospel through specific signs, declarations, and claims of Christ.

John admits the incompleteness of his Gospel in the conclusion of his book. "There are also many other things which Jesus did," John writes, "the which, if they should be written every one, I suppose that even the world itself could not contain the books that should be written" (John 21:25). John is very selective about what he writes. Much is left out, such as the genealogy and childhood of Christ. These things are not crucial to the development of John's theme. Instead, John chose to include "these things" that we might believe that Jesus is the Christ, the Son of God.

Let me speak to your heart for a moment. The Lord Jesus, as the Son of God, came out from the very heart of God. He came not so much to reveal the power of God, nor to reveal the character of God. He came to reveal the very heart of God. He wants you to know God personally, intimately, surely.

And I want to say at the outset, very frankly, that if we do not know God intimately and personally, it is not because He has not revealed Himself. If you do not know the Lord Jesus Christ as your own personal Savior, if you have never come into relationship with Him, and if your joy is not filled full and your peace is not there, it is because you have not accepted the marvelous provision that Christ came to make for you, whereby you can be brought into fellowship and relationship with God.

I say it is a wonderful thing that this Jesus of Nazareth wants you to know that He was in the beginning with God, that He was preexistent, that even before Abraham was born into the world, Jesus could say, "I am." He was made manifest. He came into the human race as a Man in the midst of men, and He came for the express purpose of revealing the very heart of God to man.

You see, in your Old Testament you have the revelation of God's power and character in everything from Genesis to Malachi. For example, the power of God is displayed in creation. Men should know God through His creative acts; they should know that He is a Person and that He is God. For we read that "the heavens declare the glory of God; and the firmament sheweth his handy-work" (Psalm 19:1). As Paul could write, "the invisible things of him from the creation of the world are clearly seen, being understood by the things that are made, even his eternal power and Godhead; so that they are without excuse" (Romans 1:20).

And God also revealed to man His own character. Even the pagan world knows this. Read, for example, the laws of Hammurabi, the great Babylonian lawgiver, who lived before the time of Moses. When Hammurabi gave his code for his nation, he gave it on the basis of the light he had received, even though he was a pagan.

Read the books of Exodus and Leviticus and see something of the holy character of God. "Neither shall ye profane my holy name" (Leviticus 22:32). "I am the Lord, and there is none else, there is no God beside me," Isaiah reported of Him (45:5). The revelation of God's character—that He is holy, righteous, and just—is revealed throughout your Old Testament.

Now when you come to John's Gospel, you find that Christ came out from the very heart of God to reveal God's heart for you.

The yearning of God's heart is for men and women to know Him and to fellowship with Him. God's great desire for every Christian is twofold; it covers the whole of Christian life and ministry. First, God yearns for your ultimate, continual fellowship, and has made provision for it if you are His child. Second, God desires that the life of His Son might be evident through you. God wants your generation to see the Gospel through you.

Jesus Christ did not come merely to reveal the power or character of God, but to reveal His heart. He doesn't just want us to know facts *about* Him. God longs for us to know Him personally and intimately.

Christ's Pre-incarnation (1:1-5)

Before Jesus Christ was manifested to men to reveal the heart of God, He was already the Son of God. Christ was active as God long before His incarnation. John uses four different titles to describe Christ's Person and work in the opening verses of his Gospel (1:1-5).

First, Christ is introduced as the Word.

> **1:1-2.** *In the beginning was the Word, and the Word was with God, and the Word was God. The same was in the beginning with God.*

Each phrase of verse 1 reveals an important aspect about the Word, Jesus Christ. "In the beginning was the Word. . . ." John attracts you to the One who is the Word, the divine expression of God. The Word contains the totality of the wisdom of God. The Lord is elsewhere described as "Christ the power of God, and the wisdom of God" (1 Corinthians 1:24). Colossians 2:3 goes on to say that God has hidden in Christ all the treasures of wisdom and knowledge.

". . . and the Word was with God. . . ." The plurality of the Godhead is clearly seen here. Christ was *with* God. Go back to Genesis. Mark the plural pronouns used in these verses where God is speaking: "Let *us* make man in *our* image, after *our* likeness. . . . Behold, the man is become as one of *us*. . . . Let *us* go down, and there confound their language" (Genesis 1:26; 3:22; 11:7). Colossians 1:19 says: "For it pleased the Father that in him should all fulness dwell." Christ is a full and distinct person in the Godhead.

". . . and the Word was God." This is perhaps the most straight-forward statement of Christ's deity that John could make. Christ was (and is) God. The New Testament affirms this declaration many times over. Colossians 1:15 says that He is "the image of the invisible God," God manifest to men. Hebrews 1:3 describes Christ as "the express image" of God's character and person.

A second title is now used for Christ's Person. He is presented as the Creator.

> **1:3.** *All things were made by him; and without him was not any thing made that was made.*

Proverbs 8 speaks of Christ as being intimately involved with God the Father in creation. Hebrews says that God has spoken to us by His Son, "by whom also he made the worlds" (1:2), and that "the worlds were framed by the word of God" (11:3). By Christ "were all things created, that are in heaven, and that are in earth" (Colossians 1:16).

Third, Christ is spoken of as the Life. **1:4.** *In him was life. . . .* This is the key verse of the Gospel through John. In Christ is life. Apart from Him there is no life. This concept continues throughout John's writings.

The Gospel through John repeatedly speaks of Christ as the life. "He that believeth on the Son hath everlasting life: and he that be-lieveth not the Son shall not see life" (3:36). "He that heareth my word, and believeth on him that sent me, hath everlasting life, and . . . is passed from death unto life" (5:24). "If a man keep my say-ing, he shall never see death" (8:51). The life that Christ gives is His own life eternal.

The first epistle of John likewise refers to Christ as the source of life. "He that hath the Son hath life; and he that hath not the Son of God hath not life. These things have I written unto you that believe on the name of the Son of God; that ye may know that ye have eter-nal life" (5:12-13). While the Gospel through John tells us how to *receive* life, this epistle tells us how to *enjoy* life in Christ.

A person never really lives—he has no spiritual life—until he is in Christ. You may be good; you may be moral; you may be religious; you may be a wonderful man or woman. But unless you are in Christ, you have no life.

"Well," you say, "Mr. Mitchell, you are kind of narrow in your thinking, aren't you?"

That's right. Broad is the way that leads to destruction. Narrow is the way that leads to life eternal. If Jesus does not give us life, then tell me, my friend, where are you going to get it? Study all the philosophers. They cannot give you life. They don't even offer it. Study your pagan religions. They have no life. It is a hopeless situation without Christ. In Him and only in Him is life.

Fourth, Christ is revealed as the Light.

1:4-5. . . . *and the life was the light of men. And the light shineth in darkness; and the darkness comprehended it not.*

Christ who is the life is also the light. This is not the only time God is pictured as the source of both life and light. The psalmist says of God, "With thee is the fountain of life: in thy light shall we see light" (Psalm 36:9).

Christ is the light of the world. All of the truth that man has learned from Adam until now has come from Him. Any light that man has about God and morality, he has received from Christ. Where did Hammurabi gain the insights he did on morality? What light he had on morality he received. It was planted in him from the Lord. No matter where you go in the world today, all men still have some light, deep down in their hearts, about what God expects of them.

All men have some light from Christ. It's not that the world can't comprehend the light. Verse 5 better reads that they could not "apprehend" it. The world cannot put the light out. Men have tried since the days of Cain to apprehend and eliminate the light. When men are exposed to the light, they protest: "Don't talk to me about Christ. Don't talk to me about your Savior. I don't want to listen to you. I'd rather not know. . . ."

If you do personal work, you will discover this. With some of these men you can talk about anything under heaven. They will listen to you. But it is a strange thing that, when you mention the name of the Lord Jesus with reverence, and suggest their responsibility to Him, they do not want to hear about it. They are unresponsive to the light of Christ.

John the Baptist's Preparation (1:6-36)

John Attracts Others to Christ (1:6-13)

> **1:6-13.** *There was a man sent from God, whose name was John. The same came for a witness, to bear witness of the Light, that all men through him might believe. He was not that Light, but was sent to bear witness of that Light. That was the true Light, which lighteth every man that cometh into the world.*
>
> *He was in the world, and the world was made by him, and the world knew him not. He came unto his own, and his own received him not. But as many as received him, to them gave he power to become the sons of God, even to them that believe on his name: Which were born, not of blood, nor of the will of the flesh, nor of the will of man, but of God.*

Mark that man is in such darkness that God had to send a witness to the light. God sent a man named John the Baptist. Imagine the darkness of the world that God would need to send a witness to Christ, the light!

You would probably call me a fool if I were to stand outside on a sunny day and say, "Do you see the sun up there? That is a light." Everyone already knows that. A light does not need a witness to attract others to it. People already recognize it as a light. But man is in such moral and spiritual darkness that God had to send a messenger to men to bear witness to the light.

Who was John? He was just a witness. John came to attract others to Jesus Christ, for Jesus is the light. Christ repeatedly claimed to be the light. "I am the light of the world" (John 8:12). "As long as I am in the world, I am the light of the world" (John

9:5). "Yet a little while is the light with you. . . . While ye have light, believe in the light" (John 12:35-36). John's responsibility was not to attract other people to himself. John's responsibility was to attract others to Christ, the light of the world.

My Christian friend, that's *our* responsibility as well. It is not our responsibility to attract others to ourselves. We do that naturally. Some people go out of their way to do that. But notice that John's great responsibility was to attract others to Christ, the light of the world. John was faithful to fulfill his responsibility, even though it cost him his life.

May I ask you a question? Are you faithful in fulfilling your responsibility? God sent John as a witness of the light. He has sent each one of us as witnesses as well. Why didn't you live one hundred years ago? Why didn't you live nineteen hundred years ago? God put you in this generation, at this time, with a distinct personality. He has redeemed you and saved you. He has indwelt you by His Spirit for one job: To bear witness of the light, that all men through you might believe. Our Lord said, "Ye are witnesses" (Luke 24:48). He went on to say, "Ye shall receive power, after that the Holy Ghost is come upon you: and ye shall be witnesses unto me both in Jerusalem, and in all Judaea, and in Samaria, and unto the uttermost part of the earth" (Acts 1:8). "We are ambassadors for Christ" (2 Corinthians 5:20), beseeching men in Christ's stead to be reconciled to God.

John was a witness of the light in the midst of moral darkness. In the same way we are God's witnesses in the midst of moral and spiritual darkness. Christ sent Paul to be a witness and to turn men "from darkness to light" (Acts 26:18). This darkness is produced by Satan, who "hath blinded the minds of them which believe not, lest the light of the glorious gospel of Christ . . . should shine unto them" (2 Corinthians 4:4). We not only wrestle against Satan, but "against the rulers of the darkness of this world" (Ephesians 6:12). The world is in darkness morally and spiritually. We cannot let men go on in their darkness. We must be lights shining in a dark place until the day dawns.

A friend once said to me, "I wish you would pray for me that I might have another job."

I said, "Why do you want another job? You already have a good one."

He said, "Well, I'm the only Christian in the plant."

"I'm going to pray that you will stay," I responded.

"Don't pray that," he protested.

"I'm going to pray that you will stick with your job. What would you want instead?"

"I want a job where there are other Christians."

"Well, that's very nice. That would be wonderful. But why do you suppose God has put you there in that particular plant? You are the only light that is there."

"But I'm a very, very small light."

"Yes, but if you go into a dark room and strike a match, the little match will light up the whole room."

Perhaps you are only a little old match where you live or work, but you are a light. Strike the match, and shine!

"There was a man (or woman) sent from God, whose name was . . . ." What is your name? Put your name at the end of that verse. You have been sent from God to attract others to the Savior. You have been sent to bear witness of the light that all men might believe.

John Worships Christ (1:15-28)

> **1:15-17.** *John bare witness of him, and cried, saying, This was he of whom I spake, He that cometh after me is preferred before me: for he was before me. And of his fulness have all we received, and grace for grace. For the law was given by Moses, but grace and truth came by Jesus Christ.*

Here you have John as a worshiper. Remember that Christ said of John, "Among them that are born of women there hath not risen a greater than John the Baptist" (Matthew 11:11). John was the greatest born of women! And yet, John did not seek to exalt himself, but humbly magnified Christ.

I want you to mark that, as a worshiper, John hides behind the Savior. In verse 7 we read that John came "to bear witness of the Light." Now in verse 15 we have his witness, what he has to say about Christ. If I may take the sense of the passage, John was continually, everlastingly talking about one Person—Jesus Christ. John hides behind the Savior, saying, "He is the preferred One. He was before me."

John is declaring two things about the Lord. He observes that Jesus Christ is unique because He is the preeminent One. John calls Him the preferred One again in verse 27: "He it is, who coming after me is preferred before me, whose shoe's latchet I am not worthy to unloose."

Notice the remarkable humility of John! Matthew and Luke record that John was not afraid to thunder at the Pharisees and say, "O generation of vipers, who hath warned you to flee from the wrath to come?" (Matthew 3:7; Luke 3:7). But you don't find that here. John is the worshiper in this passage. *He* is the preeminent One. "I am not even fit to untie His shoelace."

John also observes that Christ is unique because He is the preexistent One. "He was before me." John doesn't see the Lord as just a man who happened to be born before John was born. Luke records that John was born some three months before Christ's birth. Instead, John worships Christ as the preexistent Son of God.

> **1:19-28.** *And this is the record of John, when the Jews sent priests and Levites from Jerusalem to ask him, Who art Thou? And he confessed, and denied not; but confessed, I am not the Christ. And they asked him, What then? Art thou Elias? And he saith, I am not. Art thou that prophet? And he answered, No. Then said they unto him, Who art thou? that we may give an answer to them that sent us. What sayest thou of thyself? He said, I am the voice of one crying in the wilderness, Make straight the way of the Lord, as said the prophet Esaias. And they which were sent were of*

the Pharisees. And they asked him, and said unto
him, Why baptizest thou then, if thou be not that
Christ, not Elias, neither that prophet? John an-
swered them, saying, I baptize with water: but there
standeth one among you, whom ye know not; He it is,
who coming after me is preferred before me, whose
shoe's latchet I am not worthy to unloose. These
things were done in Bethabara beyond Jordan, where
John was baptizing.

While John was observing the uniqueness of Christ, he was the center of attraction among the Jews. The great multitudes were following John. He was in Bethabara near the Jordan preaching repentance and baptizing those who came confessing their sins. John caused such a stir across the whole nation that the Pharisees sent a committee of priests and Levites to talk to him. You can just see them dressed in their priestly robes, going down from Jerusalem to the Jordan to find out who this man is who is baptizing. Apparently there was some intimation among the Jews that, when the Messiah finally came, this would be one of the manifestations.

"Who are you?" they asked.

John's answer is very simple. He confessed and said, "I am not the Christ."

John recognized that these men had one thing in their minds: Is this the Messiah? The time was ripe for the coming of the Messiah. The Jews were groaning under the heel of Rome. They yearned for the Deliverer. They were looking for the coming of the Messiah. This was in their minds when they asked John, "Who are you?"

John said, "I am not the Christ."

They asked him, "Who are you? Are you Elijah?" This committee of priests and Levites referred to Malachi 4:5, where the Lord says, "Behold, I will send you Elijah the prophet before the coming of the great and dreadful day of the Lord." "Are you Elijah?" they asked.

John said, "I am not."

Notice that these men were seeking to get John occupied with

John. This is a common thing. Go back to the book of Genesis, chapter 3. All the devil had to do was to get Eve occupied with Eve, and she was deceived into sinning. But John is so occupied with the Savior that he is a worshiper, and he is not going to let anything stand between him and his occupation with the Lord.

How easy it is for us to be sidetracked from worshiping the Son of God. How much do we really worship the Savior? Let us examine our hearts and be honest before God. Things tend to pile up in our lives and obscure our vision of the Savior. John refused to have his vision filled with anyone but Christ.

"Who are you, John?"

"I am not the Christ."

"Well, then, are you Elijah?" They were sticking to their Old Testament.

"I am not."

"Are you that prophet?" Now they were thinking of Deuteronomy 18:18, where the Lord told Moses, "I will raise them up a Prophet from among their brethren, like unto thee. . . ."

John's answer this time is extremely brief. First he said, "I am not the Christ." Are you Elijah? "I am not." Are you that prophet?

"No." John refused to become self-occupied. John denied any claims to be someone he was not. John simply said of himself, "I am the voice of one crying in the wilderness." He draws them back to Isaiah 40:3. I say, I love this man John. John was not introspective and egotistical. "I am only a voice. I am satisfied to be just a voice."

Believer, would you be satisfied to be just a voice?

Oh, I want a big church, you say.

Do you?

I want to be a great missionary.

Do you?

I want to be a great leader.

Do you? Then you are not a worshiper. Jeremiah wisely warned his servant Baruch, "Seekest thou great things for thyself? seek them not" (Jeremiah 45:5). If we are worshipers, then we must be content to be just voices crying in the wilderness.

Crying where? In Jerusalem?

No.

In the temple?

No. In the wilderness. John was preaching in a vast wilderness. Whether you take it geographically or whether you take it morally and spiritually, there was a need for a voice in that wilderness. Similarly, what a need there is for voices, yours and mine, to exalt the Savior because of the spiritual and moral wilderness in which we live today.

Oh, that we would be worshipers. We cannot divorce testimony from worship. Just as much as we really worship the Lord, just that far we will bear testimony for Him!

John Bears Testimony Concerning Christ (1:29-36)

> **1:29-36.** *The next day John seeth Jesus coming unto him, and saith, Behold the Lamb of God, which taketh away the sin of the world. This is he of whom I said, After me cometh a man which is preferred before me: for he was before me. And I knew him not: but that he should be made manifest to Israel, therefore am I come baptizing with water. And John bare record, saying, I saw the Spirit descending from heaven like a dove, and it abode upon him. And I knew him not: but he that sent me to baptize with water, the same said unto me, Upon whom thou shalt see the Spirit descending, and remaining on him, the same is he which baptizeth with the Holy Ghost. And I saw, and bare record that this is the Son of God.*
>
> *Again the next day after John stood, and two of his disciples; And looking upon Jesus as he walked, he saith, Behold the Lamb of God!*

Not only did John give Christ the preferred place and hide behind Him, not only was John the worshiper being occupied with Him, but he bore testimony concerning His person. He proclaimed three important facts about Christ's identity.

First, John testified that Christ is the Lamb of God. In verse 29 John saw Jesus and said, "Behold the Lamb of God, which taketh away the sin of the world." Jesus is the One who was predicted to be the great sacrifice for the sins of others. He is the One of whom the prophets wrote.

The ram that God provided for Abraham, as well as Isaac his son, are types of Christ (Genesis 22). The passover lamb is another type of Christ (Exodus 12). The various sacrifices instituted by Moses are even more elaborate types of Christ (Leviticus 1-7).

Later, when the Jews had corrupted the sacrificial system and forgotten its true meaning, Isaiah predicted the coming of the Messiah as one who "was afflicted, yet he opened not his mouth: he is brought as a lamb to the slaughter, and as a sheep before her shearers is dumb, so he openeth not his mouth" (Isaiah 53:7). Christ came centuries later as the fulfillment of this prophecy. John told the crowds, "Behold the Lamb of God, which taketh away the sin of the world."

In verse 36 John saw Jesus again and repeated his statement, "Behold the Lamb of God." When John said this, two of his disciples realized what he was saying, and they left John to follow Christ. Have you ever stopped to consider that John preached in such a way that he lost his followers? What humility John must have had.

What would you think of a preacher who told his congregation, "Now next Sunday go over to the church down the street and hear Brother So-and-so. He will tell you more about Christ than I can tell you, and that is where you ought to go"? Have you ever heard a preacher say that? Go elsewhere? Never! This always gets into my heart, that dear John was willing to lose his own disciples, if they followed Jesus.

The second fact about Christ's identity is John's testimony that Christ is the Baptizer with the Spirit. In verse 33 John said that Jesus "is he which baptizeth with the Holy Ghost." John could say this because he had seen the Spirit descend on Jesus, coming down like a dove. John points to Jesus as the only One who could say, "I

will pour out my spirit upon all flesh" (Joel 2:28; see John 20:22).
"I can indeed baptize you with water," John said. "That is as far as I
can go. But He is the only One who can baptize you with the Holy
Spirit."

In these days of confusion, I want to make this very clear. God is
the *only* one who can baptize with the Spirit. A person can't work
up to it. As Christians, we all have been baptized by one Spirit into
one body, and we all have been made to drink of that same Spirit
(1 Corinthians 12:13). Christ is the One who shall baptize you with
the Holy Spirit, John says.

Third, John testified that Christ is the Son of God. In verse 34
John gave record "that this is the Son of God." This was a tremendous statement for John to make as a Jew. He was saying that Jesus
was none other than God incarnate. What an impact this testimony
must have had on those who heard John. John had been gathering
the people of Israel together. He had been looked upon as a
prophet. He had taken the country by storm. And then he turned
around and said, "I bare record that this Jesus is the Son of God."
No wonder John's disciples left him and followed Christ.

Four Who Found Christ (1:37-51)

1:37-51. *And the two disciples heard him speak,
and they followed Jesus. Then Jesus turned, and saw
them following, and saith unto them, What seek ye?
They said unto him, Rabbi, (which is to say, being interpreted, Master,) where dwellest thou? He saith
unto them, Come and see. They came and saw where
he dwelt, and abode with him that day: for it was about
the tenth hour. One of the two which heard John
speak, and followed him, was Andrew, Simon Peter's
brother. He first findeth his own brother Simon, and
saith unto him, We have found the Messias, which is,
being interpreted, the Christ. And he brought him to
Jesus. And when Jesus beheld him, he said, Thou art
Simon the son of Jona: thou shalt be called Cephas,*

which is by interpretation, A stone.

The day following Jesus would go forth into Galilee, and findeth Philip, and saith unto him, Follow me. Now Philip was of Bethsaida, the city of Andrew and Peter. Philip findeth Nathanael, and saith unto him, We have found him, of whom Moses in the law, and the prophets, did write, Jesus of Nazareth, the son of Joseph. And Nathanael said unto him, Can there any good thing come out of Nazareth? Philip saith unto him, Come and see. Jesus saw Nathanael coming to him, and saith of him, Behold an Israelite indeed, in whom is no guile! Nathanael saith unto him, Whence knowest thou me? Jesus answered and said unto him, Before that Philip called thee, when thou wast under the fig tree, I saw thee. Nathanael answered and saith unto him, Rabbi, thou art the Son of God; thou art the King of Israel. Jesus answered and said unto him, Because I said unto thee, I saw thee under the fig tree, believest thou? thou shalt see greater things than these. And he saith unto him, Verily, verily, I say unto you, Hereafter ye shall see heaven open, and the angels of God ascending and descending upon the Son of man.

After John the Baptist testified publicly concerning Christ's identity (as the Lamb of God, the Baptizer with the Spirit, and the Son of God), John fades out of the picture in the Gospel through John. He appears only one more time at the end of chapter 3. Christ's public ministry is about to start. Before Christ begins, however, He gathers several disciples.

In this passage we read of four different individuals who come to the Savior in four different ways. The longing of each of their hearts was to see the Messiah, and to know Him. After meeting Christ, each man professed faith in Jesus of Nazareth, the Son of God. Every one of them was satisfied when he met the Lord.

The first man who came to Christ and became one of His disciples was Andrew. He was brought to Christ through the testimony of John the Baptist, for he was one of the two disciples that heard John's testimony (1:35-36). Who was the other disciple of John the Baptist who followed Christ? I feel it may have been John who became an apostle, and later wrote this Gospel.

Andrew spent the latter part of the afternoon with Christ, from 4:00 P.M. until later that day (1:39). After Andrew had a glimpse of the Savior, he was never the same. Andrew never went back to John the Baptist. After meeting Christ, no one else could ever satisfy him.

After a few hours with the Savior, Andrew could contain himself no longer. He immediately went out to find his brother Simon. "We have found the Messiah!" Andrew told Simon (1:41). "We have found Him!"

Peter became the second man to come to Christ. The witness of his brother Andrew was all he needed to be brought to Jesus. Little is recorded of Peter's encounter with Christ, except that Christ gave him a new name—Cephas, which means a stone (1:42). Peter's confession is omitted here, although another confession by Peter is recorded later (John 6:68-69).

The third man who came to Christ was Philip. He became a disciple of Christ after hearing the call of Christ to "Follow me" (1:43). Like Andrew, Philip was an evangelist. After spending a little time with Christ, Philip went out to find his friend Nathanael. "Nathanael, we have found him," Philip said. "Him of whom Moses in the law, and the prophets, did write, Jesus of Nazareth" (1:45). Philip professed that Christ was the predicted Messiah.

Nathanael, as we considered earlier, was quite reluctant to come to Christ. Notice that Philip didn't try to argue with him. He simply said, "Come and see" (1:46). The truth is never imparted by argument. Instead, it is imparted to open hearts.

After hearing the words of Christ, Nathanael recognized the omniscience of Christ. "How do you know me?" Nathanael asked. Christ replied, "Before Philip called you, while you were under the fig tree, I saw you" (1:48). Nathanael was astonished at this sign of Christ's deity, and professed, "Rabbi, thou art the Son of God;

thou art the King of Israel" (1:49).

What was Nathanael doing under the fig tree? I believe he was alone worshiping God. A short time later he was with Philip, worshiping Christ as the Son of God. That one encounter with Christ changed his life. And Christ predicted that he would "see heaven open, and the angels of God ascending and descending upon the Son of man" (1:51). This refers to Christ's second coming to the earth as the King of Kings and Lord of Lords.

Andrew. Peter. Philip. Nathanael. They were four men who longed to find the Messiah. Notice that although each man found Christ in a different way, they all came to Christ. The only way we can find God is to come to Christ. There is no other way.

The cry of Job is the cry of men down through the ages: "Oh that I knew where I might find him!" (Job 23:3). Oh that I might find God! And yet David wisely counseled Solomon, "If thou seek him, he will be found of thee" (1 Chronicles 28:9). Imagine the excitement of Philip when he told Nathanael, "We have found him!" (1:45). Wherever there is a heart that means business and wants to meet the Lord, He will be found of him. The great desire of the heart of God is that He might bring people to Himself, whether it is through the testimony or preaching of men, or through the conviction of His Word. Hungry hearts are always filled.

Today there are many hungry hearts. Let us present to these people the precious Word of God so that they can say with Philip, "We have found Him!"

John 2

Christ, The Creator

The Prophetic Picture in John 1-2

The very first picture of Jesus Christ in the Gospel through John, after the declaration of His person and the drawing of disciples to Himself, is at a marriage feast where He makes everyone happy. It is a wonderful picture.

But before I take it up, it might be well to notice the wonderful dispensational picture that is given to us in John 1-2. You have at the end of the first chapter the restoration of Israel's joy at His second coming (1:51). In 1:29 you have the cross: "Behold the Lamb of God, which taketh away the sin of the world." After John the Baptist's testimony about Jesus, Christ becomes the center of gathering for two blessed days. No longer is John the Baptist gathering disciples, but the Lord Jesus becomes the center of attraction. John, the announcer, becomes the worshiper.

John 2 begins, "The third day there was a marriage in Cana of Galilee," and He manifested forth His glory. His mother, and brethren, and disciples were there. I say it is a wonderful picture of the program of God, reminding one of Hosea 5:15-6:2—

> I will go and return to my place, till they acknowledge their offense, and seek my face: in their affliction they will seek me early.
>
> Come, and let us return unto the Lord: for he hath torn, and he will heal us; he hath smitten, and he will

bind us up. After two days will he revive us: in the third
day he will raise us up, and we shall live in his sight.

And our Lord could say at the end of Matthew 23, "Ye shall not
see me henceforth, till ye shall say, Blessed is he that cometh in the
name of the Lord" (23:39). If you want to follow through on the
prophetic picture, there it is.

The First Sign: Turning Water into Wine (2:1-11)
—Christ at a Wedding in Cana

Christ's Presence at the Wedding (2:1-2)

2:1-2. *And the third day there was a marriage in
Cana of Galilee; and the mother of Jesus was there:
And both Jesus was called, and his disciples, to the
marriage.*

Let us come back to John 2 with respect to a personal word for
our hearts. The marriage was held in Cana of Galilee. There is a
possibility that this may have come about because of Nathanael. At
the end of John 1 you have Nathanael's coming to the Lord; in John
21:2 we read that Nathanael was of Cana of Galilee. Now there is
no question in my mind that Mary had relatives there as well, and
that this was a family affair. Mark that the marriage was not in the
temple; it was in a home.

The Lord Jesus went to the wedding feast to make Himself
known and to enjoy the fellowship of other people. I am glad for
this. A wedding is a place of joy and thanksgiving. And the Lord
was there. He did not put Himself off in a corner to hide. He went
where people were. One of the first things our Lord did was to
sanctify and bless the marriage of a young couple. It is a wonderful
thing to have the Lord there to sanctify that union with His own
presence.

Mary's Petition at the Wedding (2:3-5)

> **2:3-5.** *And when they wanted wine, the mother of Jesus saith unto him, They have no wine. Jesus saith unto her, Woman, what have I to do with thee? mine hour is not yet come. His mother saith unto the servants, Whatsoever he saith unto you, do it.*

Sometime during the wedding feast, Mary came to the Savior and said, "They have no wine." I think her statement indicates what was in her heart and mind. For almost thirty years Mary and Jesus (and His brothers) had been in Nazareth. Mary had seen the wonderful perfection of His character. She remembered the angel Gabriel had said that the holy thing that was to be born of her "shall be called the Son of the Highest: and the Lord God shall give unto him the throne of his father David: And he shall reign over the house of Jacob forever; and of his kingdom there shall be no end" (Luke 1:32-33).

"But they have no wine." I think the implication was, "Son, it is about time You revealed who You are to others." Mary had kept this knowledge deep within her heart. She had a secret. She had not publicized the fact that her firstborn son was the Messiah, born of the Spirit. She was saying in effect, "Son, they have no wine. Isn't it time You displayed Your power? Isn't it time You revealed Yourself as the Messiah, as the One who is going to reign upon David's throne? Isn't it time to do this?"

He had been baptized by John who had declared, "I saw, and bear record that this is the Son of God." "Now," Mary says, "manifest yourself. They have no wine."

The Lord's answer amazes me. He said, "Woman, what have I to do with thee? mine hour is not yet come." When He called His mother "Woman," I do not believe He said it disrespectfully. In John 19, for instance, He said to John while He hung on the cross, "Behold thy *mother!*" (19:27). On the other hand, He said to Mary, *"Woman, behold thy son!"* (19:26).

"Woman, what have I to do with thee?" Jesus was not being rude to His mother. He was simply saying, "Woman, your purpose and

My purpose do not agree. We are not one as to when I should reveal Myself for who I am. What do My purposes have to do with yours? Woman, what have I to do with thee?"

"Mine hour is not yet come." Jesus was not putting His mother off, or stalling for time. Rather He was saying, "We do not have the same thought in this matter. It is not My time to reveal Myself. I will say when it is time to reveal Myself. Mine hour is not yet come."

Three times in this Gospel John records that Christ's hour had not come. The first time, He made this statement to His mother (2:4). Later, He twice eluded capture because "his hour was not yet come" (7:30; 8:20). Mark that it wasn't until the end of His ministry that He could say, "The hour is come, that the Son of man should be glorified," (12:23). The night of His betrayal He prayed, "Father, the hour is come; glorify thy Son, that thy Son also may glorify thee" (17:1). The hour for the glorification of the Father through the Son was at the cross and in the resurrection, but in John 2, that hour had not yet come.

Mary did not argue. She merely said to the servants, "Whatever he says, you do." Isn't that good advice? And may I suggest that full obedience brings joy, satisfaction, and transformation. Too many Christians are only partial in their obedience. They will do certain things, but not others. But Christ asks for complete obedience. Now remember, He is God. Because He has absolute authority, He demands absolute obedience. *Whatever* He says, you do it."

Christ's Power as the Creator (2:6-10)

2:6-10. *And there were set there six waterpots of stone, after the manner of the purifying of the Jews, containing two or three firkins apiece. Jesus saith unto them, Fill the waterpots with water. And they filled them up to the brim. And he saith unto them, Draw out now, and bear unto the governor of the feast. And they bare it. When the ruler of the feast had* *tasted the water that was made wine, and knew not whence it was: (but the servants which drew the water knew;) the governor of the feast called the bridegroom, And saith unto him, Every man at the beginning doth set forth good wine; and when men have well drunk, then that which is worse: but thou hast kept the good wine until now.*

Now let us all see what took place. The six waterpots of stone that Jesus used for this first sign of His deity were ceremonial pots for cleansing. They were common in Jewish homes. The Jews were quite particular about washing their hands before they ate, and they always had an abundance of water nearby. But these ceremonial waterpots were empty. Jesus said, "Fill them up."

The servants filled the waterpots up to the brim. They didn't fill them half full. They filled them up to the brim. And the servants received according to the measure of their obedience. If they had filled the waterpots half full, they would have found the pots only half full of wine. I believe that most of our lives are destitute of power, of joy, of blessing, and of peace because we are not fully obedient. "If a man love me, he will keep my words" (John 14:23). The key to the Christian life—the key to power, joy, blessing, and peace—is obedience. And transformation is the fruitage of obedience.

Jesus gave the servants a second command. He said, "Draw out now, and bear unto the governor of the feast." The servants again obeyed Jesus, although they knew they had only put water into the pots. I want you to mark the deity of our Savior. He didn't speak to the water. He didn't touch the water. He merely said, "Draw it out." And it was wine! My friend, only God can do that.

In many of Christ's later miracles He touched people. Take the first miracle recorded in Matthew, for example. Christ reached out and touched a leper, and he was made whole. Matthew portrays Christ in that sign as the Messiah, for the Messiah was predicted to come and cleanse lepers. That is why the Lord told the leper to "go thy way, shew thyself to the priest . . . for a testimony unto them"

(8:4). The Jews were ruled by the priests in Christ's day. He was saying, "Go and show yourself to the priest. Show him that the Messiah is here!"

In other miracles, He sometimes simply spoke a word instead of touching people. This was the case in the first miracle recorded by both Mark and Luke. The Lord entered a synagogue on the sabbath. A demon-possessed man cried out "Let us alone; what have we to do with thee, thou Jesus of Nazareth? . . . I know thee who thou art; the Holy One of God" (Mark 1:24; Luke 4:34). Jesus said, "Hold thy peace, and come out of him" (Mark 1:25; Luke 4:35), and the demon departed from the man. Christ demonstrated that He was the Great Deliverer by healing this demoniac with the word of His mouth.

Christ did perform miracles by touching a leper or by speaking to a demon-possessed man. But when we come to this first miracle in John's Gospel, we find none of that. There isn't any record in this Gospel of Christ healing a leper or a demoniac. This is an astounding thing to me. John gives us a revelation of our Lord as God. For this reason, John selected Christ's first public miracle to present Him as the Creator.

Jesus merely said, "Fill the pots with water." And the servants obeyed. "Now ladle it out." He didn't even speak to the water. The very thought of the Savior was sufficient. This is the act of a Creator. If He is God, then there is one thing He ought to do—create. This is what He did. The result? The water turned to wine.

Christ's Purpose as the Creator (2:11)

> **2:11. *This beginning of miracles did Jesus in Cana of Galilee, and manifested forth his glory; and his disciples believed on him.***

Jesus deliberately performed this first of many miracles at a wedding in Cana of Galilee. May I suggest something again? He did not come to the wedding merely to perform the miracle and then to leave, for He was present as a guest. And He did not perform the miracle merely to please His mother. Christ's purpose as the Creator was to reveal Himself as God come in the flesh, and to cause men to put their trust in Him. Mark the result of this first sign.

Christ "manifested forth his glory." He will do that again when He returns to the earth and restores the nation of Israel. The Jews had a wonderful time under David and Solomon. They are going to have a more wonderful time when the Lord returns, and the nation is redeemed, and the wine pots are no longer empty. The Jews will no longer follow empty ceremonies; for, my friend, any ceremony apart from the Word of God is empty. Christ manifested His glory by filling the empty ceremonial waterpots. How we need to be filled with the Word of God, so that God may work through us to His own glory and praise.

When Christ manifested His glory, "his disciples believed on him." This is the first of about fifteen instances in the Gospel through John where individuals are said to have put their trust in Christ. I don't think that John is referring to all twelve disciples at this point. These disciples may have been just the men mentioned in the latter part of John 1: Andrew, Peter, Philip, Nathanael, and the other disciple of John the Baptist (possibly John who became an apostle, and later wrote this Gospel).

Whoever these disciples were, they believed on Christ when they saw this first sign. Many more proofs of His deity were to follow.

The First Confrontation: Cleansing the Temple (2:12-17) —Christ Arrives at a Passover in Jerusalem

Christ's Discovery of the Merchandisers (2:12-14)

2:12-14. *After this he went down to Capernaum, he, and his mother, and his brethren, and his disciples: and they continued there not many days.*

And the Jews' passover was at hand, and Jesus went up to Jerusalem, And found in the temple those

that sold oxen and sheep and doves, and the changers
of money sitting.

It was time for the Passover. Jews were coming from all over the country and also from overseas. They were coming to the temple to offer sacrifices. Unfortunately, God's Passover had degenerated into a mere feast of the Jews. In the outer court of the temple, possibly the Gentile court, the Jewish leaders were making it easy for those who came to Jerusalem to keep the Passover. They were making religion easy. It was a rational operation, but it was also a racket. Be careful of anything that makes religion easy.

When the Lord Jesus came to Jerusalem for the Passover, He found these men making merchandise of the people of God in the temple court. There were the cattle, and sheep, and doves, and the money-changers. As the worshipers came from other countries, they had to change their money into the shekel of the treasury of the temple. You could not take Roman or Greek money in there. You simply came to the temple and changed your money, and bought a sheep or ox—or a dove if you were poor.

But you can see the trouble with this. The Jewish leaders had a racket going. You could not offer your household lamb, and you could not go outside to buy a lamb. They wouldn't accept that. You had to buy an animal from them. You can see how they were manipulating the people with religion to become rich.

The Jewish leaders in Jesus' day have not been the only ones to exploit people in the name of religion for their own gain. Long before, Balaam had done this and was severely rebuked by the Lord (Numbers 22). In the last days the ecclesiastical leaders in the professing church will be doing the same thing, following the "error of Balaam for reward" (Jude 11). What is this "error of Balaam"? It is the commercializing of spiritual things. The Lord is against such exploitation.

Christ Drives Out the Merchandisers (2:15-17)

2:15-17. *And when he had made a scourge of small*

> *cords, he drove them all out of the temple, and the*
> *sheep, and the oxen; and poured out the changers'*
> *money, and overthrew the tables; And said unto them*
> *that sold doves, Take these things hence; make not my*
> *Father's house an house of merchandise. And his dis-*
> *ciples remembered that it was written, The zeal of*
> *thine house hath eaten me up.*

Now remember, the Lord Jesus had been to Jerusalem for the
Passover many times before. In Luke 2 He came as a boy, and I'm
sure that conditions were the same then. When Joseph and Mary
left to go back to Nazareth, you remember, they missed Him and
came back to Jerusalem to hunt for Him. They found Jesus in the
midst of the doctors in the temple, confounding them with His
questions and answers. Now I'm sure the Jews were merchandis-
ing the things of God in those days. And more than likely, while He
was at Nazareth with Mary, He went up to the temple possibly
every year as other good Jews did. But nothing was done then concerning the cleansing of the temple.

This was the first time, however, that Jesus had come to
Jerusalem for the Passover since His baptism by John. This was the
first time He had come to reveal Himself as God manifest in the
flesh. When He walked into the temple that day, He came in His
official capacity as the Son of God. He came with absolute authority over His Father's house, and He came to drive out the merchandisers.

In Cana Jesus manifested His power as the Creator. Now He
came to manifest His authority as the Messiah, the Son of God. Not
only did He drive the sheep and oxen out of the temple, but He
whipped the merchants out of the place. These Jews knew that He
was right. The law and their consciences were witnesses against
them. Christ was filled with *righteous* indignation in His zeal for
His Father's house.

Christ cleansed the temple by crying, "Make not my Father's
house an house of merchandise." Mark that He calls the temple,
"My Father's house." Christ was claiming a unique relationship

with the Living God. To the Jews this was a terrific thing. When Jesus made this claim again in John 5, the Jews sought to kill Him because He "said also that God was his Father, making himself equal with God" (5:18). That is exactly what Christ is claiming here in John 2. He was saying in effect, "Because of My relationship with the Father, because I in fact am the Son of God, I have the right and authority to clean My Father's house."

When Christ drove the merchandisers out of the temple, they experienced something of the terror of the Lord. In the future men will cry to the mountains and rocks to hide them "from the face of him that sitteth on the throne, and from the wrath of the Lamb: For the great day of his wrath is come; and who shall be able to stand?" (Revelation 6:16-17).

Sometimes we forget that He is a righteous God and that every one of us must one day stand in His presence and give an account to Him. "It is a fearful thing to fall into the hands of the living God" (Hebrews 10:31).

If our Lord was jealous for His Father's house, would He not be just as jealous over you and me? Your body is also the temple of God. "Therefore," Paul could say, "glorify God in your body, and in your spirit, which are God's" (1 Corinthians 6:20). Think about it! Your body is the sanctuary of God. It belongs to Him. Like the temple of old, we exist for the express purpose of glorifying and praising God. May God grant that we who profess His name, we who know that these bodies are the sanctuary of God, might walk before Him in praise, in adoration, and for the glory of God.

We are to "Awake to righteousness, and sin not" (1 Corinthians 15:34) so that our temple will remain pure. Christ cleansed the temple when men sinned and made it unclean. Similarly, the Lord has a right to cleanse us when we sin. It is much better for us to willingly confess our sins so that He may forgive and cleanse us. And He is willing and ready to do just that. How wonderful it is to know that the blood of Jesus Christ, God's Son, cleanseth us from all sin (1 John 1:7).

If we revert back to our old ways, the Lord will have to do the same thing in our lives that He did in the temple long ago. He cleansed the temple at the beginning of His ministry, but as soon as He left they were back making merchandise of the people again. Three years later He returned and found they had made His Father's house a "den of thieves" (Matthew 21:13; Mark 11:17; Luke 19:46). The unbelief of their hearts was evidenced by the disobedience of their lives.

This is the way with evil. But the Lord is ever faithful to His promise. He is always willing to restore our soul as He cleanses us. He can turn a "den of thieves" into a "house of prayer."

The First Controversy: The Resurrection Predicted (2:18-25) —Christ Remains at a Passover in Jerusalem

Christ's Prediction to the Leaders (2:18-21)

2:18-21. *Then answered the Jews and said unto him, What sign shewest thou unto us, seeing that thou doest these things? Jesus answered and said unto them, Destroy this temple, and in three days I will raise it up. Then said the Jews, Forty and six years was this temple in building, and wilt thou rear it up in three days? But he spake of the temple of his body.*

"What sign shewest thou unto us?" The Jews were outraged at what the Lord Jesus had done. He had completely disrupted the observance of the Passover in the temple. They were demanding an explanation. "Who do you think you are? Who told you to do this? Where did you get the authority to do this? Who are you, anyway?" Paul wisely observed that "the Jews require a sign" (1 Corinthians 1:22). Mark Christ's answer.

"Destroy this temple, and in three days I will raise it up." His answer is an amazing response to their challenge. Not only did He predict His ultimate death and resurrection at the end of His ministry, but He declared that His death and resurrection were the very foundation of all His work. Christ didn't base His authority on His miracles, but on His work on the cross and His resurrection three days later.

Notice the great place Jesus Christ gave to this question of His resurrection. His Person, His whole ministry, and especially His work at the cross were based upon the fact that He would rise from the dead. This was His greatest sign to the Jews that He was who He claimed to be (see Matthew 12:39-40).

"Wilt thou rear it up in three days?" The Jews completely misunderstood the sign Jesus had given them. They were thinking of the literal temple, which had taken forty-six years to build, and wouldn't be finished for another ten years.

You can hear the sarcasm in their voices: "You say you want us to destroy the temple? Do you mean to tell us you can rebuild it in *three days?*" Of course, Jesus wasn't referring to Herod's temple at all, but to the temple of His body. But to the Jews, His prediction seemed absurd.

Christ's Preparation of the Disciples (2:22)

> **2:22. *When therefore he was risen from the dead, his disciples remembered that he had said this unto them; and they believed the scripture, and the word which Jesus had said.***

It is interesting that the disciples were also confused by the Lord's prediction. But Christ was starting to prepare them for those crucial events, so that afterwards they would understand that He was the fulfillment of the prophecies given in the Old Testament and repeated by Himself. It wasn't until after the resurrection that the faith of the disciples was made secure and steadfast.

There was no question in the disciples' minds after the resurrection, however, about the identity of Jesus Christ. They knew that He was God manifest in the flesh to reveal the heart of God to men. And based on that knowledge, they put their complete belief and trust in Him. Everywhere they went they preached the risen Christ. They did not argue but merely declared the reality of the resurrection of Christ from the dead. They boldly declared what they had seen and heard. Their entire ministry and message were based on

His resurrection.

It is the same for us today. The church stands or comes crashing down depending on the resurrection, for it is the heart of Christianity.

What makes Christianity different from any religion in the world is the death, burial, and resurrection of Jesus Christ. It is foreign to the thinking of Muslims, Hindus, Buddhists, or Shintoists. What marks out Christ from any other man that has ever lived is His resurrection.

Paul made this clear when he wrote that Christ was "declared to be the Son of God with power . . . by the resurrection from the dead" (Romans 1:4). Because of Christ's resurrection, His disciples had all the evidence they needed to believe.

Christ and the Crowd's Superficial Belief (2:23-25)

> **2:23-25.** *Now when he was in Jerusalem at the passover, in the feast day, many believed in his name, when they saw the miracles which he did. But Jesus did not commit himself unto them, because he knew all men, And needed not that any should testify of man: for he knew what was in man.*

The disciples were just beginning to grasp *who* He was: God manifest in the flesh. The crowds, however, had a superficial belief in Christ. All they could see was what Jesus did: signs and miracles.

The people were intellectually persuaded that the things Jesus did were miracles, but their faith was not in the Person who performed those miracles. Because their faith was based on the spectacular (and Jesus knew this), it was not real. Later, most of these people turned back, and walked with Christ no more (John 6:66). This is always the case with a faith that is based on the spectacular, for it is never a saving faith.

"Show us a sign! Give us a miracle!" the Jews had cried. "We'll believe if we see a miracle!" Jesus knew they wouldn't believe.

I remember years ago that, during a flu epidemic in Saskatchewan, people were dying on the prairies. There were few doctors or nurses to attend to the sick. I stayed up every night for three weeks, nursing a family—a man and his wife and six children—out on the prairie.

When the little baby became ill, the mother said to me, "Mr. Mitchell, if God heals my baby, I'll believe." God graciously healed her little one. But the mother scoffed and said, "But I thought God would do it in a minute."

I told her, "You remind me of what Jesus said: 'If they hear not Moses and the prophets, neither will they be persuaded, though one rose from the dead' " (Luke 16:31).

Faith that is based upon the spectacular is not faith at all. Faith must be in a Person, not in some experience. And I repeat that statement because today there are so many who are basing their faith upon some spectacular experience or sign or miracle that someone has performed. The Lord Jesus would not commit Himself to these people because they were shallow in their faith. John literally said that although they believed in His name, Jesus did not believe in them.

Jesus must personally be the center and object of our faith and trust. But there was a man to whom Jesus could commit Himself. This man was a ruler of the Jews, as we see in the next chapter.

John 3

Christ, The Savior

The Dilemma of Nicodemus (3:1-13)

Nicodemus's Initial Query (3:1-3)

> **3:1-2.** *There was a man of the Pharisees, named Nicodemus, a ruler of the Jews: The same came to Jesus. . . .*

Nicodemus was possibly one of the most popular and outstanding teachers of the people of Israel. As a Pharisee, he was looked up to and admired by the crowds. And then Jesus came to Jerusalem, and astonished the crowds and the Jewish leaders by His miracles, and by cleansing the temple. There is no question that Nicodemus had seen the Lord do these things, presenting His credentials. That is why he came to Him . . .

> **3:2.** *. . . by night, and said unto him, Rabbi, we know that thou art a teacher come from God: for no man can do these miracles that thou doest, except God be with him.*

Nicodemus came to the Lord by night, I believe, because he was a busy man. Besides, he needed to be able to talk without interruption. He could not do that with the crowd in the temple. So he came by night and had the Lord all to Himself. Nicodemus came with a heart open to know the truth. He wanted to know who this Man is and what message He had for him.

3:3. *Jesus answered and said unto him, Verily, verily, I say unto thee, Except a man be born again, he cannot see the kingdom of God.*

Now this was a strange thing for the Lord to say to Nicodemus. "Nicodemus, do you know what's the matter with you? Except a man be born again, he cannot see the kingdom of God."

Like other Jews, Nicodemus had been hoping to see God establish His kingdom on earth. He was a teacher of the things of God, an instructor of the Old Testament. He had been looking for the Messiah. He had seen the Lord Jesus perform miracles and cleanse the temple. "Will this be the One to bring in the kingdom? Is this to be our leader?"

The Lord knew what Nicodemus was thinking and startled him with his answer: "Nicodemus, you'll never even see the kingdom of God unless you're born again. Your trouble is that you were born wrong, and there is nothing you can do with the old. You must be born again."

Nicodemus needed to be born again. His dilemma is the dilemma of every man. Man's condition demands that he be born again if he is going to see or enter the kingdom of God. This is not a popular doctrine. Most people don't believe it. Instead, they believe that if a person does something of merit, he or she will qualify to enter God's kingdom. The problem, however, is that all of us are born with an old sin nature, and there is nothing we can do to change it.

"If you knew your Bible, Nicodemus, you would have known that," Jesus was saying. "Haven't you ever read, Nicodemus, that the thoughts and imaginations of the heart of man are evil continually?" (Genesis 6:5). "And did not Job say, 'Who can bring a clean thing out of an unclean? not one'?" (Job 14:4). "Did not King David say, 'I was shapen in iniquity; and in sin did my mother conceive me'?" (Psalm 51:5). "And did not Jeremiah say, 'Can the Ethiopian change his skin, or the leopard his spots? then may ye also do good, that are accustomed to do evil'?" (Jeremiah 13:23).

There is not one thing that man can do of himself that would make him fit to even see the kingdom of God, much less enter it. This is also taught in the New Testament. "The carnal mind is enmity against God: for it is not subject to the law of God, neither indeed can be. So then they that are in the flesh cannot please God" (Romans 8:7-8). "The natural man receiveth not the things of the Spirit of God: for they are foolishness unto him: neither can he know them, because they are spiritually discerned" (1 Corinthians 2:14). The scriptures could be multiplied. Every man is born wrong, like Nicodemus. None of us are naturally fit to see the kingdom of God, much less enter it. Now Jesus said that!

And then I think of the holy character of God. "Without holiness," we read, "no man shall see the Lord" (Hebrews 12:14). God cannot open the door to any man who would try to enter His kingdom on his own merit. The standard is God Himself, and we all "come short of the glory of God" (Romans 3:23).

Consider the apostle Paul, for example. He was well born. He was a Pharisee, like Nicodemus. He was a zealot for God. He considered himself blameless before the law. And yet later Paul wrote, "This is a faithful saying, and worthy of all acceptation, that Christ Jesus came into the world to save sinners; of whom I am chief" (1 Timothy 1:15). Paul's eyes were opened when he met the Lord.

You see, there must be a new nature. Everything that was from Adam or from my parents is sinful. The old nature is of the flesh. The new nature is from God. Peter wrote that by many exceeding precious promises we have been made "partakers of the divine nature" (2 Peter 1:4). Being born a Jew or a Gentile profits nothing, but whether or not you have been reborn as "a new creature" (Galatians 6:15). "If any man be in Christ," Paul said, "he is a new creature" (2 Corinthians 5:17). The new nature is "born, not of blood, nor of the will of the flesh, nor of the will of man, but of God" (John 1:13).

The new nature is the product of the new birth—being born from above, being born of God. That's why our Lord told Nicodemus, "If you are going to see the kingdom of God, you must be born again. You must be born from above."

Nicodemus's First Question (3:4-8)

3:4. *Nicodemus saith unto him, How can a man be born when he is old? can he enter the second time into his mother's womb, and be born?*

"It's impossible!" Nicodemus exclaimed. "I can't go back to my mother's womb and be reborn."

3:5-8. *Jesus answered, Verily, verily, I say unto thee, Except a man be born of water and of the Spirit, he cannot enter into the kingdom of God. That which is born of the flesh is flesh; and that which is born of the Spirit is spirit. Marvel not that I said unto thee, Ye must be born again. The wind bloweth where it listeth, and thou hearest the sound therof, but canst not tell whence it cometh, and whither it goeth: so is every one that is born of the Spirit.*

"Nicodemus, you don't understand," Jesus replied. "Even though you are a teacher of Israel, you have missed what the Scriptures declare. You must be born again to enter the kingdom of God. This is something entirely new. It hasn't a thing to do with the flesh. You must be born of water and of the Spirit."

A man must be "born of water." Now what does the water signify? Does not water mean water? I would say that in Scripture, oftentimes, the word "water" is used as a picture of some spiritual truth. For example, in John 4, in the very next chapter, Jesus tells a woman at the well, "If you drink of the water that I shall give you, you will never thirst."

"Well," the woman said, "you have no pitcher to draw with, and the well is deep. How are you going to get that water?"

And the Lord said, "If you drink of this water, what will happen? You will thirst again. But if you drink of the water that I will give you, you will never thirst. It will be in you a well of water springing up into everlasting life." Is that literal water?

"If any man thirst," Jesus said, "let him come unto me, and drink. He that believeth on me, as the scripture hath said, out of his belly shall flow rivers of living water. (But this spake he of the Spirit, which they that believe on him should receive. . . .)" (John 7:37-39). He identified the water He offered with the Holy Spirit and with belief in Himself (based on God's Word).

Paul wrote, "That he might sanctify and cleanse it (the church) with the washing of water by the word" (Ephesians 5:26). The Word of God (water) cleanses those who place their trust in Christ. Christ said this in John 15:3, "Now ye are clean through the word." We are born again of the water of God's Word.

God's method for bringing men and women into a personal relationship with Himself is simple: the Spirit of God uses the Word of God (through the man of God). We have this in such passages as 1 Thessalonians 1:5-6. God uses the Word of God to produce the new birth. James wrote: "Of his own will begat he us with the word of truth" (1:18). Peter declared that we are "born again, not of corruptible seed, but of incorruptible, by the word of God" (1 Peter 1:23).

We must be "born of water" by the cleansing power of the Word of God as we trust in Him.

We must also be "born of the Spirit," where we come into a new relationship, into a new life. Life comes through relationship, not through the knowledge or efforts of man. The Holy Spirit is the One who gives us life.

The wind comes and goes and blows where it wishes. We cannot see the wind. We don't know where it comes from, or where it is going. But we can experience its power. In the same way, the Spirit works in the hearts of men. We cannot see the Holy Spirit, much less explain everything He does. We cannot begin to fathom the moving of the Spirit of God in taking a sinner and transforming him into a child of God. We cannot see His movement, but we can see the fruitage of it as men are transformed.

The Holy Spirit comes into any heart that is open to Him, and He makes that individual a new creation. He does not patch up the old nature. Thank God, the patching days are over! The Holy Spirit gives us new life based on a new relationship with the Lord.

Man cannot be born of his own efforts. You had nothing to do with being born the first time. And there is nothing you can do to be born the second time. God does it all. You cannot become a Christian by trying to remove your sins.

There are those who say, "Well, I'm going to give up my sin." Well, that's wonderful, my friend. Give up your sin. You ought to give it up anyway. But that doesn't make you fit to enter the presence of God. Except a man be born of water and of the Spirit, he cannot see or enter the kingdom of God.

Nicodemus's Second Question (3:9-13)

> **3:9.** *Nicodemus answered and said unto him, How can these things be?*

"How can this be accomplished?" Nicodemus asked. "What do you mean that I was born wrong? What about all of my effort and work and religious feelings as a teacher of Israel? Don't they merit anything at all? Why can't I enter the kingdom of God now? Why must I be born of water and of the Spirit? How does that happen? How can these things be?"

> **3:10.** *Jesus answered and said unto him, Art thou a master of Israel, and knowest not these things?*

Nicodemus was an important teacher of the Jews, yet he did not know one of the most basic teachings of the Old Testament. He did not understand that God desires to give every man a new nature as a result of the new birth.

This teaching is found throughout the Old Testament. For example, after David realized his basic nature was sinful, he prayed, "Create in me a clean heart, O God; and renew a right spirit within me" (Psalm 51:10). The Lord Himself spoke of the days when, "I will put my law in their inward parts, and write it in their hearts; and will be their God, and they shall be my people" (Jeremiah 31:33). The Lord pleaded with Israel to recognize her sinfulness, and to turn to God to receive "a new heart and a new spirit" (Ezekiel 18:31).

3:11-13. *Verily, verily, I say unto thee, We speak that we do know, and testify that we have seen; and ye receive not our witness. If I have told you earthly things, and ye believe not, how shall ye believe, if I tell you of heavenly things? And no man hath ascended up to heaven, but he that came down from heaven, even the Son of man which is in heaven.*

In other words, Christ was telling Nicodemus, "Not only can I tell you how to get into the kingdom of God, but I came from heaven as God. I am uniquely qualified to teach you about how to be born again so that you can enter the kingdom of God." Christ's authority as the teacher sent from God is unlimited, for He is God. Oh, the blessedness of our Savior in His omnipresence.

Christ's Discourse (3:14-21)

Jesus: the Substitute, the Son, the Savior (3:14-17)

During His interview with Nicodemus, the Lord explained the need for every man to be born again. He also revealed that the Spirit of God uses the Word of God to produce the new birth. Now we have Christ presenting the heart of the gospel.

Nicodemus was confused by the things Jesus had said. "How can these things be? What is the method whereby I, Nicodemus, can be born of water and of the Spirit? How can I be born again? How can I get into the kingdom of God? How can I see it? How can I enter it?" In verses 14 through 17, the Lord gives us three amazing answers. The first answer is found in verses 14 and 15.

3:14-15. *And as Moses lifted up the serpent in the wilderness, even so must the Son of man be lifted up: That whosoever believeth in him should not perish, but have eternal life.*

Now mark His first answer to Nicodemus's questions. We have Jesus here as the Substitute. You all know the story He is referring to in these verses. In Numbers 21 we read that the people of Israel

57

had murmured against God because of the manna. They had said, "Our soul loatheth this light bread" (21:5).

Think of this! They despised the divine provision for their daily needs. And the Lord sent serpents among the people of Israel, and many of them died because of the poison. And they cried to Moses. Moses came to God, and God said, "Make thee a fiery serpent, and set it upon a pole" because "every one that is bitten, when he looketh upon it, shall live" (21:8).

So we read that every Jew who was smitten with the serpents and was dying of the poison, if he merely looked, he lived. God provided a remedy for their affliction. He sent a savior from death.

"Now," the Lord said to Nicodemus, "God has provided a remedy for *your* condition. As Moses lifted up the serpent in the wilderness, even so must the Son of Man be lifted up. He must die on a cross. And everyone who puts his trust in this One who is to be lifted up will live. So now, the Son of Man will be lifted up, that whosoever believes in Him may have everlasting life."

> **3:16. *For God so loved the world, that he gave his only begotten Son, that whosoever believeth in him should not perish, but have everlasting life.***

And then the Lord gave His second answer. "You want to know how you can be born again, Nicodemus?" Here it is: "God so loved the world." This is the crux of it. Love provided a way for men to be delivered from their sin, and to be born of water and of the Spirit. Love stepped into the picture and provided a Gift, Jesus, God's only begotten Son, "that whosoever believeth in him should not perish, but have everlasting life."

> **3:17. *For God sent not his Son into the world to condemn the world; but that the world through him might be saved.***

Here is the third answer. The Lord Jesus came to be the Savior. May I say this, my Christian friend? When you accepted the Savior, you heard some good news about God sending His Son. This Son was sent to die on your behalf, not only for your sins, but for *you*. You heard that if you put your trust in Him, you would pass from death to life, that you would be born from above, and that you would be fitted to see and enter the kingdom of God.

How did this happen? You heard the Word. The Word attracted you to a Person. You put your trust in that Person. And immediately you were born of water and of the Spirit. The Spirit quickened the Word to your heart, and thus you passed from death to life. You became a child of God.

The Necessity for Belief (3:18-21)

> **3:18-21.** *He that believeth on him is not condemned: but he that believeth not is condemned already, because he hath not believed in the name of the only begotten Son of God. And this is the condemnation, that light is come into the world, and men loved darkness rather than light, because their deeds were evil. For every one that doeth evil hateth the light, neither cometh to the light, lest his deeds should be reproved. But he that doeth truth cometh to the light, that his deeds may be made manifest, that they are wrought in God.*

Mark the importance of belief in Christ. "He that believeth on him is not condemned." The question of salvation does not primarily hinge for us on the fact that God loves us or that Christ died for us. These facts are true. But a person can believe these facts and yet not be born from above.

If you are moral and religious and give an intellectual assent to all the wonderful doctrines of Scripture, that does not mean that you are saved. You must do more than believe that He did the right thing. You must put your faith and trust in the Savior. There must be a relationship between you and Him if there is to be salvation.

Twice Jesus said, "Whosoever believeth in him should not perish" (3:15, 16). Twice He promised "everlasting life" to those who believe on Him (3:16, 36). Belief in Christ is vitally important, for when we put our trust in Him we pass from death to life.

"But he that believeth not is condemned already." The wrath of God is already come on him (3:36). Why doesn't the judgment of God fall today? Because "the Lord is not slack concerning his promise, as some men count slackness; but is longsuffering to us-ward, not willing that any should perish, but that all should come to repentance" (2 Peter 3:9).

John the Baptist's Last Testimony (3:22-30)

The Jealousy of John's Disciples (3:22-27)

3:22-24. After these things came Jesus and his disciples into the land of Judaea; and there he tarried with them, and baptized.

And John also was baptizing in Aenon near to Salim, because there was much water there: and they came, and were baptized. For John was not yet cast into prison.

Apparently John the Baptist and Jesus Christ interlocked their ministry together until John was cast into prison. They were both baptizing for the remission of sins. You find that in the book of Matthew. And then I read of a little confusion in the minds of John's disciples.

3:25-27. Then there arose a question between some of John's disciples and the Jews about purifying. And they came unto John, and said unto him, Rabbi, he that was with thee beyond Jordan, to whom thou bearest witness, behold, the same baptizeth, and all men come to him. John answered and said, A man can receive nothing, except it be given him from heaven.

I can appreciate the concern of John's disciples. John had been the center of attraction in Israel. Great multitudes had come around him, and he had preached, "Repent ye: for the kingdom of heaven is at hand" (Matthew 3:2). John had baptized the people for the remission of sins in moral preparation for the coming Messiah. "The King is on His way. Be ready for Him!" John had told the crowds.

But then Jesus came on the scene. John testified that He was "the Lamb of God, which taketh away the sin of the world" (1:29). John lost two of his disciples. He also lost much of his popularity when the crowds went to Jesus. These dear disciples were simply jealous for John's reputation.

Remember when the seventy elders had gone up with Moses and Joshua into the mountain? When they came down two began to prophesy. Joshua said to Moses, "You'd better do something about these two fellows. They're prophesying in the camp" (see Numbers 11:28).

Moses replied, "Would to God that all His people were prophets and had the Spirit of God upon them" (see 11:29). Moses had no room for jealousy or envy. Scripture records that "Moses was very meek, above all the men which were upon the face of the earth" (Numbers 12:3). He rejoiced to see others successfully carrying out the work of God.

John the Baptist was like Moses, for he did not have any room for competition or rivalry. "If I have any ministry at all," John said, "I have received it from heaven. The ministry of Jesus is from heaven as well." John was like a star disappearing from sight as the sun rises in the morning. The star is still there, but the glory of the sun surpasses the shining of its light. John was a star, and as Christ (the Sun) came on the scene and began to manifest Himself, John began to disappear. John was not jealous of Jesus, but instead rejoiced to see Him. John was a worshiper, clothed with humility in the presence of his Lord.

As Christians we are also to be clothed with humility. "Likewise, ye younger, submit yourselves unto the elder," Peter exhorted. "Yea, all of you be subject one to another, and be clothed with humility, for God resisteth the proud, and giveth grace to the humble. Humble yourselves therefore under the mighty hand of God, that he may exalt you in due time" (1 Peter 5:5-6).

Are you worried about your reputation in the eyes of others? It would be very easy to be jealous for our reputation as a church, for instance, when we should rather rejoice whenever we hear of people accepting the Savior, or whenever we hear of God blessing someone else's ministry. God does not want us to be concerned about our reputation. We are to acknowledge, like John, that, "A man can receive nothing, except it be given him from heaven."

The Joy of John the Baptist (3:28-30)

In the first chapter, the Pharisees tried to get John the Baptist occupied with himself, but John would have none of it. In this chapter, his own disciples tried to get John occupied with himself. Again, John would have none of it. Once John caught a glimpse of Christ, everything else faded out of the picture. John's joy was made complete by merely being known as the Bridegroom's friend.

> **3:28-30.** *Ye yourselves bear me witness, that I said, I am not the Christ, but that I am sent before him. He that hath the bride is the bridegroom: but the friend of the bridegroom, which standeth and heareth him, rejoiceth greatly because of the bridegroom's voice: this my joy therefore is fulfilled. He must increase, but I must decrease.*

What an amazing statement John made! He said, "I am perfectly satisfied. My joy is filled full. I have seen the Bridegroom. As the friend of the Bridegroom, I rejoice just to be in His presence. Now that He has come on the scene, He is the Preeminent One. Never mind me. I am only the friend of the Bridegroom. He must increase. I must get out of the way."

Do you know how to decrease by letting Him increase? The more He fills your vision, the more He is the object of your love and your worship and your devotion, the more you will get out of the way, and the more you will want Him to be preeminent. John is the worshiper in love with the Lord Jesus, and nothing is going to interfere with that.

My Christian friend, have you seen Jesus? Is He the object of your worship? When you come to the Lord's table, remembering the terrible price He paid for you, can you honestly say, "Father, I want the Lord Jesus to be the perfect object of my love and my devotion. I want Him to be the object of my faith, of all that I am. He must increase. I must decrease"? This ought to be your experience and mine, whatever failures or blessings we may have had in the past.

But why should the Lord be first? Why should He increase? Why should He be the center? John cites His preeminence as the Divine One.

Christ's Divinity:
A Heavenly Origin, a Heavenly Testimony,
a Heavenly Authority (3:31-36)

3:31. *He that cometh from above is above all: he that is of the earth is earthly, and speaketh of the earth: he that cometh from heaven is above all.*

First, John spoke of Jesus' heavenly origin. John's ministry was limited to the earth. But our Lord's ministry was a heavenly ministry. Why? Because He came from heaven. Some forty times in the Gospel through John, Christ is spoken of as being sent from heaven or going back to heaven. He is the Heavenly One.

3:32-34. *And what he hath seen and heard, that he testifieth; and no man receiveth his testimony. He that hath received his testimony hath set to his seal that God is true. For he whom God hath sent speaketh the words of God: for God giveth not the Spirit by measure unto him.*

Second, John spoke of Jesus' heavenly testimony. We can talk about heaven. We can speak the words He gives us to speak. But He came as the Heavenly One. He came as God's divine Word to man. Everyone who believes in Him and His testimony has "set to

63

his seal that God is true." Paul said, "Let God be true, but every man a liar" (Romans 3:4). God cannot lie (Titus 1:2). His word is always true (Psalm 19:9). When Christ spoke, God spoke. His words are all true. Christ's testimony is heavenly; it is God's testimony to man.

Jesus said, "The Son can do nothing of himself, but what he seeth the Father do" (John 5:19). Later Jesus said, "I do nothing of myself; but as my Father hath taught me, I speak these things" (John 8:28). On the night of His betrayal, Jesus likewise affirmed, "the words that I speak unto you I speak not of myself: but the Father that dwelleth in me, he doeth the works" (John 14:10). We can talk about the Word of God, but Jesus could say, "When I speak, it is God speaking. . . ." There you have the heavenly testimony.

> **3:35-36.** *The Father loveth the Son, and hath given all things into his hand. He that believeth on the Son hath everlasting life: and he that believeth not the Son shall not see life; but the wrath of God abideth on him.*

Third, John spoke of Jesus' heavenly authority. His authority is based on the Father's love and what the Father has given Him.

"The Father loveth the Son." When Jesus was baptized by John in the Jordan, there came a voice from heaven, saying, "This is my beloved Son, in whom I am well pleased" (Matthew 3:17). The Lord Himself acknowledged back to the Father that "thou lovedst me before the foundation of the world" (John 17:24).

The Father loves the Son. The Father also loves you and me because we love the Son. We have become the objects of God's love if we have put our trust in His Son, for the Son is the object and center of the Father's love (see John 16:27).

"The Father . . . hath given all things into his hand." The Father has delegated all authority to the Son. "He that cometh from above is above all" (3:31). Jesus has all authority. He is above all things. Many New Testament passages indicate the absolute authority that the Father delegated to Jesus, the Son.

In the book of Hebrews we find that Jesus sat down at the right hand of the majesty on high (1:3; 8:1; 10:12; 12:2). What does that mean? He has all authority over every bit of creation—the universe, the earth, man, angels, demons, principalities, powers, seraphim, and cherubim. He has been given the place of ultimate power.

In the book of Colossians, as well, Christ is spoken of as being over all thrones, dominions, principalities, and powers, for "all things were created by him, and for him: And he is before all things, and by him all things consist. And he is the head of the body, the church: who is the beginning, the firstborn from the dead; that in all things he might have the preeminence" (1:16-18). Having been raised from the dead, Christ now "sitteth on the right hand of God" (3:1). The right hand of God is the most awesome place imaginable. It refers to the unique position of power and authority that is God's alone. Christ is in authority over everything in creation.

That is why Christ made a whip and cleansed the temple. He has all authority as the Son of God. Christ spoke authoritatively to Nicodemus, and He continues to speak authoritatively to us today, for He speaks God's words as the One sent from God. May we consider, and understand, and obey Christ's divine Word today.

John 4

Christ, The Water of Life

The Second Interview: Meeting a Woman (4:1-14)
—Jesus Travels in Samaria

Jesus, the Well, and the Woman (4:1-6)

In chapter 3 a religious leader received the marvelous, wonderful message of the new birth. The Lord revealed to him that unless a man was born from above—born again of the Spirit—he could neither see nor enter the kingdom of God. The chapter ended with the preeminence of Christ, His heavenly origin, witness, and authority. And now we are taken into Samaria where the Lord deals with a sinful woman.

If you and I were preaching, if we were to go down to the Gospel mission, for example, to reach the men of the street, we would preach on the new birth. You wouldn't expect me to go down to the mission and preach to these men on the Godhead, that God is Spirit and that they that worship Him must worship Him in Spirit and truth. We'd preach the new birth! I say, not so the Lord.

What Nicodemus had to learn was that he needed to be born again, because God has no confidence in the flesh. The Samaritan woman did not need to be told not to have any confidence in the flesh. She had none already. What she needed was a revelation of God.

So when we come to this fourth chapter, we have a three-fold revelation in the passage. There is the revelation of the woman, the revelation of the Father, and the revelation of the Son. As well, there are three missions in the chapter. There is the woman's mission, the Lord's mission, and the believer's mission.

It is a wonderful passage on soul winning. It is a wonderful passage on psychology. It's a great passage, this fourth chapter of John, and I would suggest that those of you who are hungry to win souls for Christ spend some time in thinking about how the Lord dealt with this woman. I am amazed the more I read the chapter at the tenderness and the patience and the compassion of the Savior as he deals with this dear woman, this dear woman who needs the Lord so badly.

> **4:1-6.** *When therefore the Lord knew how the Pharisees had heard that Jesus made and baptized more disciples than John, (Though Jesus himself baptized not, but his disciples,) He left Judaea, and departed again into Galilee. And He must needs go through Samaria. Then cometh he to a city of Samaria, which is called Sychar, near to the parcel of ground that Jacob gave to his son Joseph. Now Jacob's well was there. Jesus therefore, being wearied with his journey, sat thus on the well: and it was about the sixth hour.*

You will notice that our Lord, when He knew that the Pharisees were still cultivating the undercurrent of hatred and opposition they exhibited in chapter 2, left Judaea and went to Galilee. And, "he must needs go through Samaria."

Jews customarily had no dealings with Samaritans. They felt superior to Samaritans. And the Samaritans were suffering with an inferiority complex in the presence of the Jews. They loved each other "afar off."

But our Lord "must needs go through Samaria." They was a sinful woman there. There was a woman hungry for reality, tired of her sin and needing a Savior. The Lord must go through Samaria to meet her need, despite the fact that the Jews as a rule went up the Jordan Valley into Perea instead, and then crossed over that way into Galilee. They were willing to take the longer route rather than go through Samaria because of the tenseness of the opposition between the Jews and Samaritans.

I might add in connection with this that the Lord, looking down upon the earth, "must needs" come to the earth because you are here, because I am here. We needed a Savior. We needed a Lord. So He came, because He loved us. He came that we might have a Savior.

Jesus Breaks Down the Barriers (4:7-9)

> **4:7.** *There cometh a woman of Samaria to draw water. . . .*

And Jesus made the first move.

> **4:7.** *. . . Jesus saith unto her, Give me to drink.*

And John adds in verse 8 a very simple little thing.

> **4:8.** *(For his disciples were gone away unto the city to buy meat.)*

When Nicodemus came to Jesus in John 3, he had much in common with Jesus. They were both mature men. They were both Jews. They were both teachers. They were both considered to be godly, holy men. In contrast, when the Samaritan woman came to draw water, she met someone who was much different from herself.

When the Samaritan woman came to the well, Jesus was alone. The woman would not have come to the well if thirteen Jews were around it. She would have gone back to Sychar. Jesus had sent the twelve disciples into the city to buy food.

I've always been amused at this. If you were in a group of thirteen, and it was time to eat, how many would you send to the store to get something to eat? You would only need to send two—one to buy the food, and one for fellowship and assistance in carrying the food back. But the Lord sent all twelve of them. "Well, you fellows go," can't you hear Him say? And Jesus sat down on the well. It was then that the woman came.

This particular woman came alone. Normally, women from the city came to the well of Sychar in a group to wash their clothes, draw water, and fellowship together. I have seen this myself in Israel and other parts of the world. But this Samaritan woman came alone. She was an outcast. She came at noon. She came at a time when the other women of the city normally were not at the well.

This time when she came to the well, however, Someone else was already there. It was a Man who had stopped there to rest from His journey. And He was a Jew. She could tell by the way He dressed. To her utter amazement, this man turned to her and said, "Give me a drink."

4:9. *Then saith the woman of Samaria unto him, How is it that thou, being a Jew, asketh drink of me, which am a woman of Samaria? for the Jews have no dealings with the Samaritans.*

In other words, she was saying, "Why are you (a Jewish man) asking me (a Samaritan woman) for a drink?" Here the sex barrier was broken down. For a Jewish rabbi, a teacher, to speak to a woman was unheard of in the first place. And He broke down the national barrier—she was a Samaritan. And He broke down the sin barrier—He was the Savior.

"Woman, give me a drink." The Lord Jesus put Himself under obligation to this woman.

You who are soul winners mark this, how the Lord dealt with this woman. He knew all about her. He knew she was a sinful woman, even by the very fact that she came at the time of the day so she wouldn't have to meet the other women at the well. And the sweetness of it, the tenderness of it, when the Lord said, "Woman, give me a drink."

"You, a Jew, asking me, a Samaritan woman, for a drink?" His first step was to speak of the thing in which *she* was interested. This is a good soul-winning tactic. Don't go to a sinner to condemn him. Don't knock him on the head and say, "Are you saved?"

"Woman, give me a drink." How sweet for the Lord to discuss the matter which was so close to her heart. She came to get water, so the Lord asked her for water.

The Woman and the Water (4:10-15)

"You ask drink of *me*?" asked the Samaritan woman as she stood by the well. And note our Lord's answer in verse 10.

> **4:10.** *Jesus answered and said unto her, If thou knewest the gift of God, and who it is that saith to thee, Give me to drink; thou wouldest have asked of him, and he would have given thee living water.*

You see He had aroused the woman's curiosity. "Woman," He said, "If you knew the gift of God—if you knew who was talking to you—you would ask Him for living water."

> **4:11.** *The woman saith unto him, Sir, thou hast nothing to draw with, and the well is deep: from whence then hast thou that living water?*

"Sir, where do you have that living water? The well is deep, and you have nothing to draw with. Where do you have that living water? I'd like to get some of that."

> **4:12.** *Art thou greater than our father Jacob, which gave us the well, and drank thereof himself, and his children, and his cattle?*

"Are you greater than Jacob? Who are you, anyhow?" And here you can see her mind. Here is a strange thing. "This Jew puts himself under obligation to me and wants a drink of water—and he tells me if I knew who he was, I would ask of him and he would give me living water. But he doesn't even have a water pot. Where's your pot? Where are you going to get the living water? Who are you? Are you greater than Jacob who gave us the well and from here watered his cattle and his stock?"

71

> **4:13-15.** *Jesus answered and said unto her, Whoso-*
> *ever drinketh of this water shall thirst again: But who-*
> *soever drinketh of the water that I shall give him shall*
> *never thirst; but the water that I shall give him shall be*
> *in him a well of water springing up into everlasting*
> *life. The woman saith unto him, Sir, give me this*
> *water, that I thirst not, neither come hither to draw.*

"Sir, give me this water." The Lord had the woman's full attention. Every day she needed to come alone to get her water. Every
day she needed to carry the water home. It was quite a chore. Jesus
offered her living water to satisfy her thirst.

"This man offers me living water," she mused. "Water that will
take away my thirst forever. Every day I come here to this well to
draw water, but it never satisfies me. How well I know that! I never
have enough."

My friend, the world has many wells of water, but none will ever
satisfy your heart and soul. The world is running hither and yon
trying everything under heaven. They are like bees going from
flower to flower, trying to find enough honey to be satisfied. Whoever drinks of this water shall thirst again. You can go to a dance on
Monday, a show on Tuesday, a party on Wednesday, and something else every other night. You go the regular round, week after
week, trying to find satisfaction—but you will never find it.

"If I only had money," you say. If you had money, you wouldn't
be satisfied. Instead, you would be more dissatisfied than you are
today.

"If I only had a place of honor," you say. Even that wouldn't
satisfy you.

"If I only had all the pleasure I want. . . ." Still you wouldn't be
satisfied. "He that drinketh of this water shall thirst again." You
can't find satisfaction outside of yourself, or produce it within
yourself. "But if you drink of the water I'll give you, you will never
thirst again. It will be in you a well of water."

This is not the only time Jesus made this offer during His ministry. In John 7:37-38 He will say, "If any man thirst, let him come

unto me, and drink. He that believeth on me, as the scripture hath said, out of his belly shall flow rivers of living water."

Three Revelations Given (4:16-26)

Revelation of the Woman (4:16-19)

Here we have the revelation of the woman. This is the first of three revelations in this portion, after she said, "Sir, give me this water that I thirst not, neither come hither to draw."

> **4:16-19. *Jesus saith unto her, Go, call thy husband, and come hither. The woman answered and said, I have no husband. Jesus said unto her, Thou hast well said, I have no husband: For thou hast had five husbands; and he whom thou now hast is not thy husband: in that saidst thou truly. The woman saith unto him, Sir, I perceive that thou art a prophet.***

Here we have the revelation of the woman. Notice the change in her last response to Jesus. The woman had answered before, "Sir, thou hast nothing to draw with." She was respectful. Then she said, "Sir, give me this water." Again she was showing respect. But when He said to her, "Go and call your husband," she was a changed woman.

"I haven't any husband. Why bring that matter up? Why bring that into the question? I haven't any husband. Why talk about that?" She didn't call Him "Sir" this time.

What did He say in response? Did He say, "You old sinner! Lady, you're an awful woman"? Is that what He said? No. He did not condemn her, but gently laid her heart bare. He said, "You are right in saying, 'I have no husband.' But you know, you have already had five husbands, and the man you're living with now is not your husband. What you have said is true."

"Sir, I perceive you are a prophet," the woman said out loud. But inside she was saying, "How did this Jew know this about me? What have I got myself into this morning?"

There can be no reception of living water until we see ourselves as God sees us.

"Go and call your husband."

"I haven't any."

And the woman stood before Him with her heart laid bare. Her whole life was an open book to Him. She stood before her Judge (see John 5:22), but she didn't run away. If Jesus had been hard on her, if He had accused her of sin, she might have said, "Mind your own business," picked up her pot, and gone away without her water. Instead, the woman stood there with her heart bare before Him, and she didn't run away.

I am reminded, by the way, of three other confessions. Job said, "I have heard of thee by the hearing of the ear: but now mine eye seeth thee. Wherefore I abhor myself" (Job 42:5-6). There was no restoration for Job until you have his confession.

The same thing is true in Isaiah 6. The great prophet, who as a courtier prophesied in the reign of four kings, said when he saw the Lord, "Woe is me! for I am undone" (6:5). And on that confession the angel came and touched his lips, and cleansed him of his sin.

Dear Peter in Luke 5 said, "Depart from me; for I am a sinful man, O Lord" (Luke 5:8).

Whether it be Job or Isaiah or Peter or the woman—or you: the revelation of God always brings the revelation of yourself.

There can be no reception of living water until we see ourselves as God sees us. We can have no appreciation of all that God is, until we see ourselves as God sees us. Why is it today that so many have no appreciation of the Savior? It is because we have never seen ourselves as God sees us. We are not willing to declare that there is no good thing in us. We need a revelation of ourselves. Like Nicodemus, we need to understand that we cannot please God by anything we do. We need to be born again.

Revelation of the Father (4:20-24)

This dear woman. She knew her condition as she stood before Christ. "Sir," she said, "I perceive that thou art a prophet." **4:20.**

Our fathers worshipped in this mountain; and ye say, that in Jerusalem is the place where men ought to worship. "I want reality. But what can a person do? Where can I really worship God? We say it must be in this mountain. You Jews say it must be in Jerusalem. What am I to do?"

> *4:21-24. Jesus saith unto her, Woman, believe me, the hour cometh, when ye shall neither in this mountain, nor yet at Jerusalem, worship the Father. Ye worship ye know not what: we know what we worship: for salvation is of the Jews. But the hour cometh, and now is, when the true worshippers shall worship the Father in spirit and in truth: for the Father seeketh such to worship him. God is a Spirit: and they that worship him must worship him in spirit and in truth.*

Here is the revelation of God as Spirit and as Father to the poor Samaritan woman. Having had a revelation of her own heart, she receives the revelation of God. Before there can be cleansing and reality of life, there must be a recognition that we're sinful. She recognizes that.

Now the Lord says, "Woman, I will answer your questions. This mountain isn't the only place to worship God. Neither is Jerusalem. It doesn't matter where you worship God."

Places disappear before the God of all grace. How wonderful! The important thing is not where we worship. It's not a question of location, or ceremony, or ordinance. Instead, Jesus said, "You are to worship the Father. Places do not matter, for God is Spirit. The Father wants men and women to enter into a right relationship with Him and worship Him in spirit and in truth."

"Worship the Father in spirit and in truth." Jesus spoke of God in a new way. He is the Father. And He seeks for men and women to worship Him in spirit and in truth. God is not seeking servants. He is not seeking for people to work. He is looking for worshipers. Service is the outflow of worship. In other words, worship is the important thing. And when you and I are really in "worship" with Him, there will flow from us a logical service.

Now I am well aware of the fact today that in many Christian churches throughout the land, service seems most important. I want to say this to you: as far as I can read my Bible, the first important thing for a man to do is to accept the Savior. The next is to worship.

Revelation of the Son (4:25-26)

By this point in their conversation, the woman at the well was troubled. "I can see my sinfulness and the emptiness of my life," she thought to herself. "I want the living water this man is talking about. I want to worship the Father. But I still don't understand how this is supposed to happen."

4:25. *I know that Messias cometh, which is called Christ: when he is come, he will tell us all things.*

"All I know," the woman said, "is that when the Messiah comes, he will straighten this out. He will explain everything to us." The Samaritans were anticipating the coming of the Messiah, as were the Jews.

4:26. *Jesus saith unto her, I that speak unto thee am he.*

This is the revelation of the Son. You can just see the movement in this woman's experience. You can just see her thinking, and see how the Lord in His patience, in His tenderness, in His love is just guiding her along.

What a wonderful picture of the Savior! There is no judging of the woman. He doesn't damn her. He doesn't condemn her. He doesn't tell her to go away from Him, that she would defile Him. He just guides her along.

When she came to the well, she came with an empty waterpot to draw natural water. When Jesus told her who He was, she left her waterpot and ran back to Sychar to tell everyone about the Savior. For years her life had been empty. Sin had never satisfied her. She had drunk that water again and again, but she was never satisfied.

After meeting with the Savior, however, she became a waterpot filled with living water. She was satisfied.

My friend, does this apply to you? Have you longed for reality? Have you longed for something where you could put your hand and say, "I know where I am. I know my relationship to my Father and to my Savior, but I would like to have in my daily walk and conversation this living water"?

Go through this passage and examine the experience of this woman and the questions that were raised in her heart and mind. Then watch the Lord meet the need. Might I say, it is a wonderful picture. Our Lord "must needs" go through Samaria. There's a woman there, a woman who's hungry for reality. She doesn't know what she needs or wants, but she knows that her life is empty. Sin has never satisfied her. She has drunk and drunk and drunk of that water, and she has never been satisfied.

And I say to you, that you can try everything that man offers, everything the world offers, everything that religion offers, and never be satisfied. For although this woman was a sinful woman, she knew something about the Old Testament. She knew something about the coming Messiah. She knew about the worship they had on the mountain. But she was never satisfied.

If you want living water, if you want perfect satisfaction, if you want peace and forgiveness for the sins that so easily beset you, then there is only—absolutely only—one place to find it. And you will find it in a Person.

As we let Him lay our hearts bare, and as we let Him reveal the Father and the Son to us, we are letting Him prepare us for the inflow—and outflow—of living water to us and through us. Knowing who He is, is a prerequisite for having the living water (4:10). He has given us the Scriptures and the Holy Spirit that we might know Him, and it is His purpose that we know Him in spirit and in truth. As we know the Father and the Son, our lives will flourish, and become fruitful, and we will be fitted to carry the water of life to others.

The world is filled with unsatisfied people. They have tried everything. We need to reach out to others as Jesus did.

Oh, His patience, and tenderness, and sweetness in talking to the woman at the well. He met her on her own ground, and talked to her about something she was interested in. He did not condemn her, but brought her into an understanding of the glorious gospel of Christ.

We should never judge people or condemn them because of their sinfulness. Instead we should point them to the Savior. He is the only one who can truly satisfy.

My, what a Savior we have. What a Lord we have. What a lesson we have—the revelation of the woman, of the Father, and of the Son. May God open our eyes to see the glories and the beauties of our Savior, that we may serve Him in spirit and in truth.

Three Missions Given (4:27-42)

Mission of the Woman (4:27-30, 39-42)

The next portion gives us a revelation of three missions. First of all, we shall take up the woman's mission.

She had come to the well, this sinful woman, for natural water. But now she leaves her water pot and goes into the city to speak to the men.

> **4:27-30.** *And upon this came his disciples, and marvelled that he talked with the woman: yet no man said, What seekest thou? or, Why talkest thou with her? The woman then left her waterpot, and went her way into the city, and saith to the men, Come, see a man, which told me all things that ever I did: is not this the Christ? Then they went out of the city, and came unto him.*

Notice the simplicity of this woman's testimony: "Come, see a man who knows all about me. Isn't this the Messiah?" She didn't argue about Christ's identity, or make a long story out of her testimony. She merely made a wonderful, simple statement.

My friend, I believe that there are more people saved through the simple testimony of newborn babies in Christ, than through all the flowery sermons preachers give. The gospel isn't shared through intellectual persuasion or scholastic presentations of the truth. The woman who met Jesus at the well didn't split hairs. She simply announced: "I found a man who told me all about myself. Is this not the Christ?"

The zeal of this woman for the Savior was a demonstration of her love. She was so filled with the joy of salvation that she had to pass it on to somebody else. The Lord Jesus rebuked the Ephesian church for losing that first love for the Savior. He said, "I have somewhat against thee, because thou hast left thy first love. Remember therefore from whence thou art fallen, and repent, and do the first works" (Revelation 2:4-5). How easy it is for those of us who have been Christians for some time to lose that fervency of love in seeking to reach friends with the gospel of Christ. May the Lord restore you and me to that first love.

I wish that we would find the Lord so precious that it would be our delight to regularly share Christ with others. I wish it would be our delight not to argue with them or confuse them with our knowledge, but to give them a simple, blessed statement of Jesus Christ as the Savior. That was the mission of the woman who met Christ. She immediately ran with joy to tell others of the Savior.

4:31-38. *See page 81-86.*

4:39-42. *And many of the Samaritans of that city believed on him for the saying of the woman, which testified, He told me all that ever I did. So when the Samaritans were come unto him, they besought him that he would tarry with them: and he abode there two days. And many more believed because of his own word; And said unto the woman, Now we believe, not because of thy saying: for we have heard him ourselves, and know that this is indeed the Christ, the Savior of the world.*

The day the woman met the Savior she became a witness and

many believed on Him because of her word. You know, I was struck with one thing. There are no miracles here. He didn't perform any miracles. In chapter 2, you remember, after He had cleansed the temple, the Jews said, "Where do you get your authority for cleansing the temple?" And He said, "Destroy this temple, and in three days I will raise it up." The chapter ends, "Many believed in his name, when they saw the miracles which he did. But Jesus did not commit himself unto them."

Theirs was a persuasion, not of love for Him, but of faith based on the spectacular—a very shallow faith. But not here. There are no miracles here. There are no signs. He didn't do some supernatural thing. They came to Him on the testimony of a woman.

In chapters 2 and 3 you have Him in Judaea. You have Him in Jerusalem. You have Him dealing with the Jews, performing miracles, presenting the credentials of His Messiahship. And they didn't believe on Him. He came down to the hated Samaritans, the despised Samaritans, and without even one miracle they believed the Word of God. My friend, there is nothing that delights the heart of God more than to have people just believe His Word.

Quite often people have said to me, "Why Mr. Mitchell, if God would perform a miracle, I'd believe."

No, you wouldn't. No, you wouldn't.

One day, as we read in Luke 16, Jesus told the account of Lazarus the beggar and the rich man. They were both in the abode of the dead, but only Lazarus was in Abraham's bosom. The rich man besought Abraham to send someone from the dead so that his brother would repent. And the answer came: "They will not be persuaded through one rose from the dead." The Lord was saying, "If you're not attracted to My person, you will not believe the things I do."

In Samaria, however, God used the poor woman, and He had such fruitage through her testimony that His heart, I am sure, was filled with joy. She now, having met the Savior, had something to live for. What was her mission? Telling her friends and neighbors of the Savior. Is that your mission?

Mission of the Savior (4:31-34)

4:31-34. *In the mean while his disciples prayed him, saying, Master, eat. But he said unto them, I have meat to eat that ye know not of. Therefore said the disciples one to another, Hath any man brought him ought to eat? Jesus saith unto them, My meat is to do the will of him that sent me, and to finish his work.*

When the disciples came back, Jesus was finishing His conversation with the woman at the well. They had been into town to buy food. That's what Jesus had sent them to do. But when they came back, Jesus ignored their request to come and eat. "Has someone given Him something to eat?" they thought. "Why, when we left He was hungry. And He stayed here the whole time to talk to the woman. Why isn't He hungry now? Who gave Him some food to eat?"

Jesus explained to the disciples what He meant by saying, "My meat is to do the will of Him that sent Me, and to finish His work. My Father sent Me on a mission. My joy and satisfaction are not in material things. My meat is to complete the work He gave Me to do."

Reaching hungry hearts was meat and drink to the Lord. It is the same for anyone who has a yearning to do the Father's will, for reaching hearts for Him gives more satisfaction than having a meal. Have you experienced that? Have you forgotten to eat at times because you have been used of God in leading someone to Him? Is your meat to do the will of the One who sent you?

The Lord Jesus left glory and came to earth because He had a great mission to accomplish. The will of the Father was for Him to be the Savior of the world. "God sent not his Son into the world to condemn the world; but that the world through him might be saved" (John 3:17). "The Father sent the Son to be the Saviour of the world" (1 John 4:14). Jesus Himself said, "I seek not mine own will, but the will of the Father which hath sent me" (John 5:30). "I do always those things that please him" (John 8:29). The driving force in the life of our Savior was the will of His Father. His mission was to become the Savior of all men. No wonder the men of Sychar told the woman, "Now we believe . . . and know that this is indeed the Christ, the Saviour of the world" (4:42).

"This is a faithful saying," Paul wrote, "and worthy of all acceptation, that Christ Jesus came into the world to save sinners" (1 Timothy 1:15). He came to seek and to save that which was lost. The Jewish leaders murmured, saying, "This man receiveth sinners, and eateth with them" (Luke 15:2). "Why do ye eat and drink with publicans and sinners?" (Luke 5:30). Jesus told them, "I came not to call the righteous, but sinners to repentance" (Luke 5:32). Jesus came into the world, my friend, to save you and me.

"My meat is to do the will of him that sent me, and to finish his work," Jesus said. Note his complete satisfaction with doing God's will. No wonder He rejoiced on the night of His betrayal, "I have finished the work which thou gavest me to do" (John 17:4). He cried from the cross, "It is finished" (John 19:30). Jesus came to die that men might live. He came to become our Savior.

Mission of the Believer (4:35-38)

The mission of Jesus was to be our Savior, which leads me to the third mission.

> **4:35-38. *Say not ye, There are yet four months, and then cometh harvest? behold, I say unto you, Lift up your eyes, and look on the fields; for they are white already to harvest. And he that reapeth receiveth wages, and gathereth fruit unto life eternal: that both he that soweth and he that reapeth may rejoice together. And herein is that saying true, One soweth, and another reapeth. I sent you to reap that whereon ye bestowed no labour: other men laboured, and ye are entered into their labours.***

There are several things I want to impress upon your heart about our mission. First, we all have a mission as believers. Jesus said, "As thou hast sent me into the world, even so have I also sent them into the world" (John 17:18). He didn't send only a couple of disciples; He has sent us all into the world. In another place He said, "As my Father hath sent me, even so send I you" (John 20:21). All of the saints are to do the work of the ministry so that the body may increase in love (Ephesians 4:12-16).

My friend, do you have a project? Do you have a mission? If you are a believer, then you have a mission. I think it is time we became busy fulfilling our mission. The moment the woman came into a right relationship with the Savior, she couldn't rest until she went back to tell others about Him. Dear Andrew and Philip were like that as well. "We have found Him," they said. "We have found the Messiah!" Have You?

William Carey of India said, "My job as a missionary is to tell people about the Savior. I just cobble shoes to pay the way." I don't know what your job is. That's not important. Maybe God gave you that job to help pay the way for yourself or others to share the gospel. But your primary job, from the moment you accepted the Savior, is to do the will of your Father.

What is God's will? "The Lord is . . . not willing that any should perish, but that all should come to repentance" (2 Peter 3:9). God has sent all of us as believers out into the world with the mission of sharing Christ with others.

I want you to mark, in the second place, how the Spirit of God rules out any room for envy or for jealousy or for egotism in the mission of a believer. Paul said, "I have planted, Apollos watered; but God gave the increase. So then neither is he that planteth any thing, neither he that watereth; but God that giveth the increase" (1 Corinthians 3:6-7). We don't rejoice in the tool that is used. We don't rejoice in the sickle, but in the wheat. We don't glory in the pen that writes the letter. We are not to glory in ourselves because we are just the tools, the channels which God uses.

And third He says, "Lift up your eyes and look because the fields are already white to harvest." Here is an urgency of mission. I take it from the context that when the woman went back to the city of Sychar, out came the men. Oh, I wouldn't be surprised if there were women there as well. Here came some of the people from

Sychar out to the well. As they were coming up the road to the well, the Lord said, "You say there are four months and then the harvest. I say, look, the harvest is already here. The field is white unto harvest." The trouble is not that there is no harvest. The trouble is there are no reapers. Your sickles are dull.

May I tell you, my friends, that today after we have had the Word of God for almost two thousand years, the field is still white unto harvest. Our Lord could say in Matthew 9:38, "Pray ye therefore the Lord of the harvest," for I read He had compassion on the multitudes. They were as sheep having no shepherd. Pray ye the Lord of the harvest to thrust forth laborers into His harvest. The harvest is here. The reapers are few.

If I were to ask you now how many have you reaped this year, how many have you witnessed to concerning the Savior, what could you say? Have you had a harvest? Have you sown the seed? Now, remember that all do not harvest. Some plow the field. Some sow the grain. Others have to reap the harvest. But they all share in the harvest and they all rejoice in the fruitage.

Some men have a propensity for personal work. Others don't. Others have the joy of sowing the seed of the Word of God, scattering the seed, giving a testimony by life as well as by word. Others rejoice in teaching the Word to others in homes, classes, and churches. But everyone of us has a part in this thing. You either plow or sow or reap. But I tell you today that the harvest is white.

The thing that amazed me during a trip I took to Southeast Asia was the great hunger in the hearts of the Asian evangelists. One after the other they stood up and pleaded for help for their country. One from Hong Kong stood up and said, "My brethren, my brethren," with tears running down his cheeks, "remember there are over 700 million Chinese. My people need the gospel."

And the next hour an evangelist from India stood up and said, "May I remind you, gentlemen, that there are over 450 million people in India, and this year there will be thousands who pass over to eternity without ever hearing the gospel of Christ." His heart was broken as he spoke about India. Evangelist after evangelist spoke. These men had a vision. They saw a need. They saw the fields white unto harvest, but no one there to harvest.

Some of us were active at one time as reapers for the Lord. We used to bear witness and be used of the Lord to bring in a harvest for Him. But then we put our sickle to one side, and now it has become dull and rusty. We haven't kept in the Word of God. We haven't kept in close fellowship with Him. We have allowed the ridicule of the world to make us ashamed of the gospel. Consequently, we have lost our desire to reach men and women for Christ.

We will face hardships in the world if we try to fulfill the mission God has given to us. This is a fourth aspect of the believer's mission. The apostle Paul was rebuffed and persecuted in every city he entered to share the gospel. Certain ones believed. But few, in fact, believed. Our Savior had three and a half years of public ministry. After Christ spent all of that time presenting His credentials as the Son of God, how many followed Him? Very few. In John 6 Jesus said, "Unless you are joined to me, you have no life."

Those who were following Jesus said, "This is a hard saying. Who can receive it?" From that time forth many of His disciples walked no more with Him.

Jesus turned to the twelve. "Are you going to leave me as well?"

Peter said, "Lord, where can we go? You alone have the words of eternal life." The hardships go hand in hand with the mission.

And in the fifth place, prayer is connected with our mission. Can you pray? Jesus said, "The harvest is plenteous. The laborers are few. Therefore, pray to the Lord of the harvest. Ask Him to send forth more laborers."

People tell me, "Oh, I can't go to the mission field, and I don't have much to give." But can you pray?

"But I don't even know how to pray."

All right. Read Romans 8:26, where Paul wrote, "We know not what we should pray for as we ought: but the Spirit itself maketh intercession for us with groanings which cannot be uttered." The question is not whether or not you can pray. The question is whether or not you are giving yourself to God for the Spirit of God to pray.

We don't take time to pray. We dash into God's presence and

dash out again. We know so little of waiting on the Lord. One could not begin to imagine what God could do in the midst of a church if two dozen people were to give themselves to intercession for lost souls, and another two dozen believers were to ready their sickles for the harvest. My, what God could do!

We have a mission from God, whether we were sent to sow or reap. We each have a responsibility to reach our generation for Christ. I wish we would stop playing Christianity and be like the dear woman who met Jesus at the well. She wasn't profound. She wasn't a great teacher. She was a simple woman. But she knew one thing—she had met the Savior. "Come, see a man . . . is this not the Christ?" she told her friends. The people of the town came out to see Jesus, and a large number believed because of her simple testimony.

4:39-42. *See pages 78-80.*

The Second Sign: Healing the Nobleman's Son (4:43-54) —Jesus Returns to Galilee

Jesus stayed two days among the Samaritans after meeting the woman at the well. He revealed Himself to them, and many believed on Him. The amazing this is that there was no need for Him to perform any miracles. It must have rejoiced His heart that they believed when they saw Him. They didn't demand a sign first. He later said, "You are blessed, Thomas, because you have seen and believed. Blessed are they that have not seen, and yet have believed" (John 20:29).

4:43-44. *Now after two days he departed thence, and went into Galilee. For Jesus himself testified, that a prophet hath no honour in his own country.*

I take it that He was referring to Nazareth because the next verse says that when He came into Galilee, the Galileans received Him. But not in Nazareth.

The other three Gospels make this clear. When Jesus taught in the synagogue in "his own country," the people of Nazareth scoffed at Him (Matthew 13:54-58). Mark records the same incident, and adds that "he marvelled because of their unbelief" (Mark 6:6). Luke records what He said in the synagogue, and how the people tried to throw Him over a cliff in their anger (Luke 4:16-30).

> **4:45-46.** *Then when he was come into Galilee, the Galilaeans received Him, having seen all the things that he did at Jerusalem at the feast: for they also went unto the feast. So Jesus came again into Cana of Galilee, where he made the water wine. And there was a certain nobleman, whose son was sick at Capernaum.*

Note the mention of this town of Capernaum. Capernaum was the Lord's home during the three and a half years of His ministry. There He performed three tremendous miracles as signs of His deity, yet the people spurned Him. It was at Capernaum that He healed the centurion's servant. It was at Capernaum where He raised the daughter of Jairus from the dead. And now you have a nobleman and his son. These were three remarkable miracles Jesus performed at Capernaum.

Yet the Lord Jesus had this to say about Capernaum: "And thou, Capernaum, which art exalted unto heaven, shalt be brought down to hell: for if the mighty works, which have been done in thee, had been done in Sodom, it would have remained until this day. But I say unto you, That it shall be more tolerable for the land of Sodom in the day of judgment, than for thee" (Matthew 11:23-24).

> **4:47-48.** *When he (the nobleman) heard that Jesus was come out of Judaea into Galilee, he went unto him, and besought him that he would come down, and heal his son: for he was at the point of death. Then said Jesus unto him, Except ye see signs and wonders, ye will not believe.*

From a city that had rejected the Savior a certain man came to Jesus in desperate need. He knew the Lord could perform miracles, and he wanted Him to come and heal his dying son. Jesus said to him, however, "You won't believe unless you see signs." He did not say that in Samaria. But this man was apparently a Jew. Paul wrote, "The Jews require a sign" (1 Corinthians 1:22). He questioned the man about the sincerity of his belief.

4:49. *The nobleman saith unto him, Sir, come down ere my child die.*

A man's need is his plea. "I have no time to argue this question," the nobleman said. "Sir, come to Capernaum before my son dies. I don't care about signs. Please, just come!"

4:50-54. *Jesus saith unto him, Go thy way; thy son liveth. And the man believed the word that Jesus had spoken unto him, and he went his way. And as he was now going down, his servants met him, and told him, saying, Thy son liveth. Then enquired he of them the hour when he began to amend. And they said unto him, Yesterday at the seventh hour the fever left him. So the father knew that it was at the same hour, in the which Jesus said unto him, Thy son liveth: and himself believed, and his whole house. This is again the second miracle that Jesus did, when he was come out of Judaea into Galilee.*

It is rather remarkable to me how the Lord deals with people. In the Gospel through John we have seen how He dealt with fishermen, a leading rabbi of Israel, a Samaritan woman, and now a nobleman from Capernaum. The Lord dealt with all levels of society. It makes no difference who you are. If you have a need, the Lord will meet that need.

May I suggest something else? Sometimes the Lord allows you to have a need in order to cause you to seek Him. This nobleman would not have left home to seek Jesus if his son wasn't sick. Sometimes the Lord uses afflictions and sorrow to bring us to Himself. It was a blessing for the nobleman that his son was sick, because through the incident he met the Savior. What a wonderful thing it is to take the various afflictions of life and find in them God's purpose to bring you closer to Himself.

Do you have a need? Do you have a problem? Do you have an affliction? Are you in sorrow? Can you say with the psalmist, "Thou in faithfulness hast afflicted me" (Psalm 119:75)? What for? To draw us closer to Himself. The great desire of the heart of God is to bring us close to Himself.

John 5

Christ, The Judge

Overview of John's Gospel

By way of review, let's consider John 1-4 again. In these chapters the Lord Jesus worked among every level of society. In chapter 1 we have Him dealing with fishermen. In chapter 2 He talks with His mother and with the leaders of Israel. He conversed with Nicodemus in chapter 3, and with the Samaritan woman and the nobleman in chapter 4. He could reach into every level of society because the message of the gospel of the Savior of men is for everyone.

Now when we come to chapters 5 through 8, we have the very heart of the Gospel through John, and here He begins to deal with the multitudes. Here you have His many claims, as John begins to press this very fact that Jesus is indeed God.

Who is this Jesus who was asking men to put their trust in Him? Is He a real Savior? Is He who He claimed to be? Is He God manifest in the flesh? Does He have all authority? Does He have all power? Can He save sinners? Can He give life eternal? Can He free us from judgment? Can He raise us from the dead? These are the issues addressed in these chapters, beginning with chapter 5.

When you come to chapter 6, He manifests Himself as the Creator: when He fed the five thousand with five loaves and two fish, when He walked the water and stilled the storm, and when He declared that the life He gives is eternal, satisfying life. It is indwelling life. All you need of life is in Him.

In chapter 7 He is the Heavenly One. He came from heaven. His message is from heaven. He is going back to heaven. He is going to send the Spirit of God from heaven.

In chapter 8, He is the light of the world. He is the One who has authority over death. He can deliver us from both sin and death. He is the sinless One. He is El Shaddai, Abraham's God. He is the Eternal One.

It is at this point that His hearers realized that they had to make a decision. They must either fall down and worship Him, or they must kill Him. They chose to pick up stones. This is the crux of the whole situation. Either Jesus Christ, the Son of God, is worthy of your trust, and worship, and praise, or He ought to be taken out and stoned. And that's really the end of the argument of John.

In chapter 9 He opens the eyes of a man born blind. In chapter 10 He is the Good Shepherd. In chapter 11 He raises Lazarus from the dead. In chapter 12 He entered Jerusalem as the King. And He's on the way to be crucified.

In chapter 13 to 17 He's with the disciples. In chapter 13, He is the Advocate. In chapter 14 He is the Coming One. In chapter 15 He is the Vine. In chapter 16 He is the Preeminent One. In chapter 17 He is our High Priest. In chapters 18 and 19 He is taken and crucified. It's finished. In chapter 20 He is raised from the dead. In chapter 21 we have His final word to His disciples.

You see, this is John. You have another simple division of the book. In the first 4 chapters, Jesus talks to individuals. Then He teaches the multitudes. Then He teaches His disciples. And in every passage—He's the center.

Background of John 5

May I suggest, first of all, that here we have the revelation of Jesus Christ as Jehovah Rapha. You will find that term used in Exodus 15, and it means, "I am the Lord that healeth thee."

You remember the account. The people of Israel had come out of Egypt and had crossed the Red Sea. They had taken a three-day journey into the wilderness and had found no water. When you take a lot of people three days without water, you have a problem. So they murmured. They were wishing they were back in Egypt. And then, when they did come to water, it was very bitter. They called it "Marah," which means "bitter."

And the Lord said to Moses, "Take a tree and throw it in, and the water will be sweetened." So the waters were healed of their bitterness, and God revealed Himself to them as Jehovah Rapha. And then He said, "If you will obey my voice and do what I tell you to do, I will not bring upon you the diseases of the Egyptians, for I am the Lord that healeth thee" (see Exodus 15:26). And remember, they are going to spend forty years in the wilderness with no corner drugstores, no drugs, no vitamins, no doctors, no nurses. Nothing. God was their only hope for healing.

God first revealed Himself as Jehovah Rapha by the pools of water in the wilderness. But what I am after is this. God revealed Himself again as Jehovah Rapha by the pool of water called Bathesda in Jerusalem.

For further information, I would like you to read Exodus 15, 16, and 17. Exodus 15 is comparable to John 5, Exodus 16 to John 6, and Exodus 17 to John 7. John 8 has to do with Him as the Great Light. In Exodus, God had a pillar of fire by night to guide them and to lighten their way.

When Mrs. Mitchell and I were in Jerusalem, we went to see the pool of Bethesda. You see, a great many of the critics of the Bible said that this account in John 5 could not be true because there wasn't a pool in Jerusalem that has five porches and was big enough for a multitude of sick people. When we were there, however, the archaeologists were excavating the site of this pool. They had dug down deep into the ground, into layers through a couple of thousand years. And they had found the pool of Bethesda, including all five porches. There was plenty of room there for a great crowd of sick people. Believer, you can stay by your Bible, and the account in John 5.

The Third Sign: Healing a Sick Man (5:1-16)
—Jesus Returns to Jerusalem

Why Jesus Selected One Man (5:1-9)

5:1-5. *After this there was a feast of the Jews; and Jesus went up to Jerusalem. Now there is at Jerusalem by the sheep market a pool, which is called in the Hebrew tongue Bethesda, having five porches. In these lay a great multitude of impotent folk, of blind, halt, withered, waiting for the moving of the water. For an angel went down at a certain season into the pool, and troubled the water: whosoever then first after the troubling of the water stepped in was made whole of whatsoever disease he had. And a certain man was there, which had an infirmity thirty and eight years.*

Along came our Lord and He did an unusual thing. In His first miracle in chapter 2, His mother said, "They have no wine." In chapter 4, the second miracle, a nobleman came and asked Him to heal his son. In this third miracle, however, no one asks anything of the Lord. Of His own volition He comes to the pool of Bethesda.

5:6-9. *When Jesus saw him lie, and knew that he had been now a long time in that case, he saith unto him, Wilt thou be made whole? The impotent man answered him, Sir, I have no man, when the water is troubled, to put me into the pool: but while I am coming, another steppeth down before me. Jesus saith unto him, Rise, take up thy bed, and walk. And immediately the man was made whole, and took up his bed, and walked: and on the same day was the sabbath.*

Now, when the Lord came, here was a crowd of sick people, and they were all waiting to get into the pool. It says that the first one who got in was made whole. But here's a man who has no one to help him. His friends and his family have given him up in despair, and he is left alone to die. For thirty-eight years he has lain there. For thirty-eight years he hasn't been in the temple . . . thirty-eight years in helplessness, thirty-eight years experiencing the fruitage of sin.

But the Lord came and found this man. He said to him, "Do you want to be made whole?"

And the man said, "Sir, I have no man, when the water is troubled, to put me into the pool; but while I am coming, another steppeth down before me."

Jesus said, "Rise, take up thy bed, and walk." And the same day was the sabbath.

My question is this: Why didn't Jesus heal the whole crowd? I'd like to put you on the spot, dear reader. Wouldn't you like to see people healed?

When you go down to the hospitals, don't you wish you could just heal every one of them? Or are you different from me? I go in and sometimes I feel so helpless. The dear saints of God and others are suffering so. It's true we pray and the Lord wonderfully answers prayer. We thank God for that and for His faithfulness in raising up people. But don't you just wish you could touch every one of them?

And if you had been here at this pool, how many would you have healed? All of them? Would you have healed all of them? You mean to tell me you have more compassion than the Lord? He healed only one! I repeat the question: Do you have more compassion than Jesus? Then why did He heal just one man?

There was only one who had given up hope of getting into the pool. All of them were still hoping to get in. They had their friends, their families. They had their different ones to help them. But this man said, "Sir, I have no one. I've given up hope."

Why the Sick Man Had Suffered (5:10-14)

5:10-14. *The Jews therefore said unto him that was cured, It is the sabbath day: it is not lawful for thee to* *carry thy bed. He answered them, He that made me whole, the same said unto me, Take up thy bed, and walk. Then asked they him, What man is that which said unto thee, Take up thy bed, and walk? And he that was healed wist not who it was: for Jesus had conveyed himself away, a multitude being in that place. Afterward Jesus findeth him in the temple, and said unto him, Behold, thou art made whole: sin no more, lest a worse thing come unto thee.*

For thirty-eight years the man whom Jesus healed had been sick. Why did he suffer for so long like that? Jesus made it clear that this man had suffered because of his own sin, although this isn't the case for everyone (see John 9:3).

When God made man, He never intended that man would experience sickness and weakness, disease and affliction. That was not His purpose. These things are the fruit of sin in the human race. When we were born into Adam's race, we were born with the seed of death in us. Thank God, the day is coming when our Savior will return, and we will have new bodies that know nothing of disease or frailty or affliction or sorrow or suffering.

"Afterward Jesus findeth him in the temple. . . ." Rather precious, is it not? The moment the man is healed, he goes right to the temple. He goes to worship. He goes to thank God. Now he is in the temple, worshiping God. And the Lord found him in the temple, and said to him, "Behold, thou art made whole: sin no more, lest a worse thing come unto thee."

Why the Lord Had Healed on the Sabbath (5:15-16)

5:15-16. *The man departed, and told the Jews that it was Jesus, which had made him whole. And therefore did the Jews persecute Jesus, and sought to slay him, because he had done these things on the sabbath day.*

Jesus said, "Take up your bed and walk." And when He said that, He started an opposition that never ended until He was nailed to the cross. I want you to mark this. There is something in chapter 5 that you do not have preceding this. You have an opposition, a hatred, a desire that will never be satisfied until Jesus is put out of the way. He deliberately healed this man on the sabbath day.

Why didn't the Lord wait until the next day? The man would still have been there, wouldn't he? Or why didn't the Lord simply will that he be made whole, and pass on by without creating all this fuss? That's what He did in Cana of Galilee when He quietly turned the water into wine. That's what He did in Cana when He sent the nobleman home to his healed son.

Why then did He tell this man not only to rise up, but to carry his bed as well? He knew how the Jews interpreted such passages as Jeremiah 17:21, where the Lord said to the Jews, "Take heed to yourselves, and bear no burden on the sabbath day." Why didn't Jesus have the man leave his bed behind? Perhaps He knew that if the man left his bed, he might think he was coming back to it.

Now mark the opposition. These Jews were not concerned about the man being made whole. They didn't care whether he stayed there thirty-eight years more or not. They were more concerned about their tradition, and about the things that were added to the law.

"You're carrying your bed on the sabbath day. What are you doing that for?"

The man replied, "Well, the one that healed me told me to do this. I figured it must have been all right." The man wanted them to see the fact that he had been healed.

"Who is this man that told you to carry your bed?" They were more concerned about keeping the law than about thanking God for such a miracle. They had a distorted idea of the meaning of the sabbath. Jesus repeatedly confronted them about this issue, as He did again in John 9. Jesus wanted them to see that true rest comes from cooperating with God in the work that He wants done.

The Jews were ignorant of the value of the sabbath. They only thought it was a day of rest. Actually, it was the sign of their national covenant with God. God did not give the law of the sabbath day to the church or to the Gentiles. It was a sign of a covenant between God and the people of Israel.

Wherever Israel went, the question came up: "Why don't you work on this day? Why is this day so special? Why do you all rest?" They were to keep it because it was a sign of their relationship between God and their nation (Exodus 31:13-17). But they forgot that, and made it a burdensome thing instead. Important things, such as healing the sick, were forbidden. Less important things, such as helping endangered animals, were permitted.

It was because of Israel's corruption of the sabbath that the judgments of God came upon them. Over and over again the prophets went after Israel for defiling the sabbath. When Israel rejected her Messiah, the covenant was broken. The sabbath sign was no longer in effect. Jesus could not rest until He finished the work His Father had sent Him to accomplish.

The Witness of Christ: Three Claims of Deity (5:17-30)

Christ's Equality in Nature (5:17-18)

5:17-18. *But Jesus answered them, My Father worketh hitherto, and I work. Therefore the Jews sought the more to kill him, because he not only had broken the sabbath, but said also that God was his Father, making himself equal with God.*

"My Father worketh hitherto, and I work." Here we have the first claim of Christ that He is equal with God in nature. Later He said, "I and my Father are one" (John 10:30). He claimed to have a personal relationship with the Father. These Jews knew what He was saying. "You make yourself equal with God," they accused. And they picked up stones to kill Him.

Now I know that in Genesis 2 God hallowed the sabbath day, and rested from all His work (2:1-3). But in Genesis 3, God started working again. He took the skins of animals and clothed Adam and Eve. Down through the centuries God has not rested. He does not rest today. There is no rest for God as long as men are under the bondage and the fruitage of sin. As long as people are in sorrow and affliction, He must work. "And as long as My Father works, I work," Christ said.

When Jesus said this, claiming to be equal in nature with God, He brought the opposition of the Jews up front. Indeed, He was saying here, "As long as My Father has to work, as long as men such as this man lay sick and suffering, I must work. I am one with My Father. I go right along with Him. Whatever He does, that's what I'm going to do. And if there is no rest for My Father, then there is no rest for Me."

It is folly for us to rejoice in our union with Christ unless we work as He worked. In the last chapter He said, "My meat is to do the will of him that sent me, and to finish his work" (4:34). The driving force in His life was to do His Father's will. He could say, "I do always those things that please Him. My meat is to do His will. I have only one ambition in life as a man among men—to do His will." This should be *our* purpose in life. If we love God and are in union with Him through Christ, then we should seek always to do those things which are pleasing to Him.

Jesus worked to please His Father. It cost Him His life. What is it costing you? Dear saints of God, let us redeem the time. Let us buy up every opportunity to witness to others. As long as there are sinful, hurting people, there is a job to be done. God is still saving. He is still transforming. He is still bringing peace and rest to troubled hearts. Let us not waste the time. "My Father worketh hitherto, and I work." May God grant that you and I will be faithful in doing the job He wants us to do.

Christ's Equality in Power (5:19-21)

> **5:19-21. *Then answered Jesus and said unto them, Verily, verily, I say unto you, The Son can do nothing of himself, but what he seeth the Father do: for what things soever he doeth, these also doeth the Son likewise. For the Father loveth the Son, and sheweth***

him all things that himself doeth: and he will shew
him greater works than these, that ye may marvel. For
as the Father raiseth up the dead, and quickeneth
them; even so the Son quickeneth whom he will.

Do you know what He is saying? "Everything that God does, I
can do. God can raise the dead and make them live, and that's what
I can do." He is saying that He has equality with God in power.
And by the way, when you come to chapter 11, our Lord proves
this when He says to Lazarus, who had been four days in the tomb
and was in corruption, "Lazarus, come forth" (John 11:43).

And Lazarus came forth! Jesus did not say, "I will pray to the
Father that you might come forth." He did not say, "In the name of
the Father come forth." He said, "Lazarus, come forth." At His
word Lazarus was raised from the dead and given life.

When Jesus healed the man on the sabbath, the Jews sought to
slay Him. He was deliberately challenging them. He did not beat
around the bush. He claimed to be equal with God in nature by calling God His Father. The Jewish leaders sought the more to kill
Him. But He did not stop and tell them, "Pardon Me, sirs, but you
seem to have misunderstood Me. I didn't mean what you think I
said. I wasn't claiming to be equal with God."

He didn't say that at all. He said, "You're perfectly correct. Not
only am I one with the Father in nature, but I am also one with God
in power. Anything that God does I can and will do. Just as the
Father has power to raise the dead, so do I." The Father has not
given the Son power, but the Son in Himself has divine power.

Why did the Jews crucify Christ? What was their argument before Pilate? They said, "He made himself the Son of God" (John
19:7). And I say to you, that either Jesus Christ is worthy of all
your trust and worship and praise, or He isn't worthy at all. You
have to make your choice. Is Jesus God manifest in the flesh? Are
His claims true? Did He present His credentials? John wrote this
Gospel as proof "that Jesus is the Christ, the Son of God" (John
20:31).

The intensity of the hatred of the Jews for Jesus is evident as we go through this book. When Pilate said, "I will scourge Him" that wasn't enough. They cried, "Away with Him! Crucify Him!" They chose to kill the Son of God.

And you must make a choice as well. Either you must stand today with the Jews who opposed and eventually crucified the Savior, or you must bow in simple faith with the children of God, putting your faith and trust in Him. You must worship Him in spirit and truth. He is worthy of your worship. He is worthy of your trust.

Christ's Equality in Authority (5:22-30)

Not only did the Lord Jesus claim to be equal with God in nature and power, but He claimed to be equal with God in authority. Instead of taking up right at 5:22, I would like to go straight to 5:24, because this verse is the center of the message as far as you and I are concerned.

Quite a few of you do personal work, or you teach a Bible class, or you deal with people. And quite often in dealing with people, possibly down at a mission or in a Bible class, you will use this verse.

> **5:24.** *Verily, verily, I say unto you, He that heareth my word, and believeth on him that sent me, hath everlasting life, and shall not come into condemnation; but is passed from death unto life.*

Where do you receive the authority to say to any sinner—man or woman, boy or girl—that "If you put your trust in Jesus Christ as your own personal Savior, I will guarantee to you that you will receive eternal life right now. And I will guarantee that you will never come into judgment, but that you are passed right now from death to life?" What right do you have to say that? What is behind this verse?

This promise is made to anyone who "heareth my word, and believeth on him that sent me." We can give this promise to anyone who does those two things. To "hear" is not merely to give mental assent to doctrine and truth. Instead, this is the hearing of faith. It is a hearing that responds to the message that is heard. To "believe" means to put your trust in someone. It doesn't simply mean to give assent to certain historical facts. To believe is to trust your eternal welfare to what Christ is and what He has done. That's what it means to believe.

There are those who can quote John 5:24 forwards and backwards, and who say, "Why, I've always believed that." But how they say that often indicates to me how real it is to them. I must do more than know the facts of the gospel. I must do more than know I need to believe in Christ. Unless a person actually trusts the Savior, he isn't "believing"; at least he isn't believing according to the sense that this word is used ninety-eight times in the Gospel of John. Jesus says in 5:24, however, that if a person truly believes in Him, He will do three things for us.

1. Life Is in His Authority. His first claim in John 5:24 is that He will give us life. Jesus promised, "He that heareth my word, and believeth on him that sent me, hath everlasting life." He is not talking about physical resurrection here. (He deals with that in 5:28-29.) He is talking about those who are dead in their sins, and yet who hear His words and respond in belief. Because He is God, He can give life to those He wishes to make alive (5:21).

Look at these verses.

> **5:25-26.** *Verily, verily, I say unto you, The hour is coming, and now is, when the dead shall hear the voice of the Son of God: and they that hear shall live. For as the Father hath life in himself; so hath he given to the Son to have life in himself.*

What is He claiming? Jesus is saying, "I too have this authority. Just as the Father is the source of life, so does the Son have the source of life. And if anyone has eternal life, it is because of his relationship to the Son."

Eternal, satisfying life is only found in Jesus Christ. You remember in John 1:4: "In him was life." Jesus offered the Samaritan woman "a well of water springing up into everlasting life" (4:14).

In John chapter 10, the tenth verse: "I am come that they might have life, and that they might have it more abundantly."

In the upper room the Lord Jesus told the disciples, "I am the way, the truth, and the life" (14:6). "This is life eternal," He said, "that they might know thee the only true God, and Jesus Christ, whom thou hast sent" (17:3). In 1 John 5:12 we read, "He that hath the Son hath life; and he that hath not the Son of God hath not life."

Life—eternal life, spiritual life—is in Jesus Christ. He is the source of it. The Lord Jesus is saying, "All life—real life—is in My hands."

Jesus claimed to be the source of life based on His union with the Father. Life is in His authority because He is God the Son. One cannot have life from the Father without having life from the Son. He made this clear.

5:23. *That all men should honour the Son, even as they honour the Father. He that honoureth not the Son honoureth not the Father which hath sent him.*

To reject the Son is to reject the Father. There are those who say, "I believe in God as the source of life, but I do not believe in Jesus Christ." If we spurn the Son, we spurn the Father. Jesus said that we must honor the Son to honor the Father. There is an indissoluble union between the Father and the Son. You cannot have one without the other. you cannot know God except through Christ. And what I know of Christ is what I know of God.

As the Father gives life, the Son gives life. He is the source of it. And Jesus is saying here, "All life is in my hands." Life can only come through relationship to the Son of God. This is His first claim here.

2. Judgment Is in His Authority. His second claim in John 5:24 is that He will not bring us into judgment. Jesus not only promised that we shall receive eternal life if we believe in Him, but that we "shall not come into condemnation." Our Lord is claiming that all judgment is in His hands.

Mark what Jesus claimed about His authority to judge.

5:22, 5:27, 5:30. *For the Father judgeth no man,*
but hath committed all judgment unto the Son: And
hath given him authority to execute judgment also,
because he is the Son of man. I can of mine own self
do nothing: as I hear, I judge: and my judgment is
just; because I seek not mine own will, but the will of
the Father which hath sent me.

The Father has committed all judgment to the Son because He is
the Son of Man.

Some question the fairness of God's judgment. "Well," they
say, "how can God judge me? God doesn't know what I go
through. He is holy and righteous, but He is way off somewhere
running the universe. What does He know about me and my tests?
What does He know about me and my afflictions? How can God
fairly judge me without righteousness and sympathy?"

The Father has committed all judgment to the Son because He is
the Son of Man, God manifest in the flesh. He was made in the
likeness of men (Philippians 2:7). He experienced the tests and
trials of life as a man. He knows what it is to suffer and be tempted.
He came into the human family and was tested in all points as we
are, yet without sin (Hebrews 4:15).

In the preceeding part of the chapter, these Jews had sat in judgment on Christ. They said, "You're a blasphemer." Their judgment was completely in error. They rejected the Lamb of God who
came to take away the sin of the world.

When Jesus came the first time, He came as the Lamb of God—
in humiliation to put away sin. In the future He will come again,
this time as the Lion of the tribe of Judah. He will come as the great
Judge of men. God has "appointed a day, in the which he will judge
the world in righteousness by that man whom he hath ordained"
(Acts 17:31). The Father ordained the Son of man to judge men,
and guaranteed that fact by raising Christ from the dead. In that day
there will be a summons, not to receive life, but to face judgment.

Jesus is saying, "I am the One who is going to give that summons. I am the One who is the Judge. And you Jews, who are sit-

ting in judgment on Me today, will stand before Me in that day when I am the Judge." All judgment is in His hands. For that reason, God today is inviting men and women to accept the Savior and receive life.

When a person receives the Savior, God forgives him of every sin. He gives him a divine pardon, and pronounces him righteous. If we have accepted Christ, there is no way we will ever have to stand before God in judgment for our sins.

Romans 8:1 assures us that, "There is therefore now no condemnation to them which are in Christ Jesus." And Romans 8:32-34 indicates that God spared not His Son, but delivered Him up for us all. Who can lay anything as a charge against God's elect? It is God who has pronounced us righteous. It is Christ who died and rose again for us. He sits at God's right hand interceding for us. There is no judgment.

I say all judgment is in Jesus' hands. Isn't it wonderful that when sinners accept the Savior, they not only receive eternal life, but are guaranteed that they will not come into judgment? My, what a wonderful truth!

3. Resurrection Is in His Authority. The Lord's third claim in verse 24 is that He will raise us again from the dead. Not only do we have eternal life now, but we are "passed from death unto life."

Notice what Jesus said about His authority to raise everyone from the dead.

5:28-29. *Marvel not at this: for the hour is coming, in the which all that are in the graves shall hear his voice, and shall come forth; they that have done good, unto the resurrection of life; and they that have done evil, unto the resurrection of damnation.*

Do you know what the Lord is saying to these Jews? "Listen, I have just informed you, gentlemen, that I am equal with God in nature. I and my Father are one. I am equal with God in authority and power. I can raise the dead just as He does. All life is in My hands. Listen, you haven't heard the rest of it yet. Marvel not at this. For the hour is coming in which all who are in their graves shall hear the voice of the Son of God. Everyone."

Here is an astounding fact. Death has infected the whole human race. There is no one on earth you can turn to, to avoid it. When you are in trouble, you call in the preacher or a lawyer. When you are sick, you call in a doctor. But when death comes, there's no one to call but the undertaker. Death reigns today because of sin, and there isn't a doctor that can do a thing about it.

Death is inevitable. But our Lord made an amazing statement. He said, "If you will accept Me as your personal Savior, I will guarantee that you will immediately pass from death to life. Death will have no authority over you." That is what He is saying. "I have all authority over resurrection."

How are we going to be raised? Jesus said, "Everyone who is going to be raised from the dead is going to be raised by My voice." Life comes through His voice. This is evident in each of the three passages where our Savior raised someone from the dead. In chapter 5 of Mark, for example, you have the resurrection of the daughter of Jairus. Jesus took the little girl by the hand and said to her, "Talitha cumi, which is, being interpreted, Damsel, I say unto thee, arise" (5:41). The little girl heard the voice of Jesus saying, "Arise," and she sat up and began to walk.

In chapter 7 of Luke you have the resurrection of the widow's son. He was a young man who had died. The people were carrying him out of the city to bury him. And his mother was in deep sorrow. Jesus comforted her, then walked to the bier and said, "Young man, I say unto thee, Arise" (7:14). The widow's son heard Jesus' voice and sat up, causing fear among all the people. The people said, "God hath visited his people" (7:16).

In chapter 11 of John you have the resurrection of Lazarus. Lazarus was a grown man. He had been dead for four days. He was already in corruption. (The little girl had just died. The widow's son was on the way to the tomb, on the way to corruption. But Lazarus was already in corruption.) Jesus comforted the hearts of Mary and Martha, and went to the tomb where Lazarus' body lay. He said, "Lazarus, come forth" (11:43). And he that was dead came forth from the tomb. It has been well said that if the Lord had not singly called out to Lazarus, the whole graveyard would have come forth. That's true; all are going to hear the voice of the Son of God.

Now it's true, Jesus varied His method of healing the sick. He varied His method of opening blind eyes. He varied His method of cleansing lepers. But He never varied His method of raising the dead. He raises the dead by His voice. He speaks, and it is done. And one day, my friend, He is going to descend from heaven with a shout!

The Lord will descend from heaven with a shout, "and the dead in Christ shall rise first: then we which are alive and remain shall be caught up together with them in the clouds, to meet the Lord in the air: and so shall we ever be with the Lord" (1 Thessalonians 4:16-17). We all want to be raptured, don't we? We all want to be translated. Wouldn't that be wonderful? And maybe we shall. But even if we die before Christ comes again, we can be sure that death is a defeated foe.

My Christian friend, if you have any fear of death, may I say to you, that death is already a conquered foe. Death is today the open door into His presence. The resurrection is the hope of all believers.

Some have told me, "Mr. Mitchell, I don't believe in resurrection. When I'm dead, I'm dead." I tell them, "Yes, when you're dead, you're dead. And I can tell you Who is going to raise you from the dead. And if your name is not found written in the Book of Life, you will be cast into the lake of fire. This is the second death."

"All" that are dead shall hear Christ's voice and rise: "They that have done good, unto the resurrection of life; and they that have done evil, unto the resurrection of damnation." There is this two-fold aspect to the resurrection. There is a resurrection of the saved, and a resurrection of the unsaved. "They that have done good" are those that have put their trust in the Savior. The first good thing any person can do is to accept the Savior. "They that have done evil" are intrinsically evil. Their whole nature is evil, and they will be raised for their final judgment.

The Lord Jesus said, "He that heareth my word, and believeth on him that sent me, hath everlasting life, and shall not come into condemnation; but is passed from death unto life" (5:24). By hearing God's Word, we are brought to faith in Christ. "Faith cometh by hearing, and hearing by the word of God" (Romans 10:17). He said, "The words that I speak unto you, they are spirit, and they are life" (John 6:63). The Bible itself doesn't give us life. The Bible brings us to Him who is life.

If you, my friend, have read this far and are realizing that you have never accepted the Savior, I would plead with you to take John 5:24 and make it your own. This precious promise can be yours. I can guarantee to you that the moment you put your trust in Jesus Christ, God's Son, as your own personal Savior, you will receive eternal life. You will never come into judgment, but will pass from death to life. Jesus has guaranteed it.

My, what a solemn thing it is to realize that Jesus Christ is not only the Savior, but He is the Judge. And for those who believe in Him, He is also the One who is going to raise us, and transform us, and make us just like Himself. We shall pass from death to life!

The Witness of Others: Five Evidences of Jesus' Claims (5:31-37)

Witness of John (5:31-35)

We have considered the three claims of Christ to be equal with God. He claimed equality with God in nature, in power, and in authority. But Jesus knew that the Jews would not accept His witness concerning Himself. So here we have the evidences of those claims.

Mark the unbelief of the Jews. **5:31. *If I bear witness of myself, my witness is not true*.** Jesus wasn't saying that His claims were invalid (see 8:14). Instead, He was saying, "If I bear witness of Myself, you won't believe it to be true." For this reason, He gave them the guarantees of His claims.

He cited John the Baptist as one of His witnesses.

> **5:32-35.** *There is another that beareth witness of me; and I know that the witness which he witnesseth of me is true. Ye sent unto John, and he bare witness unto the truth. But I receive not testimony from man; but these things I say, that ye might be saved. He was a burning and shining light: and ye were willing for a season to rejoice in his light.*

We have the testimony of John the Baptist in Matthew 3, Luke 3, and John 1 and 3. He is presented in these passages as the forerunner of Christ. His testimony was that Jesus of Nazareth is the Son of God. He called Jesus the Lamb of God, the preferred One. If the Jews would have accepted the testimony of John, they would have accepted Jesus Christ as the Messiah. They did call John a prophet, but they had nothing to do with Jesus.

Witness of Jesus' Works (5:36)

The works of Jesus were His credentials that He was the Son of God.

> **5:36.** *But I have greater witness than that of John: for the works which the Father hath given me to finish, the same works that I do, bear witness of me, that the Father hath sent me.*

In the Gospel through John, seven signs are recorded to show that Jesus is God manifest in the flesh. Three of these signs show His power as the Creator. He turned the water into wine in chapter 2. He fed the five thousand in chapter 6. He also walked on water in chapter 6.

Three of the signs recorded in John's Gospel reveal His power to heal the sick. He healed a nobleman's son while He was in Cana of Galilee (John 4). He returned to Jerusalem in chapter 5 to heal a man sick for thirty-eight years at the pool of Bethesda. He healed a blind man in chapter 9 by sending him to the pool of Siloam.

The seventh sign presents His power to raise the dead. The tremendous account of the resurrection of Lazarus from the dead is found in John 11. This miracle foreshadowed Jesus' own resurrection from the dead, found in chapter 20.

Each sign recorded in John's Gospel was carefully selected "that ye might believe that Jesus is the Christ, the Son of God; and that believing ye might have life through his name" (John 20:31). Jesus Himself appealed to His works as a sufficient reason to believe in Him. He said, "Believe me that I am in the Father, and the Father in me: or else believe me for the very works' sake" (John 14:11).

Witness of the Father (5:37)

Here we have the Father as another important witness of His claims to deity.

> **5:37. And the Father himself, which hath sent me, hath borne witness of me. Ye have neither heard his voice at any time, nor seen his shape.**

Because "no man hath seen God at any time" (John 1:18), Jesus as God manifested Himself in the flesh to men. He veiled His glory to appear to men (see John 17:5). He came in the likeness of men (Philippians 2:7).

The Jews with whom He spoke had not heard the Father's voice as well. They apparently weren't at His baptism, where a voice came from heaven and said, "This is my beloved Son, in whom I am well pleased" (Matthew 3:17). They had not heard God's voice. The reason for their unbelief was their willful ignorance of God. They chose not to know God.

What a need we have today in our present generation for men and women to know God personally. If we draw nigh to God, He will draw nigh to us (James 4:8). God is more desirous of revealing Himself to us than we are to have that revelation. Let us not excuse our unbelief by saying we can't know God. God is no longer hidden behind a cloud or concealed behind a veil. He has come out to man and revealed Himself. Our Lord could say, "He that hath seen me hath seen the Father" (John 14:9). There are no barriers between God and the soul that means business with Him.

Witness of God's Word (5:38-44)

The reason the Jews did not accept Jesus as the Christ was because of their refusal to believe God's Word.

> **5:38-40.** *And ye have not his word abiding in you: for whom he hath sent, him ye believe not. Search the scriptures; for in them ye think ye have eternal life: and they are they which testify of me. And ye will not come to me, that ye might have life.*

The Jews had the truth of God. "You do search the scriptures," Jesus acknowledged. "Why don't you believe their testimony about Me? Why won't you come to Me?" Jesus wept over Jerusalem and said, "How often would I have gathered thy children together, even as a hen gathereth her chickens under her wings, and *ye would not!*" (Matthew 23:37).

It wasn't that the Jews couldn't come to Jesus; they *wouldn't* come. God wants all men to be saved, and to come to the knowledge of the truth. It's not that men and women cannot come to Christ. They simply will not come. It's not that you can't be saved, but that you don't want to be saved.

Am I talking to you, my friend? God has made all the provision for you to be saved. He offers you eternal life and peace. He offers to join you to His Son. Will you put your trust in Him today?

The Jews refused to believe in the One God had sent. They rejected the witness of the Scriptures concerning Jesus' deity. They selfishly sought status and honor from others instead.

> **5:41-44.** *I receive not honour from men. But I know you, that ye have not the love of God in you. I am come in my Father's name, and ye receive me not: if another shall come in his own name, him ye will receive. How can ye believe, which receive honour one*

of another, and seek not the honour that cometh from God only?

The Lord Jesus accused the Jewish leaders for their unbelief. They knew not God. And because they knew not God, they did not know Christ. If they had known God, they would have known His Son.

May I make this applicable to us today? There are many ecclesiastical leaders in Christendom today who despise the Word of God. And the reason they despise the Word of God is because they do not know God. Jesus said, "If you knew the Scriptures, you would know God. If you knew God, you would know His Son."

May I say something emphatically? We are living in days when many go by the name of Christian, but the Word of God has lost its authenticity and authority in their lives. They know not God. If they knew God, they would know His Son. If they knew His Son, they would love His Word. And our Savior stands as One speaking with authority when He accuses them, not only of unbelief, but of insincerity and ignorance of the knowledge of God.

Jesus went right down to the hearts of these Jewish leaders in accusing them. They would not receive Him. Instead, "if another shall come in his own name, him ye will receive." I don't want to go into the field of prophecy except to answer this question: Whom will the Jews receive? The Jews spurned the Savior, but they will someday make a covenant with the antichrist (see Daniel 9:27). They will accept a counterfeit.

Witness of Moses (5:45-47)

Here we have Jesus pointing out the unbelief of the Jews. He cites Moses as a further witness of His deity.

> **5:45-47. *Do not think that I will accuse you to the Father: there is one that accuseth you, even Moses, in whom ye trust. For had ye believed Moses, ye would have believed me: for he wrote of me. But if ye believe not his writings, how shall ye believe my words?***

The Jews knew what Moses had written, but they didn't believe it. From the time they were children they were taught to read the scriptures, and they knew them by rote. If they had searched the Scriptures with an open heart, they would not have been opposed to Christ. But they didn't accept what Moses wrote about the coming Messiah.

Jesus did accept the writings of Moses, from Genesis 1:1 through Deuteronomy. Critics today dismiss the first eleven chapters of Genesis, and further say that Joshua wrote the Pentateuch instead of Moses. They deny that the Pentateuch is inspired by God. But may I suggest this? Jesus put His stamp of approval on the authenticity of the Pentateuch and on its Mosaic authorship. We can believe the Word.

The Jews said they believed the Scriptures, but they refused to see Jesus in the Pentateuch. My friends, when you read the Bible, read it to see Jesus. Don't read it to bolster your own ideas. Read it to see Jesus. Fall in love with the Savior.

May I ask you a question? Is Jesus the center of your love and devotion? If He is, talk about the Savior. Attract others to the Savior. Make Christ the center of your life.

John 6

Christ, The Bread of Life

The Fourth Sign: Feeding the Multitude (6:1-13)
—Jesus Returns to Galilee

Crowds Attracted to Jesus (6:1-2)

Now when you come to chapter 6, you come to an amazing story. It is the account of the Lord's feeding the five thousand. This is the only miracle that is recorded in all four Gospels, and it has tremendous import in the teaching of our Savior. In chapter 6 He also gives us that marvelous discourse of Himself as the Bread of Life.

In the first few verses the crowds gather around our Lord as He teaches and heals the people.

> **6:1-2.** *After these things Jesus went over the sea of Galilee, which is the sea of Tiberias. And a great multitude followed him, because they saw his miracles which he did on them that were diseased.*

If you want to follow through all the detail of it, I would suggest you go to Matthew 14, Mark 6, and Luke 9. Each Gospel gives a little different aspect of the story, but on the whole they are the same. Luke tells us He healed all who had need of healing. And toward the end of the day He was tired and the people were hungry. This is the setting for this tremendous miracle.

Now our Lord was performing miracles all day, healing all that had need of healing. He was full of compassion, full of tenderness. He didn't say, "Come back next week and I'll pray for you." He didn't say, "Come down to the meeting and I'll pray for you." The Lord never did that. Whenever He found a need, He met that need immediately. He healed all that had need of healing. He had compassion for them all.

The great multitude followed Jesus because they saw the miracles He performed for the diseased. They did not follow Him for His own Person. They were following Him because of the spectacular.

May I say a word of warning here? Please do not follow the spectacular. Faith based upon the spectacular is shallow and empty. Now I recognize that we all love the spectacular; we all love to have our emotions worked on. And I'm not opposed to emotional feeling. That's the way we're designed. But don't build your faith upon either an emotional experience or the spectacular.

Problem of a Hungry Throng (6:3-7)

After teaching and healing the people, Jesus left them that evening to rest with His disciples. The people forgot about their need for food as they sought Jesus.

> **6:3-6.** *And Jesus went up into a mountain, and there he sat with his disciples. And the passover, a feast of the Jews, was nigh. When Jesus then lifted up his eyes, and saw a great company come unto him, he saith unto Philip, Whence shall we buy bread, that these may eat? And this he said to prove him: for he himself knew what he would do.*

When the disciples saw the crowds gathered around Jesus, they said, "Send the multitude away, that they may go into the towns and country round about, and lodge, and get victuals" (Luke 9:12). The disciples wanted to send the people away from Christ. That's sometimes true today as well.

But when Jesus saw this great company of people, He lifted up

His eyes in compassion. Then He said, "Philip, where can we buy bread to feed this crowd?" Why did Jesus turn to Philip? Perhaps it may have been because they were not far from Bethsaida, and Philip was from Bethsaida. If anyone knew where to buy bread, it would have been Philip.

> **6:7.** *Philip answered him, Two hundred pennyworth of bread is not sufficient for them, that every one of them may take a little.*

Philip couldn't imagine even giving a little bit of food to everyone. But, you know, the Lord never gives you little wee bits. Jesus was only testing Philip, for He knew what He would do to fully satisfy the people's hunger.

A Boy Shares His Lunch (6:8-9)

> **6:8-9.** *One of his disciples, Andrew, Simon Peter's brother, saith unto him, There is a lad here, which hath five barley loaves, and two small fishes: but what are they among so many?*

I think Andrew felt a little ashamed that he even brought the boy's lunch to the Lord's attention. What use was the boy's lunch when so many needed to be fed?

This lad gave up all that he had. I like this little chap, and I want to point out a very human thing. How did the lad ever get to be near Andrew? You know how a boy is . . . he always has to be on the inside of the crowd. You can just see this lad working his way along through the crowd between legs and around feet. Do you think that little fellow would have gone near Peter? Hah! If he had stood by Peter, Peter would have said, "Get out of the way! Don't push around here!" That's what Peter would have done. But not Andrew. The lad came along beside Andrew.

How did Andrew know that the boy even had five barley loaves and two fishes? All day long the boy had carried his little lunch, and when evening came, he held on to them as he stood by Andrew. My, the Lord must have been wonderful in His ministry, if the boy went through the day without eating his bread and fish! When I'm outdoors for the day, I've eaten everything in my lunch box before noon. You can just see the two of them standing there together.

"Do you have any lunch?" the boy asks.

"No, do you?"

"My mom gave me five barley loaves and two fishes. I will share it with you."

And then Andrew and the lad heard Philip being made responsible to feed the crowds. And you know the rest.

I have a notion that this little fellow tagged along with Andrew when the disciples were feeding the crowd. Don't you think so? And when they came back, they had twelve baskets full. Every apostle had a basket. I love to think the Lord doesn't care for waste. "Pick up the fragments that remain, that nothing be lost," He said.

I think the little fellow went right along with Andrew and his basket. I'm just suggesting this. But that's life, isn't it? My, what a privilege this little fellow had. He gave up five loaves and his two fishes, and in the process he cooperated with the Son of God. Afterward, he shared a whole basket of food with Andrew.

Am I talking to you? Do you have something precious to your heart? Will you cooperate with the Lord? He wants to feed the masses with the Word of God. Why won't we cooperate? This little fellow gave up his five loaves and two fishes. But he didn't lose by the transaction. He became a fellow worker with God. Think of it. When the lad left home that day, he had no thought of such things. But before the day was out, he was a fellow worker with the Son of God.

All God asks us to give him is what we have. As Paul said in Romans 1:15, "As much as in me is, I am ready to preach the gospel to you that are at Rome also." That is all God asks: "As much as in me is."

I marvel when I think of the tremendous ministry of Tommy Titcomb in Africa. As far as background is concerned, he had nothing; but he gave God what he had. To think that he was only an engine wiper in a round house, wiping the oil off the engines when they came off the road! And yet, God took that fellow. And the result was that he became a mighty man of God in Nigeria, and represented a dozen tribes before the Parliament of Great Britain. My, how God used an engine wiper!

What do you have? All He wants is a channel through which He can express Himself, through which He can make known His power and grace. He's looking for channels. He's looking for people to cooperate with Him. God has all the supply. It is for us to distribute what He gives. He does the multiplying. But He wants us to be real disciples, willing and available.

Responsibility of the Disciples (6:10)

Now we have the Savior ready to feed the multitudes.

> **6:10. *And Jesus said, Make the men sit down. Now there was much grass in the place. So the men sat down, in number about five thousand.***

The other Gospels record Jesus' specific command to the disciples: "Give ye them to eat." Jesus made the disciples responsible to feed the crowd.

"Lord, how can we feed this crowd? We only have five loaves and two fish?" When the disciples had their eyes on the hungry crowd, and on what they themselves had, they realized their inadequacy. "What are these among so many? Lord, we can't feed the crowd on this. This is all we have. We are inadequate to feed such a multitude of people."

My friends, you and I see the hungry throngs of people every day. We are inadequate to meet all the needs. I felt deeply inadequate as I stood in Singapore, and Hong Kong, and Bombay, and other cities around the world where there are people by the millions. You can stand on a street and watch masses of people going by. You wonder what they do, where they live, where they're going. You feel so inadequate. Yet, their needs must be met and they must be fed.

"Lord, what can I do? I haven't any gifts. I can't do much. I haven't very much, and I can't even see all the needs. Lord, what can I do?" That was the attitude of the disciples. And that's how we feel today. Paul wisely said, "Not that we are sufficient of ourselves to think any thing as of ourselves" (2 Corinthians 3:5). But the Lord still calls us to feed the multitudes, for our sufficiency is from Him.

May I suggest something else? The Lord did not call for volunteers. He never calls for volunteers. He made the disciples responsible to feed the group. Jesus divided the people into companies of hundreds and fifties, and told the disciples to take food to them.

Did you ever wait on tables? I worked two years through college waiting on tables. I had three tables, with ten to a table. When I brought the tray around, they all ducked their heads. I only had thirty people to wait on, and I barely kept on my feet long enough to get through with them. But here were five thousand to feed. And Jesus made the twelve disciples responsible to feed them. I repeat: He never calls for volunteers.

Oh, just a minute, you say. There is one place where the Lord said, "Whom shall I send, and who will go for us?" (Isaiah 6:8). Yes, that's right, and will you tell me how many were there when God said that? Just one! But the Lord challenged the disciples, "Give ye them to eat." And if you claim to be a disciple of the Son of God, you have a responsibility to feed the multitudes with the Word of God, and to bring them to the saving knowledge of Christ.

Jesus Feeds the Multitudes (6:11-13)

6:11-13. *And Jesus took the loaves; and when he had given thanks, he distributed to the disciples, and the disciples to them that were set down; and likewise of the fishes as much as they would. When they were filled, he said unto his disciples, Gather up the fragments that remain, that nothing be lost. Therefore they gathered them together, and filled twelve baskets with the fragments of the five barley loaves, which re-*

mained over and above unto them that had eaten.

When the disciples centered their eyes on *Whom* they had, instead of *what* they had, they could have fed five million as well as five thousand. Here the Lord Jesus revealed Himself to them as Jehovah Raah, the One Who is the Shepherd of His people, the One Who is sufficient for every need.

The Lord *is* sufficient. He is the mighty God Who can create to meet the needs of His people. We read in Psalm 23:1, "The Lord is my shepherd; I shall not want." Now here is something new. No wonder it is in all four Gospels. Jesus takes five loaves and two fishes—just a little wee bit of stuff—and, as it leaves His hands, it multiplies and multiplies. This is an act of the Creator. As long as there were hungry mouths to feed, there was always an abundant supply.

Mark the difference between our efforts and God's sufficiency. You and I can bake bread for five thousand and then we are out of bread. We might be able to catch enough fish to feed a certain crowd, and then we're out of fish. But the Lord never ran out. He kept on creating more food. Whether it is for one, or more, God is sufficient for your need. Whether it is for five thousand or five million, God is sufficient for your need. He is the Creator and He is your Shepherd. He is Jehovah Raah. I do not know what your need is, but God does. He is sufficient for your need, whatever it may be.

The Fifth Sign: Walking on Water (6:14-21)
—Jesus Crosses Over to Northern Galilee

The Crowds and the King (6:14-15)

In the feeding of the five thousand, our Lord revealed Himself to the multitudes as Jehovah Raah, the Lord our Shepherd (see Psalm 23:1). Here we read of another incident where He revealed Himself as God manifest in the flesh. By walking on the water, He revealed Himself as El Elyon, the possessor of heaven and earth (see Genesis 14:19). This revelation was only given to the disciples—

partly for their encouragement, and partly as a rebuke for their lack of faith. Read Matthew 14:22-33 as a corresponding passage for details omitted in John's Gospel.

> **6:14-15.** *Then those men, when they had seen the miracle that Jesus did, said, This is of a truth that prophet that should come into the world. When Jesus therefore perceived that they would come and take him by force, to make him a king, he departed again into a mountain himself alone.*

The people offered the Lord a kingdom. The crowd was saying, "Let's make Jesus our king. We need a king. We're ruled over by willful, sinful, powerful Rome. Here is one who can be our king and set us free. He can feed us. He can heal us. He can raise our dead. He can open our blind eyes. He can meet our every need. This must be 'that prophet.' Let's make Him our king!"

May I remind you of the fact that when our Lord came the first time, He did not come to raise up a material kingdom. He came in humiliation. He was born in a manger. His first companions were cattle. His last companions were thieves. His university, someone has said, was a carpenter's shop. He had no place to lay His head. He used a borrowed boat to sail the Sea of Galilee. He used a borrowed ass to go into the city of Jerusalem. He was buried in a borrowed tomb. Our Lord came in humiliation.

Besides, He could not be the king without a kingdom of people that were spiritually right with God. These people wanted a king because they were concerned about food. They were following Him because they were being fed. They decided that He must be "that prophet" spoken of in Deuteronomy 18:18, because He was meeting their temporal needs. These people were not seeking Him because of *Who* He was, but because of *what* He could do. They wanted Him to wait on their every need. Later He said, "You are not seeking Me because you saw the miracles that reveal My identity, but because your stomachs were filled."

Do you go to church for some material need? social need? religious need? Or do you go to meet Him? Remember, a faith that is based on the spectacular, on the sensational, on the emotional, is not real faith. Christ Himself must be the object of our faith, not some experience.

The Disciples Sent into the Storm (6:16-18)

The Lord had perceived that the people wanted to take Him by force and make Him a king. He would have none of it, so He dismissed the crowds.

> **6:16-18.** *And when even was now come, his disciples went down unto the sea, And entered into a ship, and went over the sea toward Capernaum. And it was now dark, and Jesus was not come to them. And the sea arose by reason of a great wind that blew.*

I wouldn't be at all surprised if the disciples themselves wondered if Jesus was a king. I'm sure Peter and the other disciples would have been more than happy to have joined with the crowd in making their master king. Jesus sent them into the storm to keep them out of temptation. He sent them from the test of feeding the multitudes into the tempest of the storm at sea.

Jesus knew what was going on. He was well aware that a storm would come suddenly down upon them. And He knew exactly where they were. Jesus allowed the disciples to experience the storm to teach them more about His identity. They had seen Him feed the five thousand, revealing Himself as Jehovah Raah. But all too soon they forgot, for Jesus reminded them, "Do ye not remember? When I brake the five loaves among five thousand, how many baskets full of fragments took ye up?" (Mark 8:18-19). Jesus used the storm experience to teach them that He was also El Elyon, the possessor of heaven and earth.

Most of us don't like rough weather. We don't like stormy lives. We don't like affliction and sorrow. When the sea is calm and the Lord is right there with us, filling us with joy and blessing, we think that it is wonderful. But our faith never grows that way. We never see His authority and power that way.

It is in the storms of life, when sorrow and affliction are crashing against us, that we see God more clearly. God uses the sorrows and tests of life to sharpen us as tools He can use for His glory. The Lord often permits us to go into times of distress and affliction to keep us from something that could be infinitely worse. For this reason, He sent the disciples into the storm to keep them from temptation.

A Walk upon the Waters (6:19-21)

> **6:19-21.** *So when they had rowed about five and twenty or thirty furlongs, they see Jesus walking on the sea, and drawing nigh unto the ship: and they were afraid. But he saith unto them, It is I; be not afraid. Then they willingly received him into the ship: and immediately the ship was at the land whither they went.*

Now when the disciples saw the Lord come on the water, walking as if He were going to go by them, they were afraid. They thought He was a spirit, an apparition, a ghost. I maintain that they were more afraid of what they saw than of the storm which they felt. They had been in storms before, but they had never seen a ghost before. No wonder they were afraid!

I love the tenderness of the Savior here, for He said, "It is I; be not afraid," and stilled the storm. He rebuked the wind and the waves, and there was a calm.

I say, what a wonderful thing! Even though we may not experience His presence, and the heavens are black, and we feel so frail as if the end has come, God is on His throne working all things out after the counsel of His own will. Our Lord was on the mountain with His Father. He was fully aware of the storm the disciples faced, and He knew that He would come down and deliver them. It was only to the disciples that He revealed Himself as El Elyon, possessor of heaven and earth, Who has authority over the elements. He muzzled the winds and there was a calm. My, how wonderful it is.

You and I go through times of darkness and despair. Sometimes we wonder if our prayers ever go beyond our lips. We wonder if the Lord ever hears us. We go on and it becomes darker and darker. And yet, my friend, God knows about you. He understands. And at the right time—He's never ahead of time, He's never behind time—He comes to meet you in your need. He says with that gentleness, that blessed sweetness of His, "It is I; be not afraid."

I wish we as believers could come to the place of seeing the tenderness and compassion of our Lord as He came to them. There is no rebuke here. "It is I; be not afraid." I say, what a wonderful thing.

No wonder we read in Hebrews 13:5-6, "For he hath said, I will never leave thee, nor forsake thee. So that we may boldly say, The Lord is my helper, and I will not fear what man shall do unto me." This is the wonderful experience of the presence of God when everything seems as black as night. We can say with Job, even in the midst of our sorrow and confusion, "yet will I trust in him" (Job 13:15). It is then that His calmness, His peace that passeth understanding, comes in to garrison and guard our hearts and minds (Philippians 4:7).

May this word come to you as a word of comfort, as a word of strength, as a word of hope and assurance. The Savior who stilled the storm and rebuked the waves is the same One who is with you today and tomorrow, and until He comes. He is with us when it is dark, holding us by the hand. He who leads us into the storm will bring us through the storm.

Hallelujah, what a Savior! He is Jehovah Raah, the Shepherd of His people, caring for them in their need. And He is El Elyon, the One who is the possessor of heaven and earth. He not only creates but possesses the heavens and the earth; and in these two names we have the manifestation of His person as the Son of the Highest. The first one was to the multitudes. The second one was for the comfort and encouragement of His own disciples.

The Bread of Life Discourse (6:22-59)
—Jesus Teaches in Nearby Capernaum

The Crowds Seek Jesus for Miracles (6:22-26)

Following feeding the five thousand and walking on water, our Lord gave the Bread of Life discourse. In this passage we have the first "I am" statement of Christ: "I am the bread of life" (6:35). Notice the setting of this.

> **6:22-25.** *The day following, when the people which stood on the other side of the sea saw that there was none other boat there, save that one whereinto his disciples were entered, and that Jesus went not with his disciples into the boat, but that his disciples were gone away alone; (Howbeit there came other boats from Tiberias nigh unto the place where they did eat bread, after that the Lord had given thanks:) When the people therefore saw that Jesus was not there, neither his disciples, they also took shipping, and came to Capernaum, seeking for Jesus. And when they had found him on the other side of the sea, they said unto him, Rabbi, when camest thou hither?*

You notice that Jesus ignores their question.

> **6:26.** *Jesus answered them and said, Verily, verily, I say unto you, Ye seek me, not because ye saw the miracles, but because ye did eat of the loaves, and were filled.*

After the Lord met the disciples in the midst of the sea, they landed and came over to Capernaum. The people knew that the disciples had gone into the boat without the Lord, so they asked Him how He got there. He avoided their question by making a statement. He told them, "You folk are seeking something you need, but you don't know your greatest need. You are seeking the physical instead of the spiritual. Your life is occupied with the materialistic side of life, and you have missed the important thing, the spiritual."

If there is no spirituality, there is no morality. Morality comes out of spirituality. The reason we are where we are today in this country is because we have despised the spiritual life that is only found in Christ. As a result, morality has gone out the window. What a challenge we have to present before people the great need of the human heart—not the physical or the material, but the spiritual.

The people wanted Jesus to serve them. They weren't seeking Jesus for Himself. They didn't care about the Person of the Lord. All they wanted was physical satisfaction. This attitude among the Jews caused the Lord Jesus to seek to attract them to Himself by manifesting Himself as God incarnate. The people saw the miracles, but they never realized that they were given to exalt His Person. They wanted the physical, but they didn't want Him. They wanted the experiential, but they didn't want Him.

May I say this? This same attitude is true today in many places among professing Christians. We want the physical. We want the material. We want the spectacular and the experiential. I am not opposed to these things, but the important thing is the spiritual— that which is eternal, which goes on forever.

Our danger today is to be so occupied with the material and the physical that we miss the important thing—our fellowship and communion with Him. Do we seek Jesus for Himself or do we seek Him for what we can get? Do we seek to serve the Lord, or to be served?

Jesus Offers Eternal Life (6:27-34)

Jesus rebuked the people, saying, "You don't seek Me for Myself. You seek Me because you want to be filled."

> **6:27-29. Labour not for the meat which perisheth,
> but for that meat which endureth unto everlasting life,
> which the Son of man shall give unto you: for him
> hath God the Father sealed. Then said they unto him,**

What shall we do, that we might work the works of God? Jesus answered and said unto them, This is the work of God, that ye believe on him whom he hath sent.

I want you to notice that the Lord Jesus started attracting these people to that spiritual food which is eternal. Isaiah 55 speaks of the same thing: "Ho, everyone one that thirsteth, come ye to the waters, and he that hath no money; come ye, buy, and eat; yea, come, buy wine and milk without money and without price. Wherefore do ye spend money for that which is not bread? and your labour for that which satisfieth not? hearken diligently unto me . . ." (55:1-2).

"Don't labor for things that pass away," He is saying. "Look at Me. I will give you bread that endures eternally. This bread is a gift I will give to you. I am the One who has come from God. I am the One who has come from heaven. Believe on Me." The great desire of His heart, I repeat, is not to attract people to what He gives, but to Himself. Mark the times all through this chapter where He spoke about His identity as the bread of life come down from heaven and used personal pronouns referring to Himself.

I have the feeling concerning these people that they were perplexed. "This man Jesus has fed us bread from heaven. He has multiplied the loaves and fishes. He has healed our sick, cleansed our lepers, and has met all our needs. Now He says not to labor for these things, but for eternal life, which the Son of man shall give us. But how can we labor for it? What shall we do to do the works of God?"

These people were Jews. They knew about the "doing" business. The law said this about God's commandments: "Which if a man do, he shall live in them" (Leviticus 18:5). Moses warned the people, "Observe to do all the words of this law" (Deuteronomy 31:12). Their whole life was filled with doing. This is why they asked, "What shall we *do,* that we might work the works of God?" In other words, "How can we please God? What did the law forget to tell us to do? How can we obtain life eternal?"

Jesus' amazing answer was this: "This is the work of God, that ye believe on him whom he hath sent." Rituals and works will not satisfy God. There is nothing that satisfies the heart of God more than faith. Hebrews 11:6 reads, "But without faith it is impossible to please him: for he that cometh to God must believe that he is, and that he is a rewarder of them that diligently seek him." Faith says that God is accessible. The only access we have to God is through faith in the Lord Jesus Christ. "This is the work of God."

Mark what unbelief does.

6:30-31. *They said therefore unto him, What sign shewest thou then, that we may see, and believe thee? what dost thou work? Our fathers did eat manna in the desert; as it is written, He gave them bread from heaven to eat.*

"You have shown us some signs, Jesus, but can you do a greater work than this? Moses gave our fathers bread from heaven for forty years. Can you match that? Are you greater than Moses?"

The problem here is not signs. Jesus had performed incredible miracles. The issue now is His Person. He attracted them to Himself and challenged them to believe in Him. But do you sense the challenge? "Why should we believe in you? Are you greater than Moses?"

Now remember that this incident occurred during the passover time. The minds of the people were filled with the history of Israel as their forefathers came out of Egypt and crossed the Red Sea into the wilderness. No doubt Exodus 16 was fresh in their minds, where the people went out every morning for forty years and gathered manna according to their appetites. They were always filled, but their experience led them to a wrong philosophy of life. They thought that "seeing is believing." That's a wrong philosophy. Seeing is not believing.

The Lord said, "Ye also have seen me, and believe not" (6:36). The people had plenty of evidence to believe in Him. But they turned away from Him in unbelief. Hebrews 3:12 says, "Take heed, brethren, lest there be in any of you an evil heart of unbelief, in departing from the living God." There is no reason why any person today should be an atheist. The reason people don't respond to Jesus is not lack of evidence. The cause is unbelief.

My friend, don't for one moment begin to minimize unbelief or look on it as a light thing. Unbelief is a terrible thing. It is the product of an evil heart. And that's the score here. The people asked, "Are you greater than Moses?" Mark what Jesus replied.

> **6:32-33.** *Then Jesus said unto them, Verily, verily, I say unto you, Moses gave you not that bread from heaven; but my Father giveth you the true bread from heaven. For the bread of God is he which cometh down from heaven, and giveth life unto the world.*

Jesus was saying, "My Father is the One who gives the true bread. All Moses could do was give you bread for the body, a passing thing. And the time came when the manna ceased. It was just a temporary thing. It was only meant to meet immediate physical needs. But the true bread from heaven is eternal. It lasts forever." He was offering them eternal life in Himself (6:47, 51). **6:34.** *Then said they unto him, Lord, evermore give us this bread.* Now He has stirred up something.

But notice that the people did not grasp the significance of the bread the Lord was offering them. All through the chapter you find these Jews groping along without any trust or admiration for Christ, and in the end all left Him except for the twelve.

Do you see the movement of the people as the Lord reveals Himself? The more He manifested His true identity, the further away the people went from Him. They wanted Him to serve their physical needs, but He had no time for it. He comes right out now boldly and says, "That true bread is the Son of Man which comes from heaven."

Jesus Offers Satisfying Life (6:35)

Mark what Jesus said when the people asked for the bread from heaven.

6:35. *And Jesus said unto them, I am the bread of life: he that cometh to me shall never hunger; and he that believeth on me shall never thirst.*

Jesus spoke of everlasting life in 6:27. Now we have Jesus offering satisfying life in this verse. Jesus is the bread of life that satisfies!

God has so made our hearts that we are never perfectly satisfied until we put our trust in Christ. None of the material things we run after ever satisfy. Oh, there might be a little satisfaction for a fraction of time, but the satisfaction fades away. Perfect, continual, everlasting satisfaction is only found in one place. It is found in a Person, not in an object or experience. It is found in the Lord Jesus. He is the only One who can satisfy.

Whatever our lot in life, we can always find in Him One who can truly satisfy our hearts. "I am the bread of life," Jesus said. "He that cometh to me shall never hunger; and he that believeth on me shall never thirst." My, what a passage! No human mind can begin to delve into the depths and the wonders of this little statement. "I am the bread of life. I am the only One who can really satisfy the human heart." What a statement!

Does Jesus Christ satisfy you? The happiest and most satisfied people are not the millionaires. Some of the most contented people I have met in my life lived in a sod shack with the walls simply whitewashed on the inside. These people had perfect satisfaction as they daily, continually enjoyed the Lord. Their cup was filled full with His joy, peace, and satisfaction. They weren't free from tests and trials, but they rejoiced in God who had given them a well of water springing up, a joy and satisfaction that lasts through eternity. My, what a prospect for you and me.

But many of us have only had a little wee taste of the satisfaction God offers us. All we have had are little tastes. But the psalmist wrote, "In thy presence is fulness of joy; at thy right hand there are pleasures for evermore" (Psalm 16:11). David also wrote, "O taste and see that the Lord is good: blessed is the man that trusteth in him" (Psalm 34:8). And consider what dear Peter said, "As newborn babes, desire the sincere milk of the word, that ye may grow thereby: If so be ye have tasted that the Lord is gracious" (1 Peter 2:2-3).

"I am the bread of life," Jesus says. "He that cometh to Me shall never hunger, and he that believeth on me shall never thirst."

Jesus Offers Resurrection Life (6:36-40)

The third thing Jesus offered the people is resurrection life, a life over which death does not even cast a shadow.

> **6:36-40.** *But I said unto you, That ye also have seen me, and believe not. All that the Father giveth me shall come to me; and him that cometh to me I will in no wise cast out. For I came down from heaven, not to do mine own will, but the will of him that sent me. And this is the Father's will which hath sent me, that of all which he hath given me I should lose nothing, but should raise it up again at the last day. And this is the will of him that sent me, that every one which seeth the Son, and believeth on him, may have everlasting life: and I will raise him up at the last day.*

To me, it is marvelous to rethink and meditate on the wonderful fact from this passage that God Himself is the One who gives us this life. Not only is it eternal, satisfying life, but it's a resurrection life as well.

Our Lord is the bread of resurrection life. In 6:37, He is the One who receives everyone who comes to Him. He will in no wise cast you out. He promises life to all that come to Him.

In 6:38, He is the One who always does His Father's will. He did not come from heaven to do His own will, but the will of His Father. And what is His Father's will? We have this in 6:39, where He is the One who guarantees the security and preservation of His people. He declared that His Father's will is to keep all that come to Him. The Lord preserves His people.

In 6:40, He is the One who guarantees the resurrection of His people. The resurrection is the completion of our experience in Him, when our bodies will be redeemed, raised from the dead, and made like His. Jesus promises to raise us and bring us to Himself, as we have in John 14:1-3. No other person could make such a claim except for Jesus, for He alone is God the Son.

Four times Jesus repeats that He will raise us up at the last day (6:39, 40, 44, 54). The ultimate of all eternal, satisfying life is resurrection and glorification. This is what Jesus is saying.

Consider the tremendous offer He made to the people. Jesus said, "I am the bread of life. I will not, under any circumstances, turn away anyone who comes to Me. I guarantee I will keep him. And not only that, but I will raise him from the dead."

My friend, what a Savior! No wonder Paul could say in 2 Timothy 1:12, "I know whom I have believed, and am persuaded that he is able to keep that which I have committed unto him against that day."

Do you know whom you have believed? And don't put that little word "in" into my question, will you? Don't read the verse today, "I know in whom I have believed." You have missed the whole point. I know Whom I have believed. He is the One who is the bread of life. He is the One who has promised to never turn anyone away. He is the One who guarantees the preservation of all His children, and He is the One who guarantees the culmination and completion of their salvation by raising their bodies from the dead. I say, what a Savior!

Murmurings among the Jews (6:41-47)

> **6:41-42. *The Jews then murmured at him, because he said, I am the bread which came down from heaven. And they said, Is not this Jesus, the son of Joseph, whose father and mother we know? how is it then that he saith, I came down from heaven?***

Human nature is so strange. The people murmured at Jesus when He revealed His true identity as the bread of life. "You're just the son of Joseph," they said. "We know your father and mother. We know all about you. We know who you are." To them, Jesus was only the son of a man named Joseph.

The question of the incarnation, I believe, was wrapped up in Mary's heart. All through her life she lived under the cloud of conceiving a child before her marriage to Joseph. Possibly this was the sword Simeon prophesied of when he said, "A sword shall pierce through thy own soul also" (Luke 2:35). They would have laughed her out of court if she had told others that this Jesus, her first-born son, was begotten of the Holy Spirit while she was a virgin. They would have taunted her and mocked her.

Jesus Himself had to live under this cloud of misunderstanding as well. But notice that He did not try to argue the point. Instead, He continued His tremendous offer of eternal, resurrection life. He refused to excuse their unbelief.

> **6:43-47.** *Jesus therefore answered and said unto them, Murmur not among yourselves. No man can come to me, except the Father which hath sent me draw him: and I will raise him up at the last day. It is written in the prophets, And they shall be all taught of God. Every man therefore that hath heard, and hath learned of the Father, cometh unto me. Not that any man hath seen the Father, save he which is of God, he hath seen the Father. Verily, verily, I say unto you, He that believeth on me hath everlasting life.*

Now please don't take 6:44—"No man can come to me, except the Father which hath sent me draw him"—out of its context to stress the sovereignty of God and to deny the free will of man. The more I see of human nature, and the more I see the sinful heart of man, the more positive I am that God is sovereign. He is the only One who can provide a salvation from the world. Our Lord said, "And I, if I be lifted up from the earth, will draw all men unto me" (John 12:32). God draws in 6:44. He teaches in 6:45.

What is the human responsibility? We have this in 6:40 and 6:45. Men must come to Christ and believe. Everyone who sees the

Son comes to Him. This is why Jesus came to manifest Himself among men, that all might see Him and believe.

You say, "Well these Jews saw Jesus. Why didn't they believe Him?" No, my friend, they didn't see Jesus. Oh, they did see Him as the son of Joseph. But they never did see Him as the Son of God. When Pilate sought to release Jesus, the Jews cried, "We have a law, and by our law he ought to die, because he made himself the Son of God" (John 19:7). They knew that Jesus claimed to be the Son of God, but they never saw Him as such. For this reason they did not believe on Him, and were without eternal, resurrection life.

Now, it wasn't that the Jews couldn't come to Jesus in belief. It was that they wouldn't come. Every time a person hears the Gospel, God is teaching men: "This is My Son. This is the One who can save. This is the One who can give life." Everyone has the right to come to Jesus, but many refuse to do so.

I hope I have made myself clear on this matter. I find myself between two extremes. There are some who believe that God is going to save only those He has predestined to be saved. They have no choice in the matter because He has elected them. The Bible doesn't teach that. On the other hand, there are those who deny the sovereignty of God and say salvation is all in man. This too is wrong.

The more you see the utter sinfulness of the human heart, the more you realize God must do the drawing. How does He do it? By giving forth the blessed Word of life. Your response to His offer will determine whether you have life or not.

We have man's responsibility to choose salvation back in John 5. Jesus told the Jews, "Search the scriptures; for in them ye think ye have eternal life: and they are they which testify of me. And ye *will not* come to me, that ye might have life" (5:39-40). Salvation is not a matter of moral or intellectual persuasion. It is a thing of the heart and will. It's a question of a relationship between a sinner and the Savior. There is no excuse for anyone reading this book, for example, to say, "I don't believe in Jesus Christ because God never chose me." That is an excuse for your unbelief.

Jesus said, "Whoever comes to Me, I will not cast out. Whoever comes to Me, I will give eternal life. Whoever comes to Me, I will give satisfying life. Whoever comes to Me, I will give resurrection life."

The Jews turned down Jesus' offer, because they refused to see Him as He is and believe on Him. They murmured instead: "We know who you are. You can't fool us with your talk. You're only Jesus, the son of Joseph. You're the carpenter from Nazareth. You're no better than the rest of us." That's the human heart. The people had no desire, or hunger, or yearning for the Savior. Jesus sought to draw them to Himself, but they refused in unbelief.

Jesus Offers Indwelling Life (6:48-58)

Jesus came from Heaven to offer Himself as the bread of life so that others could find life in Him. He knew that in order to accomplish this He would have to give His life for the world.

> **6:48-51.** *I am that bread of life. Your fathers did eat manna in the wilderness, and are dead. This is the bread which cometh down from heaven, that a man may eat thereof, and not die. I am the living bread which came down from heaven: if any man eat of this bread, he shall live for ever: and the bread that I will give is my flesh, which I will give for the life of the world.*

There is no question that the Lord Jesus was speaking of His sacrifice on the Cross for the sins of the world. How is it that we are going to get eternal, satisfying, resurrection life when we are dead in trespasses and sins? Jesus said He would give His life for the life of the world. Here is the cross. "God commendeth his love toward us, in that, while we were yet sinners, Christ died for us" (Romans 5:8). Jesus' offer of life to others in this passage is based on His death, burial, and resurrection.

Jesus told the Jews that a man must eat of Him, the bread of heaven, in order to receive this life. **6:52.** *The Jews therefore strove among themselves, saying, How can this man give us his* *flesh to eat?* Now, the Jews were not fighting among themselves. They were stirred up by what Jesus was saying.

> **6:53-58.** *Then Jesus said unto them, Verily, verily, I say unto you, Except ye eat the flesh of the Son of man, and drink his blood, ye have no life in you. Whoso eateth my flesh, and drinketh my blood, hath eternal life; and I will raise him up at the last day. For my flesh is meat indeed, and my blood is drink indeed. He that eateth my flesh, and drinketh my blood, dwelleth in me, and I in him. As the living Father hath sent me, and I live by the Father: so he that eateth me, even he shall live by me. This is that bread which came down from heaven: not as your fathers did eat manna, and are dead: he that eateth of this bread shall live for ever.*

Now we have come to our Lord's purpose in coming to earth. He came to bring men into perfect union with Himself. We enter into union with Him by eating His flesh and drinking his blood. And lest I be misunderstood, Jesus is not referring to the breaking of bread at the Lord's table. That is a remembrance we observe until He comes. But I question if that were even in the mind of the Lord. He was delving into something far deeper.

He had just said, "If you eat this bread, you will be satisfied and live forever. If you put your trust in Me, you will be raised from the dead." Now Jesus states a fourth thing: "You have to be in vital union with Me to have life." You do not receive life through moral persuasion or through intellectual persuasion. You receive life through union. "Except you eat the flesh of the Son of man, and drink His blood, you are without life. You have no life residing within you."

In other words, He was saying, "You have to be part and parcel with Me."

Then He goes on to say that this union is linked to the union that exists between the Father and the Son. There is a oneness between the Father, and the Son, and the believer. This indwelling life Jesus offers comes only through a relationship with the living God. Because of this union, we have an eternal, satisfying oneness that is going to last through eternity. This is communion. What a tremendous statement our Savior is making here! His purpose was to die in order to bring to Himself a people in vital union with Him.

I sometimes get discouraged at the lightness and shallowness of present day Christianity when I consider the deep, deep claims of Christ. We look at the miraculous. If we have seen the Lord feed five thousand with five loaves and two fishes, we would live on the joy of that experience for a year. "I saw the Lord feed the multitudes," we would say with amazement. "And He had twelve baskets full left over!"

Yet, I say that what Jesus is revealing to us here is far greater than any miracle He ever performed. His works were great. But His words are even greater. When our Lord spoke of "eating My flesh, and drinking My blood," He was not speaking of something material. He was speaking of the spiritual reality of a life of union and oneness with Himself.

May I repeat something? I want to get this in your heart. Jesus said, "I am the bread of life." The bread of life is a Person, the Son of God. He is in vital union with the eternal God. He is one with the Father. And Jesus went on to say, "I'm going to the cross. I'm going to give My body, My flesh, for the life of the world. And through this sacrifice I am going to bring to Myself anyone who will come. And I will give them life. I will give them eternal, satisfying, resurrection, indwelling life. I will bring them into vital union with Myself."

Reactions to Jesus' Discourse (6:59-71)

6:59-66. *These things said he in the synagogue, as he taught in Capernaum. Many therefore of his disciples, when they had heard this, said, This is an hard saying; who can hear it? When Jesus knew in himself that his disciples murmured at it, he said unto them, Doth this offend you? What and if ye shall see the Son*

of man ascend up where he was before? It is the spirit
that quickeneth; the flesh profiteth nothing: the words
that I speak unto you, they are spirit, and they are life.
But there are some of you that believe not. For Jesus
knew from the beginning who they were that believed
not, and who should betray him. And he said, There-
fore said I unto you, that no man can come unto me,
except it were given unto him of my Father. From that
time many of his disciples went back, and walked no
more with him.

These people said that Jesus' offer was "a hard saying." And
from that time forth, many walked no more with Him.

Jesus turned to the twelve apostles to get their reaction.

6:67-71. *Then said Jesus unto the twelve, Will ye*
also go away? Then Simon Peter answered him, Lord,
to whom shall we go? thou hast the words of eternal
life. And we believe and are sure that thou art that
Christ, the Son of the living God. Jesus answered
them, Have not I chosen you twelve, and one of you is
a devil? He spake of Judas Iscariot the son of Simon:
for he it was that should betray him, being one of the
twelve.

Jesus turned and asked them, "Will you also go away? Do you
want to go as well?"

Peter threw up his hands and said, "Lord, well, where can we
go? You have just declared to us that you alone have the words that
are spirit and that are life. Lord, where else can we go? You alone
have the words of eternal life. And we believe without a shadow of
doubt that You are the Christ, the Son of the living God."

My friend, what is your reaction to the offer of Jesus? You either
stand with the Jews and resist salvation through His blood. Or you
stand with Peter and say, "Lord, where can we go? You alone have
the words of eternal life. We believe and are sure that You are the
Christ, the Son of the living God."

I suggest you come to Him. Jesus said, "He that cometh to Me, no matter who it is, I will in no wise cast out. Whoever comes to Me, I will preserve. I won't lose them. I will raise them from the dead. And I will join them to Myself in a union that is eternal and that is perfect." He offers you satisfying, eternal life. My, what a privilege. My, what a joy!

John 7

Christ, The Heavenly One

Jesus Attends the Feast of Tabernacles (7:1-13)
—Jesus Waits Beforehand in Galilee

Jesus Waits in Galilee Before the Feast (7:1-2)

> **7:1-2.** *After these things Jesus walked in Galilee:*
> *for he would not walk in Jewry, because the Jews*
> *sought to kill him. Now the Jews' feast of tabernacles*
> *was at hand.*

Between chapters 6 and 7 you have a period of several months. In chapter 6, you have the Passover, held in the spring, and in chapter 7 you have the Feast of Tabernacles, held in the fall. At this time they had three feasts—the Feast of Atonement, the First Fruits, and the Tabernacles—one after the other.

Tabernacles was one of three feasts (with Passover and the Feast of Atonement) that every Jew in Israel sought to observe. Tabernacles had reference to the Lord's coming to earth to reign, when every man would sit under his own vine and fig tree. No man would build a house only to have someone else live in it. This is what the prophets declared about the kingdom age, and the Feast of Tabernacles was a foreshadowing of that time. The people took palm leaves and went out of the city and made themselves booths.

Unbelief of Jesus' Brothers (7:3-5)

Our Lord was in Galilee, and His brethren came to Him.

> **7:3-4.** *His brethren therefore said unto him, Depart hence, and go into Judaea, that thy disciples also may see the works that thou doest. For there is no man that doeth any thing in secret, and he himself seeketh to be known openly. If thou do these things, shew thyself to the world.*

"Now, if you are really the Messiah," they said to Him, "if you are what you claim to be, go on up to the feast and show yourself. Hiding up here in Galilee performing miracles won't do you any good. Go to Jerusalem. Go up to the feast. There will be multitudes there. If you want to be a king, then be one, and show yourself."

> **7:5.** *For neither did his brethren believe in him.*

Now, whether they were members of His family and children of Mary, or whether they were just His kinfolk, I don't know. They are called "his brethren." We do know that James the just and Jude were two of the brothers of the Lord. But here's an astounding thing when you think of it. Our Lord lived a pure, sinless, righteous life as the compassionate, tender Son of God before them for nearly thirty years. He worked in the carpenter shop, lived in a humble abode in the bosom of His family, and still, after thirty years, they did not believe in Him.

Possibly you are the only Christian in your family. It's a strange feeling. May the Lord come to you in real comfort. He perfectly understands what you go through. I know of precious youngsters in the Orient who accepted the Savior and came out of paganism and idolatry. When they went home and gave a testimony for the Lord Jesus, they were beaten and kicked out of the house. They were told, "Come back when you are able to bow down to the gods." We know nothing of that, but we do know something of being ostracized, of feeling alone.

And our Lord is touched with the feeling of our infirmities. He knows exactly what we go through. "He is able to succour them that are tempted" (Hebrews 2:18). And Hebrews 4:16 says, "Let us therefore come boldly unto the throne of grace, that we may obtain mercy, and find grace to help in time of need." Why should we? Why can we? Because He understands. He went through it. He knows what it is to be ostracized and not believed, even though He lived thirty years with them in sinlessness, in purity, in a town like Nazareth. "Can any good thing come out of Nazareth?" Yes. But it is hard to believe that there were those in His family who did not believe in Him.

I repeat it. His brethren did not believe on Him. They had no place for Him. The astounding thing is that people can live month after month, and sometimes year after year, under the sound of the gospel, and can hear of the glories of the Savior who can save sinners and satisfy them, and yet go on without commiting themselves to Him. These men lived thirty years with the Savior Himself and still didn't trust Him.

Hatred of the World (7:6-9)

7:6-9. *Then Jesus said unto them, My time is not yet come: but your time is alway ready. The world cannot hate you; but me it hateth, because I testify of it, that the works thereof are evil. Go ye up unto this feast: I go not up yet unto this feast; for my time is not yet full come. When he had said these words unto them, he abode still in Galilee.*

Jesus didn't say He wasn't going up, but that "I'm not going up when you say so." The brethren did not know who He was; they were blind to the Person in their midst. They didn't understand why He came, and they didn't understand the religious world to which they belonged. How true that is today.

"The world will not hate you," He told his brethren. "But the world hates Me." Why did His world hate Him? Because He testified of it, that its works were evil. His life and His ministry were an open rebuke to the world. He showed the evil in men's hearts and they hated Him without a cause.

You know, before you became a Christian, you were part of a circle of friends. As stories were told and things were done, you just sat there and everyone freely talked about evil. Then you accepted the Savior, and you gave a testimony. Immediately there was a barrier. It's not because of some doctrine. It's because the life of Jesus in you is a continual rebuke to men in sin. That's why they don't like Christians. Evil men and women are uneasy in the presence of real Christians.

Now, if that's true of us, how true it was about Him! He was absolutely sinless, harmless, holy, righteous, and pure. "The world doesn't hate you. The world hates Me," He told His unconverted brethren.

Don't be surprised then, my Christian friends. When you take a stand for the Savior, don't expect the world to come and pat you on the back. A tremendous barrier stands between the world and the believer. As Paul said in Galatians 6:14, "God forbid that I should glory, save in the cross of our Lord Jesus Christ, by whom the world is crucified unto me, and I unto the world." And John wrote in 1 John 2:15, "Love not the world, neither the things that are in the world. If any man love the world, the love of the Father is not in him."

The world is a religious system that is opposed to Jesus Christ, to the people of Christ, and to the Word of Christ. It is a willful system, despising the person of Christ, the work of Christ, and the Spirit of Christ.

Jesus Goes to Jerusalem for the Feast (7:10-13)

Now, notice the reaction of the people to Christ. Verse 43 says, "There was a division among the people because of him." The truth concerning Christ is divisive.

7:10-13. *But when his brethren were gone up, then went he also up unto the feast, not openly, but as it were in secret. Then the Jews sought him at the feast, and said, Where is he? And there was much murmuring among the people concerning him: for some said, He is a good man: others said, Nay; but he deceiveth the people. Howbeit no man spake openly of him for fear of the Jews.*

Jesus' Claims During the Feast (7:14-36)
—Jesus Teaches in Jerusalem

Claim 1: "My Message Is from Above" (7:14-18)

7:14-18. *Now about the midst of the feast Jesus went up into the temple, and taught. And the Jews marvelled, saying, How knoweth this man letters, having never learned? Jesus answered them, and said, My doctrine is not mine, but his that sent me. If any man will do his will, he shall know of the doctrine, whether it be of God, or whether I speak of myself. He that speaketh of himself seeketh his own glory: but he that seeketh his glory that sent him, the same is true, and no unrighteousness is in him.*

In other words, Jesus spoke to test the teachers. If a man is preaching for his own glory, then he's not speaking as a messenger of God. That kind of draws the line, doesn't it?

As the Lord was speaking, though, He had before Him the Jewish leaders who were always after one thing—self-glory. When these Pharisees came with their gifts to the temple, they blew the trumpet so everyone could see what they did. When they stood and taught in the synagogue or temple courtyard, they were seeking their own glory.

Jesus said, "Let's prove it. Am I seeking My glory or the glory of Him that sent Me? I'm pointing you to Him, the living God. My message is from Him." His is a heavenly message given by a heavenly Messenger. The proof? He sought the glory of God.

I wouldn't ask you to try to judge everyone you hear, because the danger is you will not judge righteously. You cannot see what's in the heart. But you can mark what place the messenger gives to Christ. That's the measurement.

Leaders Want to Kill Jesus (7:19-27)

7:19-20. Jesus went on to say, *Did not Moses give you the law, and yet none of you keepeth the law? Why go ye about to kill me? The people answered and said, Thou hast a devil: who goeth about to kill thee?*

Jesus said, "Why are you going about to kill Me?"

This made them mad. They said, "You have a devil. You're out of your head. Who goes about to kill you? Where did you get that idea about people trying to kill you?" Now it may be that the common people didn't know at this time what the leaders of Israel were going to do, but Jesus did.

When you come to the next chapter, He declares, "I am without sin." They replied, "Say we not well unto thee that thou art a Samaritan?" See the issue? Either you accept the Son of God and go on with Him (as Peter in the last chapter said, "Lord, where can we go? Thou hast the words of eternal life") or your opposition to Christ increases.

"He is a good man."

"No, he isn't."

"Jesus, you're demon possessed!" (Just think of that accusation against the Son of God. Demon possessed!)

Do you see their perplexity and growing hatred for Him? The issue is the same today in society and in the church. Christ must be the center. "What think ye of Christ?" ought to be the question we ask one another. What think ye of Christ? Who is He? What is He?

Our answers will determine our eternal destiny. Our answers will determine our spiritual life. Our answers will determine how much we will serve Him. Our answers will determine whether we are real disciples or not.

Christ—He's the issue.

He who wills to do His will shall know of the doctrine. And the obedient heart is the heart that grows. The obedient heart is one to whom God reveals Himself. It's the obedient heart that enjoys the intimacy of His fellowship. It's the obedient heart that becomes a channel of blessing to others.

Put the Lord Jesus at the very center of your affection and then gladly obey Him, feasting upon His Word and finding His purpose in your life. Then you will go forth to be a real channel of blessing to your generation.

> **7:21-26.** *Jesus answered and said unto them, I have done one work, and ye all marvel. Moses therefore gave unto you circumcision; (not because it is of Moses, but of the fathers;) and ye on the sabbath day circumcise a man. If a man on the sabbath day receive circumcision, that the law of Moses should not be broken; are ye angry at me, because I have made a man every whit whole on the sabbath day? Judge not according to the appearance, but judge righteous judgment. Then said some of them of Jerusalem, Is not this he, whom they seek to kill? But lo, he speaketh boldly, and they say nothing unto him. Do the rulers know indeed that this is the very Christ?*

The people now know that the rulers are determined to kill the Savior. But they see Him standing in the temple courtyard boldly teaching the people, and nothing is being done. So they raise the issue. "Have the rulers changed their minds? Have they lost their desire to kill Him? Or are they changing? Are they beginning to realize this is the Messiah? Is this why they are holding back?"

7:27. They went on to say, *Howbeit we know this man whence he is: but when Christ cometh, no man knoweth whence he is.* Had these Jews wanted to know the truth concerning our Savior's birth, they could have found out that He came from Bethlehem. The temple records of births were right there in their city. And they knew Micah 5:2, which reads, "But thou, Bethlehem Ephratah, though thou be little among the thousands of Judah, yet out of thee shall he come forth unto me that is to be ruler in Israel; whose goings forth have been from of old, from everlasting.

But they said, "We know where this man comes from. He's from Nazareth. He's a Galilean. But when Messiah comes, nobody knows where he is going to come from."

I take it they had in their minds Malachi 3:1, which says that the Messiah is going to "suddenly come to his temple." These were Jews who claimed to know the Bible! It is very easy to use the Bible to suit your own whims and to back up unbelief. And today there is just as much perversion of the gospel of Christ.

Claim 2: "I Am from Above" (7:28-29)

Mark the Lord's answer.

> **7:28-29.** *Then cried Jesus in the temple as he taught, saying, Ye both know me, and ye know whence I am: and I am not come of myself, but he that sent me is true, whom ye know not. But I know him: for I am from him, and he hath sent me.*

Christ's first claim was that His message is from above. His second claim here is that He Himself is from heaven.

If Jesus is not from heaven, if His message is not from heaven, if He is not God incarnate, then we have no actual revelation of God, nor can we ever know God. You can point to creation if you want to, but you don't know God through creation. You only see His handiwork. You see the demonstration of His power. You see the revelation of His Godhead, that there is a God.

But to know Him, to know what He is, to know what He wants, we need Jesus. We need the One who says, "I am the One. I've come from heaven. I know the Father."

You see, the Lord is making the issue very clear. I'm not surprised there was a division among the people because of Him. Here He is in the courtyard teaching the people with authority just a few weeks before He is going to be crucified. And the more they oppose Him, the more He speaks of His deity. And the more He makes His claims that He is one with the Father. This makes them angry. They want to take Him, but they can't.

Leaders Try to Capture Jesus (7:30-36)

Notice the reaction of the Jews to Jesus' statement. **7:30.** *Then they sought to take him: but no man laid hands on him, because his hour was not yet come.* What made them desire to take hold of Him? If I could put it in my own words, He was saying this: "I am the One who is from heaven, and My message is from heaven. I am the One who knows the Father and am joined to Him. My Father and I are one."

> **7:31-32.** *And many of the people* (possibly these are the Galilean Jews who came down for the feast) *believed on him, and said, When Christ cometh, will he do more miracles than these which this man hath done? The Pharisees heard that the people murmured such things concerning him; and the Pharisees and the chief priests sent officers* (I take it they were the temple officers) *to take him.*

Do you see the picture? The Pharisees didn't come themselves; they sent officers to take Him. And when the Lord saw these officers coming to take Him, He made this amazing statement. **7:33-34.** *Then said Jesus unto them, Yet a little while am I with you, and then I go unto him that sent me. Ye shall seek me, and shall not find me: and where I am, thither ye cannot come.*

Jesus is very bold in making these statements. "I am only going to be with you a little while, and then I'm going back to Him that sent Me. I'm going back to heaven. And where I am, there you cannot come."

I do not know what the Universalist does with a verse like this. There are those who teach that eventually everyone is going to be saved. Everyone is going to be reconciled to Him, and everyone, including Satan himself, is going to be brought back into the picture. This is what they call "universal salvation" and "universal reconciliation."

But Jesus said, "Where I'm going, you cannot come." This is definite. There are no strings attached to it. "You have shut your heart to Me. You are opposed to Me personally. You don't want Me. In that case, you can't come where I'm going. Where I go, you cannot come."

> **7:35-36.** *Then said the Jews among themselves, Whither will he go, that we shall not find him? will he go unto the dispersed among the Gentiles, and teach the Gentiles? What manner of saying is this that he said, Ye shall seek me, and shall not find me: and where I am, thither ye cannot come?*

May I refresh your memory on this one fact? All through these chapters—five, six, seven, and eight—the appeal is not to some doctrine. The appeal is to a Person. Unless you have come to Him personally, you have no life in you.

Jesus' Proclamation at the End of the Feast (7:37-53) —Jesus Continues in Jerusalem

Proclamation: "Come and Drink" (7:37-39)

Verses 37 through 39 contain the next great truth, and this to my mind is one of the most marvelous statements of our Lord in the whole Bible.

> **7:37-39.** *In the last day, that great day of the feast, Jesus stood and cried, saying, If any man thirst, let him come unto me, and drink. He that believeth on me, as the scripture hath said, out of his belly shall flow rivers of living water.* John the apostle, years afterwards, added the next verse. *(But this spake he of the Spirit, which they that believe on him should re-*

*ceive: for the Holy Ghost was not yet given: because
that Jesus was not yet glorified.)*

It is the last day of the feast. The Lord Jesus had been sitting down, according to the custom, teaching the people the Word of God, bringing His Father's message to their hearts. Now, on the last day of the feast, the great day of the feast, Jesus stood (He's no longer teaching) and cried out, "If any man thirst, let him come unto me, and drink." This is a proclamation by the Son of God.

You see, He was at the Feast of Tabernacles, the only feast of eight days. Each day for seven days, the people went down to the pool of Siloam, filled their silver pitchers with water, and walked up toward the temple. As they walked into the temple courtyard and into the temple itself, they sang Psalms 103 through 118 to refresh their memory. Psalms 103 through 107 give the history of God's dealings with the children of Israel from the Passover (their deliverance from judgment and the crossing of the Red Sea) to their wilderness wanderings and their preservation by God. Read Exodus 12 through 18. Their minds were filled with both the past history of God's faithfulness and the coming kingdom.

As the people came up into the temple, they poured the water on the altar. This was done for seven days. But on the eighth day, the great day of the feast, they did not go down to the pool for water. This was a day for rejoicing, a day of expectation.

Now right in the very middle of this, the Lord Jesus stood and cried out, proclaiming, "If any man thirst, let him come unto me and drink. He that believeth on me, as the scripture hath said, out of his belly shall flow rivers of living water."

It's not surprising, a little later in the passage to find that the policemen of the temple said, "Never man spake like this man." They had gone to take Jesus captive. Instead, He captivated them. "Never man spake like this man." They had heard rabbis and teachers who daily taught in the temple, but this Man was different. How true. He was God.

"If any man thirst. . . ." Is there a person that has no craving of heart, no thirst? Some are thirsting for wealth, for popularity, for

151

pleasures, for position. God has so made man that he will never be satisfied except with eternal truths.

"If any man thirst. . . ." I am reminded of John 6:37, "Him that cometh to Me I will in no wise cast out."

"If any man thirst. . . ." This is not the voice of a man. This is the voice of One who is in the heart of God, giving the pleading of the heart of God to humanity in its sin . . . in its lack of peace and joy and blessing and spiritual reality. "Come to Me."

"If any man thirst. . . ." No wonder in Matthew 11:27 He could say, "No man knoweth the Father, save the Son, and he to whomsoever the Son will reveal Him." "Come unto Me." Do you want to know God? "Come unto Me . . . and I will give you rest" (Matthew 11:28).

"If any man thirst. . . ." Oh, I'm glad He said "any man." That lets you and me in no matter what our condition or our background.

"If any man thirst. . . ." All He wants is that we be thirsty. Isn't it simple? "If you want satisfying life, come to Me. Do you want eternal life? Come to Me. Pardon, forgiveness, peace? Come to Me."

"If any man thirst. . . ." Remember John 4:13-15? "He that drinketh of this water shall thirst again. But if you drink of the water that I will give you, you will never thirst again. It will be in you a well of water springing up." Here in chapter 7 He says it will be a river flowing. "Out of his innermost being shall flow rivers of living water."

And may I suggest this? If there is an intake, there must be an outflow. Otherwise the water gets stagnant. Do you say you are indwelt by the Spirit of God? The next verse says, "This spake he of the Spirit, which they that believe on him should receive: for the Holy Spirit was not yet given; because that Jesus was not yet glorified." John is writing from the other side of Pentecost as he looks back to what our Lord had said. Whoever comes to Him receives life—satisfying, everlasting, wonderful, abundant life. We not only receive an intake of the Spirit of God, but there is a flow of blessing to others, the outflow of the Spirit of God.

Here's a commercial fisherman called Peter. A girl says to him,

"You're a Galilean. You're one of his disciples." He says, "I'm not! I don't even know him!" And he curses and swears.

But when the Spirit of God comes and indwells Peter, there's an outflow. He spoke to the multitude. Three thousand were saved (Acts 2). He spoke again. Five thousand were saved (Acts 4). He spoke before the Sanhedrin, the same men who put Christ to death, and accused them of killing the Prince of Life (Acts 5).

Are you thirsty? What is lacking in your life? I do not know what your thirst is as a Christian. Are you thirsting for knowledge? For power? Thirsting to be used? Thirsting to know the purpose of God? He says, "Come to Me. Come to Me." That's where the believer should be—in His presence—for He is the One who meets every need.

Someone may ask, "What if I'm thirsty for something that is not of God? Why come to Him?" So He can change your thirst. He will give you something better than a thirst for things not of God.

May I say just this and pass it along? Every believer in Christ receives the Spirit of God the moment he accepts Jesus as Savior. Romans 8:9 says, "If any man have not the Spirit of Christ, he is none of his." To the Corinthian church Paul wrote, "Know ye not that your body is the temple of the Holy Ghost which is in you?" (1 Corinthians 6:19). Our Lord could say in John 14:17, "The Spirit of God is with you, but he shall be in you." The same is found in John 15:26 and 16:7, 13-15.

Wonder of wonders! He wants to live in you and through you, for from you shall flow rivers of living water. What an opportunity. What a privilege of committing our lives and all that we are to Him, Who will flow through us like a stream of blessing to our generation.

And, my friend, our generation needs it. If we do not flow with blessing from God to men, they will never have it. God does not give this honor, this privilege, this responsibility to angels—but to you and me. "Out of your innermost being shall flow rivers of living water." Its destination is the parched ground. Thousands upon thousands of parched people, thirsty for something, live around us. They don't know what they thirst for because their thirst has never been quenched. Jesus said, "I will quench your thirst. You come to Me."

I say, what a proclamation! May we heed it.

The People's Search for Truth (7:40-53)

7:40-46. *Many of the people therefore, when they heard this saying, said, Of a truth this is the Prophet. Others said, This is the Christ. But some said, Shall Christ come out of Galilee? Hath not the scripture said, That Christ cometh of the seed of David, and out of the town of Bethlehem, where David was? So there was a division among the people because of him. And some of them would have taken him; but no man laid hands on him.*

Then came the officers to the chief priests and Pharisees; and they said unto them, Why have ye not brought him? The officers answered, Never man spake like this man.

In their attitude to Christ the people were theological gypsies. We have the same kind among us today. They are people who don't know what to believe. One day, they believe one thing, and another day they believe something else. They are never established in their faith. And there is no reason why every Christian should not be established. God deliver us from being theological gypsies, running from church to church, group to group, doctrine to doctrine, never stable, full of perplexity.

"When Christ cometh, will he do more miracles than these?"

"But then again, shall Christ come out of Galilee?"

"Surely this is the Christ." And so there was a division among the people. They were unsettled in their minds.

Some people say to me, "You you preach one thing, and so-and-so preaches something else, and Doctor So-and-so preaches something else. What can a poor fellow do?"

I tell them, "Do you really want the truth or are you excusing your unbelief by saying, 'What can a fellow believe when you are all preaching something different?'?"

The Lord Jesus said, "Do you really want to know if My teaching is from heaven? If any man will do God's will—if you really want the truth—you shall know whether I am speaking from God or not."

In chapter 6, you remember, the appeal was to the heart. He "that cometh to me I will in no wise cast out." It is the same thing here in chapter 7. If your heart is yearning for reality, for life, for God, and if you really mean business with God, God means business with you. If you really want to know, "you will know that My teaching is from heaven, from My Father."

You have it in chapter 6 when they said to Him, "What shall we do to do the works of God?"

He said, "This is the work of God, that ye believe on Him whom He hath sent."

Do you want reality? Do you really want to know? The revelation of truth is given to the believer, and only to the believer who is willing to walk in the truth that God has already given to him. If you don't walk in the truth God has given you, He won't give you any more truth.

Why are Christians so ignorant? It is because they do not walk in that which God has already revealed to them. If I cease walking in the truth as I have seen it in God's Word, there will be no more further revelation of truth. But as I do what I see to be the will of God, then He keeps opening doors to further truth and further revelation. There has to be that personal cooperation, that personal hunger, that heart yearning for the Savior Himself if there is to be the revelation of Himself to our hearts.

We are living in a day of compromise, a day of shallow Christianity, a day when so many people are confused. And the tragedy of our day is that the average Christian has lost this hunger, this yearning for the living God.

7:47-52. *Then answered them the Pharisees, Are ye*

also deceived? Have any of the rulers or of the Pharisees believed on him? But this people who knoweth not the law are cursed. Nicodemus saith unto them, (he that came to Jesus by night, being one of them,) Doth our law judge any man, before it hear him, and know what he doeth? They answered and said unto him, Art thou also of Galilee? Search, and look: for out of Galilee ariseth no prophet.

The Pharisees would have found, had they searched their records, that Jonah came from Galilee. Nahum came from Galilee. These two men prophesied to Nineveh.

7:53. *And every man went unto his own house.*

And Jesus went to the Mount of Olives. They had a home to go to, but He didn't. "Foxes have holes. The birds of the air have nests. But the Son of man hath not where to lay his head." The crowd went to their homes. He went to the Mount of Olives to be with His Father.

Christ, The Light of the World

(Part 1)

Review of John 5-7

The eighth chapter ends this section of four chapters which have given us the tremendous claims of the Son of God. The opposition to Him, which started building in chapter 5, comes to a climax at the end of chapter 8 when they accuse Him of blasphemy and seek to kill Him.

You remember in chapter 5 that the Lord claimed equality with God in nature, equality with God in power, and equality with God in authority. It wasn't that God had given Him the power or the authority, but that He in Himself has power and authority equal with God.

In chapter 6—after having manifested Himself in blessed omnipotence by multiplying the bread and the fish, stilling the storm, and setting His disciples free from their terror—the Lord gives the great discourse on the bread of life. "I am the bread of life, and the life that I give to you is eternal life." It is satisfying life. It is resurrection life, a life over which death doesn't even cast a shadow. It is indwelling life, a life in union with God the Father and God the Son.

No wonder Peter cried out, "Lord, where can we go? You alone have the words of eternal life. And we believe and are sure that You are the Christ, the Son of the living God."

In chapter 7, Jesus is the heavenly One. He came from heaven.

His message was from heaven. He was going back to heaven. He would send the Holy Spirit from heaven.

He was the One who would be the fulfiller of Joel chapter 2. He would pour out His Spirit on all flesh. And the astounding thing to me in chapters 6 and 7 is that our Savior didn't look on the people as run of the mill. Everyone is an individual person to Him, having a peculiar, individual need. And He meets each one on this level.

Chapter 7 closes with Jesus standing, making a proclamation: "If any man thirst, let him come to Me, and drink." Any man, irrespective of who or what he is, can come and drink and be satisfied.

Background of John 8

Now when we come to chapter 8, the great discourse of our Lord ("I am the light of the world") is preceded by a moral issue concerning a sinful woman. The discourse concludes in chapter 9 with a physical issue when He heals the eyes of a man born blind. It starts with a sinful woman about to be stoned, and it ends with a sinless Man about to be stoned.

On the day after the last day of the great Feast of Tabernacles, the Lord came down from the Mount of Olives early in the morning. He walked into the temple courtyard to the treasury and there He sat down again to teach the people. You remember that in the Feast of Tabernacles they had carried the water for seven days from the pool of Siloam to the temple. And the last day, when they did not carry the water, He cried out, "If any man thirst, let him come to Me, and drink." Now in chapter 8, when the special lights of the Tabernacle feasts had been put out, He cried and said, "I am the light of the world."

The occasion which brings out the message, "I am the light of the world," is a situation involving the Pharisees and a woman caught in adultery. If you remember the background of the other Gospels, the Lord in a great many of these discourses revealed the fact that He was the friend of publicans and sinners. He said, "I am not come to call the righteous, but sinners to repentance" (Matthew 9:13). People accused Him by saying, "This man receiveth sinners" (Luke 15:2). He said, "The Son of man is come to seek and to save that which was lost" (Luke 19:10).

With this background, you can appreciate the situation in John 8 at the point in time near the end of our Lord's ministry. While He is teaching the people, the Pharisees and scribes bring to Him a woman caught in the act of adultery.

The Woman Caught in Adultery (8:1-11)

The Leader's Ploy, the Lord's Reply (8:1-9)

8:1-6. *Jesus went unto the mount of Olives. And early in the morning he came into the temple, and all the people came unto him; and he sat down, and taught them. And the scribes and Pharisees brought unto him a woman taken in adultery; and when they had set her in the midst, They say unto him, Master, this woman was taken in adultery, in the very act. Now Moses in the law commanded us, that such should be stoned: but what sayest thou? This they said, tempting him, that they might have to accuse him. But Jesus stooped down, and with his finger wrote on the ground, as though he heard them not.*

Now notice these wily Jews set a trap for the Lord. They threw the woman down and said, "Rabbi, according to Moses' law this woman should be stoned. What do you say about it?" And the Lord did a wonderful thing.

Remember, He is seated. He has been teaching these people. He bowed Himself down and wrote on the ground, and absolutely ignored them. What can you say to such evil-hearted men as these?

It's true that in Leviticus 20 and in Deuteronomy 22 those who committed adultery, the man and the woman, were to be taken out and killed. Mark that they didn't bring the man, these peeping Toms. They brought the woman. According to the law the man should have been there, and the man should have been stoned as well as the woman.

There was no need for the Lord to interpret the law, for Him to tell them what He thought about it. The law was very clear. These folk should not have brought the woman to Him. They should have taken her to the Sanhedrin. Christ wasn't the judge of the Jews. The Sanhedrin judged the people. But they brought her and threw her down before Him.

And I say I just love this picture of the Lord Jesus Christ as He wrote on the ground. And please don't ask me what He wrote, because I don't know. Neither does anyone else. Suffice it for me to say that He ignored such people, and such people ought to be ignored or dismissed without a word.

But they refused to be dismissed. They persisted that He answer them. You see, they thought the Lord was in a trap. If He says, "Obey Moses' law; take her out and stone her," then He is no longer the sinner's friend. And not only so, He would have come under the jurisdiction of Rome, for Jews had no right to stone without permission from Rome. So He would be in the wrong with the Roman leaders. But if He says, "Let her go," then He is opposed to the law of Moses. You can see the Jews rubbing their hands. "Whatever His answer may be, we have Him this time. We have Him this time."

8:7-9. *So when they continued asking him, he lifted up himself, and said unto them, He that is without sin among you, let him first cast a stone at her. And again he stooped down, and wrote on the ground. And they which heard it, being convicted by their own conscience, went out one by one, beginning at the eldest, even unto the last: and Jesus was left alone, and the woman standing in the midst.*

The Lord looked up and said, "Let him that is without sin cast a stone." In other words, if I may put it this way, "All right, gentlemen, I appoint you men as executioners of this woman—on one condition. . . ." And I personally believe His implication here is this, "If any of you men have not committed the same sin that this woman has committed, cast your stone."

Whether He wrote what they had done or not, I don't know. Suffice to say this, when He wrote the second time with His head down, the Pharisees and scribes left, from the oldest to the youngest.

Jesus is going to proclaim: "I am the light of the world." So what did He do? He let the light shine on the consciences of these Jewish leaders. And when the light shone into their hearts, they left as fast as they could. Now they didn't go out in a crowd. That would have been very noticeable. They slipped out one by one.

Listen, if religious leaders in Christ's day could not stand the light of Jesus Christ in veiled glory as the Man in the midst of men, please tell me how in the world will men stand in the presence of God in unveiled glory?

You say, "I don't believe that God will send a man to hell." You don't need to believe that, my friend. A man will be glad to go to hell in preference to standing before a holy God in the blaze of His glory. No sinner could ever stand in the presence of a holy God—not even Moses, the man of God, the servant of God. He said, "Show me your glory," and God said, "No man can see Me and live" (Exodus 33:18, 20).

The Woman Transformed (8:10-11)

> **8:10-11.** *When Jesus had lifted up himself, and saw none but the woman, he said unto her, Woman, where are those thine accusers? hath no man condemned thee? She said, No man, Lord. And Jesus said unto her, Neither do I condemn thee: go, and sin no more.*

The Lord turned to the woman. "Where are your accusers?"

"There are none, Lord."

Then, if there are no accusers, sentence cannot be passed. According to the law of Moses, you had to have witnesses. If there are no witnesses, if there is no one to accuse you, then no judgment can be passed. So He said, "Neither do I condemn thee."

Now the Lord was not glossing over her sin. By no means. But

He refused to sit as a judge with no witnesses.

The Lord did say something, however, far more important. *"Woman,* where are your accusers?" He didn't say, "Sinful woman." He didn't say, "Prostitute." He didn't say, "Adulteress." He said, "Woman." My, what it must have meant to her. This is the same word used in John 2 when Jesus said to His mother, "Woman, what have I to do with thee?" There is no condemnation, no Phariseeism, no self-righteousness here. He just said, "Woman, where are your accusers?"

"There are none, Lord."

You know, I am of the persuasion that there was a tremendous transformation in this woman. When she came, she was dragged by those self-righteous religionists. You can just see her fighting her way. Such a woman would fight. Who wants to be made an object of shame? But when she looked into His face and heard His gracious, tender words, she said, "No man, Lord." And Jesus said to her, "Neither do I condemn you." Go home and repent? No. Go in peace? No. "Go and sin no more." It is far stronger. The Lord never condoned the sin, but He did love this woman, the sinner. He wanted her to be a transformed woman, free from such a life to live for the glory of God.

You know, it's an amazing thing, if I may just digress here for a second, how some people will come along right here and attack the grace of God. They say that if you're saved eternally and become a child of God forever, you can go out and do anything you want to do. What we want to do is to glorify God. You can't look into the face of the Son of God, receive of His mercy, His grace, and His love, and then want to go out and continue to live in sin. Not when you've seen Him. The tragedy is that too few of us have really looked into His face and appreciated His grace and His mercy and His love. Here it is. "Go and sin no more."

Now I haven't taken the time to be a critic on this first portion. I'm well aware of the fact that so many have written that this should not be in the Book, that this was just pushed in here, that John didn't write it, and that it has no place in his Gospel.

I'm not going to discuss this matter in detail. But, if you remove it, you have a hard time making a smooth transition from chapter 7 into chapter 8 and His discourse on the light of the world. It has a real bearing on the passage, and such men as Augustine and Jerome believed this was in the Book. We accept it as such. It has a real place in the connection between His great discourse on the water of life and His discourse now on the light of the world.

Proclamation: "I am the Light of the World" (8:12-20)

Out of this situation with the Pharisees and the woman comes Jesus' next statement.

8:12. *Then spake Jesus again unto them, saying, I am the light of the world: he that followeth me shall not walk in darkness, but shall have the light of life.*

Jesus said, "I am the light of the world."

If you read down through this chapter, the Pharisees go after the Savior time and again as He speaks. Here we have their first interruption. **8:13.** *The Pharisees therefore said unto him, Thou bearest record of thyself; thy record is not true.* The Pharisees were saying, "You have to have two witnesses." And as Jesus goes on in His claims, you will notice that ten times between verse 12 and the end of the chapter these Jews interrupt His messages. And before He is through, they are extremely mad, hateful, and full of sneering for Him. On this occasion He makes some of the strongest statements in the Bible.

8:14-19. *Jesus answered and said unto them, Though I bear record of myself, yet my record is true: for I know whence I came, and whither I go; but ye cannot tell whence I come, and whither I go.* Why? You're in the dark. *Ye judge after the flesh; I judge no man. And yet if I judge, my judgment is true: for I am not alone, but I and the Father that sent me. It is also written in your law, that the testimony of two men is true. I am one that bear witness of myself, and the*

*Father that sent me beareth witness of me. Then said
they unto him, Where is thy Father? Jesus answered,
Ye neither know me, nor my Father: if ye had known
me, ye should have known my Father also.*

May I suggest one or two things? In chapter 6 He said, "I am the
bread of life." In chapter 7, "If any man thirst, let him come to Me
and drink. Out of his belly shall flow rivers of living water." Now
He says here in chapter 8, "I am the light of the world." There is no
question that the issue is a Person. "I am the light of the world. Not
to follow Me means to walk in darkness; not to follow Me means
death."

But to follow Christ means trust. It means to believe and to trust
Him. You won't follow Him without trusting Him. If you trust
Him, you will follow Him. In Colossians 1:13 we read that He
"hath delivered us from the power of darkness, and hath translated
us into the kingdom of his dear Son." These Jews arguing with
Christ were in darkness. They did not know from whence they
came. They didn't know where they were going. Jesus said, "I
know where I came from. I know where I am going. And my witness is true. My Father bears witness of Me. We are one."

I am not surprised at the end of this section. **8:20.** *These words
spake Jesus in the treasury, as he taught in the temple: and no
man laid hands on him; for his hour was not yet come.* They
would have taken and torn Him to pieces if they could, but His time
wasn't ready. They couldn't touch Him. And for your comfort, my
Christian friend, the world can't touch you and Satan can't touch
you until your job is finished.

Why are these men in the dark? "Because they know not the
Father, nor Me." Ignorance of Christ is the root of not knowing
God. People today say, "Well, I believe in God, but I don't believe
in Christ." They're talking in a riddle. You can't know God with-
out Christ. And when you come to know Christ, you come to know
God. These are inseparable.

In chapter 14 Philip said, "Show us the Father and it sufficeth
us."

Jesus said, "Have I been so long time with you, Philip, and yet thou hast not known Me? He that hath seen Me hath seen the Father. No man cometh unto the Father but by Me. If ye had known Me, ye should have known My Father also."

These religious leaders of Israel were in the kingdom of darkness. They lived in the darkness. Their actions were in the dark. And they didn't know where they were going. Why? Because they didn't know Christ, the Light of the world.

The Liberator Revealed (8:21-36)

Jesus Liberates from Death (8:21-27)

Starting at verse 21 and running down through verse 36, we have the Lord Jesus revealed as the great Liberator. He liberates from death. He liberates from slavery. And in between those two aspects of liberation we have the ground of that liberation, which is the cross. We have seen all the way through the Gospel that the Lord (from chapter 2 when He said to His mother, "My time is not yet come") has the cross before Him. Even in this passage, there can be no deliverance from death or from slavery, except on the ground that He is going to die.

Will you notice, first of all, that Jesus is the great Liberator from death?

> **8:21-24.** *Then said Jesus again unto them, I go my way, and ye shall seek me, and shall die in your sins: whither I go, ye cannot come. Then said the Jews, Will he kill himself? because he saith, Whither I go, ye cannot come. And he said unto them, Ye are from beneath; I am from above: ye are of this world; I am not of this world. I said therefore unto you, that ye shall die in your sins: for if ye believe not that I am he, ye shall die in your sins.*

Then they interrupted again. I want you to notice the emphatic statements of our Savior here.

8:25-27. *Then said they unto him, Who art thou? And Jesus saith unto them, Even the same that I said unto you from the beginning. I have many things to say and to judge of you: but he that sent me is true; and I speak to the world those things which I have heard of him. They understood not that he spake to them of the Father.*

It is not that the Father taught Him. He was one with God. He was one with the Father. But He is accommodating Himself to human language with these who stood before Him. And the reason for their blindness was because they didn't know the Father. Yet to know God—to come into relationship with Him—to have the life of God: this is impossible without Christ.

So I say, unbelief in Him is a terrible thing. Don't you for one moment minimize the terribleness of unbelief. Hebrews 3 and 4 both say that unbelief is the product of an evil heart. And the root of it is unbelief in the Savior. Now I may be frail. I may be weak. I may stumble. But there is no unbelief in me concerning the Person of our Savior. I'm trusting Him. It is only as I know Him that I come in the presence of God and know God.

Jesus Liberates by the Cross (8:28-30)

Second, we have the foundation of our liberation.

8:28-30. *Then Jesus said unto them, When ye have lifted up the Son of man, then shall ye know that I am he, and that I do nothing of myself; but as my Father hath taught me, I speak these things. And he that sent me is with me: the Father hath not left me alone; for I do always those things that please him. As he spake these words, many believed on him.*

Notice that the foundation of deliverance is the cross. Here we have it again: "When ye have lifted up the Son of man, then shall ye know that I am he." When did they know this? It was fulfilled in

Acts 2 when Peter preached: "This Jesus, whom ye took by wicked hands and crucified, hath God raised up, whereof we all are witnesses. Therefore being by the right hand of God exalted . . . he hath shed forth this, which ye now see and hear." And when they heard of their crucifying Him and of God's raising Him from the dead, they cried out, "Men and brethren, what shall we do?"

"When ye have lifted up the Son of man, then shall ye know that I am he."

In John 12:31-33 the Lord Jesus said, "Now is the judgment of this world: now shall the prince of this world be cast out. And I, if I be lifted up from the earth, will draw all men unto me. This he said, signifying what death he should die."

"When ye have lifted up the Son of man, then shall ye know that I am he."

And He goes on, "The Father hath not left me alone; for I do always those things that please him." This to me is the most precious thought concerning the sacrifice of Christ. In Matthew and Mark our Savior died as the trespass offering and as the sin offering, respectively, the offerings for sin. Sin—that which brings separation from God. That's why He cried out, "My God, my God, why hast thou forsaken me?" You have it in Psalm 22:1; Matthew 27:46; and Mark 15:34.

But when you come to John's Gospel, He doesn't say that. John presents our Lord as the burnt offering, the offering of worship, the offering of submission. Take John 16:32: "This night you are all going to be scattered, every one to his own, and shall leave me alone: and yet I am not alone, because the Father is with Me."

In Matthew and Mark you have God in His governmental dealings with men; hence, you have separation. He was a sin offering, a non-sweet-savor offering. He became sin for us that we might be delivered from sin. But not in John's Gospel. "When you have lifted up the Son of man, then shall ye know that I am he . . . the Father hath not left me alone. I do always those things that please Him."

There is no separation in John. Jesus Christ is revealed here in two aspects of the offering: He is the burnt offering (the One pleasing to the Father), and He is the meal offering (the One whose life and sinless character always bring pleasure to God).

Jesus Liberates from Salvery (8:31-36)

Third, Jesus is the great Liberator not only from death, but from slavery.

> **8:31-36.** *Then said Jesus to those Jews which believed on him, If ye continue in my word, then are ye my disciples indeed; And ye shall know the truth, and the truth shall make you free. They answered him, We be Abraham's seed, and were never in bondage to any man: how sayest thou, Ye shall be made free? Jesus answered them, Verily, verily, I say unto you, Whosoever committeth sin is the servant of sin. And the servant abideth not in the house for ever: but the Son abideth ever. If the Son therefore shall make you free, ye shall be free indeed.*

Jesus is the great Deliverer from slavery. May I give you two aspects of this truth here, as our Lord declared them? First of all, true discipleship is evidenced by continuing in the Word of God. If you are not continuing in the Word, then you are not His disciple. One of the great characteristics of a follower, of a real disciple of the Son of God, is abiding in His Word. How can I know the will of God if I do not stay in the Word of God where it has been revealed?

And notice the result. If you and I stay in the Word of God as disciples, we shall experience liberation, freedom. Do you have in your life things that sap spiritual strength? Have you become bound somewhat by some sin? There is deliverance for you, daily deliverance through the Word of God.

May I say this to you as well? There is not one man on the face of the earth today who knows the full power of the Word of God in his life. If we had a real inkling of the power of the Word of God, we would spend more time in it. This is one thing that Satan hates.

You remember the 119th Psalm: "Wherewithal shall a young

man cleanse his way? by taking heed thereto according to thy word. Thy word have I hid in mine heart, that I might not sin against thee" (119:9, 11).

Our Lord could say in John 15:3, "Now are ye clean through the word which I have spoken unto you."

Ephesians 5:26 reads, "That he might sanctify and cleanse it (the church) with the washing of water by the word."

"If ye continue in my word, then are ye my disciples indeed; and ye shall know the truth, and the truth shall set you free. They answered him, We be Abraham's seed, and were never in bondage to any man. . . ." It's an amazing thing how blind people can be, how self-deceptive these Jews were. Never in bondage to any man? They must have forgotten their four hundred years in Egypt. They must have forgotten their seventy years in Babylonian captivity. And while they were boasting of their religious relationship to Abraham and to God, they were groaning under bondage to Rome. And not only so, but they were slaves to sin. Slaves, for "whosoever committeth sin is the servant of sin. . . . If the Son therefore shall make you free, ye shall be free indeed."

May I suggest to you 1 John 3:9? "Whosoever is born of God doth not commit sin." He is not dealing with us who fail God now and then. He is talking about a life that is dominated by sin, a life controlled by sin. A person can be a moralist in his actions, he can even be an exemplary man in his actions before men; but he still can be a slave to the lusts of the flesh and the lusts of the mind. There is only One who can actually set us free, and whoever the Son sets free, is free indeed.

If you're bound by sin, by habits, there is only one Person who can set you free, and that is the Lord Jesus Christ. The only One who can put away sin is the One who died for you and me. He died that we might be the righteousness of God in Him. He became what I was—sin, that I might become what He is—righteousness.

The Liberator Challenged (8:37-59)

Now follow through this passage and watch these Jews go after the Son of God. They interrupt Him. They begin to malign Him. They begin to call Him names. They have no argument against Him. So they begin to be personal in their venom.

> **8:37-40.** *I know that ye are Abraham's seed; but ye seek to kill me, because my word hath no place in you. I speak that which I have seen with my Father: and ye do that which ye have seen with your father. They answered and said unto him, Abraham is our father. Jesus saith unto them, If ye were Abraham's children, ye would do the works of Abraham. But now ye seek to kill me, a man that hath told you the truth, which I have heard of God: this did not Abraham.*

Mark this conflict between the religious leaders and Christ. The Jews claimed to be Abraham's seed. We have this in verse 33. They told Jesus, "We be Abraham's seed. Why are you talking about being made free? We were never in bondage to any man."

Jesus replied: "I know you are Abraham's seed. But if you were Abraham's children, you would do the works of Abraham." When He spoke of being Abraham's children, Jesus meant children of faith. We have this elsewhere: "They which are of faith, the same are the children of Abraham" (Galatians 3:7). Abraham is given to us in Scripture as an example of faith. The Jews claimed that Abraham was their father, but Jesus did not believe them.

> **8:41-45.** *Ye do the deeds of your father. Then said they to him, We be not born of fornication; we have one Father, even God. Jesus said unto them, If God were your Father, ye would love me: for I proceeded forth and came from God; neither came I of myself, but he sent me. Why do ye not understand my speech? even because ye cannot hear my word. Ye are of your father the devil, and the lusts of your father ye will do. He was a murderer from the beginning, and abode not in the truth, because there is no truth in him. When he speaketh a lie, he speaketh of his own: for he is a liar,*

and the father of it.

These Jews were glorying in the fact that God was also their Father, but Jesus is revealing very clearly to them, "If God were your Father, you would believe in Me. But you seek to kill Me instead. You are of your father the devil. He was a murderer from the beginning. This is why you don't believe in Me."

Then Jesus makes this tremendous claim. **8:46-47. *Which of you convinceth me of sin? And if I say the truth, why do ye not believe me? He that is of God heareth God's words: ye therefore hear them not, because ye are not of God.*** Jesus was saying, "I am the sinless One. Who can convince Me of any sin?"

And their reaction to that was this. **8:48. *Then answered the Jews, and said unto him, Say we not well that thou art a Samaritan, and hast a devil?*** As you study these ten interruptions of Christ's message by the Jews, you see they have come to the place where they must either acknowledge Him as coming from God or from hell. His message and His life were absolutely supernatural. They recognized this and said, "You are from hell! You are demon possessed." This is what we have in Matthew 12, where they said, "This fellow doth not cast out devils, but by Beelzebub the prince of the devils" (12:24). "He is from hell." This is what they were saying. But Jesus was claiming, "No, I am from heaven."

> **8:49-51. *Jesus answered, "I have not a devil; but I honour my Father, and ye do dishonour me. And I seek not mine own glory: there is one that seeketh and judgeth. Verily, verily, I say unto you, If a man keep my saying, he shall never see death.***

Mark what Jesus is claiming here. "If a man keep my saying, he shall never see death." You see, my friend, Jesus Christ is the difference between death and life. You remember, we have this in Deuteronomy 30, where Moses said, "See, I have set before thee this day life and good, and death and evil. . . . I call heaven and earth to record this day against you, that I have set before you life and death . . . therefore choose life, that both thou and thy seed

171

may live" (30:15, 19).

Our Savior is doing the same thing here. In verse 24 He said, "for if ye believe not that I am he, ye shall die in your sins." Here is death. On the other hand, He offers life in verse 51: "If a man keep my saying, he shall never see death."

8:52-53. *Then said the Jews unto him, Now we know that thou hast a devil. Abraham is dead, and the prophets; and thou sayest, If a man keep my saying, he shall never taste of death. Art thou greater than our father Abraham, which is dead? and the prophets are dead: whom makest thou thyself?*

"Who do you think you are? God?! Abraham is dead. The prophets are dead. Who do you think you are, saying that if a man keeps your saying, he will never taste of death?" Notice all the way through this passage there is a rift between the Jewish leaders and Jesus. "Who do you think you are? God?"

Let me tell you, my friends, I have had people today, even preachers, tell me that Jesus Christ never claimed to be God. But there was absolutely no question in the minds of the Jewish leaders about what He was claiming. We have this in chapter 5. Jesus said, "My Father worketh hitherto, and I work." The Jews sought to kill Him, because He made Himself equal with God. And Jesus didn't deny it. He didn't say, "Pardon me, but you misunderstood what I said. I didn't claim to be equal with God." No, that's not what He said. "You're right! I am equal with God in nature, in power, and in authority."

You have this again in chapter 6. "I am the bread of life. The life that I give is eternal life. It is satisfying life." In chapter 7 He says, "I am the One who is going to send the Holy Spirit." Only God could do that. And now in chapter 8: "I am the light of the world. I am the great Liberator from sin and death and slavery." What did they say? You're demon possessed! You are from hell."

8:54-56. *Jesus answered, If I honour myself, my honour is nothing; it is my Father that honoureth me;*

> *of whom ye say, that he is your God: Yet ye have not*
> *known him; but I know him: and if I should say, I*
> *know him not, I shall be a liar like unto you: but I*
> *know him, and keep his saying. Your father Abraham*
> *rejoiced to see my day: and he saw it, and was glad.*

Now remember, they had said, "Who do you think you are?
God?" Jesus said, "Yes, I am Abraham's God. I am El Shaddai,
the Almighty God."

In Genesis 17 God revealed Himself to Abraham as El Shaddai:
"I am the Almighty God" (17:1). You remember the account. In
chapter 16, there was no hope for Sarah to have a child. She was
seventy-five years old. So Abraham had a son through her hand-
maid. Between chapter 16 and 17 we have thirteen long years . . .
thirteen years of silence, thirteen years with no revelation from
God. Finally, when Abraham was ninety-nine years old, and there
was no hope for him to have a son, God said, "You are going to
have a son. I am God Almighty." And that's where you have the
Abrahamic covenant. God revealed Himself to Abraham as El
Shaddai.

> **8:57-58.** *Then said the Jews unto him, Thou art not*
> *yet fifty years old, and hast thou seen Abraham? Jesus*
> *said unto them, Verily, verily, I say unto you, Before*
> *Abraham was, I am.*

Mark that Jesus didn't say, "I *was* Abraham's God." Instead, He
said, "I *am*." This is a revelation of God's eternal name, Jehovah.
Jehovah is the name for the eternal, unchanging God. He is without
beginning and end. You have this in Exodus 6. God spoke to
Moses and said, "I appeared unto Abraham, unto Isaac, and unto
Jacob, by the name of God Almighty, but by my name JEHOVAH
was I not known to them" (6:3).

This is the same name you have in Exodus 3, where we read,
"God said unto Moses, I AM THAT I AM: and he said, Thus shalt
thou say unto the children of Israel, I AM hath sent me unto you"
(3:14).

When Jesus said, "Before Abraham was, I am," there's only one thing left to do, and that is to worship Him. Or stone Him.

8:59. *Then took they up stones to cast at him: but Jesus hid himself, and went out of the temple, going through the midst of them, and so passed by.*

And, that, as I have said, is the end of the argument of the Gospel of John. With the crowd ready to stone the Son of God, rejecting His claims.

Oh, the terribleness of unbelief that would pick up stones to kill the sinless, holy Son of God. This is how far unbelief goes. It would slay the Son of God. What a terrible thing!

Let us continue in the Word of God. Faith cometh by hearing, and hearing by the Word of God. Abide in the Word of God because unbelief is tricky. It is subtle. Satan, the devil, the adversary, will do anything under heaven to keep you from dwelling in that Book, to keep you from being occupied with the Son of God.

I say it again, unbelief is a terrible thing. May God deliver us from it, and may we as His people have a consuming passion to get into this Book. May we desire to know the purpose of God, and get into the stream of His purpose, and live to the praise of the glory of His grace.

John 9

Christ, The Light of the World

(Part 2)

Introduction to John 9

This chapter illustrates the truth of chapter 8. John not only gives us the healing of a man born blind, but also the reaction of his neighbors, the Pharisees, his parents, and the blind man himself. The chapter ends with the man cast out of the temple, repudiated, excommunicated, but on his knees in front of the Savior, worshiping Him as the Son of God. The One who has been spurned by the nation and the leaders is worshiped by a man, a blind beggar, whose eyes He has opened. Following this, Christ never again pleads with Israel, and Israel is also through with Him.

In chapter 10 you have the revelation of the Shepherd who is going to have His sheep. In chapter 11 He is on the road to Jerusalem and he raises Lazarus from the dead. In chapter 12 He is the center of attraction on His way to Jerusalem. In chapters 13 through 17 He is with His disciples. In chapters 18 and 19 He is betrayed and crucified. In chapter 20 He is raised from the dead. In chapter 21 the Chief Shepherd gives His final words to His undershepherds.

But here in chapter 9 there is absolutely no desire in the hearts of these leaders for Christ. They are determined not to believe on Him, and they are determined to excommunicate anyone who would even think of believing on Him. The matter is closed. They are through with Him. Nothing will satisfy them but His death.

The Sixth Sign: Healing a Blind Man (9:1-7)

Jesus, Sickness, and the Sabbath (9:1-5)

At the end of chapter 8, when the Jews picked up stones to cast at Jesus, He hid Himself and went out of the temple, going through the midst of them.

> **9:1.** *And as Jesus passed by, he saw a man which was blind from his birth.*

Now, some say there was a time element between the two chapters. To me, it is just as easy for Him to see the man as He came out of the temple as later. He had found one of His sheep, one who was born blind. The chapter is full of suggestions of practical truth for us.

> **9:2-3.** *And his disciples asked him, saying, Master, who did sin, this man, or his parents, that he was born blind? Jesus answered, Neither hath this man sinned, nor his parents: but that the works of God should be made manifest in him.*

The disciples manifested ignorance of the ways of God. They ask a question that the Lord is not going to discuss. His statement, "Neither hath this man sinned, nor his parents," doesn't mean they were sinless, but that He is dealing with the man's blindness "that the works of God should be made manifest in him."

The beggar's blindness was not due to any sin he or his parents had committed. He was blind for the glory of God. There is such a thing, you know, as being sick for God's glory.

Take Job, for instance. He was a righteous man, yet he was smitten with a loathsome disease. Why? For the glory of God. Satan learned a lesson. He learned that Job didn't love God for what he received in return. He loved the Lord for Himself.

Paul could say, "we are made a spectacle unto the world, and to angels" (1 Corinthians 4:9). We are on the stage to instruct angels, demons, and men. When a Christian is sick, some people say,

"Well, he must have sinned a great deal." That isn't so. May God is honoring that believer, for He knows He can trust him with affliction, that He might be glorified. Don't be too quick to judge.

There are three reasons for sickness, while I'm discussing it. There is sickness caused by folly. You eat the wrong things and feel poorly. Don't blame the devil. Next, there is sickness caused by the chastisement of God. We find this in 1 Corinthians 11:30, where Paul wrote, "For this cause many are weak and sickly among you." Why? Because they did not discern the Lord's body. Finally, there is sickness caused for the glory of God. This is what we have here. "Neither hath this man sinned, nor his parents: but that the works of God should be made manifest in him."

And may I suggest three reasons for death? First, death comes for the believer whose work on earth is finished. Paul told Timothy, "the time of my departure is at hand. I have fought a good fight, I have finished my course, I have kept the faith" (2 Timothy 4:7-8). Peter said the same thing in 2 Peter 1:14, "Knowing that shortly I must put off this my tabernacle, even as our Lord Jesus Christ hath shewed me." Peter had fed the flock. He had finished his work. It was time for the Lord to say, "Come on home!"

Then there is death caused by God's chastening hand. We have this in Acts 5, where Ananias and Sapphira lied to Peter and to the Holy Ghost. The young men carried them out and buried them. John could write in his first epistle, "There is a sin unto death" (1 John 5:16).

Finally, there is death for the glory of God. These saints will receive the martyr's crown. Jesus told Peter, "When you were young, you did what you wished. But when you are old, they will take you where you don't want to go." Jesus said this, "signifying by what death he should glorify God" (John 21:19). Some die when their work is done. Others die because of sin. Still others die for the glory of God. But don't you be the judge in any case.

As I said, here we have the ignorance of the disciples as to God's way of dealing with people. Mark what Jesus says in verses 4 and 5.

9:4-5. *I must work the works of him that sent me, while it is day: the night cometh, when no man can work. As long as I am in the world, I am the light of the world.*

"My work is delivering people from the thing in which they find themselves." And as long as we are here on earth, we Christians also have a job to do. We are surrounded by people in affliction, in sin, in despair, in darkness. They are lost. And as long as people are suffering because of sin, we have a job to do.

In chapter 5 Jesus said at the healing of a man thirty-eight years infirm, "My Father worketh hitherto, and I work." He healed that man and made him carry his bed on the sabbath day. The issue then was the sabbath. The leaders didn't care about the man as long as their traditions were kept. Let the man stay in his defiled, reprobate condition.

But now, this man was a well-known beggar. Why didn't the Lord wait until the next day? The fellow would still have been there. But He deliberately performed the miracle on the sabbath day. After all, the sabbath day was made for man, not man for the sabbath. The sabbath was a day of rest. What better day to heal this man than on the sabbath day and bring him into the enjoyment of his rest in God.

In the first chapter of John, the Jew is seen as a reprobate. "He came unto his own, and his own received him not" (1:11). Then why should he keep up the sabbath day sign of the covenant? They have broken the covenant and refused to obey the Lord of the covenant. Why worry about the sign?

"The night cometh, when no man can work. As long as I am in the world, I am the light of the world." Note the urgency. I question if God has given us very much more time to reach our generation with the Word of God, the message that Christ Jesus came into the world to save sinners. How much have we done this last month in trying to reach someone for Christ? Paul tells us to redeem the time, because the days are evil (Ephesians 5:16). Christ says, "As long as I am here, I must do the work. I must reach people in need."

This ties in to John 4:34: "My meat is to do the will of him that sent me, and to finish his work."

The danger is to fall asleep. The danger is to become sluggish. Oh, that we might redeem the time. Buy up all the opportunities God gives to you of witnessing about the Lord and glorifying Him. Buy up the opportunities He gives you.

Eye-Opening Clay (9:6-7)

9:6-7. *When he had thus spoken, he spat on the ground, and made clay of the spittle, and he anointed the eyes of the blind man with the clay, And said unto him, Go, wash in the pool of Siloam, (which is by interpretation, Sent.) He went his way therefore, and washed, and came seeing.*

You will notice that the man didn't ask to have his eyes opened. The Lord loves to do things differently. At least four times He opened blind eyes, and He does it a different way each time, depending on the personality and the circumstances.

In Matthew chapter 9 we read that Jesus touched the eyes of two blind men. In Mark 8 we have the account of Jesus spitting in the eyes of a blind man. He looked up and said, "I see men as trees, walking." Jesus put His hands on his eyes, and made him look up, and his sight was restored. In Luke 18 a certain blind man cried, saying, "Jesus, thou son of David, have mercy on me." Jesus simply said, "Receive thy sight," and the man was made whole.

But here in chapter 9 Jesus made clay and put it in this man's eyes. Now, if he wasn't blind before, he's blind now! And Jesus sent him to the pool of Siloam to wash. And he came away seeing. Obedience brought liberation.

The Lord deals with each of us, not *en masse*, but as individuals. Each of us is a special object of the grace and care and faithfulness of God. If you were the only one on the face of the earth, He would still take care of you. This is demonstrated here. He made clay and put it on the man's eyes. And this calls for two things from the man:

faith and obedience. The moment he obeyed, he had deliverance. Deliverance comes from obedience.

You remember in chapter 8 that the Lord Jesus said to the Jews who believed on Him, "If ye continue in my word, then are ye my disciples indeed; and ye shall know the truth, and the truth shall set you free" (8:31-32). And in verse 36 we read, "If the Son therefore shall make you free, ye shall be free indeed." This passage in John 9 is the illustration of John 8. To follow Him means not to walk in darkness. Here is a man who has never seen the light of day, or seen a tree or a flower, or seen his mother. He has never seen anything. He has always lived in the dark. How glad I am the Savior is the light of the world and can come into any darkened heart that wants to know God. The moment your heart is open to Him, the light shines in.

Obedience brings deliverance. This blind man had to manifest faith. He had never seen Jesus. As far as I know, he may have heard the name, but he didn't know who it was who put His hand on him and said, "You go and wash." He just obeyed. And when the Word of God speaks to us, let us believe it. Our believing will be evident by our obedience, and obedience brings freedom, emancipation, and liberation.

Various People React to the Sign (9:8-34)

Reaction of the Neighbors (9:8-12)

Now we have some trouble on our hands. Notice, first of all, the neighbors.

> **9:8-12.** The *neighbours therefore, and they which before had seen him that he was blind, said, Is not this he that sat and begged? Some said, This is he: others said, He is like him: but he said, I am he. Therefore said they unto him, How were thine eyes opened? He answered and said, A man that is called Jesus made lay, and anointed mine eyes, and said unto me, Go to the pool of Siloam, and wash: and I went and washed,*

*and I received sight. Then said they unto him, Where
is he? He said, I know not.*

They were not so much occupied with the fact that his eyes were
open. They were concerned about how it happened. This is unbelief. Faith looks to the fruit. The man of faith rejoices, "My, the
man's eyes are open. We don't care how they were opened. They
are open. That's the important thing." Unbelief goes the other way
around. Unbelief is not concerned with the result, but with the
manner in which it was done.

This is one of our dangers today. We are more occupied with the
methods and manner than we are with life in Christ. I don't care
what experience you have had. I care that you really know Him.
Do you have life in Him? Are you joined to Him, related to Him?
That's the important thing.

The important thing here is not the clay, not the pool of Siloam,
but that his eyes were opened.

Reaction of the Pharisees (9:13-17)

Now these neighbors couldn't understand this, so they brought
him to their leaders, the Pharisees.

**9:13-14. *They brought to the Pharisees him that
aforetime was blind. And it was the sabbath day when
Jesus made the clay, and opened his eyes.***

I repeat, why didn't the Lord heal the man on the first day of the
week? Why didn't He do it on some other day than the sabbath? It's
the same question we ask about His healing of the man at the pool
of Bethesda in chapter 5. (Jesus just seemed to love to do something like this to bring out truth.)

This man had never in all his life seen the light of day or the face
of his parents. Why not wait and avoid trouble, or at least only
speak the word and slip away? Why did Jesus both work and cause
the man to work as well on the sabbath?

Again, the sabbath was the sign and seal of the covenant between the Jews and God. The Jewish people had rejected the God of the sabbath, so why should Jesus keep up the sign of that broken covenant?

> **9:15-17.** *Then again the Pharisees also asked him how he had received his sight. He said unto them, He put clay upon mine eyes, and I washed, and do see. Therefore said some the Pharisees, This man is not of God, because he keepeth not the sabbath day. Others said, How can a man that is a sinner do such miracles? And there was a division among them. They say unto the blind man again, What sayest thou of him, that he hath opened thine eyes? He said, He is a prophet.*

You remember in chapter 7 there was a division among them because of Jesus. Here the division is not caused by the blind man. The division is again because of Jesus. They didn't know what to make of the Man Jesus.

Reaction of His Parents (9:18-23)

The Pharisees thought it was impossible for one who was born blind to now see, so they brought in the man's parents.

> **9:18-19.** *But the Jews did not believe concerning him, that he had been blind, and received his sight, until they called the parents of him that had received his sight. And they asked them, saying, Is this your son, who ye say was born blind? how then doth he now see?*

The parents of this man were scared. It had gone around that if anyone claimed that Jesus Christ was the Messiah he would be excommunicated. Now that doesn't sound like much to us. We would just leave one church and go to another. But a Jew couldn't do this. A Jew belongs to the temple. When he has been excom-

municated, he can't enter any temple or synagogue. He is cut off
from the worship of God and the reading of God's Word. He is cut
off from social life with his people. He's an outcast. The parents
were afraid of this.

9:20. *His parents answered them and said, We*
know that this is our son, and that he was born blind.

You couldn't fool that mother. If anyone knew he was born
blind, she did. My, what years upon years of sorrow these parents
must have had. And now their son stands before them with his eyes
open. But they are scared.

9:21-23. *But by what means he now seeth, we know*
not; or who hath opened his eyes, we know not: he is
of age; ask him: he shall speak for himself. These
words spake his parents, because they feared the
Jews: for the Jews had agreed already, that if any man
did confess that he was Christ; he should be put out of
the synagogue. Therefore said his parents, He is of
age; ask him.

Is this your son?"
"Yes."
"Was he born blind?"
"Yes."
"Well, how does he now see?"
"We don't know. We can't say. You better ask him." They were
scared.

Reaction of the Man (9:24-34)

The Pharisees spoke again to the man.

9:24. *Then again called they the man that was*
blind, and said unto him, Give God the praise: we
know that this man is a sinner.

"Give God the praise. Give God the glory." That sounds nice and religious. Isn't that a nice thing to say? "Ignore this one who opened your eyes. We want to glorify God." It is all words.

Listen to this man's testimony.

9:25. *He answered and said, Whether he be a sinner or no, I know not: one thing I know, that, whereas I was blind, now I see.*

"Brother, you can't fool me! Once I was blind, but now I see. Once I was lost, and now I'm found. Once I was a child of wrath, and now I'm a child of God. Once I was bound for hell, and now I'm bound for heaven. You can bring all the intellectual arguments you want to, but one thing I know: I was blind, and now I see."

You know, friends, people ask me if I know I'm saved. Of course, I'm sure. I was there when He saved me. I know what I was like before, and I know what I am now in Christ. Oh, this wonderful thing of assurance. Say, do you have that assurance?

They said, "Give God the glory."

But he said, "Whether he be a sinner or no, I know not: one thing I know: once I was blind, and now I see." Oh, what blessed assurance! We can say with Paul in 2 Timothy 1:12, "I know whom I have believed, and am persuaded that he is able to keep that which I have committed unto him against that day." We are "confident of this very thing, that he which hath begun a good work in you will perform it until the day of Jesus Christ" (Philippians 1:6). I love that verse in Ecclesiastes: "I know that, whatsoever God doeth, it shall be for ever: nothing can be put to it, nor any thing taken from it: and God doeth it, that men should fear before him" (3:14).

"Once I was blind, but now I see." I tell you, my friend, assurance of salvation is a wonderful thing. I have met some Christians that aren't so sure about it. They try to fight it. They take some obscure verse out of its setting and try to prove that a man can be saved and then lost. But Romans 8 is rich in assurance. "Who is he that condemneth?" No one. "Who can separate us from the love of Christ?" No one. "I am persuaded," Paul could say, that nothing in heaven or earth "shall be able to separate us from the love of God, which is in Christ Jesus our Lord" (8:38-39).

I tell you, it's a wonderful thing to say, "Once I was blind, but now I see. Once I was lost, but now I'm alive forevermore." Can you say that, my friend? Do you know Him? Do you know the Savior? Oh, friend, why don't you come to Him today?

"Once I was blind, but now I see." After this testimony, the man feels pretty good. Listen to him as he challenges the Pharisees.

> **9:26-30.** *Then said they to him again, What did he to thee? how opened he thine eyes? He answered them, I have told you already, and ye did not hear: wherefore would ye hear it again? will ye also be his disciples?* He's getting a little sarcastic here. *Then they reviled him, and said, Thou art his disciple; but we are Moses' disciples. We know that God spake unto Moses: as for this fellow, we know not from whence he is. The man answered and said unto them, Why herein is a marvellous thing, that ye know not from whence he is, and yet he hath opened mine eyes.*

"You're religious leaders and yet you don't know the things of God?" He's beginning to irritate them.

> **9:31-33.** *Now we know that God heareth not sinners: but if any man be a worshipper of God, and doeth his will, him he heareth. Since the world began was it not heard that any man opened the eyes of one that was born blind. If this man were not of God, he could do nothing.*

This man was beginning to crow a little bit. Watch as these religious leaders press harder and harder on him and try in their unbelief to push Christ out of his thinking.

> **9:34.** *They answered and said unto him, Thou wast altogether born in sins, and dost thou teach us? And they cast him out.*

They want him to deny that Jesus had done this miracle. Unbelief is such a terrible thing. A closed heart to the Savior is an awful calamity. The Pharisees couldn't deny the evidence of the man before them, so they cast him out. They did the same thing in Acts 3 and 4 to the apostles. Oh, the awfulness of unbelief!

Results of the Sign (9:35-41)

The Man's Response to Jesus (9:35-38)

> **9:35.** *Jesus heard that they had cast him out; and when he had found him, he said unto him, Dost thou believe on the Son of God?*

I believe the Lord went right out and found him. It's wonderful. Even though one may be kicked out by the world and scorned by friends, the Lord Jesus is always there. As Hebrews 13:5-6 says, "I will never leave thee, nor forsake thee. So that we may boldly say, The Lord is my helper, and I will not fear what man shall do unto me."

We have this in Isaiah 41:10 as well: "Fear thou not; for I am with thee . . ." in the factory, in the shop, in your neighborhood, in your home. If you take a stand for the Savior, if you love Him and worship Him, you may be ostracized by your unsaved friends. But He has said, "Be not afraid. I am with you. I will never leave you. I will never forsake you." I love this little picture.

Notice that the Lord is always willing to add further truth. In verse 11 the man said, "A *man* that is called Jesus made clay and opened my eyes." In verse 17, when they asked what he thought about Jesus, he said, "He is a *prophet*." Now Jesus asks him, "Do you believe on the *Son of God?*" Mark his answer. **9:36-38.** *He answered and said, Who is he, Lord, that I might believe on him? And Jesus said unto him, Thou hast both seen him, and it is he that talketh with thee. And he said, Lord, I believe. And he worshipped him.*

"Lord, I believe." Do you notice the movement? First he said that Jesus was a man, then a prophet, and now the Son of God. He worshiped Him.

When you and I walk in the truth God gives us, He will add truth. But there is no further revelation of truth to your heart until you walk in the truth you already know. He is a man. He is a prophet. He is the Son of God. Worship Him.

Do you want to know more of the intimacy of the heart of God and His purposes and counsels? Then walk in obedience to the truth that you know. He will unfold it, enlarge it, and increase your capacity until you become a mature man or woman in Christ.

The Pharisees Found Blind by Jesus (9:39-41)

9:39-41. And Jesus said, For judgment I am come into this world, that they which see not might see; and that they which see might be made blind. And some of the Pharisees which were with him heard these words, and said unto him, Are we blind also? Jesus said unto them, If ye were blind, ye should have no sin: but now ye say, We see; therefore your sin remaineth.

At the end of this chapter the Pharisees are asking Jesus, "Are we blind?" There is a kind of sarcasm about this question. "We are leaders. Are you accusing us of being blind?"

"Yes," said the Lord, "and your condition is bad because although you are blind, you say you can see."

John 10

Christ, The Good Shepherd

Introduction to John 10

In this wonderful portion on the shepherd work of Christ, we find the Lord gathering together a flock of sheep. Through the Old Testament, God was looked upon as the Shepherd of His people. In Psalm 22, as the good Shepherd, He dies for the sheep. In Psalm 23, as the great Shepherd, He cares for the sheep: "The Lord is my shepherd; I shall not want." In Psalm 24, as the chief Shepherd, He rewards the sheep. We have this in 1 Peter 5:4, where we read, "And when the chief Shepherd shall appear, ye shall receive a crown of glory that fadeth not away." In Isaiah 40:11, He takes the lambs to His bosom. In Ezekiel 34 and Zechariah 11, He pastures His people.

God looks upon Himself as the Shepherd of His people, and distinguishes in both Testaments between the real Shepherd and the false shepherds. Ezekiel 34:1-2 warns about the false shepherds who undermine the work of God, who have no care or desire or love for the sheep. But God loves His sheep, and cares for them, laying down His life for them.

Here in John 10 He is going to have a flock. In chapter 8 the Shepherd was cast out of the temple. In chapter 9 one of the sheep was cast out. But now He's going to have a flock. He's going to care for them. He's going to give them abundant life. He's going to protect them from their enemies. The Son of God reveals Himself as the true Shepherd, the good Shepherd, the only Shepherd, the obedient Shepherd, and the faithful Shepherd.

Jesus Is The True Shepherd (10:1-6)

In the first six verses of this chapter the Lord is revealed as the true Shepherd, in contrast to the false shepherds, and He is going to put forth His sheep out of Israel.

> **10:1-6.** *Verily, verily, I say unto you, He that entereth not by the door into the sheepfold, but climbeth up some other way, the same is a thief and a robber. But he that entereth in by the door is the shepherd of the sheep. To him the porter openeth; and the sheep hear his voice: and he calleth his own sheep by name, and leadeth them out. And when he putteth forth his own sheep, he goeth before them, and the sheep follow him: for they know his voice. And a stranger will they not follow, but will flee from him: for they know not the voice of strangers. This parable spake Jesus unto them: but they understood not what things they were which he spake unto them.*

This is the only parable you have in the Gospel through John, and they did not understand what He was getting at. Of course, you know the picture. At eventide when the sun went down, all the flocks came into the one fold. And in the morning the shepherds would come to get their own flock, and each shepherd would give his own peculiar call. His sheep, and only his sheep, would follow him. They would wend their way through the other sheep and come out of the sheepfold and follow him. Another shepherd would come along, give his peculiar call, and his sheep would come out. The sheep know their shepherd.

The Pharisees and scribes and priests of our Lord's day considered themselves to be the leaders and shepherds of God's people, but I believe the Lord is primarily referring here to these Pharisees before Him as the ones who are the false shepherds. They had no love for the man in chapter 5, a man thirty-eight years infirm. They would rather see him in his sinful and wretched physical condition by the pool, than to have the sabbath day and their traditions broken. It's the same also in chapter 8 where they caught a woman in the act of adultery. They became her critics and judges. They didn't come as shepherds caring for the sheep. Nor had they any interest in the man born blind, who had never seen the light of day. They had no care for the sheep. They were false shepherds.

Now we have six things before us in this parable. We have a true Shepherd and false shepherds. We have sheep, a sheepfold, and a door. And we have one who is the porter.

The shepherd is the Lord Jesus Christ. The sheep are His people. The fold is Israel. We have this in verse 16, where He says, "Other sheep I have, which are not of this fold: them also I must bring, and they shall hear my voice; and there shall be one fold, and one shepherd." You remember in Matthew 10 that the Lord said to the disciples, as He sent them out two by two, "Do not go to the Gentiles. Do not go to the Samaritans. Only go to the lost sheep of the house of Israel."

In Matthew 15 a Syrophoenician woman came to the Lord and said, "Thou Son of David, have mercy on me and heal my daughter. She is grievously vexed with a devil."

You remember the Lord's answer: "I can't take the children's bread and cast it to the dogs. I am sent but to the lost sheep of the house of Israel."

And who is the porter? May I suggest this? The porter would be John the Baptist who, by preaching the baptism of repentance for the remission of sins, first prepared the way of the Lord and opened the door of the sheepfold to Him. He introduced our Lord officially to Israel when he said, "Behold the Lamb of God which taketh away the sin of the world" (1:29).

But what would the door represent? It describes the way the Messiah was to come to fulfill the promises to Israel.

There was no question in the minds of the Jews how the Messiah would come. When Herod went to the scribes and leaders of Israel in Matthew 2 and asked them where the Son of David would be born, they knew the answer. Isaiah 7:14 says, "Therefore the Lord himself shall give you a sign; Behold, a virgin shall conceive, and bear a son, and shall call his name Immanuel." Isaiah 9:6 says, "For unto us a child is born, unto us a son is given: and the government shall be upon his shoulder: and his name shall be called Wonderful, Counsellor, The mighty God, The everlasting Father, The Prince of Peace." Micah 5:2 says, "But thou, Bethlehem Ephratah, though thou be little among the thousands of Judah, yet out of thee shall he come forth unto me that is to be ruler in Israel; whose goings forth have been from of old, from everlasting." I could multiply the passages.

The Jewish leaders never challenged the Lord Jesus concerning His right to the throne. All they needed to do was go down to the archives in the temple and follow through the genealogy of David. They would have had to come to Mary.

He says, "I am the only true Shepherd." He is the One who "calleth his own sheep by name and leadeth them out. And when he putteth forth his own sheep, he goeth before them, and the sheep follow him: for they know his voice." He is putting forth His sheep, leaving them out of Israel. And He is starting a new flock, as we will see in verse 16.

Jesus Is the Good Shepherd (10:7-11)

In verses 7 through 11 Jesus is the good Shepherd.

> **10:7-8.** *Then said Jesus unto them again, Verily, verily, I say unto you, I am the door of the sheep. All that ever came before me are thieves and robbers: but the sheep did not hear them.*

God is going to begin to give us two things: His purpose and His program. His purpose is to gather out a flock. How can He gather a flock when they need life, when they need cleansing, when they need liberation? So starting at verse 9 you have His program.

10:9. *I am the door: by me if any man enter in, he shall be saved, and shall go in and out, and find pasture.*

He is declaring that He is the only One who can save. He will say it again in John 14:6, "I am the way, the truth, and the life: no man cometh unto the Father, but by me." That's why Peter could say before the Sanhedrin in Acts 4:12, "Neither is there salvation in any other: for there is none other name under heaven given among men, whereby we must be saved."

Now remember, the Lord is standing up before these leaders. He is claiming authority over the souls of men ("if any man enter in"), authority in the salvation of men ("he shall be saved"), authority in the liberation of men ("and shall go in and out"), and authority in sustenance of men ("and find pasture"). He is not a hireling. He is not someone hired to do a job. Here is the manifestation of His love. He is the door of the sheep, and everyone who enters into Him has salvation, liberation, and sustenance.

There is plenty of pasture today for God's people. We go in and out of the Scriptures, out of the Old Testament into the New Testament and back, to find our pasture. Remember the book of Ruth? Boaz said to her, "Stay by my maidens. Do not go into another field." There is abundant pasture. You do not need to leave His field. If you studied and fed on this Book for a hundred years, you would still find the pastures green.

I remember a statement by dear W. R. Newell, a man who wrote on the book of Romans. We were together one day at a Bible conference, and I said to him, "W. R., how often have you taught the book of Romans?"

He looked at me with those deep set eyes and said, "John, I have taught the book of Romans some eighty times, and the pastures are still green." And if our Savior in the first Psalm could say that He did meditate day and night upon the Word of God, shall we do less? Let us be well-fed sheep. Search the Scriptures. In them you will find life and strength. You will have that wonderful peace that passeth all understanding because they always point to Him who is the Living Word. He gives peace.

What was His program? He came that we might have life and that we might have it more abundantly. How? "The good shepherd giveth his life for the sheep."

Now go to verses 10 and 11.

10:10-11. *The thief cometh not, but for to steal, and to kill, and to destroy: I am come that they might have life, and that they might have it more abundantly. I am the good shepherd: the good shepherd giveth his life for the sheep.*

He is saying, "I am the Shepherd, the good One, in contrast to the hirelings, the thieves, and the robbers. And as the good Shepherd, I manifest My goodness, My love, and My care for the sheep by giving My life for them that they might have abundant, overflowing life." This is divine life, eternal life. This is the life He has been talking about in chapters 4, 5, 6, and 8. Indeed, it starts in chapter 1, verse 4: "In him was life."

But how can those who are dead in sins receive life? "I am the Shepherd, the good One, and I lay down My life. I give My life." What for? That we might live? Yes. That we might have an overflowing, abundant, satisfying, resurrection life, an indwelling life in union with God Himself.

Now go to your Old Testament. In Genesis 22, when Abraham was willing to offer up his son, God stopped him. Abraham took the ram caught in the thicket and offered it instead of his son. In Exodus 12 we have the Passover lamb. The Jews slew a lamb, applied the blood, and then the death angel passed over. All through the Old Testament it is the sheep that die for the shepherd. But when we come to this picture, it is the other way around. This is an amazing thing, that He should lay down His life that the sheep might not only be saved, but might have an abundant, overflowing life.

Jesus Is the Only Shepherd (10:12-16)

In verses 12 through 16 Jesus is the only Shepherd. He loves the sheep. The hireling doesn't. The good Shepherd lays down His life for the sheep. The hireling runs away.

I wonder if we Christians appreciate such love, a love evident in sacrifice? What is its value to us? That we might just be saved from sin? That we might just get to heaven? Those are wonderful things. Its value to us is that we might be partakers of an abundant, eternal, divine life . . . an overflowing life, a life that goes out to others.

How much do you love the Savior? He lay down His life for you because He loves you, cares for you, knows you, wants you, and owns you. How do you respond to His love?

10:12-13. *But he that is an hireling, and not the shepherd, whose own the sheep are not, seeth the wolf coming, and leaveth the sheep, and fleeth: and the wolf catcheth them, and scattereth the sheep. The hireling fleeth, because he is an hireling, and careth not for the sheep.*

The hireling is not the shepherd and doesn't own the sheep. He has no love for the sheep; he doesn't care for the sheep. And when the wolf comes and scatters the sheep, he's gone as well. Why? Because he doesn't own or love the sheep. He flees because he is a hireling.

10:14-15. *I am the good shepherd, and know my sheep, and am known of mine. As the Father knoweth me, even so know I the Father: and I lay down my life for the sheep.*

Oh, this is a wonderful thing, this union between the Father and the Son. The Lord says, "I know My Father, and the Father knows Me, and I know My sheep. But I love My sheep, and I lay down My life for the sheep, and I care for the sheep. And no one is ever going to take My sheep. Don't you know your Shepherd? I own you. You are mine. I know you intimately by name. I love you. I manifested My love by dying for you."

When the wolves come, He doesn't run away. When opposition comes, He is right by your side. He is your Shepherd. And if He were to leave you for one moment, He would not be a keeper of sheep. He wouldn't be the Shepherd, the good One. As John 13:1 says, "Having loved his own which were in the world, he loved them unto the end." Why, even dear Jeremiah, the weeping prophet, could write, "The Lord hath appeared of old unto me, saying, yea I have loved thee with an everlasting love" (Jeremiah 31:3). That is the only kind of love God has . . . a perfect, complete, eternal love.

10:16. *And other sheep I have, which are not of this fold: them also I must bring, and they shall hear my voice; and there shall be one fold, and one shepherd.*

I love this relationship between the Lord Jesus and His people. He knows each individual believer by name. He is the One who leads His sheep out of the fold of Israel and into the flock of God.

"And they shall hear my voice; and there shall be one *flock*." Jesus uses a different word here than He uses for "fold" earlier in the verse. He isn't referring to the fold, but to the flock. No longer is the flock restricted to Israel. It's international. It's for anyone, Jew or Gentile, who will become a member of His flock. He knows them all by name, and they are in tune with Him, and they know His voice.

Sheep won't listen to another voice. You could put on the shepherd's cloak, take his rod, make the same cry he makes, and the sheep will just ignore you. They know his voice.

May I ask you a question? Does He have that intimacy with you? Do you know His voice? Or would you follow a stranger? In this day when so many false philosophies, so many false doctrines, so many voices are crying out, it is amazing how even God's weakest people will not be taken in.

Young people in school and college often face an anti-Christian teacher who ridicules their faith with all kinds of smooth arguments. He seeks to do one thing: destroy their faith in Christ. Now listen. Whether any of us are able to answer his arguments or not is neither here nor there, for he is blind, and leads the blind.

If you have heard the voice of the Son of God, your heart will not be open to strangers. If you get into the Word and saturate your mind (and I don't care who the teacher is or how explicit and how wonderful he may be), even though you can't explain away his arguments, the Spirit of God will move in your heart warning you there is something wrong. You may not be able to put your finger on it. You may not be able to analyze it. But you will know right down in your heart that there is something false.

Jesus said, "There shall be one flock, and one shepherd." This is God's purpose. He's gathering out a people to be a flock. In Acts 15:14-16 James said: "Simeon hath declared how God at the first did visit the Gentiles, to take out of them a people for his name. And to this agree the words of the prophets; as it is written, After this (after I have gathered out my flock of Jews and Gentiles) I will return, and will build again the tabernacle of David, which is fallen down. . . ." When He comes back to earth, He is going to rebuild Israel. But right now He is gathering out a people for His name. He is gathering out Jews and Gentiles and forming a flock.

It is not that the Gentiles are coming into the Jewish fold. We don't come into the Jewish fold, into Israel. We never were Israel, never are Israel, and never will be Israel. We belong to the Church, the flock of God today. We have become a new flock.

I want to be dogmatic about this. I want this thing to be very clear in your mind. This was one of the troubles in the early Church. In Acts chapter 15, the first Council of Jerusalem wanted the Gentiles to be saved, but they wanted the Gentiles to be saved through Judaism to Christ. That is, they wanted them to come to Christ through the Law. We are not even spiritual Israel. We are the body of Christ. We're a flock that is international. "Other sheep I have which are not of this fold, them also I must bring, and they shall hear My voice. There shall be one flock and there shall be one shepherd."

Jesus Is the Obedient Shepherd (10:17-18)

In verses 17 and 18 we have Jesus as the obedient Shepherd.

10:17-18. *Therefore doth my Father love me, because I lay down my life, that I might take it again. No man taketh it from me, but I lay it down of myself. I have power to lay it down, and I have power to take it again. This commandment have I received of my Father.*

Here is a stupendous thing. Here is something that no one else can do. Notice the authority of the Son of God, working in perfect cooperation with the desire and will of the Father. "I lay down my life that I might take it again." He only could do that. You can't do that. No man could do that. You can take your own life, but you are not laying down your life. "No man taketh my life from me."

You say, "Why, they crucified Him."

Yes, they killed His body, but not until He gave them the right to do it. All through John they picked up stones to kill Him. He slipped away through their midst. In verse 24 the Jews gathered round Him with a jealousy, with an envy, with a hatred, with an opposition that nothing would satisfy except His death. "No man taketh my life from me," He said. "I have power to lay it down."

At the cross the Lord Jesus cried, "My God, my God, why hast Thou forsaken me?" He cried out, "I thirst." He cried with a loud voice, "It is finished," and He bowed His head in resignation and yielded up the Spirit. You can't do that.

The Lord Jesus' death was both natural and supernatural. It was natural because of sin. In 1 Peter 2:24 we read that He bore "our sins in his own body on the tree." Go back to Isaiah 53:6—"All we like sheep have gone astray; we have turned every one to his own way; and the Lord hath laid on him the iniquity of us all." He died a natural death because of sin. People die because of sin. The wages of sin is death. Romans 8:10 says, "The body is dead because of sin." It is under the sentence of death because of sin. We're born into the world in sin and we're born to die.

But the Lord Jesus wasn't born in sin. He could say, "Which of you convinceth me of sin?" (8:46). He was without sin. He did no sin. In Him is no sin. He knew no sin. He was sinless. Yet He died, and He bore your sin and my sin. From that viewpoint, His death was natural.

But His death was also supernatural. "No man takes My life from Me. I have the power to lay it down. I have the power to take it up again."

Not only did He lay down His life for the sheep, but He came forth in resurrection to guarantee life to the sheep, that they in turn might enjoy divine life, eternal life, satisfying life. This is a stupendous thing.

What authority He has as the Son of God—as the Son of Man—working in perfect cooperation with the Father. This is His desire. You have here the eternal, complete obedience of the Son. And in obeying, He ignores the powers of hell. He ignores the power of men. "No man, no power, no authority can take My life from Me." What a claim.

Jesus Is the Faithful Shepherd (10:19-42)

Unbelief of the Hirelings (10:19-24)

No wonder there was a division among the Jews after Christ claimed such authority.

> **10:19-21.** *There was a division therefore again among the Jews for these sayings. And many of them said, He hath a devil, and is mad: why hear ye him? Others said, These are not the words of him that hath a devil. Can a devil open the eyes of the blind?*

Jesus said, "I have power to lay down My life. I have power to take it up again."

They said, "You're mad. You're demon possessed. You're not talking like a rational being. You're saying things that could only be said by God."

Several months went by between verse 21 and the next verse.

10:22-23. *And it was at Jerusalem the feast of the dedication, and it was winter. And Jesus walked in the temple in Solomon's porch.*

The Feast of Tabernacles is in the fall. The Feast of Dedication (or the Feast of Lights) is in the winter. In fact, some declare the Feast of Lights should be held on the twenty-fifth of December as the memorial of the cleansing of the temple by Judas Maccabaeus in 164 B.C. Since then, Jewish people all over the world have recognized this feast, called here the Feast of Dedication, remembering the cleansing of the temple when it was defiled by Antiochus Epiphanes, the one who sacrificed a pig on the altar.

As Jesus walked in the temple area, you can just see the Jews hemming Him in now on Solomon's porch. **10:24.** *Then came the Jews round about him, and said unto him, How long dost thou make us to doubt? If thou be the Christ, tell us plainly.* "Tell us now, once for all. Tell us in your own words. Are you the Christ?"

These Jews were just looking for an opportunity to challenge Jesus. As we read this, we begin to wonder about these fellows. We begin to wonder about these enemies of Christ. With all the evidence that He's presented to them, what more do they want? They have seen His spectacular miracles. They have seen Him heal the sick, open the eyes of the blind, and feed the hungry. What more do they want?

"How long do you make us to doubt?" When a person is full of unbelief, it doesn't matter what you do. They won't accept the Savior. I tell you again, my friend, unbelief in the Son of God is a terrible thing. In fact, it means one's eternal destiny. Persisting in unbelief leads to hardness. Our Lord, I say, had presented His credentials. They had heard His gracious words. Before their eyes a man born blind was healed. And still they were full of doubt. "If ye be the Christ, tell us plainly."

Security of the Sheep (10:25-30)

And I want you to mark the strong language our Lord used here. He gave them far more than they expected. **10:25-26.** *Jesus answered them, I told you, and ye believed not: the works that I do in my Father's name, they bear witness of me. But ye believe not, because ye are not of my sheep, as I said unto you.* "If you were My sheep, you would believe Me, you would heed Me. But I know you are not My sheep because you don't believe Me, you don't love Me, you don't follow Me, you don't obey Me."

His sheep have a bond, a relationship, with the faithful Shepherd.

> **10:27-30.** *My sheep hear my voice, and I know them, and they follow me: And I give unto them eternal life; and they shall never perish, neither shall any man pluck them out of my hand. My Father, which gave them me, is greater than all; and no man is able to pluck them out of my Father's hand. I and my Father are one.*

When Jesus says "never," He means exactly what He says: "My sheep hear My voice, and I know them, and they follow Me: and I give unto them eternal life; and they shall never, in no wise, under any consideration, perish." Why? Because "no man is able to plunder them out of My hand. My Father who gave them to Me is greater than all. He is omnipotent, He is God, and no man is able to plunder them out of My Father's hand.

"I am the One who gives eternal life to My sheep. I lay down My life for the sheep. I give them My life. The life I give My sheep is My own life." Some say that a Christian doesn't have eternal life. They deny the fact that Christ is eternal. But that is the only life He has to give. The very life that God gives to sinners who believe in His Son is the same life that He Himself has. In Him is life!

When you and I came as sinners and received Him as our Savior, we put our trust in Him. At that very moment He gave us His life, His divine life. We are partakers of divine nature, of a life that never ends (see 2 Peter 1:4).

Jesus could pray, "Holy Father, keep through thine own name those whom thou hast given me, that they may be one, as we are. While I was with them in the world, I kept them in thy name: those that thou gavest me I have kept, and none of them is lost" (John 17:11-12). He makes Himself responsible to keep those who put their trust in Him, "and no man is able to pluck them out of my Father's hand." In Deuteronomy 33:27 Moses wrote, "The eternal God is thy refuge, and underneath are the everlasting arms." When we put our trust in the Savior, He makes Himself responsible to keep us, everlastingly.

"But I get discouraged at times. I am full of doubts," some will say. Well, let me put it this way. The unsaved never doubt. They haven't a faith to doubt. Don't be disheartened. Doubts are Satan's tactic to discourage Christians. But if you have really put your trust in the Savior, there is nothing to doubt. He gives us eternal, everlasting life. We are kept safe in the Father's hands.

Dr. Hinson used to say, "The Lord takes you and puts you into the Father's hand, and then He covers you with His other hand. How are you going to get out?"

"No man is able to plunder them out of My Father's hand. I and My Father are one."

Rejection of the Shepherd (10:31-42)

10:31. *Then the Jews took up stones again to stone him.*

We had this back in chapter 5, when Jesus said, "My Father worketh hitherto, and I work." They picked up stones to cast at Him. They were filled with rage. They knew what He was claiming. "You make yourself to be God." And they sought to slay Him.

And my unsaved friend, what are you going to do with Him? What are you going to do? Jesus Christ is either worthy of your worship and trust, or He ought to be stoned. Are you going to stand with these Jews, or bow down and worship Him. "I and my Father are one." There was no question in their minds what He was claiming.

Mark His answer.

> **10:32-33.** *Jesus answered them, Many good works have I shewed you from my Father; for which of those works do ye stone me? The Jews answered him, saying, For a good work we stone thee not; but for blasphemy; and because that thou, being a man, makest thyself God.*

Notice their accusation. "You, being a man, make yourself out to be God." Again I repeat it, there was no question in their minds what He was claiming. "Do you know what you're doing?" they asked. "You're claiming to be God!"

And then the Lord Jesus gave this unanswerable argument.

> **10:34-38.** *Jesus answered them, Is it not written in your law, I said, Ye are gods? If he called them gods, unto whom the word of God came, and the scripture cannot be broken; Say ye of him, whom the Father hath sanctified, and sent into the world, Thou blasphemest; because I said, I am the Son of God? If I do not the works of my Father, believe me not. But if I do, though ye believe not me, believe the works: that ye may know, and believe, that the Father is in me, and I in him.*

He said, "I depend upon your infallible Word, the Scriptures. If God called the unjust judges 'gods,' what do you think of the One whom the Father has sanctified and sent into the world?"

He said, "I am the Son of God." He didn't object to the leaders of Israel, who were unjust. They were made the recipients, the caretakers, of the Word of God. But they were unjust in their dealings with God's people. "And if God called them 'gods,' why are you mad because I say I am the Son of God?"

Jesus was referring to Psalm 82:1, 6. These verses in the Psalms were a rebuke to God's people, especially the unjust judges. "You should act like children of the Most High. But you're going to die like men. Why? Because of your disobedience." And Romans 2 says that "the name of God is blasphemed among the Gentiles through you" (2:24). The Jews dishonored the Lord by their wickedness, by their disobedience. They were unrepresentative of God. And in the world today, sinners blaspheme the name of God because believers don't act like Christians.

May I remind you, that in the book of Exodus, God said to Moses, "See, I have made thee a god to Pharaoh" (7:1). In other words, Moses was the living representative of God to Pharaoh. Whatever he said came true, just as in the case of Elijah many years later. Paul could say, "As though God did beseech you by us: we pray you in Christ's stead, be ye reconciled to God" (2 Corinthians 5:20). We are God's representatives.

Here Jesus is saying, "If the Scriptures call men 'gods,' why do you try to kill Me because I say I am the Son of God?" Now let's be very clear about this. Our Savior did everything He could for the revelation of the Father to men. He could say, "I and the Father are one. We are absolutely one. We are in perfect union. Why do you want to kill Me?"

The Lord Jesus left them and went to Bethabara.

> **10:39-42.** *Therefore they sought again to take him: but he escaped out of their hand, And went away again beyond Jordan into the place where John at first baptized; and there he abode. And many resorted unto him, and said, John did no miracle: but all things that John spake of this man were true. And many believed on him there.*

The people in this area still remembered what John the Baptist had said about Jesus. They remembered that he said, "He it is, who coming after me is preferred before me, whose shoe's latchet I am not worthy to unloose" (1:27). And it was in Bethabara at this time that people believed on Him.

How does it affect your own heart, your own love for the Savior, your obedience to His Word, your desire to follow Him—when you realize that He knows you, that He loves you enough to die for you and give you His life, that He calls you by name, that you are precious in His sight, and that He cares for you?

He is the real Shepherd. He's the faithful Shepherd; faithful even unto death; faithful in caring for us. The very life which is His is the life He has given for us.

May I say this to those of you who love the Savior? Isn't it about time that we Christians really got down to business with God and appreciated His love and His care and His knowledge? To think that He calls you by name individually and personally. He loves you, cares for you, knows you, and is guaranteeing that one of these days—because you belong to His flock—you will stand in His presence conformed to the image of your Shepherd, Jesus Christ. I say, what a Savior! What a Lord!

We can say with the psalmist, "The Lord is my shepherd; I shall not want."

John 11

Christ, The Resurrection and The Life

Jesus Told of Lazarus's Illness (11:1-16)
—Jesus Stays in Bethabara

An Appeal to the Love of the Lord (11:1-3)

In this chapter we have the resurrection of Lazarus from the dead. This miracle is the last sign the Lord gave of His deity before the cross.

In chapter 10, the Jews had said to Him, "How long dost thou make us to doubt? If thou be the Christ, tell us plainly." And when He did tell them, they picked up stones to stone Him.

Now He is going to give them one last sign they must accept or reject. Oh, the awfulness of unbelief! I trust this chapter will bring to us both the revelation of the marvelous heart of God in His tremendous care and sympathy for His people in their need, and the revelation of His mighty power over man's worst enemy, death.

Mark the appeal of Mary and Martha.

> **11:1-3.** *Now a certain man was sick, named Lazarus, of Bethany, the town of Mary and her sister Martha. (It was that Mary which anointed the Lord with ointment, and wiped his feet with her hair, whose brother Lazarus was sick.) Therefore his sisters sent unto him, saying, Lord, behold, he whom thou lovest is sick.*

It wasn't that Lazarus had the flu or a cold. This man was really sick unto death, and these sisters knew it. And it would take the messenger some two or three days to get the Lord.

Now these two girls appealed to the Lord on the ground of His love. I believe this is the ground whereby we can have our requests answered. You remember in John 16:26-27 He speaks of this fact: "At that day ye shall ask in my name: and I say not unto you, that I will pray the Father for you: For the Father himself loveth you. . . ." We are to make our requests and expect them to be answered, not on the ground of our love or affection for Him, but on the ground of His devotion and infinite love for us. John 17:24 illustrates this: "Father, I will that they also, whom thou hast given me, be with me where I am; that they may behold my glory, which thou hast given me: for thou lovedst me before the foundation of the world."

This very affliction of Lazarus's drove these two girls to the Lord Jesus. Affliction often comes to God's people for the purpose of driving us to Him.

Jesus' Response for the Glory of God (11:4-6)

Note the perspective of the Lord's when He heard of Lazarus's illness.

11:4. *When Jesus heard that, he said, This sickness is not unto death, but for the glory of God, that the Son of God might be glorified thereby.*

Now the driving force in our Lord's life was the glory of God, and through that glory the Son was going to be glorified. You have that in chapter 12, verse 23: "The hour is come, that the Son of man should be glorified," and in chapter 17, verse 1: "Father, the hour is come; glorify thy Son, that thy Son also may glorify thee." The great purpose of all redemption, the purpose of all suffering for the believer, is in the final analysis for the glory of God. We may not begin to understand it, especially when we are going through it; but it is for the glory of God.

Notice the contrast between verses 3 and 5. **11:5.** *Now Jesus loved Martha, and her sister, and Lazarus.* In verse 3 we read, "Lord, behold, he whom thou lovest *(phileo)* is sick." Verse 5 reads, "Now Jesus loved *(agape)* Martha, and her sister, and Lazarus." His is a much deeper word. "Now Jesus was very devoted. . . ." Their love was an emotional thing. Verse 5 anticipates that in this chapter He is going to reveal something concerning the very heart of God that is not shown in any other place.

> **11:6.** *When he had heard therefore that he was sick, he abode two days still in the same place where he was.*

If we had been in those girls' shoes, we would have said, "Lord, hurry up. Hurry up! Every day we see our brother going further down. If you don't come soon, Lazarus will die. It's no use coming when he's dead."

What an appeal. Of course, the Lord is going to come. The girls thought He would rush right over and heal him. But, my friend, if God makes us wait, He has a far richer blessing for us through the waiting. His delays are just as important as His answers. But it is hard to wait, isn't it? It seems sometimes the Lord is so slow to answer our prayers.

We pray, "Lord, I'm in a jam. Things are just going down and down. Lord, hurry up." But it is far better for Lazarus to die and to be in corruption and be raised from the dead, than to be healed of physical infirmity. The Lord has a greater purpose and reason for the delay.

Misunderstandings About His Mission (11:7-16)

> **11:7.** *Then after that saith he to his disciples, Let us go into Judaea again.*

Oh, the wonderful desire of our Lord for the fellowship of His disciples. He's going to Jerusalem. "Let us go into Judaea again. That's where I'm going to die. That's where I'm going to be rejected and crucified. I want you to go with Me. Let us go into Judaea."

11:8-10. *His disciples say unto him, Master, the Jews of late sought to stone thee; and goest thou thither again? Jesus answered, Are there not twelve hours in the day? If any man walk in the day, he stumbleth not, because he seeth the light of this world. But if a man walk in the night, he stumbleth, because there is no light in him.*

In other words, He is saying—if I may give the implication of it—"They can't touch Me until My work is finished." You see, He is comforting the disciples. "They can't do a thing until My Father permits it."

After this Jesus revealed the condition of Lazarus.

11:11-14. *These things said he: and after that he saith unto them, Our friend Lazarus sleepeth; but I go, that I may awake him out of sleep.* The Lord knew already that Lazarus has died. *Then said his disciples, Lord, if he sleep, he shall do well. Howbeit Jesus spake of his death: but they thought that he had spoken of taking of rest in sleep. Then said Jesus unto them plainly, Lazarus is dead.*

Those dear disciples should have known about this. Peter, James, and John were with Him in Luke 7 and 8 when our Lord raised the widow's son and the daughter of Jairus. Furthermore, if Lazarus was just sleeping physical sleep, how long was he going to sleep? It would take them two or three days to walk from where they were up to Bethany. Was he going to sleep all that time? They weren't thinking. How quick we are to misunderstand. We lose sight of the purpose and presence of God.

11:15. *And I am glad for your sakes that I was not there, to the intent ye may believe; nevertheless let us go unto him.*

Not only would the resurrection of Lazarus be a sign unto Israel (especially to those leaders who said, "If thou be the Christ, tell us plainly"), it would also be a sign to inspire and give assurance to His own disciples.

11:16. *Then said Thomas, which is called Didymus, unto his fellowdisciples, Let us also go, that we may die with him.*

I know most folk don't like Thomas because he was the doubter. But I like Thomas. He was in love with the Savior. Oh, we may have some questions about what took place in chapter 20, but he really loved the Lord. And because of this, he said, "Let's go and die with Him. Let's not let Him die alone."

Now when the Lord was taken, they all forsook Him (including Thomas) and fled. Peter fled as well. Peter was the one who said, "Lord, though all these other fellows will leave You, You can sure count on me. I will stick by You, Lord. You can count on me." But he ran with the rest of them.

Jesus Comes to Lazarus's Grave (11:17-38)
—Jesus Travels to Bethany

Death Does Not End It All (11:17-27)

11:17-22. *Then when Jesus came, he found that he had lain in the grave four days already. Now Bethany was nigh unto Jerusalem, about fifteen furlongs off: And many of the Jews came to Martha and Mary, to comfort them concerning their brother. Then Martha, as soon as she heard that Jesus was coming, went and met him: but Mary sat still in the house. Then said Martha unto Jesus, Lord, if thou hadst been here, my brother had not died. But I know, that even now, whatsoever thou wilt ask of God, God will give it thee.*

Martha is saying, "I'm not going to limit You, Lord, as to what You can do. But don't You think You've come too late? He's already been in the grave four days."

Later on, she says, "Leave the stone alone. It doesn't smell very good in there. He's in corruption." And yet there was a longing in Martha's heart—shall I say a hope?—that Jesus could even yet do something. "Lord, if You had only come, my brother wouldn't have died."

Even if the Lord had left when He first got the message and had walked up the hill for two or three days to the city of Jerusalem, He would have been too late. He would have had to walk from nine hundred feet below sea level up through those canyons and caves and desert roads to approximately three thousand feet above sea level. He simply would have been too late.

11:23-24. *Jesus saith unto her, Thy brother shall rise again. Martha saith unto him, I know that he shall rise again in the resurrection at the last day.*

Now, she has a Scripture for that, Job 19:25-26: "For I know that my redeemer liveth, and that he shall stand at the latter day upon the earth: And though after my skin worms destroy this body, yet in my flesh shall I see God." And Daniel 12:2 says, "And many of them that sleep in the dust of the earth shall awake, some to everlasting life, and some to shame and everlasting contempt." And Isaiah 26:19 reads, "Thy dead men shall live, together with my dead body shall they arise."

"Oh, yes, Lord," Martha says, "I know he will be raised in the resurrection at the last day."

You see, Martha wanted her brother to be delivered *from* death. Jesus wanted Lazarus to be triumphant *over* death. There's quite a difference. Martha doubted and needed instruction, and so the Lord gives her this instruction.

11:25-26. *Jesus said unto her, I am the resurrection and the life: he that believeth in me, though he were dead, yet shall he live: and whosoever liveth and*

believeth in me shall never die. Believest thou this?

"I am the resurrection. I am the life." Here is another one of His "I am" statements. In John 5:21 Jesus had said, "As the Father hath authority and power to raise the dead, so the Son raises the dead. Just as God can raise the dead and give them life, so can I. It isn't that the Father does it through Me, but I do it."

Now Jesus is saying, "Martha, I am the resurrection and the life. If there is to be any resurrection of any kind, I am the One that is going to do it. And listen, Martha, you believe that your brother will be raised in the last day. Well, I am the resurrection and the life. I am the One who will raise him in the last day. And if I can raise him then, why can't I raise him now?"

But dear Martha didn't say, "Yes, Lord, I believe he is going to be raised now." What did she say? **11:27.** *She saith unto him, Yea, Lord: I believe that thou art the Christ, the Son of God, which should come into the world.* She gave a wonderful testimony, but she missed the issue. He had said, "I am the resurrection and the life." Death is not the end of all. The end of the natural body is death. But resurrection is the end of death. Death is a terrible enemy, but death is a defeated enemy.

When a believer leaves the earth, he goes immediately into the presence of the Lord. Paul said, "I am in a strait betwixt two, having a desire to depart, and to be with Christ" (Philippians 1:23). The psalmist could say, "Thou wilt shew me the path of life: in thy presence is fulness of joy" (Psalm 16:11). To be absent from the body is to be present with the Lord (2 Corinthians 5:8). The Lord doesn't have around Him millions of His saints asleep. They are enjoying His presence.

I wish we Christians could remember that when we accept the Savior, we are made partakers of the divine nature. We receive the very life of God. Death has no place in it. Jesus said, "If a man lives and believes in Me, he shall never die." Do you believe this?

We love to quote John 5:24, "He that heareth my word, and believeth on him that sent me, hath everlasting life, and shall not come into condemnation; but is passed from death unto life."

That's a wonderful verse, but do you believe it?

"Do you mean to tell me, sir," you say, "that you will never see death?"

"That's correct."

"You mean you will never die?"

"I will never die." Eternal life is *eternal* life, is it not? Indeed, I would say this to you: when you leave these bodies, we shall experience *real* life. Our lives today are affected by sorrows, by afflictions, by disappointments, by misunderstandings. We're full of fear. Death comes along as man's worst enemy. People are afraid to die. Too many Christians are that way. We ought to yearn for the experience of perfect, eternal, real life into which we shall enter. It may be through what man calls death.

I should remind you about the dear man of God, Dr. Sutcliffe, and the illness that took him toward death. I stood by him one day, and he held me by the wrist. He was very, very sick. The doctor had told me he wouldn't live the day, so I went over and stood by his side.

He said, "Oh, John, I'm so sick." And he looked it. He had the Bible in his lap. He was propped up. He had heart trouble and a few complications. And he dropped his head and closed his eyes.

I thought he was gone, but he still had hold of my wrist. And all of a sudden he shook himself and looked at me and said, "Is that you, John?"

And I said, "Yes."

"My, oh my, oh my, I'm so disappointed. I'm so disappointed. I was expecting to see the Lord, and all I saw was you."

Well, I would have been disappointed as well. Wouldn't you? The tragedy is that too many Christians know so little of this real life in Christ over which death doesn't even cast a shadow.

The Infinite Lord Weeps (11:28-38)

Martha has just testified of her faith in Him.

11:28. *And when she had so said, she went her way,*

and called Mary her sister secretly, saying, The Master is come, and calleth for thee.

Now Mary did the proper thing. She stayed home in the house of mourning. Martha didn't. She should have stayed in the house as well; but when she heard the Lord was coming, she had to see Him and tell Him about Lazarus.

So when Martha returned to the house, she whispered in Mary's ear, "The Lord is come and calleth for you."

11:29-32. *As soon as she heard that, she arose quickly, and came unto Him. Now Jesus was not yet come into the town, but was in that place where Martha met him. The Jews then which were with her in the house, and comforted her, when they saw Mary, that she rose up hastily and went out, followed her, saying, She goeth unto the grave to weep there. Then when Mary was come where Jesus was, and saw him, she fell down at his feet, saying unto him, Lord, if thou hadst been here, my brother had not died.*

Now Mary said the same words that Martha said, but I think with an entirely different attitude. You see, Martha doubted, and she needed instruction. Mary wept, and she needed comfort. And the Lord met both girls in their need.

You remember, this is one of three times when Mary of Bethany is found in the Scriptures. Each time she is found at the feet of Jesus. In Luke 10, she sat at His feet for instruction. As He revealed to her the things of the Father and the purpose of God for the Son, she believed. In this passage, she is at His feet for comfort. In chapter 12 of John, she will be at His feet for worship. Remarkable!

It was Mary who understood that Jesus was going to die. She had an insight into the purpose of God for the Lord that I don't believe Peter, James, or John had. She didn't go to the cross. You find Mary Magdalene, and Mary the mother of James there, but not Mary of Bethany.

11:33-38. *When Jesus therefore saw her weeping, and the Jews also weeping which came with her, he groaned in the spirit, and was troubled.* One version says He was indignant and troubled. *And said, Where have ye laid him? They said unto him, Lord, come and see. Jesus wept. Then said the Jews, Behold how he loved him! And some of them said, Could not this man, which opened the eyes of the blind, have caused that even this man should not have died? Jesus therefore again groaning in himself cometh to the grave. It was a cave, and a stone lay upon it.*

I wonder if you and I can realize what it meant to the Lord to go across the Valley of Kidron, climb up the side of the Mount of Olives on the east side, and come into the house of Mary, and Martha, and Lazarus? Jesus, the object of the hatred of the leaders, was invited home. Here was love. Outside was enmity. Here was love. Outside was opposition. Here was love. Outside was hatred. What a wonderful place for the Lord to come.

"Jesus wept." I don't know of any verse that gives to us the revelation of the heart of God more than this. Here is the infinite God, taking time out to weep with sorrowing friends. When you and I go through times of affliction, times of sorrow, the Lord Jesus is there. He is touched with the feeling of our infirmities.

Aren't you glad you have a real Man in heaven who knows, who understands, and who cares? Even though I can't understand why I go through certain things, it is enough to know that He cares, that He loves, that He weeps. Three times our Lord is said to have wept. He wept over Jerusalem (Luke 19:41). He wept in the garden (Hebrews 5:7). And here in John 11, He wept at the tomb of Lazarus. And all three passages use a different word. Here is the infinite God entering into the sorrows, the afflictions, the wounded hearts of others. He was one with them. "Jesus wept."

From our viewpoint, if you or I had been the Savior, we would have said, "Now listen, everyone. Just stop this grieving. I'm going to raise Lazarus from the dead. Now just stop your weeping." Isn't He going to return Lazarus to them? Then why doesn't He get about it and do it? This is one of the most astounding passages in all the Bible. Imagine that the infinite God, as a Man in the midst of men, would take the time out to stand by two girls in their sorrow and weep with them. My, what a Savior we have! What a Shepherd! What a Lord! As God, He is able to raise the dead and defeat the powers of hell and the grave. But as the perfect Man in the midst of men, He took this place and wept with His people.

He does this with you, my friend. Are you crushed? Are you asking, "Why doesn't He come and do something for me?" He will be right there with you, to comfort you, to give you peace in the midst of unrest, to touch that broken heart, that crushed soul. And aren't you glad that it says in Revelation, "He shall wipe away all tears from their eyes; and there shall be no more death, neither sorrow, nor crying, neither shall there be any more pain" (Revelation 21:4). No wonder John could say, "Even so, come, Lord Jesus" (Revelation 22:20).

The Seventh Sign: The Resurrection of Lazarus (11:39-57)
—Jesus Goes from Bethany to Ephraim

And Lazarus Came Forth (11:39-44)

11:39-42. *Jesus said, Take ye away the stone. Martha, the sister of him that was dead, saith unto him, Lord, by this time he stinketh: for he hath been dead four days. Jesus said unto her, said I not unto thee, that, if thou wouldest believe, thou shouldest see the glory of God? Then they took away the stone from the place where the dead was laid. And Jesus lifted up his eyes, and said, Father, I thank thee that thou hast heard me. And I knew that thou hearest me always: but because of the people which stand by I said it, that they may believe that thou hast sent me.*

"I said it, that they may believe that thou hast sent me." Now you remember that we have this over and over again in this Gospel. Everything Jesus said and did was so that men and women might believe in Him.

11:43-44. *And when he thus had spoken, he cried with a loud voice, Lazarus, come forth. And he that was dead came forth, bound hand and foot with grave-clothes: and his face was bound about with a napkin. Jesus saith unto them, Loose him, and let him go.*

Here you have our Lord proving His statement in John 5:21, where He said, "For as the Father raiseth up the dead, and quickeneth them; even so the Son quickeneth whom he will." Then in 5:28: "Marvel not at this: for the hour is coming, in the which all that are in the graves shall hear his voice." In chapter 5 Jesus made the claim. In chapter 11 He proves the claim.

And may I suggest something else here? We have wonderful co-operation here. What these people standing there could do, He did not do. What they could not do, He did. They could roll away the stone. He didn't do it. Lazarus lay there in corruption, but they could do nothing. Then Jesus said, "Lazarus, come forth," and he that was dead came forth, bound in grave clothes. Jesus told the people to loose him. Jesus didn't loose him. They could do that. Here is cooperation. Obedience to the Savior brought liberation to Lazarus.

And, by the way, I am of the persuasion that when Lazarus was raised from the dead and loosed from the grave clothes, he went back as fast as he could to Bethany. I don't think he hung around the old grave. You see, Lazarus wasn't an American. If we had a case like that, we would have put up a placard and charged twenty-five cents. "See, I was in there for four days. . . ." We would have materialistically capitalized on the situation. But not Lazarus. He left as fast as he could.

May I draw a spiritual lesson or two from that? Too many of God's people today are staying at the cross. Now, I'm well aware that Jesus died for me. I'm well aware it was there He took away my sin. But, my friend, Jesus is no longer on the cross. He is on the throne. The riches of grace proceed from the cross to reach sinners. The riches of glory proceed from the throne to build up God's people.

Many today are bound by the shackles of the law. You and I have a wonderful job to go to these people and set them free from the bondage of the law. As Paul could say, "Stand fast therefore in the liberty wherewith Christ hath made us free, and be not entangled again with the yoke of bondage" (Galatians 5:1). And "Now to him that worketh is the reward not reckoned of grace, but of debt. But to him that worketh not, but believeth on him that justifieth the ungodly, his faith is counted for righteousness" (Romans 4:4-5).

Too many are still hanging on to their grave clothes. They are wrapped in the sins of their life in the past. You and I are to "put off concerning the former conversation the old man, which is corrupt according to the deceitful lusts; And be renewed in the spirit of your mind; And that ye put on the new man, which after God is created in righteousness and true holiness" (Ephesians 4:22-24).

The Opposition Commits to Its Course (11:45-57)

11:45-53. *Then many of the Jews which came to Mary, and had seen the things which Jesus did, believed on him. But some of them went their ways to the Pharisees, and told them what things Jesus had done. Then gathered the chief priests and the Pharisees a council, and said, What do we? for this man doeth many miracles. If we let him thus alone, all men will believe on him: and the Romans shall come and take away both our place and nation. And one of them, named Caiaphas, being the high priest that same year, said unto them, Ye know nothing at all, Nor consider that it is expedient for us, that one man should die for the people, and that the whole nation perish* *not. And this spake he not of himself: but being high priest that year, he prophesied that Jesus should die for that nation; And not for that nation only, but that also he should gather together in one the children of God that were scattered abroad. Then from that day forth they took counsel together for to put him to death.*

The Council was saying, "Jesus has gone too far. If we don't stop him, we are going to have trouble with the Romans, and we will lose our jobs and all that goes with it." They were more concerned about their status than about the people knowing God. Unknowingly, the high priest prophesied a great truth: that Christ would die, not only for the nation, but for those who were scattered abroad.

At the end of this chapter we find our Lord going into the wilderness to a city called Ephraim. This was an area northeast of Jerusalem.

11:54-57. *Jesus therefore walked no more openly among the Jews; but went thence unto a country near to the wilderness, into a city called Ephraim, and there continued with his disciples. And the Jews passover was nigh at hand: and many went out of the country up to Jerusalem before the passover, to purify themselves. Then sought they for Jesus, and spake among themselves, as they stood in the temple, What think ye, that he will not come to the feast? Now both the chief priests and the Pharisees had given a commandment, that, if any man knew where he were, he should shew it, that they might take him.*

These Jewish leaders, these priests and Pharisees, are determined now to kill Jesus. It is all out in the open. The news was public. It was spread abroad through the whole city. It was one great determination to kill the Son of God. And I read that the Lord left them. He was still in control. They couldn't take Him until His hour was come. But in just a few days Jesus will say, "The hour is come" (12:23).

John 12

Christ, The Center of Attraction

Wherever you find Jesus Christ, He is the center of attraction. When He was born in Bethlehem, they worshiped Him, not Mary. When He was a boy of twelve standing in the temple teaching, He was the center of attraction, not the doctors of the law.

When John the Baptist came on the scene, they knew that he was a prophet. One day, John baptized the Lord Jesus and then left the scene. The Lord became the center of attraction.

On the Mount of Transfiguration, the three disciples saw Moses, the great lawgiver. They saw Elijah, the great prophet. Then they saw no man, save Jesus only. The Lord was declared by the Father to be the beloved Son. He was singled out as the center of attraction.

And when we come to this passage, we find people coming to see Lazarus at a supper in Bethany. The Lord is the center of attraction, however, not Lazarus.

On the road to Jerusalem, the people sang His praise: "Hosanna in the highest." During the Triumphal Entry, Jesus was the center of attraction once again. Later He prophesied, "If I be lifted up, I will draw all men unto me." He was the center of attraction even at the cross. Yet Israel rejected this One who had attracted the multitudes. They were determined to slay the Son of God.

Where is He today? He is at the right hand of God, at the right hand of the Majesty on high. He is the center of attraction. Hebrews speaks of this. "When he had by himself purged our sins, (he) sat down . . ." (1:3). "Let all the angels of God worship him" (1:6). "But unto the Son he saith, Thy throne, O God, is for ever and ever" (1:8). "We see Jesus . . . crowned" (2:9). Even when Jesus stands as Judge and judges men, they will cry out for the rocks and mountains to fall on them to hide them from the wrath of the Lamb (Revelation 6). Jesus was, and is, and always will be, the center of attraction among men.

Jesus Attracts the Members of a Home (12:1-11)
—Jesus Returns to Bethany

Martha and Lazarus Attracted to Jesus (12:1-2)

12:1. *Then Jesus six days before the passover came to Bethany, where Lazarus was which had been dead, whom he raised from the dead.*

Our Lord left Ephraim and, coming down by way of Jericho, moved on toward Bethany to meet His friends. One of the homes where He was always welcome was the home of Martha and Mary and Lazarus.

12:2. *There they made him a supper; and Martha served: but Lazarus was one of them that sat at the table with him.*

And Mary was at His feet. All three loved the Savior. Don't question Martha's love for Him. Don't question Lazarus's love, or Mary's love, either. These three really were devoted to Christ, but they manifested their love in different ways. Don't you demand of others that they love the Savior the way you love Him or show that love the way you do.

Martha? She loved to serve the Lord. Some believers express their love by continual service.

Lazarus? He sat with those at the feast. People came to see him. Why wouldn't they come? Here's a man who had been four days in the tomb, a man whose body was already in corruption. And now he's raised from the dead and is sitting at the feast. What an evident token of the power of God. He ate with them at the table, and Martha served.

Here you have the quiet adoration and love of Lazarus. As far as we know, he never said a word. Why should he speak when the One who had raised him from the dead was there? You wouldn't expect him to talk.

There are some people who are always talking about their experiences. But they never had one like this one. Lazarus never said a word. Why should he draw attention to himself? He was perfectly content to be in the presence of the Savior, enjoying Christ for Himself.

Jesus Attracts Mary; Judas Despises Jesus (12:3-8)

And Mary? **12:3.** *Then took Mary a pound of ointment of spikenard, very costly, and anointed the feet of Jesus, and wiped his feet with her hair: and the house was filled with the odour of the ointment.* In her adoration and worship of the Savior, Mary pours her love upon Him.

According to Jewish custom, she had no right to be where she was. As the men reclined around the festive board, the women waited on them. But Mary came to His feet and poured her treasures upon Him in adoration, in worship, in thanksgiving. Why shouldn't she? He had raised her brother from the dead. Nothing was too expensive, nothing too costly for the Savior.

I wish that we knew something of this generosity. Do you love someone? Then you will be generous to him. Do you love the Savior? Then you will be generous to Him. Generosity is ever the language of love.

Mary took her pound of ointment of spikenard, a very costly oil, and anointed the feet of Jesus. Mark says she also broke her alabaster box as another sacrifice for the Savior. She didn't merely pour a little out. She broke the thing to pour all that she had upon Him. The house was filled with the fragrance of the ointment.

And Judas? **12:4-5.** *Then saith one of his disciples, Judas Is-cariot, Simon's son, which should betray him, Why was not this ointment sold for three hundred pence, and given to the poor?* Now Judas wasn't philanthropic. He was a man who was sold out to money. Three hundred pence is practically a year's wages for a laborer of that day. To take your year's salary and pour the whole thing upon the Savior? "What a waste," said Judas.

> **12:6-8.** *This he said, not that he cared for the poor; but because he was a thief, and had the bag, and bare what was put therein. Then said Jesus, Let her alone: against the day of my burying hath she kept this. For the poor always ye have with you; but me ye have not always.*

The contrast here is between Mary (who showers upon the Savior all her love and devotion because there is nothing too costly to pour upon Him), and Judas (a man even worse than the priests who plotted to put the Lord to death). Judas spent three and a half years with the Savior. He traveled with Him. He had seen His wonderful miracles. He had heard His gracious words. And, you remember, "never man spake like this man."

Here was one in the intimacy of the circle with Christ. And while this woman is pouring out her love and devotion on the Savior, he stands by and criticizes with a heart that is purposing to sell and betray his Master. How much more devilish could a person be? How much more corrupt can the human heart be than to be that close to Jesus and then to plot to sell and betray Him? Judas was sold out to money. And all he received was thirty pieces of silver.

Here is Mary worshiping. Here is Judas sneering. Here is Mary attracted to the Savior. Here is Judas rejecting the Savior. Here is one worshiping. Here is one despising. She is adoring Him, and he is plotting to sell Him. The amazing thing is that when Judas asked why her gift was not sold and given to the poor, some of the other disciples agreed with him. And the Lord rebuked them for this.

It may be, Christian friend, in your desire and love and devotion to the Savior, that some other Christian will criticize you for doing something in service for Him. That person may say you're just wasting your time or your money. What of it? Others may call you a fanatic. What of it, as long as your life is poured out upon Him? And may I say very frankly, the more devoted you are to Christ, the chances are the more you will be criticized for it. But what of it as long as your heart is occupied with the Savior?

This woman Mary didn't care what they thought as long as she could be found at His feet. In Luke 10 she was at His feet as a disciple for instruction. In John 11 she was at His feet as a supplicant for comfort, and now here she is at His feet as a worshiper. And because of this, wherever the gospel has been proclaimed, her name has become immortal.

She was found at His feet. May I ask you a question? How much time do you spend at Jesus' feet? She was willing to break her alabaster box and pour her treasures upon Him. Matthew and Mark tell us she poured it upon His head. John says upon His feet. You know, there is no difference here. She took a whole pound of ointment and poured it over His head, and it came on down over His feet. And it was so much that she took her hair and wiped the excess, and the place was filled with the odor of the ointment.

May I say this to you? When our lives are poured out for Christ, our love and our life become a sweet aroma wherever we go.

Take the man, Hudson Taylor, who poured out his life at the feet of the Lord Jesus, and thousands of Chinese smelled the aroma and came to Christ. Amy Carmichael of India poured out her life, ministering with a broken, sickly body for the last twenty years of her life. And the fragrance of that life has swept through thousands of families in India. Wherever God finds a life poured out on His Son, the sweet aroma of His presence is realized, and people are brought to Him.

I wonder, my believing friend, if there is anything of the sweetness of the life of Christ manifested in your life? Is that sweetness manifested in your own family, among your neighbors, among your friends, in the office, in the shop? If there is one thing God wants, it is that the life of His Son shall be manifest in us and through us day by day. Anyone who spends time with Him, who pours out a life in behalf of the Son of God, will have a life that will be a sweet aroma of Christ.

It is so easy to be occupied with "three hundred pence." Let us not be like Judas, who was so sold out to materialism that his character dissolved and Satan took over. His was not a life poured out with the sweetness of Christ, a life sacrificed in love for Christ. His was a life lost because he was occupied with himself. The selfish life always leads to death; the life poured out always leads to life. This is the principle right through your Bible.

God grant that you and I may come and pour out our treasures upon our Lord, and that He will be the center of our devotion, of our affection, of our worship. He is always looking for poured out lives through whom He can display His Son in the sweetness of His character, in the sweetness of His own heart. But the one thing that hinders the expression of the character of the Son of God in us is that our hearts are not totally His.

God grant that each one of us may manifest something of the sweetness of the aroma of the Son of God, that in every place we go our words, our actions, and our attitudes will be such that people will see something of the character, of the sweetness, and of the grace of our Lord Jesus Christ. May we emulate Mary of Bethany. May we manifest our love for Him.

Again I say, sacrifice is ever the language of love. Gratitude and generosity are the language of love. Mary used that language with her Savior. Do you?

The Leaders Want Lazarus . . . Out of the Way (12:9-11)

> **12:9-11.** *Much people of the Jews therefore knew that he was there: and they came not for Jesus' sake only, but that they might see Lazarus also, whom he had raised from the dead. But the chief priests consulted that they might put Lazarus also to death; Because that by reason of him many of the Jews went*

away, and believed on Jesus.

"Let us get rid of the evidence," the Jewish leaders said. Lazarus was living proof of the deity of Christ. Now it is not for lack of evidence that people deny Christ. Don't be surprised if humanist leaders in America deny the evidence. Unbelief closes the heart to any evidence.

These Jewish leaders saw Lazarus who had been in the tomb in corruption. Now he's raised and sitting at the feast, eating with the rest. There's only one thing to do, and that is get rid of the evidence. These fellows were jealous, mad, and determined to kill him, simply because "by reason of him (his life) many of the Jews went away, and believed on Jesus."

Jesus Attracts the People Along the Road (12:12-19)
—Jesus Enters Jerusalem

Note the reaction of the people as Jesus goes down from Bethany to Jerusalem.

12:12-13. *On the next day much people that were come to the feast, when they heard that Jesus was coming to Jerusalem, Took branches of palm trees, and went forth to meet him, and cried, Hosanna: Blessed is the King of Israel that cometh in the name of the Lord.*

Now Josephus says that at some of these Passover feasts people would come from all over Asia Minor. Sometimes the crowds around Jerusalem would number three million people. Notice, everyone is following Jesus—the Pharisees, the priests, the crowd, the disciples—and all have a different attitude to the Son of God. In the mob are some who have seen Lazarus raised from the dead, others who have heard of it, and here comes Jesus who raised him. He's leaving Bethany and coming toward Jerusalem.

As He comes around the Mount of Olives, the people salute Him. They take their palm leaves, throw them in the way, and cry out, "Hosanna (which means, "Save us!"): Blessed is he that cometh in the name of the Lord." They called Him the King of Israel. The tragedy is that they wanted a material kingdom. They wanted to be delivered from Rome. He came with a spiritual kingdom. Many of these crying, "Hosanna!" will be crying, "Crucify Him!" in just a few hours. What a terrible thing.

But notice this truth: Before He comes to the city to be acclaimed as the King of Israel, He has been anointed. A significant truth. Mary didn't know the greatness of her act of worship, for sometimes the Lord uses us when we do not know He is using us. The law required that a king must be anointed before He is crowned. Mary had anointed Him for His coronation. He's on the way to be crowned . . . with a crown of thorns.

Mark how Jesus entered the city. **12:14-15.** *And Jesus, when he had found a young ass, sat thereon; as it is written, Fear not, daughter of Sion: behold, thy King cometh, sitting on an ass's colt.* Notice the literal fulfillment of prophecy of Zechariah 9:9: "Rejoice greatly, O daughter of Zion; shout, O daughter of Jerusalem: behold, thy King cometh unto thee: he is just, and having salvation; lowly, and riding upon an ass, and upon a colt the foal of an ass."

When Zechariah wrote that, there were no kings in Israel. He prophesied after the Babylonian captivity to encourage the remnant to rebuild the temple in the midst of the ruins. They had no king. They were without a king from the scattering by Nebuchadnezzar until the present time. Zechariah is prophesying to encourage the remnant who returned under Ezra, Nehemiah, and Zerubbabel.

Jesus did not come as a warrior on a horse, but in humility on a young ass. Oh, the literal fulfillment of it all. When one thinks of the detail of all that the Scripture said concerning His first coming, even to the last words he uttered, we ought to look with real expectancy to the Scriptures which pertain to the rapture and His return to the earth. Every detail will be fulfilled—literally. Unless it says otherwise, you always take Scripture literally.

Notice the attitudes among all these people.

12:16-18. *These things understood not his disciples at the first: but when Jesus was glorified, then remembered they that these things were written of him, and that they had done these things unto him. The people therefore that was with him when he called Lazarus out of his grave, and raised him from the dead, bare record. For this cause the people also met him, for that they heard that he had done this miracle.*

How did the people react? The mob was filled with praise. The disciples? They needed understanding. All of this was beyond them. After they received the Spirit of God in Acts 2, their minds were opened and they understood what had happened on this day.

And what about the Pharisees? **12:19.** *The Pharisees therefore said among themselves, Perceive ye how ye prevail nothing? behold, the world is gone after him.* They had seen Him take a man who was a derelict for thirty-eight years and heal him. They had seen Him take a man born blind and open his eyes. They had seen him raise a man in corruption from the dead. Talk about evidence! But their hearts were full of unbelief.

Jesus Attracts the People in the City (12:20-36)
—Jesus Stays Temporarily in Jerusalem

A Request: "We Would See Jesus" (12:20-22)

12:20-21. *And there were certain Greeks among them that came up to worship at the feast: The same came therefore to Philip, which was of Bethsaida of Galilee, and desired him, saying, Sir, we would see Jesus.*

The Lord begins now to give the last word in the Gospel of John that He has for the people of Israel. It is introduced, however, by the coming of certain Greeks to Him. This is a strange element which comes into the picture here. It is at this time that Jesus expresses that the great hour had arrived for which He had come.

231

Now these Greeks were not Jews who lived in Greece. They were Greeks who possibly had found nothing in the heathen, pagan religions in which they were born and had turned to Judaism. They possibly were proselytes, because they had come to the city to worship at the Passover. Whatever their background, these men were hungry for something real. They said, "Sir, we would see Jesus."

12:22. *Philip cometh and telleth Andrew: and again Andrew and Philip tell Jesus.*

Study these two men. In chapter 1 both men are soul winners, the only ones of the twelve who did any personal work. Andrew found Simon and brought him to Jesus. Philip found Nathanael and brought him to Jesus. In chapter 6, Andrew brought the little boy with his five loaves and two fish; and the Savior asked Philip, "Whence shall we buy bread, that these may eat?"

There is something about these two men that captivates my heart. They are not preachers like Peter and Paul. They are not writers like James or John. They are just two of the quiet ones who are devoted to the Savior, the ones people approached to find out about the Lord Jesus.

"Sir, we would see Jesus." Wouldn't that be a wonderful thing to put across the front of any church? They have it on the inside of some pulpits to remind the preacher why the people come to church and why they attend Bible classes. I trust it is the cry of your heart, as it was in the hearts of these Greeks: "Sir, we would see Jesus."

Jesus Declares that His Hour Is Come (12:23)

12:23. *And Jesus answered them, saying, The hour is come, that the Son of man should be glorified.*

We do not know whether Jesus said any word to the Greeks or not, but He did say, "The hour is come, that the Son of man should be glorified." In chapter 2 He said to His mother, "Mine hour is not yet come." In chapter 7 He said to His brethren, "My time is not yet come." Also in chapter 7 they sought to take Him, but "his hour was not yet come." It isn't until now that Jesus could say, "The hour is come."

In chapter 10 our Lord said, "No man taketh my life from Me. I have the power to lay it down, and I have the power to take it again." You see, in Matthew 26 the leaders of Israel had a committee meeting, planning and plotting Jesus' death. But they said, "Not on the feast day," for they feared the people. But the Lord Jesus said, "That's when I'm going to die. My hour is come." It wasn't the Jews who declared that, but Jesus. Have you ever stopped to realize, my Christian friend, that every page of this Gospel is a revelation of the sovereignty of Jesus Christ of Nazareth?

Take chapter 11, verse 4. Jesus said, "This sickness is not unto death, but for the glory of God, that the Son of God might be glorified thereby." In chapter 12, verse 23 we read, "The hour is come, that the Son of man should be glorified." Notice that Jesus did not say, "The hour is come, that the Son of man should be crucified." Our Lord looks beyond the suffering to the glory. He is going down into the darkest experience anyone has ever gone, "that he should taste death for every man" (Hebrews 2:9). The one thing that characterized Him in all His suffering was that He looked beyond it to the glory.

In verse 28 we read that a voice came from heaven, saying, "I have both glorified (thy name), and will glorify it again." In the next chapter we read, "Therefore, when he was gone out, Jesus said, Now is the Son of man glorified, and God is glorified in him. If God be glorified in him, God shall also glorify him in himself, and shall straightway glorify him" (13:31-32). Read chapter 17, verse 1: "These words spake Jesus, and lifted up his eyes to heaven and said, Father, the hour is come; glorify thy Son, that thy Son also may glorify thee."

The great consuming passion of the Lord Jesus, as He was going to the cross, was the glorifying of His Father, through whom He Himself would be glorified. This is an amazing answer when He said, "The hour is come."

Oh, the impossibility of the world, of men, of demons, of even

hell touching the Son of God until His hour was come! No power
on earth or in hell could touch Him until His hour was come. And
no power on earth or in hell can touch you until the job which God
has for you is completed. The believer in Christ, as he walks in the
will of God, cannot see death until his work is done.

Now Christians do die prematurely under the chastening hand of
God. "For this cause many are weak and sickly among you, and
many sleep" (1 Corinthians 11:30). "There is a sin unto death,"
(1 John 5:16). It is possible for a Christian to die ahead of the time
that God has planned for him. That's in judgment, lest he be condemned with the world, as 1 Corinthians 5:5 declares.

But if you and I seek to please Him, there's no power on earth or
in hell that can touch us. We can say just as our Savior said, "Mine
hour is not yet come." They hemmed Him in. They wanted to lay
hold of Him and slay Him, stone Him, and tear Him to pieces. He
stepped out of their midst. His hour was not yet come. They had no
authority, no power to touch Him. In Matthew 26:5 the Pharisees
did their planning. But the timing was not in their hands. The timing was in His hands, for that same night they took Him. He arranged the time in spite of all their ingenuity, and all their committee meetings, and all their devisings.

You have this in Galatians 4:4, where Paul writes, "But when
the fulness of the time was come, God sent forth his Son." We read
in Romans 5:6, "In due time (at the right time) Christ died for the
ungodly." And He's going to return for the Church at the right
time. He will not be one hour ahead of time, and He will not be one
hour late. Such a Savior! Such a Lord!

A Discussion: True Discipleship (12:24-26)

Jesus attracted certain Greeks and announced the arrival of His
hour to be glorified. Now He begins attracting disciples.

> **12:24.** *Verily, verily, I say unto you, Except a corn
> of wheat fall into the ground and die, it abideth alone:
> but if it die, it bringeth forth much fruit.*

I came across a jar of seeds the other day, seeds I used to plant when I had a little garden plot. In all these years in that jar they haven't sprouted once. They abide alone. But if you take them and put them in the ground, they die. There's no fruitage until there is death.

"Unless I die, there will be no fruitage." Jesus is talking about a spiritual kingdom. He is going to speak of the manner and extent of His death. There must be the cross before the crown, suffering before glory, death before fruitage. Out of death comes life.

12:25. *He that loveth his life shall lose it; and he that hateth his life in this world shall keep it unto life eternal.*

Jesus is saying, "If you're going to follow Me and experience this life of which I am the giver and you are the recipient, it is going to call for faith and obedience, and it may call for suffering." The selfish life ends in destruction. The spiritual life goes on through eternity. These Jews and Greeks must learn the lesson—as we must—that only out of death can come life.

And here He says, "Now mine hour is come to lay the foundation for a spiritual kingdom." This is the foundation of our Christian faith; for if there is no death, there is no resurrection. If there is no resurrection, there is no fruitage. Think of the fruitage of His death—the millions of souls saved for eternity. Our eternal life has come out of His death.

He is taking a natural event in everyday living to teach this. You must put your corn seed in the ground. Some come up and some don't. The ones that die are the ones that come up. This is true of all life. Even when a baby is born into the world, the mother goes down to the bowels of death to bring up life.

If God is going to have a spiritual kingdom, if He is going to have a people who will be fitted to spend eternity with Him—a people just like His Son—then His Son must die. If you put wheat in the ground, you get the fruitage of wheat. If you put in oats, you get oats. If Christ dies, then the fruitage of that death will parallel what He is.

That is why Paul could say in Ephesians 1:6, "He hath made us accepted in the beloved," in all that He is. That is why John says in 1 John 3:2, "When we see Him, we shall be like Him." That is why Paul says in Philippians 3:21 God is going to change these bodies and fashion them "like unto his glorious body," just as He died and came forth in resurrection. That is why Peter says that we have been "born again, not of corruptible seed, but of incorruptible, by the word of God, which liveth and abideth for ever" (1 Peter 1:23). We must be like Him if we are going to stand in His presence. Unless a person is just like the Savior, he will never see glory.

Unless you are like the Lord Jesus Christ, the Son of God, you will never see glory. As the seed is, so is the fruitage. And if He died and came forth in blessed resurrection with a body that is absolutely unlimited and glorified, that's what every believer is going to have. You are the fruitage of His death. Read Romans 6:4-11.

Now about this question of discipleship, Jesus is contrasting the material and the spiritual in verse 25. "He that loveth his life shall lose it; and he that hateth his life in this world shall keep it unto life eternal." Until a person's heart is open to what Jesus Christ is offering, he will never be saved. Unbelief closes the heart and shuts out the Son of God. The life of the unbeliever is material, physical, limited. Death is the end of it.

But if I turn my back on that which is physical and material—in the sense that my life is not wrapped up in it—and I turn to the Savior and receive Him who died for me, then I receive life. This is real life. I may be in frailty down here. I may be in sorrow. I may have my afflictions and my failures. But I have life, that eternal life which is in Christ.

> **12:26.** *If any man serve me, let him follow me; and where I am, there shall also my servant be: if any man serve me, him will my Father honour.*

Faith and obedience are the evidence of a disciple. We follow

Him. That's why He said in John 10, "My sheep hear my voice and they follow me, and I give unto them eternal life."

Jesus Sorrows as His Hour Comes (12:27-30)

Here we come to a very serious thing.

> **12:27-30.** *Now is my soul troubled; and what shall I say? Father, save me from this hour: but for this cause came I unto this hour. Father, glorify thy name. Then came there a voice from heaven, saying, I have both glorified it, and will glorify it again. The people therefore, that stood by, and heard it, said that it thundered: others said, An angel spake to him. Jesus answered and said, This voice came not because of me, but for your sakes.*

Jesus begins by saying, "My soul is exceedingly sorrowful, even unto death." You remember He had gone into the Garden of Gethsemane at the foot of the Mount of Olives. He had taken Peter, James, and John with him. And He cast Himself on the ground and prayed, "Father, if it be possible, let this cup pass from me: nevertheless not as I will, but as thou wilt" (Matthew 26:39). In Isaiah 53:12 we read, "He hath poured out his soul unto death." We're coming to something here that is beyond the physical.

Many of His people have suffered in the physical just as much (and I say this reverently) as the Lord suffered in the physical. Others have been scourged and crucified, or flayed and set afire, or torn to pieces by wild beasts. Some have been put on the rack until their bones were pulled out of joint. These people have suffered. But not what He went through. He tasted death for every man.

He cried out, "My God, my God, why hast thou forsaken me?" The sinless One, the righteous One, the One who always did the things that pleased His Father is going to become sin. Your sin, all your sin, and all my sin, and all the murder, all the adultery, all the vileness, all the perversion of the human race were put upon the

Holy One, the sinless One. You and I can't fathom this. All I know is that John the Baptist said, "Behold the Lamb of God, which taketh away the sin of the world" (1:29).

The One who had never touched sin, the One in whom there was no unrighteousness, the absolutely holy One, became this damnable thing called "sin." He was not only bearing your sin and my sin, but He was dying the death we should. He was dying, forsaken by God, cast out by man, as an accursed thing. "Father, what shall I say? What shall I say?"

I am not surprised to read in Luke 22:43 that while He was in the garden an angel came and strengthened Him. The physical couldn't begin to stand the tremendous pressure and the burden and agony of becoming a sin bearer. No human mind can fathom this.

Nothing is said in the Gospels about what Jesus experienced during those three terrible hours when He hung on the cross. The sun hid its face. A great darkness covered the earth and there was an earthquake. But you have to go back to Psalms 22 and 69, and Isaiah 50, 52, and 53 to see what He went through when He said, "My Father, what shall I say? My soul is troubled even unto death." For the first time He would be separated from God the Father.

Down through the eons of time, the Father and Son were always together in perfect, intimate fellowship. "O Father," Jesus prayed, "glorify thou me with thine own self with the glory which I had with thee before the world was" (17:5). He was with Him in the Garden of Eden when man transgressed. They were together at the Tower of Babel. When He was a babe, they were together. At the Jordan River they were together. On the Mount of Transfiguration, in the Garden of Gethsemane, and when He stood before Pilate, they were together. But at Calvary, they separated.

Why? He bore my sin. All the wrath and judgment of the holy God that should have fallen on me, fell on Him. This is the extent of the cross.

Have you ever stopped to think, when you partake of the bread and the cup, that this is the only thing the Lord Jesus asked you to remember? "This do in remembrance of me" (1 Corinthians 11:24–25). In remembrance of what? That through His death we have access into the presence of God; that through His shed blood we were cleansed from all sin; that when He died, He died in my place and yours. Not only did He die for your sins, He died for you, a sinner. He died for me, a guilty one. He became sin. Though He knew no sin, He was made sin for us. Why? To bear fruitage, that we might be made the righteousness of God in Him.

He poured out His soul unto death, right down to the very bowels of death for us. As Hebrews 2 says, He "tasted death," something you and I will never do. We will never taste death. When we leave this scene, we go immediately into the very presence of God.

A Prediction of His Own Crucifixion (12:31-33)

12:31-33. *Now is the judgment of this world: now shall the prince of this world be cast out. And I, if I be lifted up from the earth, will draw all men unto me. This he said, signifying what death he should die.*

In the manner of His death, He must die by crucifixion, fulfilling Psalm 22 and 69, which give the experience prophetically of One being crucified. Crucifixion was a Roman punishment. It was never known in the days of David. And yet, David prophesied by the Spirit of God that He would die by crucifixion; and by doing so, He judged the world.

Have no doubt about this fact. The world is already judged. It is not moving on to judgment. It is moving on to the execution of the judgment. And the believer is no more a part of the world. Paul said in Galatians 6:14, "God forbid that I should glory, save in the cross of our Lord Jesus Christ, by whom the world is crucified unto me, and I unto the world."

We are in the world, but we don't belong to the world. In John 17, our Lord clearly defines the fact that just as He is free from the world, so is the believer. Nineteen times in that passage our Savior speaks of the world and that we are not of the world. The world is judged. We have been freed from judgment.

And Satan was judged at the cross. "Now shall the prince of this world be cast out." Our Savior speaks of Satan three times in John's Gospel as the "prince of this world." Here in chapter 12 he is to be cast out at the cross. At the end of chapter 14, Jesus said, "The prince of this world cometh and hath nothing in me—nothing he can attract or deceive." And in chapter 16 Jesus said, "The prince of this world is judged." "Having spoiled principalities and powers, he made a shew of them openly, triumphing over them in it" (Colossians 2:15).

Our Savior at the cross defeated the forces of darkness. That's why in Colossians 1:13 Paul could say that God "hath delivered us from the power of darkness, and hath translated us into the kingdom of his dear Son." That's why God became a man, why He took His place in the human family, "that through death he might destroy (annul the power of) him that had the power of death, that is, the devil" (Hebrews 2:14). The captives of Satan can now be set free. His authority and power have been annulled.

Our Savior did a tremendous thing when He died on the cross. Why is it that people are ashamed of it? Because the cross is an offensive thing (Galatians 5:11). It is an offense to my morality. The cross says I haven't any. It is an offense to my philosophy of life. It says that I am absolutely no good. The cross is an accursed thing.

And please do not say that Jesus changed the cross from an accursed thing into a thing of glory. The cross is never a thing of glory. We can glory in the cross, because there Christ purchased redemption for us. But the cross itself is an accursed thing. "Cursed is every one that hangeth on a tree" (Galatians 3:13). It has a stigma, and that is one reason why men don't accept the Savior.

The average evangelical Christian hasn't begun to realize the depth, the marvel of the work our Savior accomplished on the cross. The very heavens are going to be purged from sin on the grounds of what He did on the cross. Not only were we redeemed, not only were our sins put away, not only was God's righteous character vindicated, not only was death defeated, but the world was judged, Satan was shorn of his power, and his captives were set free.

Jesus Warns Against Spurning the Light (12:34-36)

Now mark the reaction of the people to Jesus' prediction. **12:34.** *The people answered him, We have heard out of the law that Christ abideth for ever: and how sayest thou, The Son of man must be lifted up? who is this Son of man?* All down through this Gospel Jesus has revealed by His words and works that He is the Christ of God, the Son of God, the Son of man. Now they knew these titles. These people were Jews. And they knew the Scripture . . . at least some of it.

"Why are you talking about being lifted up?" they asked.

Jesus had said this in John chapter 8: "When ye have lifted up the Son of man, then shall ye know that I came from God and that the Father hath not left me alone."

But they said, "Why, when the Christ comes, He is going to live forever. He is going to abide forever. What do you mean, He shall be lifted up? And who is this Son of man? Are you talking about dying? But He doesn't die. He is eternal."

Now the Lord ignored their response. He ignored their questions. Instead, we have the Lord's last definite statement to them. It is both a warning and a plea.

> **12:35-36.** *Then Jesus said unto them, Yet a little while is the light with you. Walk while ye have the light, lest darkness come upon you: for he that walketh in darkness knoweth not whither he goeth. While ye have light, believe in the light, that ye may be the children of light. These things spake Jesus, and departed, and did hide himself from them.*

What is Jesus' warning? In a little while there will be no more light. In chapter 9 He said, "As long as I am in the world, I am the light of the world." And may I add, our generation is spurning the light and is walking in darkness.

If you were to ask me where the world is going nationally and internationally, I would say the world itself doesn't know where it is going. Our own nation, founded on the Word of God, has spurned the Word of God. The professing Christian Church in America has spurned the Light of the world and we are walking in uncertainty and fear, not knowing what tomorrow may bring.

Why?

Politically, economically, religiously, when any nation or individual rejects the Light, nothing is left but darkness. God has blessed America, but we've rejected the Blesser. He has blessed great nations that for centuries have boasted of being Christian, of having the Word of God. Where are they today morally? politically? spiritually?

Yet here is an amazing fact. In Israel, when David Ben-Gurion (who for many years was the premier of Israel) was living, more than one thousand Israeli Bible lovers would gather as guests of a little town just south of Tel Aviv. All expenses were paid by the town, and they would have four days of Bible study led by some of the political leaders of Israel.

Wouldn't it be a wonderful thing if our government were to call for a Bible conference? Perhaps the Light is beginning to break through the darkness of Israel, but the darkness is becoming more dense in hearts and lives in other nations of the world. We don't know where we are going.

I'm glad I don't belong to the world. I'm glad I belong to Him. Our redemption draweth nigh. Our only hope is in the One who nineteen hundred years ago pled with Israel: "Walk while ye have the light, lest darkness come upon you."

Israel's Rejection of Jesus (12:37-43)

Now in the next verses we have a summary of Israel's unbelief.

12:37-39. *But though he had done so many mir-*

acles before them, yet they believed not on him: That
the saying of Esaias the prophet might be fulfilled,
which he spake, Lord, who hath believed our report?
and to whom hath the arm of the Lord been revealed?
Therefore they could not believe, because that Esaias
said again, . . .

Notice the statement, "Yet they believed not on him . . . therefore they could not believe." Though Jesus had performed many miracles before them—healing a man thirty-eight years infirm, a man born blind and absolutely helpless, and raising a man dead and buried and in corruption—yet they believed not on Him.

Though He had taught many wonderful things ("I am the light of the world," "I am the good shepherd," "I am the resurrection and the life," "I am the bread of life") and although "never man spake like this man," yet for all that they believed not on Him. And because they persisted in their unbelief, they could not believe. They would not, therefore they could not. They could not because they would not. God ratified their own actions.

It is not that God prevented them from believing or forced them into a state where they wouldn't believe. This would be contrary to all the revealed truth. "If any man thirst, let him come" (7:37). "Ho, every one that thirsteth, come ye. . . ." (Isaiah 55:1). "Come unto me all ye that labour and are heavy laden, and I will give you rest" (Matthew 11:28). "Him that cometh to me I will in no wise cast out" (6:37). That's anyone! He appeals to the individual.

But when a person persistently refuses to accept the evidence and refuses the Savior, hardness sets in. God ratifies that person's own actions. Unbelief persisted in leads to hardness.

Take Hebrews chapter 3, where the Lord appeals three times to men and woman, "Harden not your hearts" (verses 8, 13, 15). Unbelief is the product of an evil heart. He pleads with them not to harden their hearts through unbelief. It is not that God doesn't want to save people. But when people won't be saved and won't believe, the Spirit of God withdraws. That was true of Pharaoh in Exodus. It was true of Israel. Why were they scattered? For this very reason.

The tragedy is that the Spirit of God prophesied not only to
Isaiah's generation but also to all succeeding generations: "Who
hath believed our report? and to whom is the arm of the Lord revealed?" (53:1). The report is here. The testimony is here. But
some will not believe.

Isaiah had said this about their unbelief. **12:40-41.** *He hath*
blinded their eyes, and hardened their heart; that they should not
see with their eyes, nor understand with their heart, and be con-
verted, and I should heal them. These things said Esaias, when
he saw his glory, and spake of him. I am so happy this is in the
Scriptures. These verses are from Isaiah chapter 6.

You remember how Isaiah chapter 6 starts: "In the year that
King Uzziah died I saw also the Lord sitting upon a throne, high
and lifted up, and his train filled the temple." Seraphim cried out,
"Holy, holy, holy, is the Lord of hosts: the whole earth is full of his
glory." Isaiah spoke of Jesus when he saw Him in His glory. I think
John is standing back, taking a retrospect of the whole thing, and
he puts in exactly what Isaiah wrote about Israel's unbelief after he
had seen our Savior. Isaiah saw Him in His glory.

In the next two verses we have a warning. **12:42-43.** *Neverthe-*
less among the chief rulers also many believed on him; but be-
cause of the Pharisees they did not confess him, lest they should
be put out of the synagogue: For they loved the praise of men
more than the praise of God. These men were convinced, but I
question if they were persuaded. They were convinced that He was
the Messiah, but they were not converted to Him. It is possible for
a person to be convinced of the truth and yet have no experience of
life. We can know the Word of God, we can know doctrine, we can
be convinced that He is the Christ; but that's not enough.

I had a two or three hour session with a young man in my office
one day. Two or three times he stood up. I thought he was going to
punch me, and I stood up as well, because if I'm going to be
punched, I'm going to be standing up. But I told him to sit down,
and he sat down.

When we finished our discussion, he said, "Dr. Mitchell, I believe that Jesus Christ died for the whole world."

I said, "I want you to be more specific than that."

He said, "I believe that Jesus Christ died for my sins. I believe that He was raised again from the dead." He accepted the evidence; he declared he believed. Did that make him a Christian? No.

I said, "Sir, you have no excuse. You have declared you believe these facts. Now will you, of your own volition, put your trust in Jesus Christ as your own personal Savior?"

He said, "I'll do no such thing."

He acknowledged the essential facts, but he wouldn't, by his own will, put his trust in Christ as Savior. Salvation doesn't come through the enlightenment of the mind. It comes through the will. I think the folk in these verses in John believed in this sense. They knew by His miracles and gracious words that He must be the Messiah. But when they thought of what it would cost them to believe, they refused to openly put their trust in Him. They thought, "It might mean I will be put out of the synagogue. I might lose some business. I may lose my popularity. I may bring down the displeasure of the Sanhedrin."

I believe that too many people in our churches have just given a mental assent to truth, and there hasn't been that realistic receiving of the Son of God into their own hearts and lives as Savior.

Jesus' Invitation to Israel (12:44-50)

From verses 44-50 we have the final word of our Savior. It's the summary of His person and work and ministry. It's the summary of our Lord's final word to the nation of Israel.

> **12:44-47.** *Jesus cried and said, He that believeth on me, believeth not on me, but on him that sent me. And he that seeth me seeth him that sent me. I am come a light into the world, that whosoever believeth on me should not abide in darkness. And if any man hear my words, and believe not, I judge him not: for I came not*

to judge the world, but to save the world.

"I came not to judge the world, but to save the world." We have that statement in John 3:17: "For God sent not his Son into the world to condemn the world; but that the world through him might be saved." We have it again in 1 John 4:14: "And we have seen and do testify that the Father sent the Son to be the Saviour of the world." Jesus came to save the world.

Jesus also insists upon the fact that He and His Father are one.

12:48-50. *He that rejecteth me, and receiveth not my words, hath one that judgeth him: the word that I have spoken, the same shall judge him in the last day. For I have not spoken of myself; but the Father which sent me, he gave me a commandment, what I should say, and what I should speak. And I know that his commandment is life everlasting: whatsoever I speak therefore, even as the Father said unto me, so I speak.*

Jesus insists upon this oneness with the Father. Not to believe Him means you don't believe in God. If you don't believe His words, you don't believe God's words. Jesus' words are His Father's words. This is His statement. His Word becomes life if I receive Him. His Word becomes my judge if I reject Him.

John 13

Christ, The Advocate

Overview of John 13-17

Of all the Scriptures between Genesis and Revelation, I know of no greater portion as far as the people of God are concerned than chapters 13 through 17 of John. I believe in these chapters we have the seed germ of all the truth concerning the Church, as well as almost all the doctrine in the New Testament. Our Lord's discourse here takes us within twenty-four hours of the crucifixion.

These disciples have walked with the Lord for three and a half years. Spiritually, they are not very mature. Their knowledge of the things of God is very meager. And now the Lord must leave them. He speaks from a heart that is absolutely full of love for His own. But what shall He say to them?

In chapter 13 Jesus is the Advocate, making provision for their communion and their fellowship. If they are to be His disciples, they will evidence it by love. In chapter 14 He speaks of His return. If He goes away, He is going to come again and receive them unto Himself. He speaks of the fact that He will send the Spirit of God to indwell them. He will not leave them comfortless. In chapter 15 He speaks of Himself as the Vine and of them as the branches. He expects much fruit-bearing from them, for "herein is my Father glorified, that ye bear much fruit."

And then in chapter 16 He declares Himself to be the preeminent One. He is the One of whom the Spirit of God will speak. Indeed, the Spirit will teach them things concerning Him, and show them things to come. When we come to chapter 17, He is revealed as the great Intercessor. He is our High Priest as He pleads with the Father in behalf of His disciples whom He is going to leave in the world. In that chapter He speaks nineteen times of the world. He knows the world. He knows what's in the world. He knows the world is a tremendous enemy against His own. So He prays for them.

It is remarkable that this section, starting in chapter 13, begins with the statement, "Having loved his own which were in the world, he loved them unto the end" (13:1). This section ends in chapter 17 with Jesus praying, "that the love wherewith thou hast loved me may be in them, and I in them" (17:26). He begins and ends with His love for His own. It's just like the Savior! And down through these five chapters we have the marvelous revelation of His love, of His concern for His own.

I wish that you could read and reread these passages as we go through them. It is a wonderful thing to know that we have a Savior who is on the throne today, who cares for us, and whose love for us is never affected by our failures or our weaknesses or our circumstances.

Revelation of the Advocate (13:1-17)

The Advocate's Sovereignty (13:1-3)

We have a revelation of the Lord as our Advocate in these first few verses of John chapter 13. Here we see His sovereignty, His heavenly origin, and His divine destiny.

> **13:1-3.** *Now before the feast of the passover, when Jesus knew that his hour was come that he should depart out of this world unto the Father, having loved his own which were in the world, he loved them unto the end. And supper being ended, the devil having now put into the heart of Judas Iscariot, Simon's son,*

> *to betray him; Jesus knowing that the Father had*
> *given all things into his hands, and that he was come*
> *from God, and went to God; . . .*

Our Lord was acutely aware of all the details concerning the next twenty-four hours. Here He manifests His sovereignty and His omniscience. Jesus knew *where* He was from. He knew He was come from God. He knew *where* He was going. He knew he should depart out of this world. He knew *when* He was going. He knew that His hour was come. He knew to *whom* He was going. He knew He was going to the Father.

He knew *why* He had come and *why* He was going. He knew the Father had given all things into His hands. He knew that the Father had such confidence in Him that He would finish the purpose for which He came. And may I say this? If the Father had confidence in Christ through it all, is it asking too much that we believers should have complete confidence in the Lord Jesus Christ? My friend, do you have confidence for your family, confidence in your home, confidence in your business, confidence in personal work, confidence in your ministry, confidence twenty-four hours a day that "he which hath begun a good work in you will perform it until the day of Jesus Christ" (Philippians 1:6)?

Jesus knew *whom* He had come to and *whom* He would leave. He knew His own which were in the world. He knew who should betray Him. He knew what Peter was going to do that night. He knew what Thomas would say after the resurrection.

He knew all about the frailty and the failures of His disciples, yet He loved them to the end. And He loves us clean through to the end, to the uttermost. I repeat, our frailty, our faults, our failures, our circumstances never affect His love for us. Now, I'm not excusing fraility, nor am I excusing failure.

But instead of becoming discouraged because of failure, we must have our eyes on Him and remember that even our failures have not affected His love for us. For, "having loved his own which were in the world, he loved them to the end."

The more I see His love for me, the more I want to obey Him.

May the Lord increase our love so that we will not want to fail Him or disappoint Him. If He loved us when we were ungodly, think of how much He loves us now (Romans 5:8ff). Why don't you tell the Lord how much you love Him?

The Advocate's Example (13:4-5)

Starting in verse 4 Jesus gives us an example, this wonderful experience of foot washing.

> **13:4-5. *He riseth from supper, and laid aside his garments; and took a towel, and girded himself. After that he poureth water into a basin, and began to wash the disciples' feet, and to wipe them with the towel wherewith he was girded.***

You can just hear John reminding himself of all the details of this evening as you read the description in these verses. They had sat down at the table and reclined to eat supper. They had come in off the street, but no one had washed their feet. They wore sandals and the very first thing to do would be to wash each other's feet or have a servant do it. This was the custom. This was the courteous thing to do. We have this in Luke 7.

But here no one washed their feet. Each disciple wondered, "Who is going to get up and wash our feet?" No one stirred. No one moved. You see, there is still a great deal of pride in the disciples. "Who is going to start washing our feet?"

Jesus Himself rose up from supper to wash their feet. My friend, consider this tremendous act of our Savior. Here is the omnipotent God. He is the One who said, "I know My hour is come. I know I am going to My Father. I know who is going to betray Me. I know the Father has utter confidence in Me." Here is the Lord of glory on His knees, washing the dirty feet of His disciples.

One is reminded of Philippians chapter 2. Paul could say, "Let this mind be in you, which was also in Christ Jesus: Who, being in the form of God, thought it not robbery to be equal with God: but made himself of no reputation, and took upon him the form of a servant . . ." (2:5-7).

Here we have love displayed in meekness and service. Did you ever think of the distance the Lord traveled? He left the glory, took His place in the human race, and was rejected and despised of men. He revealed Himself in His glory and power to the people of His day. And here I find Him on His knees washing the dirty feet of His disciples. What a sight for the angels! What a distance He traveled from the glory to the place of a slave.

Here is One before whom angels fall in worship, adoration, and praise. And if they could gaze out of the battlements of heaven and look down upon earth, they would see the Savior on His knees with a basin of water, not only washing feet, but taking a towel and wiping them. I say, what an example.

The Advocate's Work (13:6-11)

13:6. *Then cometh he to Simon Peter: and Peter saith unto him, Lord, dost thou wash my feet?*

"This can't be, Lord. You can't wash *my* feet. I should be washing Your feet. You are my Master. Do You wash my feet, Lord?"

13:7. *Jesus answered and said unto him, What I do thou knowest not now; but thou shalt know hereafter.*

"Peter, you don't understand what I'm doing now, but you will understand later." I personally believe the Lord had reference here to the time when the Spirit of God would come and indwell and teach him these things.

13:8. *Peter saith unto him, Thou shalt never wash my feet. . . .*

The English here is not strong enough. Peter was saying, "You'll never wash my feet at any time or in any place. You're never going to wash my feet. Why should I, the servant, the disciple, be washed by my Master? You will never, under any circumstances, ever wash my feet." That's just like Peter.

13:8-9. . . .*Jesus answered him, If I wash thee not, thou hast no part with me. Simon Peter saith unto him, Lord, not my feet only, but also my hands and my head.*

Peter was saying, "Lord, if it means communion, if it means relationship, if it means something to do with You, then don't stop with my feet. Do the whole business!"
Mark what Jesus says.

13:10-11. *Jesus saith to him, He that is washed* (bathed) ***needeth not save to wash his feet, but is clean every whit: and ye are clean, but not all. For he knew who should betray him; therefore said he, Ye are not all clean.***

There is a two-fold lesson that our Lord desires us to learn from His example. First, we learn the advocacy of the Savior. In verse 8 Jesus said, "If *I* wash thee not. . . ." He didn't say, "If someone else washes you, you are clean." Hebrews 10:14 says, "For by one offering *he* hath perfected for ever them that are sanctified." His work at the cross bathes people in the bath of regeneration, as Titus 3:5 declares. The Old Testament priests were ceremonially bathed just once when they were inducted into the priest's office. After that, they washed only their feet and hands at the laver of cleansing.

Let me emphasize this. There must be cleansing before there can be communion. The cross was an act that happened once— forever. Hebrews 10:10 says, "We are sanctified through the offering of the body of Jesus Christ once for all."

But daily there must be cleansing before there can be communion. Fellowship is a daily proposition. We have this in 1 John 1:9-2:2. The Lord Jesus, who is at the right hand of God, not only makes intercession for us now, but He pleads our cause. He advocates on the ground that He has already put away our sin. As our

Advocate, He always keeps us fit for heaven. "Having loved His own which were in the world, He loved them to the end."

When you and I came as sinners and accepted the Savior, God accepted us in all the righteousness and beauty and glory of His Son. Relationship was established because of His worth on the cross.

But as a believer still on earth, when I fail God, my fellowship is broken. Now, God keeps His appointment. But do we? No. We're the ones that do not keep our appointment.

After we are bathed, however, we need not save to wash our feet. We maintain fellowship with Him now through confession, forgiveness, and cleansing. There can be no fellowship or communion with Him without cleansing. "If we confess our sins, he is faithful and just to forgive us our sins, and to cleanse us from all unrighteousness" (1 John 1:9).

The Advocate's Meekness (13:12-17)

The second lesson Jesus would have His disciples learn is one of meekness. Wherever you find real love for Him, you find meekness and humility.

> **13:12-17.** *So after he had washed their feet, and had taken his garments, and was set down again, he said unto them, Know ye what I have done to you? Ye call me Master and Lord: and ye say well; for so I am. If I then, your Lord and Master, have washed your feet; ye also ought to wash one another's feet. For I have given you an example, that ye should do as I have done to you. Verily, verily, I say unto you, The servant is not greater than his lord; neither he that is sent greater than he that sent him. If ye know these things, happy are ye if ye do them.*

Jesus has washed the feet of Peter who will deny Him, of Thomas who will doubt Him, and of Judas who will betray Him.

He has more in mind here than an ordinance of foot washing. I have no argument against those who claim we should have literal foot washing services. If you feel you should do that, that's between you and the Lord. I think, however, that the Lord has a far greater matter before us here.

Peter and the disciples knew all about foot washing. This was a daily occurrence with them. But this is the only place in the New Testament where Jesus said, "I have given you an example." What was the example?

Meekness.

In Matthew 11:29 Jesus said, "Take my yoke upon you, and learn of me; for I am meek and lowly in heart: and ye shall find rest unto your souls." Only once did He ever say, "Learn of me." Learn what?

Meekness.

Peter in his first epistle reaffirmed this. "Christ also suffered for us, leaving us an example, that ye should follow his steps" (1 Peter 2:21). After this Peter discusses Christ's meekness. We also read that the fruit of the Spirit includes meekness (Galatians 5:23).

After this evening the disciples never again criticized each other or quarreled. In fact, this same Peter wrote in 1 Peter 5:6, "Humble yourselves therefore under the mighty hand of God." He also tells the brethren in verse 5, "All of you be subject one to another, and be clothed with humility," just as the Lord girded Himself with a towel. Humility is the sign of greatness in the kingdom of God. Meekness is the fruit of the Spirit. It takes a strong man to be meek. We have many *weak* Christians, but not many *meek* ones.

You say, "Well, how can I be meek?"

There are plenty of feet to be washed. Galatians 6:1 says, "If a man be overtaken in a fault (if a brother be out of joint), ye which are spiritual, restore such an one in the spirit of meekness; considering thyself, lest thou also be tempted (lest you also get out of joint)." When an arm is out of joint, do you cut the arm off? Certainly not. You put it back in. And there are a great many Christians who are out of joint, out of fellowship with God. Don't take a club to them. Don't criticize them. Don't run to the phone and tell everyone. Instead, love them. Wash their feet. Restore them.

If you are spiritual, take the Word of God. Wash the feet of other believers who have stepped out of the way and dirtied their feet. You can't go through this world without becoming dirty, and neither can they. Use the Word of God lovingly. Restore them with the spirit of meekness, for the time may come when you will need to be restored to fellowship as well.

The Lord's great desire at the beginning of this Upper Room discourse is communion. How glad I am that every one of us who has professed the name of the Lord Jesus Christ is the object of His love. And He loves us to the end in spite of all our frailty. And He made provision for the great yearning of His heart. His yearning is that you might have fellowship and communion with Him. And when you're in fellowship with Him, it is easy to be in fellowship with your brethren.

Revelation of the Betrayer (13:18-30)

The Betrayer: One of His Own (13:18-21)

Following this we have the amazing revelation of the one who would betray the Savior. Jesus knew who would betray Him. He said in verse 11, "Ye are not all clean." The omniscience of Christ is evident throughout this passage.

Notice what He said.

13:18-20. *I speak not of you all: I know whom I have chosen: but that the scripture may be fulfilled, He that eateth bread with me hath lifted up his heel against me. Now I tell you before it come, that, when it is come to pass, ye may believe that I am he. Verily, verily, I say unto you, He that receiveth whomsoever I send receiveth me; and he that receiveth me receiveth him that sent me.*

Our Lord speaks here of the union of believers, Himself, and the Father. God expects us to walk down here on earth as those who are in vital union with the Son. And our attitude one to another will reveal our relationship to our Savior and God.

Because the love the Father has for the Son is the same love the Son has for you and for me, our love for each other is the outward demonstration of our love for Him. God sees my faith, but men experience my love. God wants the life of His Son to be displayed in our love for one another.

13:21. *When Jesus had thus said, he was troubled in spirit, and testified, and said, Verily, verily, I say unto you, that one of you shall betray me.* This is the thing that troubled Him. It wasn't one of the Pharisees, or one of the Sadducees, or one of the Herodians, or one of His other enemies, but one of His own that would betray Him. What a startling statement for Him to make!

The Betrayer: The One Given the Sop (13:22-26)

If you read this story in all four Gospels, you will notice the great confusion in the minds of the disciples. **13:22.** *Then the disciples looked one on another, doubting of whom he spake.* I wouldn't be surprised if they wondered, "You mean that one of us is going to betray you, Lord? Why, we have lived with you for three and a half years. We have followed you all over this country. We have testified concerning you. We have heard your gracious words. You are our Master. You are our Teacher. You are our Lord. You mean one of us will betray You? This is unbelievable. Am I the one, Lord?"

Dear old Peter couldn't keep quiet. He had John ask the Lord who would betray Him.

> **13:23-26.** *Now there was leaning on Jesus' bosom one of his disciples, whom Jesus loved.* I believe John the apostle is referring to himself here. *Simon Peter therefore beckoned to him, that he should ask who it should be of whom he spake. He then lying on Jesus' breast saith unto him, Lord, who is it? Jesus answered, He it is, to whom I shall give a sop, when I*

have dipped it. And when he had dipped the sop, he
gave it to Judas Iscariot, the son of Simon.

It is an astounding thing that a person can be one of the twelve, and walk three and a half years with the Lord, and yet not have any love for Christ. Judas had associated with the disciples of Christ. He had gazed upon the Savior. He had heard His words and seen the miracles He performed. And yet he had no place in His heart for Christ. Is it possible?

Listen, a person can know all the doctrines and can associate with God's people and be found in the worship meetings, the prayer meetings, at the Lord's Table, and yet not know Jesus Christ as Savior. Both Jude and Peter write concerning this. Jude says, "These are spots in your feasts of charity, when they feast with you, feeding themselves without fear: clouds they are without water, carried about of winds; trees whose fruit withereth, without fruit, twice dead, plucked up by the roots" (Jude 12). Peter says the same thing in 2 Peter 2:13, 17. Their life is without Christ.

Judas had a weakness—covetousness. Now the Lord knew that Judas was a thief. But as far as I know, Judas did not know he was a thief when he became treasurer of the company. The Lord did.

You say, "Well, then, why did He allow it?"

Because He wanted Judas to see this himself so that he could be freed from his sin. Remember, he was the only one of the twelve from Judea. I take it he was a brilliant businessman and probably well thought of by the other eleven. I question if any of them ever dreamed it was Judas. He was so close to them. He was one of the executives.

I say to you solemnly that if you have some weaknesses in your life, and God puts circumstances around you that reveal it, remember it is that you might see your sin and get rid of it. Judas did not do this.

You ask, "Was Judas ever a Christian?" Very clearly, Judas was never a real disciple of Jesus Christ. In Matthew 26, when the Lord said, "One of you shall betray me," the disciples in perplexity asked, "Lord, is it I?" They called him their Lord. But Judas said,

"Rabbi, is it I?" Judas only acknowledged Him as his teacher.

In John 6 the Lord had said, "Have not I chosen you twelve, and one of you is a devil?" In John 17 He speaks of Judas as being the son of perdition. In Acts 1:25 Peter said, "Judas by transgression fell, that he might go to his own place." Here in chapter 13, the Lord is simply ratifying what was already in Judas's heart.

There is such a danger in being religious among God's people but never really knowing the Lord. This is a particular danger for second and third generation Christians.

Two things ought to have opened Judas's eyes to the deity of Christ. First, Jesus said, "One of you shall betray me." Now who knew that Judas was going to betray his Lord? The other twelve didn't. Who did? In his heart, Judas knew what he was going to do. He had determined that he was going to sell Jesus for money. And when the Lord Jesus said, "One of you shall betray me," Judas should have recognized the omniscience of his Teacher.

Second, when John asked who would betray Him, the Savior said, "The one to whom I shall give the sop." Now the custom was that the governor of the feast would honor someone by taking his own bread, dipping it in the wine, and presenting it to the one he desired to honor. The Lord said, "I know who is going to betray Me, and yet I am going to offer to him the place of honor. I am going to recognize him at the feast." He took the sop, dipped it in the vinegar, and offered it to Judas. He should have recognized that the Lord was still pleading with him.

The Betrayer: The One of Darkness (13:27-30)

13:27. And after the sop Satan entered into him. Then said Jesus unto him, That thou doest, do quickly.

When Judas took the sop, he determined to go through with his plan. Compare Psalm 41:9. He opened his heart to that determination and Satan took over.

"That thou doest, do quickly." Jesus ratified that decision.

There would be no return. Judas spurned the grace of the Savior. Judas ignored His omniscience. He made his decision. He went out and sold his Lord. As Zechariah said, they treasured God at thirty pieces of silver (11:12-13). This was the price of a slave (Exodus 21:32).

The disciples didn't realize what was going on. They thought Judas was going out to prepare for the meal.

13:28-30. *Now no man at the table knew for what intent he spake this unto him. For some of them thought, because Judas had the bag, that Jesus had said unto him, Buy those things that we have need of against the feast; or, that he should give something to the poor. He then having received the sop went immediately out: and it was night.*

"And it was night." Not to have Jesus Christ in your heart and life means night. In chapter 8 the Lord had said, "I am the light of the world: he that followeth me shall not walk in darkness, but shall have the light of life." That's why the apostle Paul calls us "children of light" (1 Thessalonians 5:5). We are not children of the night, but of the day. We have it in Romans 13. God is light. As members of His family, we are children of light.

If we spurn the light, there is nothing left but darkness. Peter could say that the unrighteous are kept in chains of darkness (2 Peter 2:4). Impenetrable darkness is the portion of those out of Christ. Here is Judas who spent three and a half years with this wonderful Savior. And when he left, he not only went out into the darkness at midnight, but he went out into impenetrable darkness.

"Judas by transgression fell." He made his choice. He went to his own place. God does not need to send men to outer darkness. They choose to go there, and God ratifies their choice. Think about that.

Revelation to the Disciples (13:31-35)

Glorification of Jesus (13:31-33)

Judas was gone. Now the Lord turned to the eleven to reveal His heart to them.

13:31-32. *Therefore, when he was gone out, Jesus said, Now is the Son of man glorified, and God is glorified in him. If God be glorified in him, God shall also glorify him in himself, and shall straightway glorify him.*

The hour is come. *"Now* is the Son of man glorified." Where? At the cross. There God was glorified in that His character was vindicated, in that redemption was completed, in that sin was put away, in that He is now free to manifest His mercy to sinners. The Son was glorified, for the Father would raise Him from the dead, the Father would glorify Him with His own glory, and the Father would give Him a name that is above every name.

The Father is glorified through the work of His Son. The Son is glorified because the Father exalted Him and has given Him a name above every name. We have this in Romans 3:25-26, where Paul speaks of Christ, "Whom God hath set forth to be a propitiation through faith in his blood, to declare his righteousness for the remission of sins that are past, through the forbearance of God; To declare, I say, at this time his righteousness: that he might be just, and the justifier of him which believeth in Jesus." I suggest for your further study Philippians 2:6-13.

13:33. *Little children, yet a little while I am with you. Ye shall seek me: and as I said unto the Jews, Whither I go, ye cannot come; so now I say to you.*

This is the only time our Lord called His disciples "little children." It is like a mother taking her little children around her and saying, "Little children, I have you all to myself now. The traitor has gone out, and here we are. I love you and you love me. Here we are, my little children, all together. I have some things to say to you personally now." You can just see the heart of Christ being poured out when Judas left.

Now there was a difference between what He said to the Jews in chapter 8 and what He said to the disciples here. In John 8:21 He told the Jews, "I go my way and you shall seek me, and shall die in your sins: whither I go, ye cannot come." (Compare 7:34.) But here Jesus is saying to His disciples, "Where I'm going you can't come now. But you will come afterwards."

The Badge of True Discipleship (13:34-35)

While Jesus was gone, the disciples were to manifest themselves to the world. Notice the commandment He gave them.

13:34-35. *A new commandment I give unto you, That ye love one another; as I have loved you, that ye also love one another. By this shall all men know that ye are my disciples, if ye have love one to another.*

The Lord doesn't criticize us. He loves us. He knows our frailty. He remembers we are dust. And oh, how compassionate, how tender He is with us in our frailty. It is when we get stiff-necked that the Lord puts out His hand in chastisement. A mother doesn't spank her child when he is weak or stumbles, only when he gets self-willed and wants his own way.

Jesus evidenced His love by sacrifice. And as 1 John 3:14-16 says, we will manifest our love for the brethren by sacrifice. Love is not evident only by service or by holding to true doctrine, but by sacrifice. This is a sad thing today among evangelicals; for we hold true doctrine and we're eager and zealous for service, but we manifest no love. "By this shall all men know that ye are my disciples, if ye have love one for another." The badge of discipleship is love.

Are you His disciple? Judas revealed what he was. He went out. He had no love. He was not a real disciple.

There are three measurements of a disciple. We had the first in chapter 8. "If ye continue in my word, then are ye my disciples indeed; And ye shall know the truth, and the truth shall make you free" (8:31-32). The second measurement is here. "By this shall all men know that ye are my disciples, if ye have love one to another." Remember, "love suffereth long, and is kind" (1 Corinthians 13:4). The third measurement of discipleship is in chapter 15. "Herein is my Father glorified, that ye bear much fruit; so shall ye be my disciples" (15:8).

God grant that we Christians, we who love Him, we who have been redeemed by His precious blood, may wear the badge of discipleship. It is genuine love one for another and especially with frail, stumbling believers.

My friend, this rules out all divisions. It rules out all bitterness and jealousy and envy among God's people. It rules out all pettiness and smallness and shallowness. How much are we to love each other? As Christ loves us. This is the measure of it.

Let us manifest love. May this be evident in our daily walk and conversation as the people of God.

13:36-38. *See pages 264-265.*

John 14

Christ, The Coming One

Introduction to John 14

In this portion we have the Lord answering the questions of His disciples. He reveals more about Himself, more about His return, and more about the indwelling Spirit whom He wants to give them. All this takes place after Judas has gone out. In a few hours another one of His disciples is going to deny Him, and all the rest are going to forsake Him and flee. And yet the Lord takes the time to comfort these perplexed disciples concerning the future.

I want you to see something of the tenderness, the compassion, the love, and the yearning heart our Savior has for these eleven men. Remember that you have now come into the same relationship, under the same care, into the same place in His heart as they did.

Life is full of tests and trials, afflictions and sorrows, as well as blessings. The Lord permits these things to come into our lives because He wants to wean us away from transient things and to fix our hearts on eternal verities. In these chapters, from 14 through 17, we have remarkable revelations of what God has in store for us. He has made provision for His disciples, and for you and me, to help us cope with tests and trials in a world that has no place for Him.

We are living in the same world as these disciples. We go through the same tests and trials of life they did. Our circumstances may be a little different, but the tests are there. The flesh is weak and frail, and we often stumble along. But He understands and has made marvelous provision for us. How glad I am that He has given assurance of the acceptance of every one of His children assured.

The disciples raise four questions. The first question is asked by Peter: "Lord, where are You going?" The second question is asked by Thomas: "Lord, how can we know the way?" The third is asked by Philip: "Won't You show us the Father?" And the fourth question is asked by Judas (not Iscariot): "How can You show Yourself to us and not to the world?"

How glad I am that the disciples interrupted the Lord here, for their questions brought out even more wonderful revelations.

Question 1: "Lord, Where are You Going?" (13:36-14:3)

Now this first question began in chapter 13.

> **13:36-14:3.** *Simon Peter said unto him, Lord, whither goest thou? Jesus answered him, Whither I go, thou canst not follow me now; but thou shalt follow me afterwards. Peter said unto him, Lord, why cannot I follow thee now? I will lay down my life for thy sake. Jesus answered him, Wilt thou lay down thy life for my sake? Verily, verily, I say unto thee, The cock shall not crow, till thou hast denied me thrice. Let not your heart be troubled: ye believe in God, believe also in me. In my Father's house are many mansions: if it were not so, I would have told you. I go to prepare a place for you. And if I go and prepare a place for you, I will come again, and receive you unto myself; that where I am, there ye may be also.*

This question of Peter's arose out of the discussion they had been having in verse 33. This dear man, Peter, how he blurts things out. You can never question Peter's love for the Savior. But I question his knowledge of spiritual things. A person can love the Savior and be zealous for God, and yet be ignorant of spiritual realities.

"Where are You going?"

"Well, where I'm going you will come afterwards, Peter."

"Why can't I go with You now? I've been three and a half years with You, Lord. I gave up my boat. I gave up my fishing. I've followed You these years and You're on my heart. You're my Master and my Lord. Why can't I go with You now?"

"You will come afterwards."

"Lord, I'm willing to die for You."

"Yes, I believe that, Peter, but I want to inform you that before this night is over, before the cock crows, that somewhere between two and three o'clock in the morning, you're going to deny Me three times."

No wonder these men were perplexed. Jesus had just said, "One of you is going to betray Me." And Judas went out. Now He says, "One of you is going to deny Me."

But then He said these gracious words: "Let not your heart be troubled: ye believe in God, believe also in me." The balm for heart trouble is a constant faith in Him. Jesus was saying, "You're believing in God whom you haven't seen. Now believe in Me, because I'm going to be unseen as well. I'm going to leave you. And just as you have faith in God, have faith in Me, for I am God. Have faith in Me."

I've been reading a book by a medical doctor who says that one of the greatest death-dealing foes we have is the heart. A great percentage of those who die of heart trouble would not have died if they were living in peace. Isaiah says, "Thou wilt keep him in perfect peace, whose mind is stayed on thee" (26:3). There is no question that strains and stress undermine the heart. But our Lord is giving us something here that is good for the body and good for the soul in times of need and sorrow and affliction.

"Let not your heart be troubled. You have put your trust in God. Put your trust in Me." Nothing delights the heart of God more than to have His people on earth living the life of faith, a life of daily trust in Him whatever the circumstances.

In a few short hours He is going to give His back to the smiters, and His cheeks to those who will pluck out His beard. He's going to be scourged and hung on a cross as a malefactor. And yet He talks to these disciples about peace and rest. That means He Himself is at perfect peace and rest even in the midst of what is coming upon Him.

If you and I knew that within a few hours we were going to suffer, we would be all torn up inside. But not Jesus. He takes the time to say to these men, "Don't be troubled. Let not your heart be troubled. You believe in God; believe also in Me." Oh, what tenderness, what love, what compassion our Savior manifests!

In Genesis, God prepared a garden, but man ruined it. Christ has gone home to prepare a place for us that man will never ruin. He created Eden with a word. He has been spending nearly two thousand years preparing a place for us. And now He is preparing us for that place!

Down through the centuries these first three verses of chapter 14 have been a tremendous comfort and strength and hope to God's people under all circumstances. Don't be troubled, they say. Don't be perplexed. Don't feel hopeless. We are just in school down here for a few years being trained by God for eternity. This life is just a fleeting shadow, in preparation for what He has up there.

And there is going to be a reception committee waiting for us. We're not unknown in heaven. If you are a Christian down here with few friends, if you feel lonely, may I tell you this? There will be a reception committee waiting for you when you get there. It is home.

Isn't it a wonderful relief for you when you leave your office or your shop or your store or whatever you're doing, and you get home? You can kick your shoes off and put your slippers on and just sit down.

"Oh boy, I'm home!" This is the place where you are guarded. This is the place of love. This is the place where you're loved for yourself. This is the place of peace, permanency, and restfulness. This is home. You might be as ornery as anyone else, but you're loved just the same when you get home.

My friends, that's what it will be like when He takes us to the place He has prepared for us.

Someone asked me, "Well, Mr. Mitchell, do you think they'll let me in?"

"Well," I said, "even if Michael the Archangel were to stand at the door of glory and say, 'Mitchell, you can't come in here,' I'll just push him to one side and say, 'Get out of my way. I'm the man Christ died for. I'm coming home.' " Heaven isn't a strange place to me. I'm not going there as a stranger. I'm going home as the son of One who is God.

Like dear Job years ago, I can say, "I know that my redeemer lives, and that I'm going to see Him face to face. And when I see Him, I won't be a stranger to Him, and He won't be a stranger to me" (see Job 19:25-27). I'm not surprised the apostle Paul could say, "I am in a strait betwixt two, having a desire to depart, and to be with Christ; which is far better" (Philippians 1:23). It's home!

Will you mark something else? He is not only preparing a place, but He is preparing a people. Men were made for the earth. I was born on the earth and I belong to the earth, physically. The day came when I became a child of the living God, and then I belonged to heaven. This is something new in the economy of God. It must be a tremendous thing for angelic beings to find people from the earth being received in glory as the children of the eternal God. He is preparing a people for that place.

"Oh," you say, "I thought I was prepared the moment I was saved."

Yes, you received eternal life. You came into right relationship with Him when you accepted the Savior. There's no question about that. If you're just a babe in Christ, you're going to go home to glory. Whether you have much faith or little faith, whether you're mature or immature, whether you are strong or weak, every believer is going to be there. But there will be differences of position in the sense of service and ministry. Some will be crowned and some will not be crowned. Suffice it to say, God today is preparing a people for that place.

But the important thing is not heaven. The important thing is being with Him. "And if I go and prepare a place for you, I will come again, and receive you unto myself; that where I am, there ye may be also." The call is not to a place; the call is to a Person. "Heaven is my Father's house. I'm going to be there," Jesus is saying. "And you're coming to be with Me."

The disciples were sad this night. They were sad at the cross. They were sad at the empty tomb. But after He for forty days instructed them, they saw their Master go to heaven. And while they were looking up, there came two men in white apparel who said, "Ye men of Galilee, why stand ye gazing up into heaven? this same Jesus, which is taken up from you into heaven, shall so come in like manner as ye have seen him go into heaven" (Acts 1:11). They went back to Jerusalem rejoicing with great joy.

And I am sure that the early disciples lived every day in the anticipation of the return of the One whom they loved. What a tragedy it is today that what we hold as a doctrine (the coming of the Lord), the early church believed as a reality.

It is easy to become so occupied here that we miss the vision of His soon return. An angel will not come for us. An angel did not die for us. The Lord Himself stands at the door. If you want to follow this wonderful truth through, I would remind you of 1 Thessalonians 4:13-17; Hebrews 10:37; and 2 Corinthians 5:1. And remember, Psalm 16:11 tells that in His presence is fullness of joy.

Question 2: "Lord, How Can We Know the Way?" (14:4-7)

Jesus continues to answer Peter. **14:4.** *And whither I go ye know, and the way ye know.* Then Thomas injects himself. **14.5.** *Thomas saith unto him, Lord, we know not whither thou goest; and how can we know the way?* In other words Thomas was saying, "Lord, if we don't know the destination, how can we know the way?"

The disciples never understood when the Lord Jesus talked of eternity. They didn't see beyond the material kingdom. When Thomas uttered the second question, it evoked this wonderful answer. **14:6-7.** *Jesus saith unto him, I am the way, the truth, and the life: no man cometh unto the Father, but by me. If ye had known me, ye should have known my Father also: and from henceforth ye know him, and have seen him.*

Jesus Christ did not say, "I am a way-shower." Not only the cults, but also some who profess to be real Christians in theological circles are declaring that Christ was a "way-shower," just as you and I are way-showers. But Jesus said of Himself, "I am the way."

This is another one of our Lord's tremendous statements. In chapter 4 He is the water of life. In chapter 5 He is the great Judge who has all resurrection and all life and judgment in His hands. In chapter 6 He said, "I am the bread of life. I am the One who can satisfy you. The life I give is a satisfying life. It's resurrection life, eternal life, indwelling life." In chapter 7 He said, "I am the One who will send the Spirit of God upon you." In chapter 8 He said, "I am the light of the world." In chapter 10 He said, "I am the good shepherd." In chapter 11 He said, "I am the resurrection and the life." Here in chapter 14 He says, "I am the way. . . ."

No mere man would say things like this. This is God speaking. "Neither is there salvation in any other: for there is none other name under heaven given among men, whereby we must be saved" (Acts 4:12).

God is going to have a people in heaven without sin. He is a holy God. He is a righteous God. And He has made the provision for us to get there. He says, "I have eternal life to give." He says, "I'm here to save." He says, "I'm going to have a people in heaven, but this is My way." And God has the right to say what that way is, since He is going to do the saving.

Our way is described in Proverbs 14:12, where we read, "There is a way which seemeth right unto a man, but the end thereof are the ways of death." But Jesus said, "I am the way to the Father." His way is the way to life.

He is not only the way, but He is also the truth. In Colossians 2:3

we read that God has hidden in Him "all the treasures of wisdom and knowledge." Do you want the truth? You will find it in Him.

And He is the life. He is the water of life. He is eternal life. "He that hath the Son hath life; and he that hath not the Son of God hath not life" (1 John 5:12).

He is the way that brings us to God. He is the truth that sets men free. And He is the life that brings men into fellowship with God. In John 17:3 Jesus says, "This is life eternal, that they might know thee the only true God, and Jesus Christ, whom thou hast sent."

Question 3: "Lord, Won't You Show Us the Father?" (14:8-20)

See the Father in the Son (14:8-11)

Jesus said, "If ye had known me, ye should have known my Father also: and from henceforth ye know him, and have seen him." This leads us to the next question, which Philip asked.

> **14:8-9.** *Philip saith unto him, Lord, shew us the Father, and it sufficeth us. Jesus saith unto him, Have I been so long time with you, and yet hast thou not known me, Philip? he that hath seen me hath seen the Father; and how sayest thou then, Shew us the Father?*

Jesus was saying, "Philip, don't you know who I am?"

Of course, the disciples knew more than the Jews did. Peter had said, "Thou art the Christ, the Son of the living God" (Matthew 16:16). But how slow they were to lay hold of the wonderful truth concerning His person. And how slow we are. Some Christians have been on the way for forty and fifty years, and yet know so little of our precious Lord and the wonderful life we have in Him.

"Show us the Father."

This request of Philip's has been the cry of thousands of people through the centuries. Moses said to God, "Shew me thy glory" (Exodus 33:18). This is the yearning of the human heart. We yearn for something that is real, something that is eternal, something that will really satisfy us.

"Show us the Father."

"Have I been so long time with you, and yet hast thou not known me, Philip?" I think this is a mild rebuke to Philip. He was one of the early disciples. "Don't *you* know Me, Philip?"

Then the Lord gives us the marvelous revelation that the Father is seen in Himself.

14:10-11. *Believest thou not that I am in the Father, and the Father in me? the words that I speak unto you I speak not of myself: but the Father that dwelleth in me, he doeth the works. Believe me that I am in the Father, and the Father in me: or else believe me for the very works' sake.*

What does He mean?

"I am so one with the Father that the words He has are My words, and the words that I speak are My Father's words." We had it again in John 5, where Jesus says, "What I see the Father do, that I do likewise. For as the Father has the authority and the power to raise the dead, and make them alive, so I have the same authority and power to raise the dead and make them alive."

The authority He has and the power He has are equal to His Father's. Throughout the Gospel of John the teaching of our Savior is far more remarkable and far more supernatural than the physical works that He performed. I think sometimes we forget that. Though John does give us seven signs to prove Christ's deity, the astounding thing is not the miracles. His words are the claims of One who is God. They are just as supernatural, just as real, just as divine as the words of the Father. All His statements, all His miracles, all His life reveal the Father.

All that we know of the Father is what we know of Jesus Christ. What I know of Jesus Christ is what I know of God. When you introduce people to Jesus Christ, you are bringing them face to face with God. We Christians fail to realize this.

The apostle Paul speaks of Jesus Christ as "the image of the invisible God" (Colossians 1:15). In Hebrews 1:2-3 He is the "heir of all things, by whom also he made the worlds; who (is) the brightness of his glory, and the express image of his person." I repeat it: all I know of the Father is what I know of Jesus Christ. To see Jesus is to see God. The more we know Christ, the more we know God.

John 1:18 says, "No man hath seen God at any time; the only begotten Son, which is in the bosom of the Father, he hath declared him." "No man hath seen God at any time," but Adam and Eve saw Jesus in the Garden. With whom did Enoch walk? With whom did Noah talk? Whom did Moses see? Whom did Isaiah behold?

They saw "the only begotten Son, which is in the bosom of the Father." Jesus has declared Him.

The God of glory appeared unto Abraham, who "rejoiced to see my day" (John 8:56). In the first chapter of Revelation, Jesus said, "I am the Alpha and Omega, the beginning and the ending, saith the Lord, which is, and which was, and which is to come, the Almighty" (1:8). Jesus declared that He was "the Almighty." This is the very name that was used for the revelation of God to Abraham in Genesis 17. God told Abraham, "I am the El Shaddai, the Almighty."

How is the Father made known? He is made known through the words and works of His Son.

See the Father in Believers (14:12-14)

The second revelation is that the Father is also made known through the believer in His words and in His works.

> **14:12-14.** *Verily, verily, I say unto you, He that believeth on me, the works that I do shall he do also; and greater works than these shall he do; because I go unto my Father. And whatsoever ye shall ask in my name, that will I do, that the Father may be glorified in the Son. If ye shall ask any thing in my name, I will do it.*

Now verse 12 has been used by some who believe that we should always be performing miracles. But are you doing the works He did? Do you feed the hungry?

"Oh," you say, "we go down and buy food for the hungry. We bought enough bread this month to feed five thousand." But He took five loaves and two fish and fed the multitudes.

Do you still the storm when the wind blows outside? You run for cover. But He stilled the storm. You may use the wind (as with an airplane), but you can't control it. He said, "Be muzzled," to the wind, and it was muzzled. He said to the storm, "Peace," and it ceased raging.

Jesus said to the dead, "Arise," and they rose. He said to the lepers, "Be thou clean," and they were whole. He said to the palsied, "Take up your bed and walk," and they stood up. He said to the blind men, "Receive your sight," and they could see.

I mention this for a reason. I have had in my ministry men who come to me and say, "You don't believe your Bible. You don't believe the miraculous." I certainly do. I don't believe the day of miracles is past by any means. We see them right along. The day of miracles is still here, but do you do the works He did?

Now, you may answer me by saying, "Well, He doesn't mean every individual will perform spectacular miracles." But that's kind of backing down, isn't it? In the book of Acts and in Hebrews 2:3-4 we read that God confirmed the message of the apostles by miracles and wonders and signs. But it is not God's purpose to keep on performing physical miracles. Christ performed them at specified times for a purpose in both the Old and New Testaments. He used them to free Israel from Egypt and to lead them through the wilderness. He closed the heavens and it rained not in Elijah's day for three and a half years. He miraculously took care of Elijah, using the ravens and then the widow. Following him, Elisha performed twice the number of miracles Elijah did.

In our Lord's day, the nation was in apostasy and declension, led by a priesthood that didn't believe in the supernatural. The Lord performed miracles to open their eyes to His fulfillment of Isaiah's prophecies. Isaiah wrote that when the Messiah comes, "Then the eyes of the blind shall be opened, and the ears of the deaf shall be unstopped. Then shall the lame man leap as an hart, and the tongue of the dumb sing" (35:5-6). These miracles carried over into the book of Acts and then ceased.

I would not for one moment exclude the fact that the Lord responds to individual faith. But by and large, the miracles passed on with the apostles. They raised the dead. They cast out demons. They healed the sick. But I believe the spiritual miracles of transforming men who are dead in sin and making them eternally alive in Christ is a far greater miracle than the resurrection of Lazarus from the tomb. Through the centuries multitudes of people have been taken out of the slavery of sin, out from under the bondage of death, and have been fitted to spend eternal glory with God.

How, then, will we do greater works than our Savior did when He walked among men?

"If ye shall ask anything in my name, I will do it." Now, don't take this prayer promise out of its context. Jesus is dealing with the revelation of the Father. When men were walking the earth in our Lord's day, if they had wanted to see God the Father, they would have seen Him through Jesus Christ His Son. Today He is seen by the words and works of His people.

Someone has written a piece that ends, "What is the Bible according to *you*?" People today are not reading their Bibles. They don't believe the Bible. They only know about the living God through you and me. That is why Jesus tells us, "If ye shall ask anything in my name, I will do it."

And don't tell me that the Lord just writes out a check and signs it and leaves it for you to fill in the blank for how much you want. That sounds very nice. But every prayer promise in your Bible has something attached to it. Here He is talking about the revelation of the Father in His people. The reason for the greater works is because Christ goes to be with His Father, giving us access into the very presence of God that these greater works may be done.

My friend, that's a tremendous promise. Is the yearning of your heart that God will be revealed through you and me by our word, our attitude, and our actions? How can I live in a world like this one? How can I work down there in the office, down there in the shop, or live among my neighbors, when all around I see things that are godless, unrighteous, unholy? You hear and see ungodly things all day long. How in the world can a man live for God in a world like this? "Whatsoever ye shall ask in my name, that will I do, that the Father may be glorified in the Son."

The great passion of the Son is the glorification of the Father through the Son. We had it in chapters 11, 12, 13, and you have it now in chapter 14. You will have it again in chapters 16 and 17. And He wants to be glorified through you and through me.

How is He going to do it? By my words. By my actions. By my attitude to people.

"But I feel so weak," you say. "I feel so frail."

"All right," He says, "I'll give you something. Whatever you ask Me, I will do it." Could I be a little blunt and ask you a question? Honestly now, do you want to live that He might be glorified? Do you want to so live that the eternal God will be revealed through you? Do you want your family to see God in you? Do you want your neighbors to see God in you? How can it be? The unsearchable resource for the Christian is to be able to come at any time under any circumstance into the very presence of God and to speak boldly and reverently to Him, "Father, this is what I want."

The Lord Jesus said, "I will do it, if it is for the glorification of My Father." This gives you assurance and certainty. Paul speaks of it in Ephesians 3:12, where he says that in Christ "we have boldness and access with confidence by the faith of him."

My, how we live like paupers when we ought to live like children of the King. We are rich in faith and in power, rich in peace and in joy because of our certainty. The Father has put all authority in the hands of the Son. The yearning of the Son is that the Father by glorified. Whenever you ask for that, He will give it to you. It is just that simple. But the trouble is that a great deal of our praying is asking for ourselves. God wants you to ask largely, but for the purpose of glorifying Him.

See the Father through the Spirit (14:15-20)

In verse 15 through 20 John gives us the marvelous revelation of the indwelling Spirit.

> **14:15-19.** *If ye love me, keep my commandments. And I will pray the Father, and he shall give you another Comforter, that he may abide with you for ever. Even the Spirit of truth; whom the world cannot receive, because it seeth him not, neither knoweth him: but ye know him; for he dwelleth with you, and shall be in you. I will not leave you comfortless: I will come to you. Yet a little while, and the world seeth me no more; but ye see me: because I live, ye shall live also.*

I love the tenderness of our Savior here. You remember in chapter 13 in verse 33 He could say, "Little children, yet a little while I am with you." Jesus wouldn't leave them orphans. Instead He says, "I will pray the Father and He will give you another Comforter, another Advocate. He will not give you a different One, but another like Myself, One equal with Myself, not someone who is a servant under Me. Just as the Son is equal with the Father, so the Spirit of God is equal with the Son. I will not leave you orphans."

It was to the advantage of believers that the Lord should leave them. The Son prays, the Father sends, and the Spirit comforts. Who is this Comforter? The One who will "abide with you for ever."

May I point out something? We have two Advocates—One in heaven pleading my cause at the throne and One in me who pleads my cause and His cause. Compare Romans 8:26-27. The Spirit of God reveals to us the very deep things of God. It is the Spirit of God indwelling the believer that makes a tremendous difference between the Christian and the non-Christian. He is the Spirit of truth whom the world cannot receive.

14:20. *At that day ye shall know that I am in my Father, and ye in me, and I in you.*

This union is absolutely indissoluble. Just as the Father and the Son are united forever, so is the believer with the Son. We have been united forever, the one to the other.

The world knows nothing of this. It is something different from all the religions of the world. The moment you and I in simple faith took the Lord Jesus Christ as Savior, that very moment we were not only redeemed and forgiven and given life eternal, but we came into a union with the Son of God comparable to that of the Father and the Son.

There could be no spirituality, no power, no salvation apart from this marvelous union. We share His resources in prayer. He indwells us by the Spirit. He gives us life eternal. We have union with Him.

The Christian life is a supernatural life. The Spirit indwells us. Our actions, attitudes, and words ought to reveal God to this world, but we can only reveal God as we yield ourselves to Him.

Let us not be too hard on these disciples. They had gone far beyond the men of their generation. But let us search our own hearts. Do we read the Word as we should? How can we know the truth unless we read it? How can we obey it unless we know it? We can't be disciples unless we are obedient.

Question 4: "How Will You Manifest Yourself to Us and Not to the World?" (14:21-31)

I Will Manifest Myself to the Obedient (14:21-23)

14:21-23. *He that hath my commandments, and keepeth them, he it is that loveth me: and he that loveth me shall be loved of my Father, and I will love him, and will manifest myself to him. Judas saith unto him, not Iscariot, Lord, how is it that thou wilt mani-*

fest thyself unto us, and not unto the world? Jesus an-
swered and said unto him, If a man love me, he will
keep my words: and my Father will love him, and we
will come unto him, and make our abode with him.

May I suggest several answers to Judas's question? First, Jesus said, "If you love Me, keep My commandments. He who has My commandments, and keeps them, he it is who loves Me. If a man loves Me, he will keep My words." We have this in verses 15, 21, and 23. Obedience and love cannot be separated. I say, Jesus will only manifest Himself to His true disciples.

What is the measure of your love for Christ? It is measured by your obedience to His Word. Obedience is the true test of love. If I say I love the Savior and you see in my life nothing but disobedience, then I'm only mouthing words.

We go to Bible conferences, New Life conferences, Keswick conferences, spiritual conferences. We have all kinds of doctrines concerning the spiritual life, and how to get it, and how to maintain it. But if you analyze it and bring it right down to the basic facts, the key is obedience.

You say, "But, Mr. Mitchell, don't you believe in discipleship?"

Yes, but the key of discipleship is obedience. The foundation of spiritual power and spiritual experience is obedience.

My friend, I don't care what ecstatic experiences you may have. They may be wonderful. They may fill you with joy and blessing. You may be in the third heaven. But if it is not the fruitage of a life of obedience, it is nothing but a fleshly, ecstatic thing.

Second, notice something else in verses 21 and 23. Jesus says, "And he that loves Me shall be loved by My Father. My Father will love him."

You say, "But, Mr. Mitchell, doesn't the Lord love us even before we are saved? Doesn't the apostle John say in 1 John 4:19 that, 'We love him, because he first loved us'? But here it says that if we prove our love by our obedience, He will love us. Why?"

This is an added love, a special love to those who are obedient.

And with it comes a revelation of His person (verse 21) and the intimacy of His fellowship (verse 23). Why do Christians know so little about Him? Why doesn't the Lord manifest Himself more? Because we are not obedient. Why don't we have more fellowship with the living God? Because we are not obedient.

May I remind you of 1 John chapter 1? In the first verse we have the apostle's great experience: "we saw Him, we heard Him, we handled Him who is the Word of life." In verse 2 he repeats this. Then in verse 3 he says his great desire is that "ye may have fellowship with us, and truly our fellowship is with the Father, and with his Son Jesus Christ." Fellowship with the Father and the Son should be the very hunger of our hearts.

Mel Trotter started the Union Gospel Mission in Grand Rapids, Michigan. The Lord saved him out of a life of sin in Chicago at a mission. He became a mighty testimony for God.

One day a man said to him, "Look here, Trotter, you've been talking to me about your God. How do you know He lives? Have you seen Him?"

"No," said Mel.

"Have you heard Him?"

"No."

"How do you know He lives."

"Why," he said, "that's very easy. I was just talking to the Lord five minutes ago."

Now the world doesn't understand that. How can the world not see Him? Judas says, "How can you make yourself known to us, and not to the world?" This is something of which the man out of Christ knows absolutely nothing. He may have all the degrees of a university after his name, but if he is out of Christ, he is totally ignorant of what I'm talking about. It is not for the world. As we are obedient, He manifests Himself to us (verse 21). And we experience His fellowship (verse 23).

I will Manifest Myself through the Spirit (14:24-28)

14:24-26. *He that loveth me not keepeth not my sayings: and the word which ye hear is not mine, but the Father's which sent me. These things have I spoken unto you, being yet present with you. But the Comforter, which is the Holy Ghost, whom the Father will send in my name, he shall teach you all things, and bring all things to your remembrance, whatsoever I have said unto you.*

Jesus promises to give the Holy Spirit to the disciples. We have the fulfillment of this in Acts 2. After the Spirit of God came to indwell His people on the day of Pentecost, dear Peter stood and said, "Ye men of Israel, hear these words; Jesus of Nazareth, a man approved of God among you by miracles and wonders and signs, which God did by him in the midst of you, as ye yourselves also know . . ." (Acts 2:22). The Lord had just revealed to him the wonders of His grace. Here is an ignorant fisherman, and his message in Acts 2 is a wonderful sample of real homiletical teaching.

Not only did Jesus promise to give the Holy Spirit to the disciples, but He also promised them His peace and joy. **14:27.** *Peace I leave with you, my peace I give unto you: not as the world giveth, give I unto you. Let not your heart be troubled, neither let it be afraid.*

The Lord is in the shadow of the cross. The disciples are greatly troubled. How can He comfort their hearts? He says, "Peace I leave with you."

Follow through the Scriptures on this question of peace. The very first words the Savior said to the disciples after the resurrection were, "Peace be unto you" (John 20:19). The first experience of a sinner coming to find the Savior is having "peace with God through our Lord Jesus Christ" (Romans 5:1). In Colossians 1:20 He made "peace through the blood of his cross." In Ephesians 2:14-17 we find that the Lord is our peace. He made peace for us. He preached peace unto us. You see, the thing that God wants to give men is peace.

In John 16:33 we read, "These things I have spoken unto you, that in me ye might have peace." Paul says, "And the peace of God, which passeth all understanding, shall guard your hearts and minds through Christ Jesus" (Philippians 4:7). And Isaiah wrote, "The work of righteousness shall be peace" (32:17).

You and I are living in a generation that has never known peace. It is absolutely impossible for the world to give you peace. I say that dogmatically. The world can give you wealth, pleasures, honor. But one thing the world cannot give you is peace.

Mark the next verse.

14:28. *Ye have heard how I said unto you, I go away, and come again unto you. If ye loved me, ye would rejoice, because I said, I go unto the Father: for my Father is greater than I.*

"My Father is greater than I." Isn't Christ equal with the Father? As a Man in the midst of men, He took the place of subservience to the Father. He is speaking here as a man. When He went back into glory and took His position of equality with the Father back again, He was given a name above every name.

But these disciples know nothing of what is beyond death. The Lord says, "I have just told you that in My Father's house are many mansions. And I'm giving you My peace no matter what the circumstances of life may be. But now I'm going to leave and I'm going to My Father. Oh, if you only knew what that meant. Then you would be filled with joy because I said I'm going to My Father."

You know, I wish I could put into words the way I feel about this. If we could only get a glimpse of what is on the other side. In the presence of the Father there is the glory of an omnipotent God. There are no more tests or trials; there is no more sickness, sorrow, death, or slavery; there are no more misunderstandings or afflictions. Instead, there is perfect love, perfect joy, perfect peace, perfect fellowship in the presence of the eternal God. If you only knew this, you would be filled with joy.

You remember that when the Lord was ascended into heaven, the disciples went back into the city with exceeding great joy. They didn't go back with their heads down, saying, "We've lost our Lord." They went back with great joy. You have this in Mark 16, Luke 24, and Acts 1.

Here in John 14, Jesus gave the disciples a little glimpse of that joy. "Not only will I give you My peace, but if you knew what was on the other side, you would be filled with joy. You would rejoice because I said, 'I go to My Father.' "

I Will Manifest Myself in Spite of Satan (14:29-31)

14:29-31. *And now I have told you before it come to pass, that, when it is come to pass, ye might believe. Hereafter I will not talk much with you: for the prince of this world cometh, and hath nothing in me. But that the world may know that I love the Father; and as the Father gave me commandment, even so I do. Arise, let us go hence.*

"The prince of this world cometh." Remember, when Jesus is saying this, Judas has bargained with the priests. In fact, while He is in the upper room, they are gathering Roman soldiers and the rabble to hunt for Jesus. That same night He is going to be scourged and then crucified. He didn't say, "The Roman soldiers are coming." He didn't say, "Judas and the priests are coming." He said, "The prince of this world cometh." It is Satan's last opportunity to find something in Him.

"He comes, and he is going to find nothing in Me." Jesus Christ is the only member of the human race in whom Satan could find nothing to which he could appeal. Jesus could say, "I'm absolutely obedient to My Father. If it means the cross, then I go to the cross. If it means death and the grave, I'll go through that. Satan finds nothing in Me. He finds no trace of rebellion, of sin, of disobedience in Me."

Satan found it in Adam and Eve in the Garden. He found it in

Abraham. He found it in Moses and in David and in all those great prophets. And down through the centuries Satan has found it in God's great men. There is only one Person in the human race of whom it can be said that Satan has nothing in Him.

My friend, if there had been something in Him to which Satan could have appealed, we would not have had a Savior. He was absolutely sinless and righteous and perfect. That's why He could die for you and for me.

"I love the Father; and as the Father gave me commandment, even so I do." We have Jesus' complete submission to His Father. His obedience revealed how He loved the Father. Have you noticed that in John 14? He mentions the Father twenty-three times. There is no chapter in the whole Bible that is as full of this relationship between the Son and the Father. All His words, all His works, all His motives, all His desires were His Father's. His complete union with His Father brought forth complete obedience.

As I've read and reread this passage, I've tried in my own heart to comprehend this amazing relationship between the Father and the Son. It is beyond the ken of men. If the Lord tarries another thousand years, and preachers and students study the Word of God, they will never begin to plumb the depths of this chapter. Oh, how the Lord loved the Father. Oh, this bond of union, of love, of obedience, of submission to His Father.

How much do we love Him? How can I measure my love? What is its true test?

It is my obedience to His Word. May the Lord in all things be preeminent in our lives. May we live a life of submission, a life of obedience to Him.

John 15

Christ, The Vine

Background of John 15

The last chapter ended as Jesus said, "Arise, let us go hence." I take it the Lord and His disciples left the upper room on their way down to the Garden of Gethsemane. Some believe it was as they passed the temple and saw the golden vine on the doors that the Lord was prompted to give the eleven an object lesson from the vine. Or it may have been sparked by a vineyard outside the gates of the city, or by a decoration in the room where they ate. Who knows? Personally, I believe He went to the Garden of Gethsemane by way of a vineyard outside the city.

As Jews, the disciples were familiar with the vine. In the Old Testament Israel was often called the unfruitful vine. Let me suggest for your study Psalm 80, Isaiah 5 and 27, Jeremiah 2, Ezekiel 15 and 19, and then Hosea 10. You can't read your Old Testament without recognizing that God looked upon Israel as a vine. Psalm 80 speaks of the fact that the Lord brought a vine out of Egypt and planted it in Canaan. He took care of it Himself, and it flourished. Then Israel rebelled against the Lord. And when He went to look for fruit and couldn't find the right kind, He pushed the vine to one side. Jesus uses this illustration in John 15 to speak prophetically of the fact that God was going to put Israel to one side and find His fruitage elsewhere.

Life in Union with the Vine (15:1-14)

15:1. *I am the true vine, and my Father is the hus-*
bandman.

Here the Lord is pictured as the true vine of God, and the Father is the husbandman, the One who cares for the vine. There were husbandmen before Jesus' parables, however, who didn't do their job. In the parable of the husbandmen and the vineyard in Matthew 21, the husbandmen beat the servants that the owner sent, and some they slew. Finally He said, "I will send my son. They will reverence my son." But when the son came, they said, "This is the heir. Let us take him and kill him."

The Lord said, "What shall the owner of the vineyard do to those husbandmen who slew his son? He will cast them out and give his vineyard to someone else."

As the husbandman, the Father is not going to trust the vine and branches to anyone else. He's not trusting it to any church leadership. He's not trusting it to angelic beings. The Father Himself is personally interested that every branch bear fruit. He is going to prune the vine. He is going to cleanse the vine. He is going to get much fruit from it.

And we are the ones who bear the fruit. We are the branches. Of course, the branches do not produce the fruit. They hold it up. We are in union with Him, and the manifestation of that union is fruit bearing. Each branch is part of the vine. It is not the vine. The branch's life is in the vine. And we, being in the vine, are to hold up the fruit. There must be union before there can be fruit. The great theme of this portion is this question of fruit bearing.

Notice that there are two kinds of branches mentioned in verse 2.
15:2. *Every branch in me that beareth not fruit he taketh away:*
and every branch that beareth fruit, he purgeth it, that it may
bring forth more fruit. There is a branch that is not bearing fruit,
and there is a branch that bears fruit.

Many expositors believe verse 2 means the Lord takes the branch away in judgment. I do not accept this. Now, as I have said before, there is no question but that the New Testament teaches that Christian can die before their job is done. They are taken home in discipline. You have this with Ananias and Sapphira in Acts 5, and with the young man in 1 Corinthians 5. You have it in 1 John 5:16. And then you have 1 Corinthians 11:30, where Paul says, "For this cause many are weak and sickly among you, and many sleep." But I do not believe this is what our Lord has reference to here. The theme of this discourse is fruit bearing that is dependent upon abiding.

"Every branch in me that beareth not fruit he taketh away." The primary meaning of the Greek here is "to raise up," not "to take away." Verse two should read this way: "Every branch in Me that does not bear fruit He raises up." What is the purpose of the husbandman? He goes through the vineyard looking for fruit. But here is a branch on the ground, not bearing any fruit. What does he do? Cut it off? No. He raises it up, so the sun can shine upon it, and the air can get to it. Then it will bear fruit.

Some Christians don't bear fruit. What's the matter with them? They need to have the Son shining on them. When a believer is out of fellowship with God and is occupied with the things of the world, he is not bearing fruit. The husbandman must come along and lift the branch, raising it up and bringing the individual believer back into fellowship in order that he or she might bear fruit. God's purpose is to gather fruit, not render judgment.

15:3. *Now ye are clean through the word which I have spoken unto you.*

When the husbandman comes to a branch that is not bearing luscious fruit, he examines it. Often he finds something is hindering the fruit. What does he do? He cleanses the vine. Some say he prunes it. The word "purgeth" (verse 2) and "clean" (verse 3) are essentially the same, and may include the idea of pruning. Certainly there are things in your life and mine that ought to be pruned. But how does the Lord do it? He cleanses us through the Word.

Have you noticed in John the marvelous place God gives to the

Word? In chapter 5 we are to believe the Word. In chapter 8 we are to abide in the Word. In chapter 14 we are to obey the Word. In this chapter we are cleansed by the Word. We also have this in Psalm 119:9, where we read, "Wherewithal shall a young man cleanse his way? by taking heed thereto according to thy word." Here Jesus says, "Ye are clean through the word."

But what does the husbandman clean off of the vine? He washes off infinitesimal bugs that get on the vine and sap out its life and prevent fruit bearing. Along comes the husbandman carrying a goatskin full of water to squirt the vine and wash off the parasites hidden there. You can't live in the world without some of those little parasites sapping out your life. They are like the little foxes that spoil the vines (Song of Solomon 2:15).

But we all excuse ourselves for having these parasites by saying, "Well, you know, I was born this way. I was born with this temper. . . ." Are you blaming God for that?

You have to confess with me that the little things that come into your life do rob you of joy, of usefulness, and of much fruit. We get occupied with material things that don't amount to anything. They become the big things in our lives that rob us of fruit.

Would you be willing to come into the presence of God alone, just you and the Lord, and ask Him to cleanse you from those things that sap out your spiritual life and power, from those things that rob you of bearing luscious fruit for Him?

I'll guarantee He will do one thing. He will send you to the Word, because it cleanses us. When you're driving your car or doing your job, let your mind be filled with some portion of the Word of God. Chew it over like chewing a cud. Chew it over and over again. Get all the meat and the honey and the life out of it. Unconsciously it will affect your language. It will affect your attitude. It will affect your whole life.

Fruit bearing depends on abiding as the Lord points out here.

15:4-5. *Abide in me, and I in you. As the branch cannot bear fruit of itself, except it abide in the vine; no more can ye, except ye abide in me. I am the vine,*

*ye are the branches: He that abideth in me, and I in
him, the same bringeth forth much fruit: for without
me ye can do nothing.*

Chapters 14 through 17 speak much of this wonderful, indissoluble union between Christ and His people. We have no life in ourselves. He has the life and the power. He does the producing. We must simply abide. The great prerequisite for fruit bearing is abiding.

All the branch needs to do to bear fruit is to abide. That's all you have to do, just abide. "Apart from Me, separated from Me, you can do absolutely nothing." The life and power are in the vine. The vine produces the fruit and the branch bears it. A vine is known by its fruit, for the fruit it produces reveals what sort of vine it is. You and I are branches in the vine. We are joined to Him. His life is our life. His power is our power. He does the producing. We do the cooperating. How? By abiding.

Jesus says to us, "Stay close to Me. Keep in close, intimate fellowship with Me. For the closer you are in fellowship with Me, the more fruit you will bear. The farther you get from Me in your fellowship, the less fruit you will bear." That's the key to the whole thing—abiding. "Abide in Me."

But the problem is this. We set our jaws and our wills and decide *we* are going to produce fruit on our own. But what we produce is not what He wants. In our own strength all we produce is of the flesh. The Spirit indwells us in order that we might produce spiritual fruit. Everyone who has really put his trust in the Lord is His child, is in the vine, is in Christ, and has His life, Spirit, and power. All we need is in Him. What He wants us to do is to rest in Him, abide in Him, stay in close proximity to Him, have fellowship with Him, and cling to Him day by day, hour by hour.

We talk about great men of God down through the centuries. You will find that the men who were usable by the Spirit of God were men who were abiding. The closer you walk with Him and stay near Him, the more evident will be the luscious fruit.

Now, you won't be looking at yourself and saying, "I wonder if I have any fruit?" You won't even be thinking about the fruit. You won't be thinking about anything else but Him. If your life is controlled by Him, you will automatically bear fruit on the job, in the factory, in the office, in the shop, washing your dishes at home, taking care of the children. You will do the everyday things of life with your heart in fellowship with Him.

And what's the fruitage? "Love, joy, peace, longsuffering, gentleness, goodness, faith, meekness, temperance" (Galatians 5:22-23). What's the fruitage? Compassion, tenderness toward others, a desire that others might know the Lord.

Watch our Savior. As He walked among men, He was a friend of publicans and sinners for the purpose of bringing them into eternal life. He could say, "I do always the things that please Him." He could say, "I and My Father are one." He could say, "My Father loves Me and I love Him." There's a oneness there. "His words are My words. His works are My works." We see real abiding between the Son and the Father.

As He prepares to leave the world—for in a few hours He is going to be nailed to a cross—He brings these disciples (and you and me) into this same blessed, wonderful relationship. It is what Paul meant when he said, "I am crucified with Christ: nevertheless I live; yet not I, but Christ liveth in me" (Galatians 2:20). This is what he wrote in Colossians 3:4, where we read, "When Christ, who is our life, shall appear, then shall ye also appear with him in glory." The only life that is worth anything is this life in Christ. And what is the evidence of such a life? It is bearing fruit.

15:6. *If a man abide not in me, he is cast forth as a branch, and is withered; and men gather them, and cast them into the fire, and they are burned.*

The word "man" here has been inserted. It should be "it," the indefinite pronoun. This verse better reads, "Whoever it is who abides not in me. . . ." Now contrast this with verse 2: "Every branch in me that beareth not fruit. . . ." I believe these are believers in verse 2. But in verse 6 you have spurious ones. They are imitations. Is it not true that many of those who profess to be followers of the Savior have never had any life in Him? They have never been in Christ.

"If any man abides not in Me, he withers." Why does he wither? Because there is no life. He is not in the vine. All he is fit for is burning.

15:7. *If ye abide in me, and my words abide in you, ye shall ask what ye will, and it shall be done unto you.*

Now please don't take verse 7 here out of its context as people do with the prayer promise in 14:13. If you stay close to Him, abiding in Him, with His Word abiding in you, what do you think you will ask? You will pray in the will of God. Abiding in Him gives us entrance into the very heart of God. There His will becomes our will. We not only have a union with Him in life, but a union with Him in communion. Life comes to us through union with Christ. Fruitage comes through communion with Christ.

Being in fellowship with Him, you will know His will. You will know what He wants done, and you will cooperate with God as a partner in revealing His character and His grace. God has chosen you out of all created beings as the channel through which He will manifest His character, grace, and mercy before men. How can the world ever see the character of God except as it is displayed in His people. And how can it be displayed except by fruit bearing, by this life of communion with Him?

15:8. *Herein is my Father glorified, that ye bear much fruit; so shall ye be my disciples.*

Jesus links discipleship with bearing much fruit in this verse. In chapter 8 abiding in the Word is the evidence of a disciple. In chapter 13, love is the badge of a disciple. Now in this chapter, bearing much fruit is the manifestation of a real disciple. In other words, if you take it all and boil it down in all these passages, discipleship is living in close, blessed, intimate fellowship with the Savior.

Discipleship involves abiding in Him with His Word abiding in us. You can't separate these two elements. The more I live in the

Word of God, the more I will abide in Him. The more I abide in Him, the more I want to be in His Word. Then will come the revelation of His will.

Do you want to know why some Christians have their prayers answered more than others? The key is abiding. We need to abide in Him and have His Word abiding in us. If the Husbandman, our loving Father, were to come through the portion of His vineyard where you are today, would He find much fruit? Would He find you abiding?

May I urge upon you who are branches in the vine to stay close to Him? Stay in His Word. Then you will understand His will. Then there will be displayed through you the luscious fruit that glorifies God, because of His life and power manifest in you.

15:9-10. *As the Father hath loved me, so have I loved you: continue ye in my love. If ye keep my commandments, ye shall abide in my love; even as I have kept my Father's commandments, and abide in his love.*

Notice that Jesus' love for the Father is a perfect, complete love. He said, "My meat is to do the will of him that sent me" (4:34). "I do always those things that please him" (8:29).

In verses 9 and 10 two words stand out: "love" and "commandments." The Lord doesn't divide them. They run together. Love keeps His commandments. Now, I'm not talking about the commandments of Moses. Love keeps God's words. I display my love for Christ by obedience. As I've stated many times already, the measure of true Christianity, of reality, of life, is the obedience of His people. Faith cements our relationship to God, but obedience is our side of the picture. It causes us to bear much fruit to His glory.

Notice the connection between "love," "commandments," and "joy" in this next portion.

15:11-14. *These things have I spoken unto you, that my joy might remain in you, and that your joy*

might be full. This is my commandment, That ye love
one another, as I have loved you. Greater love hath no
man than this, that a man lay down his life for his
friends. Ye are my friends, if ye do whatsoever I com-
mand you.

Our love is displayed by obedience to His Word. Obedience to His Word brings full joy. Why are Christians so sad, so lacking in joy and blessing? It is because they are disobedient. Obedience brings full joy, but sin never brings joy. Did you get that? Sin never brings joy.

The world outside is running hither and yon trying all kinds of sin. Worldlings go like a bee from one flower to another, trying to find satisfaction. They have no real joy. They may find a certain measure of fleshly thrill, even happiness, depending upon circumstances. But when circumstances change, their happiness is gone.

Joy, deep joy, is found only in the Lord. "My love I give to you. My commandments I give to you. And My joy I give to you." Look, my friend, you and I can rejoice in our union with Christ in life. We are children of God, and we are justified, and we are forgiven, and we have life eternal, and we are on our way to glory. His joy carries you through in the midst of affliction and deep sorrow. It brings peace and rest of heart.

As a pastor, I have been with God's people in their sorrow and suffering many times. I have seen a child of God in intense suffering smile with tears running down her cheeks. Why? Because of the love and grace of God for her. She had peace. A person like this experiences something with God that many of us never experience because we can't stand suffering. God can't trust us with it.

Here in verse 11 we have celestial joy. No human mind can begin to plumb the depths of that joy. You and I are brought into a relationship and into a fellowship with Him. In Him is fullness of joy.

Life of Love and Service as Branches (15:15-17)

Called to Be Friends (15:15)

Here we have our relationship to each other in a life of love and service. I call verses 15 through 17 the three C's. **15:15-17.** *Henceforth I call you not servants; for the servant knoweth not what his lord doeth: but I have called you friends; for all things that I have heard of my Father I have made known unto you.* In this verse we are *called* to be friends. We are also *chosen* to bear fruit. *Ye have not chosen me, but I have chosen you, and ordained you, that ye should go and bring forth fruit, and that your fruit should remain.* In verse 17 we are *commanded* to love others. *These things I command you, that ye love one another.*

Please don't switch these around. You are not commanded to be friends, but you are called to be friends. You are not commanded to bear fruit, but you are chosen to bear fruit. You are only commanded to love one another.

In verse 15 the Lord tells us first of all that we are called to be friends. He says, "I no longer call you servants. I call you friend."

God called Abraham His friend (2 Chronicles 20:7; Isaiah 41:8; James 2:23). And "the Lord spake unto Moses face to face, as a man speaketh unto his friend" (Exodus 33:11). Ah, you say, that was Abraham. That was Moses. But Jesus is saying, "I have called *you* My friends."

Someone might say, "Why, Mr. Mitchell, I'm more than a friend."

Now just a minute. We could take John 1:12-13 and say we are children of God, or the first epistle of John and say we are the children of One who is God. And you might say, "Why, I'm more than a child of God. I'm a son by adoption, and I am His heir." That's wonderful. We have that in Galatians 4. And yet the sad thing is that you and I can revel in our adoption as sons and heirs, and yet know very little about being a friend of God.

When someone says, "This is my friend," we know they share confidence, intimacy, and revelation to one another of what's on their heart. I don't tell the secrets of my heart to everyone. Do you? That's folly. You reserve those secrets for the ones in whom you have confidence, the ones who are your friends.

I was a child of my father the moment I was born. But my dad never made a confidant of me when I was a boy. It wasn't until I was grown up that my dad and I sat down and he told me what was on his heart.

Jesus first called them disciples, and now He calls them friends. "I am making you a confidant of what is in My heart, and of all that I hear from My Father. The very secrets of the eternal counsels of God I reveal to you. You are My friends."

Many of us know little of the confidence He places in His people. We have robbed ourselves of the marvelous riches of the intimacy, the fellowship, and the communion with God Himself. We fail God. We come to church Sunday morning, go to Sunday School, go to Wednesday night prayer meeting, and we feel we have done our duty. But how well do we know Him?

To think that you and I could go morning, noon, and night in perfect, blessed, intimate fellowship with God, where He will unveil before us the glories and treasures of His counsel and His heart. Whatever your job may be—in the office, the shop, the store, or at home—you can do your job with your heart still in fellowship with God.

Chosen to Bear Fruit (15:16)

Second, the Lord has chosen us to bear fruit that will last through eternity. "Ye have not chosen me, but I have chosen you, and ordained you, that ye should go and bring forth fruit, and that your fruit should remain: that whatsoever ye shall ask of the Father in my name, he may give it you."

With the innumerable company of angels and principalities and powers, and the billions on earth from which to pick, God has said, to us as a select and small group, "I have chosen you to be My channels to express My character and to reveal My life and grace to others."

I wonder sometimes what the world sees in us. You know, I read an article the other day. It just made my heart go down to my shoes. The author said this: "Christianity is on the way out. It is not able to meet the demands and the needs of our present generation." Of course, it was an unsaved man writing.

Has Christianity failed? Is it on the way out? If you go to the Far East, to Southeast Asia, you will see a tremendous revival of Buddhism. All the ideologies of men are moving like a vast wave over the earth. Have we failed?

Let me say this again: The true test of real Christianity is obedience to His Word. The secret of fruit bearing is abiding. And abiding involves intimate communion with God. Jesus is saying, "You are My friends. I've brought you into the recesses of My heart. I want to lay bare before you the secrets of God's counsel, the greatness of His heart, the marvels of His grace, and the sovereignty of His power. You're My friends, and I've chosen you. Out of all the millions, I have chosen you to bear fruit, and that your fruit should remain. And to encourage you in this fruit bearing, whatever you ask the Father in My name, He will give it to you."

Command to Love Others (15:17)

Third, we are commanded to love one another. Why are we commanded? Do you command a person to love someone else? Doesn't this verse just mean loving those believers who love you?

You know, I've often thought that the Lord has an amazing family. He has some wonderful children and He has some ornery, bad-tempered, envious, jealous, and critical children. But He gives us this command: "Love one another."

And I am of the persuasion that there are some Christians who may be unlovable or unlovely in some of the things they do. They might not be like that if someone were to love them, you know. It's amazing what a little love will do.

Wouldn't it be wonderful if we were to love the brethren as He commanded us? Wouldn't it be a wonderful thing if we were to be disciples of Christ, glorifying the Father by bearing much fruit? Wouldn't it be wonderful if we were to go out with the blessed realization that we are His friends?

I say, what a wonderful thing for you and me as God's people to go out into a world of darkness and be so in communion and fellowship with the living, eternal God—through Jesus Christ His Son—that with His Word living in us, we would become God's channels to present to the world something of His character, His mercy, and His grace.

Life of Opposition from the World (15:18-27)

Now we have the opposition of the world from verse 18 down through chapter 16 verse 4.

> **15:18-19.** *If the world hate you, ye know that it hated me before it hated you. If ye were of the world, the world would love his own: but because ye are not of the world, but I have chosen you out of the world, therefore the world hateth you.*

Our Lord is very much concerned about the world. He speaks of it more than thirty times in chapters 15 through 17. He is saying here, "Don't forget, the world hated Me before it ever hated you. And it hates you because you belong to Me, because I have chosen you."

What does Jesus mean by the "world"? Certainly He is not talking about the earth upon which we live. He's not talking about geography. Nor is He thinking about taverns, theaters, dancing, and things that are often coupled with the "world." These are "worldly things" and they may be included, but He is talking about a Satanic kingdom that is antagonistic to the kingdom of God.

Now let's get this thing clear. There are two kingdoms—the kingdom of God and a kingdom that is absolutely dominated by Satan. He is its prince and god. He is the one who energizes every one of its citizens. It is the kingdom of "darkness" (Colossians 1:13), the kingdom absolutely antagonistic to the kingdom of God. It can be moral and it can be religious at the same time that it is Satanic.

You will have that in John 16, where Jesus says, "The time is going to come when they will take you out of the synagogues. They will kill you in the name of God." This has been the experience of God's people for almost two thousand years, since our Lord died and rose again. Then when you come to chapter 17, the Lord in His prayer with His Father mentions the "world" nineteen times.

The apostle John must have had this in mind when he wrote his epistles. In 1 John 2:15-17 he said, "Love not the world, neither the things that are in the world. If any man love the world, the love of the Father is not in him. For all that is in the world, the lust of the flesh, and the lust of the eyes, and the pride of life, is not of the Father, but is of the world. And the world passeth away, and the lust thereof: but he that doeth the will of God abideth for ever."

First John 3:13 says, "Marvel not, my brethren, if the world hate you." The more the world hates the believer, the more the believer ought to love the people of God. It is a tragedy to find in this day that Christians will go to the world to criticize and condemn other Christians (1 Corinthians 6:1-8). We are to have no part, no relationship to the world.

The world is a system diametrically opposed and antagonistic to the kingdom of God. And its great venom is directed against those who have been taken out of the world by the Son of God.

Why this hostility? Why do they hate Him? Our Lord came offering love. He offered life, forgiveness, grace. He offered man a relationship with the living God. But they offered Him hate, envy, and then murder. Remember, the world that had no place for Christ has no place for me.

As Christians we are not exempt from opposition because even our Lord was persecuted by the world.

15:20-24. *Remember the word that I said unto you,*
The servant is not greater than his lord. If they have

persecuted me, they will also persecute you; if they
have kept my saying, they will keep your's also. But all
these things will they do unto you for my name's sake,
because they know not him that sent me. If I had not
come and spoken unto them, they had not sin: but now
they have no cloke for their sin. He that hateth me
hateth my Father also. If I had not done among them
the works which none other man did, they had not had
sin: but now have they both seen and hated both me
and my Father.

Here are the Pharisees and Sadducees, the Herodians and scribes in our Lord's day. They had spent their whole lifetime claiming that they served God. In chapter 8 they said sarcastically to Him, "We be not born of fornication; we have one Father, even God." They made that boast to the living God, yet they belonged to the kingdom of darkness, and He tore their mask away. Because of that they hated Him and sought to kill Him.

Why did the world hate Jesus? He knew the answer. "You hate Me because I tore your mask off. If I hadn't come and torn the mask away, you would have had no sin. It would not have been revealed. But I came and tore the mask away, and people saw you for what you are."

Someone has asked, "If Jesus Christ were to come to America, to so-called Christian America, what would we do with Him?" We would crucify Him because He would tear our mask off and show us what we are.

15:25-27. *But this cometh to pass, that the word*
might be fulfilled that is written in their law, They
hated me without a cause. But when the Comforter is
come, whom I will send unto you from the Father,
even the Spirit of truth, which proceedeth from the
Father, he shall testify of me: And ye also shall bear
witness, because ye have been with me from the beginning.

Verse 25 is a quote from Psalm 35:19. It indicates that the Lord was already rejected. They had no place for Him even though there was no reason at all why they should hate Him. He went about doing good. He healed all who were oppressed of the devil. He fed their hungry and raised their dead. He opened the eyes of the blind and cleansed the lepers. He stilled the storms. He met their need. He was a friend of publicans and sinners.

One day, the religious folk said to His disciples, "Why, look at your rabbi. He's eating with sinners. He's become a friend of publicans."

Jesus, overhearing them, said, "Listen, you fellows haven't a thing to give to sinners and publicans. But I have something to offer them. I have peace, pardon, rest, life. I have love to give to these people."

By the way, do you have a message for sinners? for outcasts? Do you claim to be joined to Christ? Do you claim to have the life of the Son of God? Do you believe that His Spirit is living in you? What is going to be the evidence of it? The evidence is being a friend to publicans and sinners. And why should we be their friend? To bring them to life through God's Son.

Why is Christianity so different from every other religion? Because it has a risen and living Savior who can give life. Religions tell you what you should do for the gods. Christianity is telling the world what God has done for man in the Person of His Son. And this makes a tremendous cleavage between those who love the Savior and those who love the world. The world is religious, whether it is the Hindus or Muslims or Buddhists or Christian Scientists and other cults, or whatever. They all belong to the same kingdom.

The great cause of the persecution and suffering of God's people in the first century A.D. was because they would not let Jesus be put among the gods. Christians said, "We can't worship the gods. There is only one true God. There is only one Savior. He is Jesus, the Son of God. He doesn't belong to the world or to its gods. He is the only living God." So the world accused them of being atheists and crucified them, burned them, threw them to the lions. The more they tried to kill them, the more they increased.

The gospel of Jesus Christ is separate from the world. The world doesn't want Him. "The world knoweth us not, because it knew him not" (1 John 3:1). The world never understood Him. The religious world wouldn't have a thing to do with Him. They killed Him. When God's people draw the same line of demarcation He drew, the world will do the same thing to us.

People who do not belong to the Savior can be wonderful, moral, religious people, and yet hate the people of God. Why? They know not God. They don't understand why you who were one time in the world no longer belong to the world. They don't understand that the One they crucified has chosen you out of the world to be His own.

For instance, if a Muslim accepts the Savior, he will have to leave his home and his district if he is going to live. His family is responsible to slay him; and if they don't do it, the town will do it. He will have to get away if he is going to continue as a Christian. The worst thing a Muslim can do is to turn to Christ. The world hates him. It kills him in the name of Allah.

God forbid that the world should hate us because of our sins (1 Peter 4:15). What a tragedy. But the world will hate you if you live for Him, for His name's sake. We will see this again in chapter 16.

But we know so little of persecution in this country. It doesn't cost a thing to be a Christian here. We don't face the cost of hurt or trouble or the sacrifice of financial reserves and sources. But there is a coldness if you are outspoken for Him, if you are His spokesman and you touch their conscience. The world will treat you as a foreigner, as someone who doesn't belong in it.

Have you tried to analyze why your non-Christian neighbors act the way they do? There is a barrier. If you were to ask your neighbors about it, they wouldn't know what you were talking about. They are in the dark. They belong to the world. They can be friendly, unfriendly, or indifferent. But there is always a barrier between. Why? Because you belong to Him.

John 16

Christ, The Preeminent One

Life of Opposition from the World [Continued] (16:1-4)

From verse 18 of chapter 15 through verse 4 of this chapter we have the world in its hatred for the disciples. The Lord is telling His disciples that these are the facts of the Christian life. "I have suffered. You will suffer as well. You can't expect any better treatment from the world than I received. If they accept My words, they wil accept your words. If they reject Me, they will reject you."

16:1. *These things have I spoken unto you, that ye should not be offended.*

My friends, we shouldn't be surprised if the world hates us. The more it hates us, the more we are to love one another. Compare 1 John 4:1-6.

Our Lord here is prophesying persecution against God's people, and the reason for it. He goes on to say that most of this hatred will come from the religious leaders.

16:2-4. *They shall put you out of the synagogues: yea, the time cometh, that whosoever killeth you will think that he doeth God service. And these things will they do unto you, because they have not known the Father, nor me. But these things have I told you, that when the time shall come, ye may remember that I told you of them. And these things I said not unto you at* *the beginning, because I was with you.*

The moment you take a stand for the Savior, you have opposition. Why does the world do that? "These things will they do unto you, because they have not known the Father, nor me." Do you remember 1 John 3:1? "The world knoweth us not, because it knew him not." The world never knew the Savior. The world never knows you and me. The world only loves its own. Once we belonged to the world. But now we belong to Christ. He has chosen us out of the world.

Look at the last verse of this chapter: "These things I have spoken unto you, that in me ye might have peace. In the world ye shall have tribulation: but be of good cheer; I have overcome the world." Victory is assured over the world. He has guaranteed the victory!

Coming of the Spirit (16:5-15)

His Coming is Dependent on Jesus' Departure (16:5-7)

Let me take up the ministry of the Spirit of God now.

> **16:5-7. But now I go my way to him that sent me; and none of you asketh me, Whither goest thou? But because I have said these things unto you, sorrow hath filled your heart. Nevertheless I tell you the truth; It is expedient for you that I go away: for if I go not away, the Comforter will not come unto you; but if I depart, I will send him unto you.**

If Christ had stayed on earth, His ministry would have been limited because of the physical. But there is a whole world needing the Savior. There are teeming hundreds of millions out of Christ, without God, without hope. How are they going to be reached?"

"It is expedient for you that I go away." Caiaphas used the same word when he said, "It is expedient for us, that one man should die for the people, and that the whole nation perish not" (11:50). An antagonistic, vile, jealous high priest unknowingly cooperated with the purpose of God. The time is going to come when God will make the wrath of man to praise Him (Psalm 76:10).

Now you will notice that in chapters 7, 14, 15, and here in 16, the Lord is speaking of the coming of the Spirit. In chapter 7 the Lord said, "If any man thirst, let him come unto me, and drink. He that believeth on me, as the scripture hath said, out of his belly shall flow rivers of living water" (7:37-38). The apostle John adds, "But this spake he of the Spirit, which they that believe on him should receive: for the Holy Ghost was not yet given; because that Jesus was not yet glorified" (7:39). I question if the disciples caught the significance of that statement when He said it.

In chapter 14 Jesus deals with the amazing truth of the indwelling Spirit of God. He said, "And I will pray the Father, and he shall give you another Comforter, that he may abide with you for ever; Even the Spirit of truth; whom the world cannot receive, because it seeth him not, neither knoweth him: but ye know him; for he dwelleth with you, and shall be in you. I will not leave you comfortless: I will come to you" (14:16-18).

In chapter 15 we read, "But when the Comforter is come, whom I will send unto you from the Father, even the Spirit of truth, which proceedeth from the Father, he shall testify of me: And ye also shall bear witness, because ye have been with me from the beginning" (15:26-27).

Here in this chapter Jesus says, "Nevertheless I tell you the truth; It is expedient for you that I go away: for if I go not away, the Comforter will not come unto you; but if I depart, I will send him unto you."

I want you to mark several things from these passages. We have the Father giving the Spirit in answer to the Lord Jesus' request. The Spirit is sent by the Son in cooperation with the Father. The Father, heeding the request of the Son, sends the Spirit. Notice the remarkable cooperation of the Godhead.

I also want you to mark something else. There is a real cooperation between the believer and the Holy Spirit. In chapter 15, verse

26 and 27, for example, we have the Spirit bearing witness (verse 26), and the believer bearing witness (verse 27). This is cooperation.

As you read the book of Acts you will notice this cooperation between the Spirit and believers. In Acts 13 you have the cooperation of Paul and Barnabas and the leaders of the church at Antioch with the Spirit of God. The church sent Paul and Barnabas out (verse 3). The Holy Spirit also sent them out (verse 4). This is wonderful cooperation.

In Acts 15 we have the cooperation of James and the council with the Spirit of God. They could write to the churches, "It seemed good to the Holy Ghost, and to us. . . " (verse 28).

Now if I were teaching the filling of the Spirit, I would go to Luke's Gospel. There you have the question, "How did Jesus Christ as a Man in the midst of men perform His ministry?" Luke records that Jesus was "full of the Holy Ghost" (4:1).

But in John's Gospel, the filling of the Spirit isn't dealt with. He's dealing with life. He's dealing with the indwelling Spirit. John is taking up the question that the Spirit is going to come and indwell every believer.

Do you remember Romans 5:5? "The love of God is shed abroad in our hearts by the Holy Ghost which is given unto us." And who gives us the Spirit? The Father sent the Spirit in answer to the request of the Son, that everyone who believes on the Son might be indwelt by the Spirit. You remember Romans 8:9, where Paul writes, "Now if any man have not the Spirit of Christ, he is none of his."

Notice that you have the "Holy Spirit," the "Spirit of God," and the "Spirit of Christ." These are used synonymously. They all refer to the same blessed Spirit. Now we may not understand all He does in and through us, but we can be sure He indwells us, and that He is working out in us His own divine purpose and plan. His coming was made possible by Jesus' departure, for "if I depart, I will send him unto you."

You see, what I'm trying to get to your heart is this. Whoever you are, you are indwelt by the Spirit of God if you are a child of God. In cooperation with the Spirit you are to bear witness to the world of the wonders of the Savior, and the marvels of His love. The world is going to hate you, but you are not alone. The Comforter has come to live within you.

I want to encourage your heart today. If you're discouraged because of opposition from the world, or if you are weak and lonely, remember that Jesus is with you and the Holy Spirit indwells you.

A dear man I knew was in a hospital. He said to his daughter, "My eyes are so bad I can't read, and I'm so weak in body I can't pray. I'm just going to put my head on Jesus' bosom and enjoy Him for Himself." Why don't you do that?

"Why," you say, "that's too simple." But that's what He wants. He loves simplicity. If it were profound, it would leave many of us out. The Spirit of God indwells us because He wants to make Christ known to us. He wants to comfort us so that we can enjoy His peace, His love, His life. The world knows nothing about this.

Ministry of Conviction in the World (16:8-11)

16:8. *And when he is come, he will reprove the world of sin, and of righteousness, and of judgment.*

The word "reprove" can also be translated "correct" or "illuminate." He rebukes the world in order to bring conviction.

First, we have the conviction of sin.

16:9. *Of sin, because they believe not on me.*

When a person preaches the gospel, some people come under what we call the "conviction of sin." We say, "That fellow is really convicted. He needs the Savior." Now, who made him convicted? The Spirit of God is the One who illuminates the heart.

Suppose someone had told you and me before we were saved, "Well, you're just an old sinner." Our immediate answer would have been, "Well, I'm just as good as you are. What do you mean, calling me a sinner? I'm just as good as you are." You see, there's no conviction.

But once the Word of God comes in the power of the Spirit of God, then comes the illuminating power of the Spirit on your conscience. You are convicted of your sin. You realize you are a sinner. Now, you're not a sinner because of the standards of men, but because you realize you're in the presence of God.

How can you stand in the presence of God without being convicted of your sin? You see, you are like Isaiah. When he saw the Lord high and lifted up, he said, "Woe is me! for I am undone; because I am a man of unclean lips" (Isaiah 6:5).

You are also like Job. Now if ever there were a self-rightous man, it was Job. But after he saw the Lord, he said, "Wherefore I abhor myself, and repent in dust and ashes" (Job 42:6).

And then there's dear old Peter. You remember, after the miraculous draft of fish, he fell at the feet of the Savior and said, "Depart from me; for I am a sinful man, O Lord" (Luke 5:8). Why did Peter say that? Because he was in the presence of the Savior.

When you give the gospel of the sinless Son of God dying for men and women, the unsaved person thinks, "Why should Jesus die for me? What's wrong with me?" Well, we read in Romans 6:23 that "the wages of sin is death." Either Christ died for me, or I have to die. If I don't die, someone else must die. Sin pays wages. God executes the penalty. You see, when you talk about sin, you're dealing with a holy, righteous God.

If you judge yourself in light of those around you, you will say, "Well, I'm just as good as anyone else." Well, I'll admit that. In fact, you might say, "Why, I'm even better than that preacher." Is that what you're going to tell God? No. When you stand in the presence of the righteous God, your lips will be sealed, your mouth will be shut. Why? Because you will see yourself as you really are when you're in the presence of a holy God.

Jesus is saying, "When the Holy Spirit comes, He is going to illuminate people's minds with respect to sin." But what kind of sin? Verse 9 tells us, "of sin, because they believe not on me." Notice He doesn't say, "of sin, because they lie," or "of sin, because they steal," or "of sin because of what they do." No. He convicts of sin "because they believe not on me."

What you do is the fruitage of your ignorance of God. Unbelief heads up all sin. Unbelief goes when you accept the Savior. The Word of God is given by the Spirit of God that people might see their need of the Savior. The issue is this: What will you do with Jesus?

Next, we have the Spirit of God reproving the world of righteousness.

16:10. *Of righteousness, because I go to my Father, and ye see me no more.*

Why is the Holy Spirit going to convince the world of righteousness? Because the Lord Jesus has been raised from the dead and exalted to God's right hand. The very resurrection of Jesus Christ is God's testimony that this Jesus is His Son, that this Jesus is righteous, that this Jesus is now on the right hand of the majesty on high. He must be righteous. But the world rejected and crucified the righteous One.

Finally, we have the Spirit reproving the world of judgment.

16:11. *Of judgment, because the prince of this world is judged.*

And since the prince of this world is judged, hence the world itself is judged. You remember our Savior said in chapter 12, "Now is the judgment of this world: now shall the prince of this world be cast out. And I, if I be lifted up from the earth, will draw all men unto me" (12:31-32). The time has come. At the cross Jesus Christ not only put away your sins and settled the sin question, He not only defeated death and afterward defeated the grave, but He also judged the world and the prince of this world.

You have this in chapter 14 as well. Jesus said, "Hereafter I will not talk much with you: for the prince of this world cometh, and hath nothing in me." Satan had nothing to which he could appeal in Christ.

For the third time Jesus declares, "the prince of this world is judged." And when the prince is judged, the world is judged. I want to tell you very frankly, my friend, that the One who is going to judge this world in righteousness is the One the world crucified.

Maybe you are still not a believer, my friend. I say, either you will stand before God in your own sin and your own unbelief, or you will stand before God in all the holiness and righteousness of Jesus Christ. The difference is Christ. The issue is Christ. You have nothing to offer God but sin. All that you try to do is of the flesh. But you must stand in the presence of God.

Hebrews 9:27 says, "it is appointed unto men once to die, but after this the judgment." I don't care how long you live. Eventually you will die. And after that you must stand in the presence of God. Jesus said to the Jews, "ye shall die in your sins" (8:24). And after death, what comes? The judgment. And who is going to judge you? A holy God.

"But He is a God of love," you say. "He wouldn't actually judge anyone. Doesn't He love me?" He certainly is a God of love, and He does love you. Look at Romans 5:8. But let me remind you that when you come to the book of Revelation, the Lord of glory comes in His wrath. He comes to judge men. Everyone will stand before the Lamb. The One the world cast out and crucified will be their judge. Jesus is the personification of love, but He is also the personification of righteousness and holiness. His very resurrection is the guarantee of His righteousness.

Isn't it wonderful that God offers you and me a salvation that is real and perfect? The Spirit is in the world today reproving and illuminating the hearts of men with respect to sin, and righteousness, and judgment.

The issue is Christ. The Holy Spirit reproves men of sin, because they don't believe in Christ. He reproves them of righteousness, for Christ is righteous. He reproves them of judgment, for Christ comes as the judge of this world. I repeat it again: The issue is Christ.

Ministry of the Spirit to Believers (16:12-15)

The Spirit of God is come into the world to illuminate the world with respect to sin, righteousness, and judgment. But He is come to do even more than that. Here we have the ministry of the Spirit of God to believers. The Lord is especially dealing with the revelation of truth to the believer.

It's a wonderful thing to know that the truth of God is only made known to us by revelation. Man doesn't know the truth of God apart from the Spirit of God. In 1 Corinthians 2:4 Paul says, "And my speech and my preaching was not with enticing words of man's wisdom, but in demonstration of the Spirit and of power." "The preaching of the cross is to them that perish foolishness; but unto us which are saved it is the power of God" (1 Corinthians 1:18). The Lord could pray, "I thank thee, O Father, Lord of heaven and earth, because thou hast hid these things from the wise and prudent, and hast revealed them unto babes" (Matthew 11:25). It is the Spirit that reveals the deep things of God.

16:12. *I have yet many things to say unto you, but ye cannot bear them now.*

In other words our Lord is saying, "You fellows don't have the capacity to receive all the truth." The Lord doesn't teach us beyond our capacity to receive it. You feed babies milk. You don't feed them steak. It is important to feed them according to their capacity to receive. When it comes to spiritual things, God is just as careful.

Now remember these disciples had been approximately three and a half years accompanying the Savior. After our Lord was baptized in the Jordan by John the Baptist, you remember, Jesus spent quite a bit of time at night in the presence of His Father. He came down the mountain; and out of those who were following Him, He chose twelve men. These men stayed with Him right through (especially the eleven, for Judas is already gone in this passage). The Lord said to them, "There's so much I would like to talk to you about, but you can't bear it now. However when He, the Spirit of truth, is come, He will guide you into all truth."

May I just stop here for a moment? Wouldn't it be a wonderful thing if you and I would ask the Lord to increase our capacity to receive the truth? Truth is only imparted by the Spirit of God. And He imparts it to open hearts.

I had a missionary say to me one time as we were discussing some truths, "You can't change me."

"Why," I said, "I don't expect to change anyone. The Spirit of God has to do that. But I wonder, my friend, if your mind is closed to truth? If we come to the place where we're not willing to sit down and examine the Word of God, then we are in a bad situation spiritually. None of us knows all the truth. You know some, and I know some. Let's share together."

If you're a new Christian, don't get discouraged if you can't understand all that is said to you. Just keep on in the Word of God. Read it. Reread it. The Spirit of God will slowly increase your capacity for truth. But you must have an open mind and an open heart for the Spirit of God to take the Word of God and make it real to you.

If you encounter false teachers and wonder who is telling the truth, I suggest you just take your Bible, and God will take His Word and make it very precious to you. If you mean business with God, then He means business with you.

May God grant you and me a real capacity to receive the truth. I repeat it, the Lord gives us truth according to our capacity to receive it. You can't pull truth out of the air. You must get down to business and discipline yourself to get into the Word of God and read it and reread it. Ask the Spirit to make the truth real to your heart. Don't study the Bible just to teach a Bible class. First, get the truth into your own heart so that the Spirit of God will make it a living reality in your life. This is what produces transformed lives. The Word of God doesn't come only in word, "but also in power, and in the Holy Ghost, and in much assurance" (1 Thessalonians 1:5).

The Spirit is come to reveal the truth of God to us as believers. Mark what His theme is.

> **16:13-15.** *Howbeit when he, the Spirit of truth, is come, he will guide you into all truth: for he shall not speak of himself; but whatsoever he shall hear, that shall he speak: and he will shew you things to come. He shall glorify me: for he shall receive of mine, and shall shew it unto you. All things that the Father hath are mine: therefore said I, that he shall take of mine, and shall shew it unto you.*

"He will guide you into all truth," Jesus says, according to our capacity to receive it. He is the only One who can guide us into truth. And thank God, He is willing to do it. The Spirit desires to make Him very real to you. His great theme is the person of the Lord Jesus Christ.

As you read your Bible, remember that the Spirit reveals Jesus Christ there as the center and object, not only of your faith, but also of your knowledge. From the beginning of Genesis to the end of Revelation, the central theme all the way through is the Person and work of Christ (either in type, or shadow, or prophecy, or instruction). You remember our Lord could say, "had ye believed Moses, ye would have believed me: for he wrote of me" (5:46).

The Spirit's purpose is to reveal the Lord Jesus Christ. There is much ministry today concerning the Spirit, but remember that the Spirit of God will not speak of Himself or from Himself. The Father and the Son and the Spirit are all of one accord. When the Spirit of God comes to indwell you, whatever He says will be in perfect accord with the purpose and will of our Father and of the Lord Jesus Christ.

"He will take the things that are mine, and show them to you," Jesus said. When a person claims to be filled with the Holy Spirit, look for the evidence of the heart and character of Christ in that person. God grant to us these days that we might be filled unto all the fullness of God, and might be taught of the Spirit of God. Oh, that He would take you and me and reveal to us the wonderful person of our Savior. The more we see the beauty and glory of the Savior, the

more we know something of an intimate fellowship with the living
God.

Departure of the Son (16:16-33)

His Departure is Necessary for the Disciples' Joy (16:16-22)

Once more we have the Lord explaining the necessity of His departure.

> **16:16-18.** *A little while, and ye shall not see me:
> and again, a little while, and ye shall see me, because
> I go to the Father. Then said some of his disciples
> among themselves, What is this that he saith unto us,
> A little while, and ye shall not see me: and again, a
> little while, and ye shall see me: and, Because I go to
> the Father? They said therefore, What is this that he
> saith, A little while? we cannot tell what he saith.*

Obviously, the disciples are perplexed. "What in the world is He
talking about?" they asked one another. They simply did not understand the plan of God. When Christ was buried, their hopes
were shattered. They admitted, "We trusted that it had been he
which should have redeemed Israel" (Luke 24:21).

Jesus answers their dilemma.

> **16:19-22.** *Now Jesus knew that they were desirous
> to ask him, and said unto them, Do ye enquire among
> yourselves of that I said, A little while, and ye shall not
> see me: and again, a little while, and ye shall see me?
> Verily, verily, I say unto you, That ye shall weep and
> lament, but the world shall rejoice: and ye shall be
> sorrowful, but your sorrow will be turned into joy. A
> woman when she is in travail hath sorrow, because
> her hour is come: but as soon as she is delivered of the
> child, she remembereth no more the anguish, for joy
> that a man is born into the world. And ye now there-*

fore have sorrow: but I will see you again, and your
heart shall rejoice, and your joy no man taketh from
you.

"A little while, and ye shall see me." Here we have the crucifixion. No wonder He speaks of their sorrow. When Jesus met the two disciples on the road to Emmaus, He asked them, "What manner of communications are these that ye have one to another, as ye walk, and are sad?" (Luke 24:17). As I said before, the cross shattered their hopes that Jesus should have been the Messiah to redeem Israel.

"Again, a little while, and ye shall see me." Here we have the resurrection. The disciples' anguish turned to joy as they saw the risen Savior. We have this in chapter 20, where we read, "Then were the disciples glad, when they saw the Lord" (20:20). When the disciples were beaten for their faith, they left "rejoicing that they were counted worthy to suffer shame for his name" (Acts 5:41).

For us today, I would take this—"ye shall see me"—as a promise concerning His return. In the world we will have tribulation and sorrow, as we read in verse 33, but we have hope of His return. We will have joy when He returns for us in the clouds. What is interesting is that those who are persecuted today experience unusual joy. We know so little of that in this country. Our brethren in other parts of the world have experiences with the Savior we know nothing about.

Promise of Privileges in Prayer (16:23-28)

Here our Lord encourages His disciples by telling them of their wonderful resources in prayer.

16:23-28. *And in that day ye shall ask me nothing.*
Verily, verily, I say unto you, Whatsoever ye shall ask
the Father in my name, he will give it you. Hitherto
have ye asked nothing in my name: ask, and ye shall

*receive, that your joy may be full. These things have I
spoken unto you in proverbs: but the time cometh,
when I shall no more speak unto you in proverbs, but I
shall shew you plainly of the Father. At that day ye
shall ask in my name: and I say not unto you, that I
will pray the Father for you: For the Father himself
loveth you, because ye have loved me, and have believed that I came out from God. I came forth from the
Father, and am come into the world: again, I leave the
world, and go to the Father.*

I want you to mark that in these six verses our Lord mentions the
Father six times. What our Lord is doing is informing the disciples
that they have the same access to the presence of the Father that He
does. He is informing them that they can enter at any time into the
throne of grace and stand before the Father in all that Jesus is to the
Father.

Three times in these verses Jesus tells them to pray "in my
name" (verses 23, 24, 26). Now what does that mean? It does *not*
mean just tacking His name to your prayers.

Our access to the presence of God is based on the ground of re-
demption. Our sins have been forgiven. We have been cleansed
from all unrighteousness. We have been brought by the work of
Christ into a real relationship with the Lord. We are children of
One who is God. He is our Father. We can say, "Abba Father"
(Mark 14:36; Romans 8:15; Galatians 4:6). This is relationship.
We can come into the very presence of God on the ground of what
Christ has done.

When you and I pray in Jesus' name, it means that we stand before God in all the merit, all the righteousness, and all the good
standing of the Savior Himself. We are asking in His name.

When you and I realize we are dealing with the living God, a
great many of our prayers will go out the window as we stand before Him. Your mouth will be sealed before God if you attempt to
pray in the power of self-will. But when you realize you are standing in the presence of God in all the beauty and merit of Christ,

fully "accepted in the beloved" (Ephesians 1:6), you will pray as if the Lord Himself were making the request.

It's not that Jesus takes your request and presents it to the Father. That's not in His mind. We are to "ask the Father in my name." We come before the Father on the ground of redemption and relationship. We come before Him in all the merit of Christ, making our requests as if He were making them.

Now we would all agree that if the Lord Himself were making the requests, they would certainly be answered. But when we make the requests, we have a question mark in our minds. "Will the Lord answer me? Do I have enough faith?" But on what ground does God answer our prayers? Is it on the ground of our faith? Notice that faith isn't even mentioned here. Instead, the Father grants our requests on the ground of His love for us. "Whatsoever ye shall ask the Father in my name, he will give it you. . . . for the Father himself loveth you."

The Father answers our requests on the ground of His love for us. Let me give you an illustration. Take John 17:24. This is one of Jesus' only requests of the Father. Notice what He says, "Father, I will that they also, whom thou hast given me, be with me where I am; that they may behold my glory, which thou hast given me: for thou lovedst me before the foundation of the world."

Upon what ground did Jesus expect the Father to grant His request? "For thou lovedst me before the foundation of the world." Upon the ground of the Father's love for Him, the Lord Jesus expected His request to be granted. In the same way, the Father answers our requests because He loves us.

As I said, it's not that Jesus presents our requests to the Father. "At that day ye shall ask in my name: and I say not unto you, that I will pray the Father for you."

"But I thought the Lord was praying for us all the time," you say. You have Hebrews 7:25 and 9:24 in mind, as well as Romans 8:34 and 1 John 2:1, where our Lord is presented as our advocate, our intercessor, our representative. In these passages He prays for us because of our frailty. He advocates for us when we sin. He represents us before the Father.

But the Lord is not talking about that here in verse 26. He's talking about our requests. When I make my request in the name of Jesus Christ, I make it on the ground of all His beauty and merit and grace. I make it on the ground of the Father's love.

This whole passage has transformed the way I pray. I don't ask for many of the things I used to request. When I go to pray, I begin to think about several questions. Is my praying for the glory of God? Is my request that the Father be glorified in the Son? Is my request that the Lord Jesus be manifested among men and women?

"I came forth from the Father, and am come into the world: again, I leave the world, and go to the Father." Here we have the coming, incarnation, ministry, leaving, and ascension of the Lord Jesus all in one verse. But there is nothing here about His love. We can know all the facts of His life, but we cannot know His love until we accept Him as our Savior.

As the objects of His love, we will have all our needs met by the Lord. Oh, sometimes He meets our needs in a different way than we expect. But a mother does that as well because she loves her child. The Lord is love personified to us. Jesus came to reveal God's love to us, and then returned to the Father that we might pray the Father on the ground of His love.

Promise of Peace in the World (16:29-33)

Our Lord also promises peace to His disciples in a world full of tribulation.

> **16:29-30.** *His disciples said unto him, Lo, now speakest thou plainly, and speakest no proverb. Now are we sure that thou knowest all things, and needest not that any man should ask thee: by this we believe that thou camest forth from God.*

They probably didn't even understand what they were saying. Mark what our Lord says.

16:31-33. *Jesus answered them, Do ye now believe? Behold, the hour cometh, yea, is now come, that ye shall be scattered, every man to his own, and shall leave me alone: and yet I am not alone, because the Father is with me. These things I have spoken unto you, that in me ye might have peace. In the world ye shall have tribulation: but be of good cheer; I have overcome the world.*

Let me suggest a contrast. Here Jesus says, "Yet I am not alone, because the Father is with me." But from the cross we hear, "My God, my God, why hast thou forsaken me?" (Matthew 27:46; Mark 15:34). In Matthew He is the trespass offering, hence the separation. In Mark He is the sin offering, bearing our sins, and hence this separation. In Luke He is the peace offering where there is no separation, so we do not have this cry from the cross. In John He is the burnt offering, completely offered to the Father. Thus Jesus could say here, "I am not alone, because the Father is with me." We also had this back in chapter 8. There Jesus said, "And he that sent me is with me: the Father hath not left me alone" (8:29). In John's Gospel, you never read of any separation between the Lord Jesus and the Father.

Jesus warns the disciples that they are going to be scattered, leaving Him alone. Yet He knew He wasn't alone, for the Father is with Him. And may I add this? The Father was also with them. They were scared in the Garden of Gethsemane, and everyone scattered and left Jesus. Jesus said to the rabble, "let these go their way" (John 18:8). But He knew the Father was with them.

John ends the chapter with a reminder that in Him we have peace. In the world we have tribulation, but He is our peace (Ephesians 2:14). He "made peace through the blood of his cross" (Colossians 1:20). "Therefore being justified by faith, we have peace with God through our Lord Jesus Christ" (Romans 5:1). He has given us peace (John 14:27). All that live godly in Christ shall suffer persecution, but those who suffer with Him shall reign with Him (2 Timothy 2:12; 3:12).

We have guaranteed victory over this antagonistic kingdom that would seek not only to kill the Son of God, but also to kill the people of God. And we have guaranteed peace. How glad I am for a Savior who is on the throne, working all things out after the counsel of His own will. The very nations of the earth are before Him as nothing. Hence, we can rest in Him.

"In Me—not in your circumstances, not even in your strong faith if you have any—in Me you will have peace. In the world you will have tribulation. But cheer up. I have overcome the world."

We walk in the triumph of the One who has overcome the world. Victory is assured. That's why we can sing that little chorus: "Cheer up, ye saints of God, there's nothing to worry about." Do you know it? "Cheer up, ye saints of God, there's nothing to worry about. There's nothing to make you feel afraid, nothing to make you doubt. Remember Jesus never fails, so why not trust Him and shout? You'll be sorry you worried at all tomorrow morning."

He has guaranteed the victory!

John 17

Christ, The Intercessor

Introduction to John 17

Now we are on holy ground. We have come within the veil. We have come into the holiest of all, and we are permitted to see the communion of the Father and the Son. One is not inferior to the other. They commune together as equals.

During His life here on earth, our Savior frequently retreated into the mountains or the wilderness to pray. Often He would spend all night in prayer, the Gospel writers record. But in this chapter we are allowed to come within the veil to hear Christ talking to the Father.

This is one of the most remarkable chapters in all the Word of God. Our Savior has opened His heart to His disciples all through the first sixteen chapters of John. He has spoken to them of His love for them, and about His Father's love for them. He has explained their unbreakable union with Him. He has told them about the Holy Spirit who would come and indwell them, and be their Comforter, Teacher, and Guide. And now He brings them into the presence of His Father.

Three times in this chapter He says, "I pray." He is not making a request of God, but is speaking what is on His heart. In fact, if there is any chapter in the Bible that would reveal the deity of the Son of God and His equality with the Father, it would be this chapter.

Jesus prays in verse 5 that He may be glorified with the glory that

He had with the Father before the world began. He asks in verse 11 that His Father take care of these disciples that they might be kept. He asks in verse 17 that they may be sanctified through the truth. Then He prays in verse 24 that they may behold His moral glory.

You see the heart of Christ poured out here, as He and His Father commune together concerning you and me. Not only has He redeemed us, but He has us upon His heart. The great yearning of our Lord's heart is for you and for me.

The chapter divides itself into three simple sections. In the first five verses, it is "Christ and His Father." The great word there is "glory." Jesus requests the Father to glorify Him with the glory they shared from eternity. And then from verse 6 through verse 19, we have "Christ and His Disciples." The great word there is "kept." Jesus asks the Father to preserve His disciples. Then from verse 20 to verse 26 we have "Christ and His Church." The great word there is "one." Jesus desires for His church to be in oneness with each other.

You will notice also that there are four great doctrines in this chapter. You have the doctrine of salvation in the first five verses, the doctrine of preservation from verse 11 to verse 16, the doctrine of sanctification from verse 17 through verse 19, and the doctrine of glorification from there to the end of the chapter.

In this chapter there are also three different kinds of glory. We have His eternal glory in verse 5 (the glory which He had with the Father before the world began), His acquired glory in verse 22 (the glory in which you and I share), and His moral glory in verse 24 (the glory we will see when we behold Him as the Man at God's right hand, glorified with all the glory of the omnipotent God).

Christ and His Father (17:1-5)

Jesus Claims Full Glory (17:1)

Let us then first consider Christ's eternal glory.

17:1. *These words spake Jesus, and lifted up his*

eyes to heaven, and said, Father, the hour is come;
glorify thy Son, that thy Son also may glorify thee.

In the preceding chapters our Lord opened His heart to the disciples concerning our oneness and our eternal union with Him, in that we are the objects of His love. Now He brings us right within the holiest of all, and we are permitted to sit down in the presence of God. We are allowed to sit there and witness this fellowship, this communion, this bond, this oneness, this equality between the Father and the Son. How much do we really know about coming within the veil of the holiest of all, and being perfectly at home in the presence of the Father and the Son?

"Father, the hour is come." We have already discussed the tremendous importance of the "hour" that was now come. You remember in chapter 2 He said to His mother, "What have I to do with thee? mine hour is not yet come." In chapter 7 He said to His brethren, "Your hour is here. My hour is not yet come." In chapter 12, when the Greeks wanted to see Jesus, He said, "Now is mine hour come, that the Son of man should be glorified." Note that it wasn't the hour that the Son should be crucified, but glorified.

When the leaders took Jesus captive in the Garden of Gethsemane shortly after this prayer, He said to them, "This is your hour, and the power of darkness" (Luke 22:53). Did you ever stop to think of the fact that the power of darkness, the forces of hell, had an hour? Their hour was the taking of the Son of God, scourging and rejecting Him, and then crucifying and killing Him. And yet the Lord took that very same thing, and showed that the ultimate purpose of Calvary is not salvation but the glorification of God.

Paul picked up this principle in Romans 8:18, where he wrote, "I reckon that the sufferings of this present time are not worthy to be compared with the glory which shall be revealed in us." And in 2 Corinthians 4:17 he wrote that, "our light affliction, which is but for a moment, worketh for us a far more exceeding and eternal weight of glory." In Romans 5:3 we read, "we glory in tribulations also."

Every sorrow, every pain, every bit of suffering, every circumstance, every joy, everything that comes into your life is going to be for the glory of God. Do you ever think of it that way? There's no place for self-sympathy, growling, and grumbling. Why? Because it is all going to "redound to the glory of God" (2 Corinthians 4:15).

The matter of the Son's being glorified started in chapter 11, carried on through chapter 12, repeated in chapter 13, and now appears again here in chapter 17. One of the most astounding things in the whole universe is that there is a Man at God's right hand, glorified with all the glory of the omnipotent God. His whole passion of life—His every word, every action, every attitude—was for the glorification of His Father.

That is why Jesus could say in chapter 4, "My meat is to do the will of him that sent me." He repeated this in chapter 5, where He says, "My Father worketh hitherto, and I work." In chapter 8 He says, "I do always those things that please him." In the Garden He will say, "Not my will, but thine, be done" (Luke 22:42).

This one hour when He was nailed to the cross is the central hour of all eternity. As a result, "God also hath highly exalted him, and given him a name which is above every name: That at the name of Jesus every knee should bow, of things in heaven, and things in earth, and things under the earth" (Philippians 2:9-10). Every created intelligence shall acknowledge that this Jesus Christ is Lord to the glory of God the Father. Again, the center of eternity is this one hour at the cross, for there can be no glorification without the cross.

"The hour is come" that the Son of Man should be glorified. And in the glorification of the Son, the Father is glorified. The One is glorified in connection with the Other. Neither is inferior nor superior to the Other. "Father, the hour is come." And Jesus could say in verse 5, *"Now,* O Father, glorify thou me with thine own self with the glory which I had with thee before the world was." Oh, the eternal thrill of this!

Why is so little place given to this very fact in our Christian churches today? May God grant to you and to me an enlarged vision of this which was planned back in eternity and revealed in Psalm 40:8, where we read, "I delight to do thy will, O my God." That will was the cross. What for? For the glorification of God. That is why we are saved. That is why He keeps us.

And don't you for one moment think, my Christian friend, that God is going to let you go. He's concerned that we be "conformed to the image of his Son" (Romans 8:29). What for? That we might glorify Him through eternity. This is the heart of the incarnation, of redemption, of the resurrection and ascension, and the plan of God for His people.

Jesus Claims Full Authority (17:2-3)

17:2-3. As thou hast given him power over all flesh, that he should give eternal life to as many as thou hast given him. And this is life eternal, that they might know thee the only true God, and Jesus Christ whom thou hast sent.

Did you notice what Jesus claims here? He has power and authority over all flesh, including yours and mine. Yes, He has power over all flesh, wherever you find it. We ought never to fear anyone. "The Lord is my helper, and I will not fear what man shall do unto me" (Hebrews 13:6). Men can rage, but they can't touch believers unless He permits it. Christ is the One who holds authority over death and hell (Revelation 1:18).

Jesus could say, "All power is given unto me in heaven and in earth" (Matthew 28:18). But He didn't say that here. Instead, He says, "Father, You have given Me power and authority over all flesh." For what purpose? "That I should give eternal life to as many as You have given to Me."

He has authority to give life instead of death, authority to save sinners instead of destroying them, authority to love them with an everlasting love instead of hating them because of their sin and corruption. He has authority over all flesh—authority over a world in chaos, and authority over your flesh.

Christ has authority over all flesh, including yours and mine. The trouble is, we don't permit Him to do what He wants to do. Now He could do it in sovereignty, but He doesn't treat you like a piece of machinery. He's not going to coerce or force His way. He tells you what He wants you to do. And if you say, "I have no power to do this," He says, "I will supply the power."

We have this all in Romans 8:11, where Paul says, "If the Spirit of him that raised up Jesus from the dead dwell in you, he that raised up Christ from the dead shall also quicken (give life to) your mortal bodies by his Spirit that dwelleth in you." And if He is going to transform the body and change it from mortal to immortal, from corruptible to incorruptible, certainly He can control that body now. And what He asks from you and me is that we yield ourselves to Him, that He may control our bodies which have become the temples of the Holy Spirit. I fear in these days we trust ourselves too much in this matter of control.

He also has authority to give life to people under bondage to sin. He has the authority to give eternal life to everyone the Father has given Him. Knowing Him is life eternal. All down through this Gospel we have dealt with this continually. "In him was life" (1:4). "The words that I speak unto you, they are spirit, and they are life" (6:63). "I am come that they might have life" (10:10). This is eternal life, satisfying life, resurrection life, indwelling life. What is life eternal but the personal knowledge of the Father and the Son? Eternal life comes through relationship with God Himself. God is not an idea. He is not a doctrine. He is not a concept. He is a living Person.

Life is not a commodity you buy, or pray for, or work for. Life only comes through relationship. This is the trouble with religions. They offer you things if you work hard enough, if you're earnest enough, if you sacrifice enough. This is not Christianity. You can't buy your way, earn your way, or argue your way into Christianity. Christianity is a life that produces fellowship and communion with the living God.

The world has nothing to offer you but empty husks. It has nothing to offer you but death. But Christ conquered death, and made death an open door into the very presence of God. Man's worst enemy has become the tool used of God to bring you to Himself. "This is life eternal, that they might know thee the only true God, and Jesus Christ whom thou hast sent."

Jesus Claims Full Obedience (17:4)

> **17:4.** *I have glorified thee on the earth: I have finished the work which thou gavest me to do.*

Jesus is the only One who could fully say that. Now there have been other men on earth who have brought glory to God, such as Abraham, Moses, David, and Elijah. God has had men who have brought Him glory, but not one has been able to say, from the moment he was born until he left this scene, "I have glorified You on the earth. Everything I have said, everything I have done, everything in my life has been for the glory of God."

As we discussed earlier, the great consuming passion of the heart of our Savior was for the glory of God. When He cleansed lepers, fed the thousands, opened blind eyes, raised the dead, stilled the storm, rebuked the wind, showed compassion on sinners, it was all for the glory of God.

Even when Jesus was being scourged, it was for the glory of God. This always causes a strange feeling in my heart when I think that they took the Son of God and scourged Him until His face was marred more than any man's face, fulfilling Isaiah 50:6. There He said, "I gave my back to the smiters, and my cheeks to them that plucked off the hair: I hid not my face from shame and spitting." This was for the glory of God. I can't understand it. I can't fathom it. Compare Isaiah 52:14.

At the cross, when they gnashed on Him with their teeth, He could cry out, "Father, forgive them; for they know not what they do" (Luke 23:34). When the dying thief said, "Lord, remember me when thou comest into thy kingdom," He said, "Today shalt thou be with me in paradise" (Luke 23:42-43). The whole thing was for the glory of God.

"I have glorified thee on the earth." Believer in Christ, could you and I come into the presence of God and say this to Him? Now, we may say, "Lord, I want to live for Your glory," and mean it. But not long afterwards we find how frail and how weak and stumbling we are. In fact, it will take eternity for us to fully appreciate this amazing statement, "I have glorified thee on the earth."

Whatever the past may have been between you and the Lord, dear reader—whether you can see only failures and weaknesses in the years behind you—may I suggest something? Get down before the Lord and say, "Lord, from here on I desire to live for the glory of Christ."

Only then can we echo the words of Christ: "Wist ye not that I must be about my Father's business?" (Luke 2:49). "My meat is to do the will of him that sent me, and to finish his work" (4:34). "I seek not mine own will, but the will of the Father which hath sent me" (5:30). "I do always those things that please him" (8:29). "I have finished the work which thou gavest me to do" (17:4).

What was the work of the Son? His work was twofold. He came to give mankind the revelation of the heart and character of God, and He came to bring men back into relationship with the Father. This now has become our twofold job. We are to bring to men the revelation of the heart of Jesus and let them see Him in our actions, in our compassion, in our tenderness, in our grace, in our love. Isn't it strange that after almost two thousand years people are still searching for God? The world needs to see in us the revelation of the very heart and character and person of the living God.

"I have finished the work which thou gavest me to do." Jesus could say this for He finished the work of *redemption*, making it possible for us to be loosed eternally from sin. He finished the work of *reconciliation*, making it possible for man to enjoy peace with God in a renewed relationship. He finished the work of *propitiation*, removing the barrier between us and God, perfectly satisfying the righteous and holy character of God by bearing our

328

sins. This is what God has in the cross.

Concerning sin, Christ made redemption by putting away our sin. Concerning man, He made reconciliation by renewing man's relationship to God. Concerning God, He made propitiation by satisfying the very character of God. Jesus could fully say, "I have finished the work which thou gavest me to do."

Jesus Claims Full Existence (17:5)

17:5. *And now, O Father, glorify thou me with thine own self with the glory which I had with thee before the world was.*

This is the first request of Jesus in his prayer. Notice the great yearning of His heart that He might again be glorified "with the glory which I had with thee before the world was." Here He is not only claiming equality with God, but He is claiming preexistence. And He is preparing to go back into heaven as a Man.

This is something new, that Jesus Christ as a Man is going to be glorified with all the eternal glory of omnipotent God. We have this fact recorded in 1 Peter 1:21, where we read, "Who by him do believe in God, that raised him up from the dead, and gave him glory." Hebrews 2:9 states, "We see Jesus . . . crowned with glory and honour." See also Philippians 2:5-11.

Glory was to be given to the Son, the Son who had become a man for His Father's glory. Did not Gabriel say to Mary, "Behold, thou shalt conceive in thy womb, and bring forth a son, and shalt call his name JESUS. He shall be great, and shall be called the Son of the Highest" (Luke 1:31-32)? And Mary became the vehicle whereby God took His place in humanity.

Now Jesus, in that humanity, is going into the glory, glorified with the eternal glory that He had before the foundation of the world. He is there at the right hand of God today as a Man, a real Man, glorified with all the glory of God. And He is going to bring a host of redeemed ones into the presence of God. Through eternity they shall magnify and glorify the Son.

I know of no better time than now for us to dedicate ourselves and lay our bodies, minds, and wills at His feet, and acclaim Him to be Lord of Lords, King of Kings.

Christ and His Disciples (17:6-19)

A Gift for the Son and for the Disciples (17:6-8)

> **17:6-8.** *I have manifested thy name unto the men which thou gavest me out of the world: thine they were, and thou gavest them me; and they have kept thy word. Now they have known that all things whatsoever thou hast given me are of thee. For I have given unto them the words which thou gavest me; and they have received them, and have known surely that I came out from thee, and they have believed that thou didst send me.*

"I have manifested thy name." What name of God did Christ reveal to His disciples? I believe the name Christ revealed here is "Father." It is a new relationship. He has made us children of One who is God. "Behold, what manner of love the Father hath bestowed upon us, that we should be called the sons of God" (1 John 3:1).

"I have manifested thy name unto the men which thou gavest me." Six times Jesus mentions that the disciples were the Father's gift to the Son (verses 2, 9, 12, 24, and John 6:37 and 39). Where did God get these men? Out of the world while they were dead in trespasses and sins (Ephesians 2:1). Nothing is said here about their failures, however, even though the Lord knew that on that same night Peter would deny Him three times, and the others would be scattered, leaving Him alone (16:32).

But still ringing in His ears is Peter's affirmation of faith, "Thou art the Christ, the Son of the living God" (Matthew 16:16). Thus Jesus could say, "They have believed that thou didst send me." Indeed, the Lord Jesus is the Father's unspeakable Gift to us (2 Corinthians 9:15). God has given us the perfect Gift. And for nearly two thousand years He has been gathering out a people for His name as a gift to His Son.

A Prayer for the Disciples (17:9-10)

17:9-10. *I pray for them: I pray not for the world, but for them which thou hast given me; for they are thine. And all mine are thine, and thine are mine; and I am glorified in them.*

"I pray for them." Think of the tremendous place these men had in the heart of the Savior. And do you realize the tremendous place you have in His heart? Look down at verse 20: "Neither pray I for these alone, but for them also which shall believe on me through their word." How many of us really know the Savior? How many of us have a real place in our heart for Him?

"I pray not for the world." The world is not on Jesus' heart. It is a foreign institution, as we noted in 15:18 through 16:4. The world is a kingdom of darkness. Satan is its prince and power. Christ has finished His work for the world, as He said in verse 4. God's only message to the world now is one of salvation and redemption through His Son.

The Savior is not working in the world today. It was wicked hands that crucified Him; it was loving hands that put Him in the tomb. He did not appear to the world after His resurrection; He appeared only to His own. Nor is He praying for the world. He prays for us.

I just love this little statement, "I pray for them." And if you have trials, tests, and sorrows, remember that He said, "I pray for them." And if you have suffered failures in days and weeks past, remember that He said, "I pray for them."

He prayed for Peter that His faith would not fail (Luke 22:32). Isn't it wonderful that He is praying for us? The man of the world can't say, "Someone is praying for me." But we can. "He ever liveth to make intercession for them" (Hebrews 7:25).

Put your name in there. "I pray for _____ . I pray not for the world, but for _____ whom thou hast given me; for _____ is mine. And all mine are thine, and thine are mine; and I am glorified in them."

Have you noticed how the Savior identifies His loved ones in this chapter? He says, "They have kept Your Word. They are not of the world. They are Your gift to Me. And they have glorified Me." Now He says, "I am glorified in them."

"I am glorified in them." My Christian friend, have you ever stopped to realize that every experience in life is an opportunity for God to be glorified in His people? At the beginning of this chapter, Jesus revealed that He was going to the cross for the glorification of God. And as we go through tests, it is also to glorify God.

Why didn't the Lord take us home when we were saved? Wouldn't it have been wonderful if the moment you received the Savior you were taken right home into the presence of God where there is fullness of joy? No, the place where we glorify God is not in heaven, it is on earth. How is the world going to know about our Savior if every believer goes home?

Some Christians say, "I'm going to ask the Lord to take me home." Listen, this is one prayer God doesn't answer. When He wants you home, He is going to take you fast enough. No pills or antibiotics are going to keep you down here when He wants to take you home.

There were three discouraged men in the Bible who asked the Lord to take them home. He never answered one of the three prayers. Do you recall who these men were?

There was Moses, the servant of God. He said, "Kill me, I pray thee . . . and let me not see my wretchedness" (Numbers 11:15).

There was Elijah, the man who shut the heavens and opened them again. He performed miracles. He raised the dead. He fed the hungry. He knew God. Yet he said, as he sat discouraged under the juniper tree, "It is enough; now, O Lord, take away my life; for I am not better than my fathers" (1 Kings 19:4).

There was Jonah, a man who preached in a city, and over half a million inhabitants repented. But Jonah moaned, "Take my life from me: for it is better for me to die than to live" (Jonah 4:3). But God didn't take him home.

He leaves us here for a purpose, that He might be glorified in us. So don't become sour because certain circumstances come into your life, and because certain people disappoint you. It is in the tests and trials of life that our faith grows. He says, "I pray for them." My, what safety. What security. What peace of heart. What joy this gives us.

A Protection for the Disciples (17:11-12)

17:11. *And now I am no more in the world, but these are in the world, and I come to thee. Holy Father, keep through thine own name those whom thou hast given me, that they may be one, as we are.*

As far as the Lord was concerned, His ministry had about come to an end. In a few hours He would be in the presence of His Father, where there is fulness of joy. He would be away from this scene with all its hatred and envy, its opposition of hell and jealousy of the Jews. He was about to be free of the whole thing.

"I'm going home to glory, Father, but I'm leaving these dear men, with all their weakness and frailty in this world that hates Me. I'm leaving them in a world that's going to crucify Me. I'm leaving them in a world of sin and opposition, in a world that is controlled and dominated by its prince, Satan. I'm leaving these dear men, Father, but they can't keep themselves. If they had a problem in the past, they came to Me. If they had a need, they came to Me. If they were hungry, they came to Me. But now I'm leaving them, Father. Where can they go?"

And I just love this: "Holy Father. . . ." It is the only time that Jesus called His Father, "holy Father." Can God in His holiness and righteousness take care of these men in their frailty and sin? Of course. "Holy Father, you keep them."

You see, we were the Father's to begin with. He loved us so

much He gave us to the Son. And now the Son loves us so much,
He's putting us right back into the heart of the Father.

"Holy Father, you keep them." All the love of God is behind
this. "Keep the ones You have given Me through Your own name.
Put Your name on these men. They are Yours. Care for them."
What a ground of comfort and safety. He doesn't trust us to keep
ourselves. That is why it is as if someone puts a knife in my heart
when I hear people say, "Ah, well, you can take yourself out of
God's hand. As long as you hang on, you're saved. But if you
don't hang on, you're not saved."

Listen, friend, there's not a man or a woman on the face of the
earth, and I don't care how godly they may be, who can keep themselves for one minute. Our security, our safety, our joy, our comfort, all we have and need is found in one place—in Him.

The Lord prays for the preservation of His disciples, "that they
may be one, as we are." Here we have the second desire of Jesus in
this chapter. During these last few hours our Lord's great desire is
that these men may know something of this union with the living
God and be brought, not only into a relationship in the family of
God, but also into a oneness with God Himself. He prays that we
might be one with Him in life, one in love, one in fellowship. We
will have this again in verses 20 and 21.

> **17:12. *While I was with them in the world, I kept
> them in thy name: those that thou gavest me I have
> kept, and none of them is lost, but the son of perdition;
> that the scripture might be fulfilled.***

"I've guarded these men. Now Father, You guard them." Jesus
again prays for the safety of His disciples. The Lord will guard that
which we have put in His hands until that day when we stand in His
presence, conformed to the image of His Son (2 Timothy 1:12).
What a Savior we have! What a salvation is this!

A World Opposed to the Disciples (17:13-16)

17:13-16. *And now come I to thee; and these things I speak in the world, that they might have my joy fulfilled in themselves. I have given them thy word; and the world hath hated them, because they are not of the world, even as I am not of the world. I pray not that thou shouldest take them out of the world, but that thou shouldest keep them from the evil. They are not of the world, even as I am not of the world.*

Here our Savior speaks of the opposition of the world to His disciples. He touched on this in chapter 15 when He said, "If the world hate you, ye know that it hated me before it hated you." I am sure one of the reasons why we Christians do not experience the enmity of the world more is because we have compromised with it. The message of God for the world is salvation. The message of God for His people is separation from the world. See 2 Corinthians 6 and 1 John 2.

Nineteen times in this passage our Savior speaks of the world as a system, a kingdom of darkness controlled and dominated by Satan. And when you and I become Christians, we are taken out of the world system. We have no relationship to this system anymore. I repeat it: God's message for the man of this world is salvation, and for the believer it is separation. We are in the world, but not of the world. The whole world lieth in the lap of the wicked one (1 John 5:19). See also Galatians 1:4 and 6:14.

One of the great tragedies is that so many professing Christians are living as those who are in the world. They have been tainted and affected by the materialistic and humanistic philosophy and morals of the world. There is no such thing as a "new" morality. The Bible doesn't speak of any new morality. Sin is sin, and you and I belong to the Savior who died to redeem us from sin. Therefore, as children of God for whom He prays and upon whom He has set His name, as those who are the object of His love and His heart, may we live for Him on earth.

But, you say, "Mr. Mitchell, I'm surrounded by tests and temptations of all kinds." I know. We're living in a world that is a moral cesspool. That is why Christ said, "I pray for them." That is why He said, "Holy Father, You keep them." That is why He said, "Father, make them one, just as We are one."

Believer in Christ, I care not what your circumstances may be, the Father has made you the object of His care. Shall we fail Him? Shall we dishonor Him? Shall we live like the world from which He has delivered us? Shall we not rather be ambassadors representing Him, showing forth the praises of Him who has called us out of darkness into His marvelous light (1 Peter 2:9)?

It is not a question of isolation from the world, but insulation from the world. When we give ourselves to God, it is amazing what He can do with us. We can witness to the world. We can have victory over the world.

Now there are some things we have in the world we will not have in glory. We can witness for Christ in the world as ambassadors for Him. We can experience the power of God to help us overcome the wicked one. We won't need that in heaven. We will be perfect there. We can experience the peace of God during affliction and sorrow. In heaven there will be no more sin, trials, sickness, or death.

This is the world that had no place for Him, the world that opposed Him, the world that eventually crucified Him. Yet in this world He came to the poor, to sinners, to publicans, to sorrowing hearts, to broken hearts, to slaves, and He set them free. And the work He started is passed on to you and to me. This is why we are here in the world today. He started the work. We carry it on until God's purpose is completed.

A Godliness for the Disciples (17:17)

17:17. *Sanctify them through thy truth: thy word is truth.*

Now to do God's work, we must be sanctified. This is the Lord's third request. He prays that we might be kept from the world, and that we might be sanctified.

Now "sanctify" is a wonderful word. It means "to be set apart." And there are two or three aspects of sanctification. For example, we've been sanctified through the offering of the body of Christ, once for all. Look at Hebrews 10:10. In the book of Hebrews sanctification is never by the Spirit. It is always on the ground of the blood of Christ and because of our relationship to Him. We have been set apart for God as an act of God, set apart for God on the ground that He died for us and that we are related to Him. We are "perfected forever" by Christ's death (Hebrews 10:14).

But Jesus could also pray, "Sanctify them through thy truth." Sanctification has a practical side, a daily sanctification, that has to do with our godly walk as Christians in the world. The very heart of Christianity is right here. A holy life in a world that hates God is God's program for His people. Obedience to His Word is a sign of discipleship (8:31).

Sanctification in this sense is not imputed. Justification is imputed to the believer. Righteousness is also imputed. But sanctification isn't imputed; it is more of an impartation, an inwrought work by the Spirit of God because we are in Christ.

If there is no godliness, you can't claim the word, "Christian." I'm not a Christian because I'm godly. But the fruitage of being in Christ is a transformed life, and it is a daily process. There are those who grow fast. And, unfortunately, there are some people who have been on the way fifty years and still act like babies, spiritually speaking.

Don't forget the fact that the more the Word of God takes its place in your life, the more it lives in you, the more like Him you will be. Our Savior walked among men, revealing the Father. As we hear Him speak, we know that He is speaking exactly what the Father would say. As we note His actions and attitudes toward people, we learn exactly what the Father would do. We have the heart of the Father manifest in the life of Christ as it is unfolded in the pages of Scripture. This is why I am so continually urging people to read and reread the Word of God.

The tragedy of the twentieth century Christian church is the fact that we neglect the Word of God. This is why, in religious and secular circles, the Word of God is being pushed out. In many of our seminaries the Word of God isn't wanted. Many of our church-related colleges and universities do not want the Scriptures. And to me the astounding thing is that sometimes the man of the world, the unsaved man, will point out the inconsistencies of religious preachers with respect to the Word of God.

If there is anything Satan and all hell hates, it is a person of Christ and the Word of Christ. And yet it is by this Word that believers are set apart and sanctified, and a godly walk that pleases Him is daily produced in their lives. A godly walk, let me say again, is a rebuke and witness to the man of the world who has no place for Christ.

A Mission for the Disciples (17:18-19)

17:18. *As thou hast sent me into the world, even so have I also sent them into the world.*

We are also sanctified for a mission. Before the Lord started His ministry, He spent all night in prayer. And when He came down from the mountain to the people, He deliberately *chose* twelve men to accompany Him as He walked among men. They didn't choose Him. Every believer in Christ has also been set apart by God for a mission (15:16). He has finished His mission. We learn in chapter 20 that we are to pick it up, for "as my Father hath sent me, even so send I you" (20:21).

I can hear you protest that you don't have any gifts. Wait a minute. What kind of people did God use when He raised up judges over His people, and what kind of instruments did they use? Shamgar had an ox goad (Judges 3:31). Gideon, the least in his father's house, gathered an army and used only lamps and trumpets to rout the enemy (Judges 7:16). Samson used a jaw bone of an ass to kill one thousand Philistines (Judges 15:15).

When God wanted to split the Red Sea, what did He use? Just a dried up old stick (Exodus 14:16). Don't limit God. Don't rationalize your disobedience by saying, "I haven't any gifts." You have been assigned by the eternal, sovereign, living God to go back into the world from which you have been redeemed. Your assignment is to manifest the character and the love and the life of the living God, and to give forth a testimony of the Savior. You are to be a bearer of good news to men who are dead in trespasses and sins.

Do you remember how the book of Acts starts? "The former treatise have I made, O Theophilus, of all that Jesus *began* both to do and teach, until the day in which he was take up. . . ." He began a job; He began a mission. He has assigned you and me to continue the mission.

In Philippians 2:15-16 we read that you and I are "the sons of God . . . in the midst of a crooked and perverse nation, among whom ye shine as lights in the world; Holding forth the word of life." I'm not asking you to be preachers, or even to be missionaries (in the sense of going from your own home to some foreign field), though it would be wonderful if you did. But wherever God has put you, you have an assignment. You are to represent the living God to men.

To me, one of the astounding challenges of the Bible is found in Luke 4:18-19, where Jesus said as He started His ministry, "The Spirit of the Lord is upon me." What for? "To preach the gospel to the poor, to heal the brokenhearted, to preach deliverance to the captives and recovering of sight to the blind, to set at liberty them that are bruised, To preach the acceptable year of the Lord." This is your job and this is my job. Everything in that passage we can do by the power of the Spirit of God who indwells us. "Father, as thou hast sent me into the world, even so have I also sent them into the world." But this is not the end.

17:19. *And for their sakes I sanctify myself, that they also might be sanctified through the truth.*

Did you ever stop to realize that the great thing upon the heart of

Christ is not the upholding of the physical universe? We have supposedly conquered the earth and the heavens, but we still can't conquer ourselves. How far man has gone in his investigation of the powers and forces of nature. How far he has gone in the sphere of medical science and the sphere of nuclear physics. The science of man has gone beyond all the dreams of men who lived just fifty years ago. But the Lord isn't concerned about that.

"By him all things consist" (Colossians 1:17). By Him all things are held together. He upholds "all things by the word of his power" (Hebrews 1:3). He not only is the Creator of all things, and the heir of all things, but He is the upholder of all things. He holds up the physical universe by the Word of His power. But that is not the important thing to Him.

He flings worlds into space at a word, but on His heart are the lives and souls of millions of people on the face of the earth. That is why He came and died for a rebellious world. He has set Himself apart that we might be separated unto the gospel of Christ and sanctified through the truth. He has set Himself apart that we might be separated unto the gospel of Christ and sanctified through the truth.

Christ and His Church (17:20-26)

Oneness for the Church (17:20-21)

From verses 20 through 26 our Savior prayed for us, the church of God today. Mark the great desire of His heart.

> **17:20-21.** *Neither pray I for these alone, but for them also which shall believe on me through their word; That they all may be one; as thou, Father, art in me, and I in thee, that they also may be one in us: that the world may believe that thou hast sent me.*

The desire of our Savior is that we might be one, even as the Father and the Son are one. This is a vital relationship. God deals with vital things, with eternal verities; and this is the great yearning of the heart of our Lord a few hours before He is to be crucified. He desires that we may be in union together as one.

We have the question of oneness all throughout this chapter. "All mine are thine, and thine are mine; and I am glorified in them" (verse 10). "Keep through thine own name those whom thou hast given me, that they may be one, as we are" (verse 11). "That they all may be one; as thou, Father, art in me, and I in thee, that they also may be one in us" (verse 21). "And the glory which thou gavest me I have given them; that they may be one, even as we are one" (verse 22). "I in them, and thou in me, that they may be made perfect in one" (verse 23). "And I have declared unto them thy name, and will declare it: that the love wherewith thou hast loved me may be in them, and I in them" (verse 26).

Notice the repetition of the word "as" or "even as" in these verses. He is dealing with an internal unity. The union of believers will be the same as the union between the Father and the Son. This is not organizational unity dealing with man-made affiliations. This is a vital relationship in life between God and the believer. The lack of this unity has been a tremendous hindrance to men and women everywhere receiving the Savior.

Now there are occasions when the divisions in Christianity occurred because of spirituality rather than carnality. The great revivals that God has brought among men through the years, instead of knitting people together, caused divisions. When Martin Luther stood out for justification by faith, another group started. When Charles and John Wesley ministered those great gospel revivals in Great Britain, it caused separation. That which was cold and worldly and carnal separated from that which was spiritual. This has been true all down through the years. A great many of the so-called denominations have come out of other denominations because of the cleavage concerning spiritual life. And today we see men trying to cause a union between all those who profess the name of Christ, irrespective of doctrine. It is a man-made thing which is doomed to failure. Christianity is centered around a Person, not an organization.

And the Son came for the express purpose of bringing into being a new race of people, separated as the apostle Paul could say, "unto the gospel of God, (Which he had promised afore by his prophets in the holy scriptures,) Concerning his Son Jesus Christ" (Romans 1:1-3). We are those that believe on His name, "which were born, not of blood, nor of the will of the flesh, nor of the will of man, but of God" (1:13). We have been made "partakers of the divine nature" (2 Peter 1:4). Paul in Ephesians 4 and Colossians 3 speaks of the new man which is created in righteousness and true holiness. "If any man be in Christ, he is a new creature" (2 Corinthians 5:17).

Christ wants this new race of people to be one. This is the yearning of His heart. He is going to a cross. He is going to be crucified. He is going to leave these men. And it is not enough for Him to pray that the Father might keep them, but He wants them to realize that "we all, with open face beholding as in a glass the glory of the Lord, are (being) changed into the same image from glory to glory, even as by the Spirit of the Lord" (2 Corinthians 3:18).

As we day by day center our hearts, our affections, our devotion on Him, we change; so that our unity in life with God evidences itself in our unity with each other. Ecclesiastical distinctions disappear when you come to the family of God. We're one in Christ.

I had fellowship the other day with a brother in Christ I've known for a great many years. He doesn't come to my church. He belongs to another. But down through the years we've had wonderful, intimate fellowship. Why? Because we don't talk about denominations or organizations. We talk about the things that knit us together in Christ. We have the same life, the same purpose, the same desires, the same devotion, the same Savior, the same destination.

You go to Africa, China, Southeast Asia, Europe, Central and South America, and you meet people of different color, different language, different culture. But the moment you find they are in Christ, there is a bond there.

I think of some Chinese in Singapore, for example, whom I had never seen before in my life. They took me right into their home, just as if we were brothers. And we are brothers in Christ. There's a oneness there. This is what the Lord is talking about. It's not union in organization, but an internal unity in love, in life, in purpose, and in desire.

I think this is in John's mind, for example, in 1 John 1:3, where he expresses his desire "that ye also may have fellowship (partnership) with us: and truly our fellowship is with the Father, and with his Son." This oneness is the great yearning of our Savior's heart. If you love the Savior, and if you are joined to Him, don't forget that you are joined to one another.

Proverbs speaks of six things God hates, but the seventh one is an abomination to Him. What is that? Sowing "discord among brethren" (Proverbs 6:19). Why? Because we are one in life. We are joined to Him. And when we're joined to Him we are joined to each other. When you sow discord among brethren, you are losing the opportunity for fellowship, for blessing, for usefulness. If you grieve the Spirit, the whole work of God is hindered.

When you and I walk in fellowship with Him, enjoying Him for Himself, we are knit together with every other believer. We yearn to encourage each other in Christ. And do you realize that when Christians are having wonderful fellowship together, it is a testimony to the world that the Father sent the Son to save sinners? The world outside is going to either say, "See how they love one another," or "See how they fight with one another." God's thought is that you and I, in union with Him, may become channels to bring good news to men—good news that Jesus Christ was sent by the Father to redeem men and women from sin, death, and hell.

Glory for the Church (17:22-24)

> **17:22-24.** *And the glory which thou gavest me I have given them; that they may be one, even as we are one; I in them, and thou in me, that they may be perfect in one; and that the world may know that thou*

hast sent me, and hast loved them, as thou hast loved me. Father, I will that they also, whom thou hast given me, be with me where I am; that they may behold my glory, which thou hast given me: for thou lovedst me before the foundation of the world.

In this our Savior deals again with His glory. We actually have two glories here. In verse 22 He *gives* His glory. This glory is His acquired glory, the glory He received from the Father because He accomplished our redemption. In verse 24 He *shows* His glory. This is His moral glory, a glory that we cannot share. We can only gaze upon it.

Paul refers to the glory Christ gives in several places. "I reckon that the sufferings of this present time are not worthy to be compared with the glory which shall be revealed in us" (Romans 8:18). "Our light affliction, which is but for a moment, worketh for us a far more exceeding and eternal weight of glory" (2 Corinthians 4:17). "When Christ, who is our life, shall appear, then shall ye also appear with him in glory" (Colossians 3:4). You and I are going to share in this glory.

In verse 24 Jesus says, "Father, I will. . . ." This is the only time in our Lord's ministry upon the earth where He said to His Father, "I will." In Isaiah 14 we read that Satan, the adversary, said, "I will exalt my throne above the stars of God. . . . I will be like the most High" (14:13-14). He said, "I will" five times in that passage. Jesus said "I will" only once, and it is concerning you and me. "Father, I will that they also, whom thou hast given me, be with me where I am; that they may behold my glory." This is Jesus' fourth and final request in this chapter.

The Lord Jesus is on His way to the cross and to the tomb. He is going to be raised and exalted to God's right hand to be a Prince and a Savior. The astounding thing in all God's universe today is that there is a real Man at God's right hand, glorified with all the glory of the omnipotent God. And you and I are going to see Him in His glory. Why, in the last chapter of your Bible, you read, "And they shall see his face" (Revelation 22:4). What a prospect!

Even David had a little glimpse of that when he said, "Surely goodness and mercy shall follow me all the days of my life: and I will dwell in the house of the Lord for ever" (Psalm 23:6). He could also say, "One thing have I desired of the Lord, that will I seek after; that I may dwell in the house of the Lord all the days of my life, to behold the beauty of the Lord, and to enquire in his temple" (Psalm 27:4). And if David caught a little glimpse and was so yearning to be with the Savior, what about us?

So, in His last words before He went to the cross, the Lord Jesus was thinking about you and me in union with Him. Every believer in Christ is going to stand in the very presence of God and gaze upon Him in His glory. Moses in Exodus 33 said, "Show me your glory." God said, "You can't see Me in My glory and live." But you and I will.

This is one of the most marvelous things, that God should not only redeem us and give us life eternal, but also bring us into this relationship. Christ could say, "Father, I want everyone who believes on Me to be with Me where I am, to see Me in My glory, because You loved Me before the foundation of the world."

Knowledge and the Church (17:25)

17:25. *O righteous Father, the world hath not known thee: but I have known thee, and these have known that thou hast sent me.*

"O righteous Father. . . ." This is the only time the Lord Jesus ever called Him "righteous Father." And the only time Jesus ever called Him "holy Father" was in verse 11, you remember, when He asked Him to care for you and me.

"The world hath not known thee." I took the time to go through these chapters again, from 13 through 17, noticing the things the world doesn't know. In chapter 14 we find that the world knows nothing about the Spirit of God. Jesus said the world cannot receive the Spirit of truth, "because it seeth him not, neither knoweth him" (14:17). When you come to chapters 15 and 16, the world hates the Son of God because it doesn't know Him either. Now He says, "O righteous Father, the world hath not known thee." And I might add, the world also hates the people of God because it doesn't know them, as we read in 1 John 3:1.

Don't be surprised at the ignorance of the world. "The natural man receiveth not the things of the Spirit of God: for they are foolishness unto him: neither can he know them, because they are spiritually discerned" (1 Corinthians 2:14). The world doesn't know the Lord.

"But I have known thee, and these have known that thou hast sent me." The disciples of Christ were the only ones who grasped who Jesus really was. You remember our Savior could pray, "I thank thee, O Father, Lord of heaven and earth, because thou hast hid these things from the wise and prudent, and hast revealed them unto babes. Even so, Father: for so it seemed good in thy sight. . . . Neither knoweth any man the Father, save the Son, and he to whomsoever the Son will reveal him" (Matthew 11:25-27).

The Lord could also say, "Blessed art thou, Simon Bar-jona: for flesh and blood hath not revealed it unto thee, but my Father which is in heaven" (Matthew 16:17). And this revelation to believers continues today as God reveals Himself through His people and through His Word. If our hearts and minds are closed, we will never learn a thing. But if our hearts and minds are open to what God wants to teach us, then He *will* teach us.

Love for the Church (17:26)

Mark how Jesus closes this section.

> **17:26. And I have declared unto them thy name, and will declare it: that the love wherewith thou hast loved me may be in them, and I in them.**

Jesus ends this section (from chapter 13 through 17) the same way He started it—with His infinite love for His disciples. "Having loved his own which were in the world, he loved them unto the end" (13:1). Now Jesus prays "that the love wherewith thou hast loved me may be in them, and I in them." This divine and perfect and eternal love that the Father has for the Son, and the Son for the Father, is the same love He has for you and me.

Indeed, this is the kind of love He wants to see displayed through you and me. You remember in Romans 5:5 we read, "The love of God is shed abroad in our hearts by the Holy Ghost which is given unto us." Paul could also say in 2 Corinthians 5:14, "The love of Christ constraineth (overmasters) us." When God's people come to the place where His love is evident in their lives, in their words, in their actions and attitudes and motives the one to the other, then you have a revival of God in the midst of His people.

If we ever want to see a great ingathering of souls, it will be when God's people get right with Him. This rules out all pettiness and all harsh criticism. It knits us together in a bond. It causes the world to wonder and say, as they said of the early church, "See how they love one another."

8/6/88

John 18

Christ, The Faithful One
(Part 1)

Introduction to John 18-21

We come to the last hours of our Savior's life here on earth. Throughout this Gospel we have seen Jesus Christ present His credentials as God manifest in the flesh. We have considered His seven great signs. We saw His power over creation in chapter 2 when He turned water into wine, and in chapter 6 when He fed the five thousand and walked on water. We saw His authority over sickness in chapters 4, 5, and 9 when He healed the sick, the lame, and the blind. Finally, we saw His power over death in chapter 11 when He raised Lazarus from the dead. Yet here Christ begins to manifest His greatest sign of all concerning His person and work.

"What sign shewest thou unto us?" the Jews demanded in chapter 2. "What authority do you have to cleanse the temple?"

Jesus replied, "Destroy this temple, and in three days I will raise it up." You remember the Jews didn't understand what He meant, but we read that "he spake of the temple of his body." That temple is about to be destroyed.

In this chapter we will find Jesus in the Garden of Gethsemane where Judas will betray Him. We will see Him stand before the religious and civil courts of His day. In chapter 19 He will be condemned and crucified. In chapters 20 and 21 we will see the risen Savior manifesting the reality of His resurrection from the dead.

Indeed, the resurrection is the greatest and final sign of His person and authority.

The rest of the New Testament is built upon the fact that we have a risen Savior. Peter finishes the very first gospel message by saying, "Therefore let all the house of Israel know assuredly, that God hath made that same Jesus, whom ye have crucified, both Lord and Christ" (Acts 2:36). And in his last recorded words to the Jewish leaders, Peter goes on to say, "The God of our fathers raised up Jesus, whom ye slew and hanged on a tree. Him hath God exalted with his right hand to be a Prince and a Saviour" (Acts 5:30-31). What was the center and focus of the early church? It was the resurrection of Christ. My friend, is it the center of your life?

The Betrayer Steps Forward (18:1-11)

Agony of Jesus (18:1)

18:1. *When Jesus had spoken these words, he went forth with his disciples over the brook Cedron, where was a garden, into the which he entered, and his disciples.*

We now come to the beginning of the last few hours of Jesus' life here on earth. Jesus moves from being an intercessor to becoming a sacrifice. He moves from being in the center of His beloved disciples to being in the midst of His enemies for the fulfillment of His redeeming work.

John does not speak of our Lord's agony in Gethsemane. It has already been mentioned in Matthew, Mark, and Luke. When John wrote many years later, he possibly did not see the need to mention it. Or perhaps it was too sacred for him to mention, for here you have the final submission of our Savior to the will of His Father.

Jesus crossed over the brook Cedron. He took His disciples into the Garden with Him. Then He took Peter, James, and John further, as we find in the other Gospels. There He tells them to watch and pray lest they enter into temptation.

He cries in prayer, "O my Father, if it be possible, let this cup pass from me: nevertheless not as I will, but as thou wilt" (Matthew

26:39). Mark records in his Gospel that Jesus' soul was "exceeding sorrowful unto death" (14:34). We had this first in Isaiah, where we read, "He hath poured out his soul unto death" (53:12). In Luke's Gospel we have Jesus in intense suffering, sweating "as it were great drops of blood" (22:44).

But as I said before, John mentions nothing of this agony. We read only that there "was a garden, into the which he entered" with his disciples. As we read of the Garden of Gethsemane we realize that we can never fathom what complete submission to the will of the Father meant to Christ. We know what Psalms 22 and 69 prophesied concerning Him. He knew this as well. And He knew what Isaiah 50:5-7, 52:14, and 53 meant. He knew the prophetic picture of the intense suffering and abuse to which He was going.

What would you and I do if we knew God wanted us to give our back to the smiters, and our cheeks to those who would pluck off the hair? What would we do if we knew the crown of thorns would bite into our heads, if we knew our face would be marred more than any man's? What would we do if we knew we would be stripped naked and nailed to a tree?

The band of men coming with Judas to the Garden could deliver Him to such a death. He knew this. Yet He could say, as was first written in Psalm 40:6-8, "Sacrifice and offering thou wouldest not, but a body hast thou prepared me. . . . Then said I, Lo, I come . . . to do thy will, O God" (Hebrews 10:5, 7).

The very center of all time is before us. The Godhead had planned in ages past that He, the holy and righteous Son of God, would be made that terrible thing called "sin" for us. No wonder He shrank; no wonder He said, "My Father, if it be possible, let this cup pass from me. . . ." But He went forth as a Conqueror. He knew the victory was won.

Wickedness of Judas (18:2-3)

I do not know how far down a person can go in sinfulness and opposition to Christ, but I think here we have one of the vilest things a person could ever do.

> **18:2-3.** *And Judas also, which betrayed him, knew the place: for Jesus ofttimes resorted thither with his disciples. Judas then, having received a band of men and officers from the chief priests and Pharisees, cometh thither with lanterns and torches and weapons.*

Judas had accompanied the Savior for over three years as one chosen for ministry by the Lord Himself. Judas had heard His gracious words and wonderful claims. Judas had seen His marvelous miracles. He had seen five thousand fed with five loaves and two fish. He had seen Lazarus raised from the dead. He had seen lepers cleansed, blind eyes opened, and the palsied healed. He knew what took place in the privacy of the Garden of Gethsemane when the Lord of glory would meet with His Father.

Is it possible for a person to live three years with the Savior, and then, because of a few shekels, betray the holy Son of God? Is it possible that a person can go to church and hear the truth of the Word of God and see the Son of God exalted week by week, but eventually be lost?

My friend, it is very possible to start in the beginner's department and go through the whole Sunday School, and live your life in the midst of the things of God, and yet not know Him. Judas never knew the Son of God in a vital relationship. Even in chapter 13, when our Savior was urging Judas to turn from the path he was taking, Judas was still set in his mind to go tell the priests where to find Him. He still brought a band of men and officers from the chief priests and Pharisees. They came with torches and weapons to capture the One who went about unarmed, "doing good, and healing all that were oppressed of the devil; for God was with him" (Acts 10:38).

Submission of Jesus (18:4-11)

Notice Jesus' reaction when Judas and the mob came.

18:4-6. *Jesus therefore, knowing all things that should come upon him, went forth, and said unto them, Whom seek ye? They answered him, Jesus of Nazareth. Jesus saith unto them, I am he. And Judas also, which betrayed him, stood with them. As soon then as he had said unto them, I am he, they went backward, and fell to the ground.*

Here we see His majesty. Before they could find Him, He went to meet them. Oh, the manifestation of His majesty, the manifestation of His person as the Son of God. What authority! He merely said, "I am he," and the whole multitude fell to the ground, including Judas.

What a time for Jesus and the disciples to run away. They could have simply slipped off and left their enemies in fear and confusion. How easy. But the Lord was completely submissive to the will of His Father. That meant the cross, and He knew it.

18:7-9. *Then asked he them again, Whom seek ye? And they said, Jesus of Nazareth. Jesus answered, I have told you that I am he: if therefore ye seek me, let these go their way: That the saying might be fulfilled, which he spake, Of them which thou gavest me have I lost none.*

Observe the Lord's concern for His own here. My Christian friend, weak though you may be, remember you are always the object of His care, of His love, of His devotion. Just think of it. You personally are the object of His devotion. He said, "I give unto them eternal life; and they shall never perish, neither shall any man pluck them out of my hand."

18:10. *Then Simon Peter having a sword drew it, and smote the high priest's servant, and cut off his right ear. The servant's name was Malchus.*

Now, dear Peter had to do something. And the final miracle our Lord performed before the cross was to repair what one of His disciples did in fleshly enthusiasm. In Luke's Gospel we are told that the Lord "touched his ear, and healed him" (22:51). It's interesting. Wherever we find the power of God at work, we also seem to find a manifestation of the flesh.

Now don't you for one moment think that Peter was a real swordsman. He was really attempting to cut the fellow's head off. Peter was a fisherman, not a swordsman.

18:11. *Then said Jesus unto Peter, Put up thy sword into the sheath: the cup which my Father hath given me, shall I not drink it?*

May I suggest two cups the Lord drank? One was the cup of suffering, which we have in Luke 22:44. "Being in an agony he prayed more earnestly: and his sweat was as it were drops of blood falling down to the ground." The other is the cup of submission, which we have here. "Shall I not drink the cup which my Father hath given me to drink?"

A Hearing Before Annas: The Beginning of the Trials (18:12-14)

18:12-14. *Then the band and the captain and officers of the Jews took Jesus, and bound him, And led him away to Annas first; for he was father in law to Caiaphas, which was the high priest that same year. Now Caiaphas was he, which gave counsel to the Jews, that it was expedient that one man should die for the people.*

"The Jews took Jesus, and bound him." I say, Jesus was bound, not so much by the fetters the soldiers put upon Him, but because of His love for sinners. Jesus could say in chapter 10, "No man taketh my life from me, but I lay it down of myself. I have power to lay it down, and I have power to take it again. This commandment have I received of my Father."

They could not have bound Him against His will. But, let me say again, it was His love for you and for me which prompted Him to submit to them. He willingly set His face to go to the cross.

The Lord Jesus was first led to Annas, the father-in-law of Caiaphas, the high priest, for a hearing. For a number of years Israel's high priest, Annas, was succeeded in that office by his sons and son-in-law, Caiaphas. Annas was really the power behind Caiaphas and the priesthood, and the brains behind the graft so evident in the temple. He was a very subtle man, full of politics, full of schemes.

Our Lord actually appeared in three courts after this hearing. He was tried before the religious court of Caiaphas. Between His trips to Pilate He came before the worldly court of Herod (Luke 23:6-12), a fact which John doesn't mention. Finally, Jesus did appear before the civil court of Pilate, the Roman governor (Matthew 27:2, 11-26). The trial before Pilate in the Gospel of John begins in verse 28 of this chapter and continues through verse 15 of the next chapter.

First Denial by Peter (18:15-18)

Calling of Peter (18:15)

18:15. *And Simon Peter followed Jesus, and so did another disciple: that disciple was known unto the high priest, and went in with Jesus into the palace of the high priest.*

I feel inclined to spend some time on Peter, because he has such a great place in my heart. He is so much like the rest of us, and we're so much like him.

When the Lord first met Peter, his name was Simon. Jesus said, "Thou shalt be called Cephas" (1:42). The word here is "stone" or "rock." This is not a large, immovable rock, but a rock you can kick around with your foot.

After the Lord charged Simon's name, I believe Peter, Andrew, James, and John went back to their fishing. The Lord met them later and said, "Follow me, and I will make you fishers of men" (Matthew 4:19).

In Luke 5, after the miraculous draft of fishes, Peter said, "Depart from me; for I am a sinful man, O Lord" (5:8). Then the Lord said, "Fear not; from henceforth thou shalt catch men" (5:10). In other words, Jesus was saying, "Peter, follow Me. From now on you are going to catch men alive."

Courage of Peter

Peter showed his courage and faith when the disciples were caught in a storm. The Lord came walking on the water in the third watch of the night. We had this in chapter 6 of this Gospel and in Matthew 14. The men were scared. They thought they saw a spirit.

Jesus said, "It is I—be not afraid."

Peter said, "Lord, if it's really You, then bid me to come to You." I love dear Peter, because he passed a test none of the others was willing to face. As his feet touched the water, he was still hanging on to the boat. But he let go, trusting in the one word of the Savior, "Come."

Peter let go, and he walked on the water. Don't you question it. He walked on the water, and he didn't have skis. But then he felt the wind blowing and saw the waves rolling high. I can just hear the others yelling, "Watch out, Pete! A wave is coming!" The moment he got his eyes off the Savior and on to his circumstances, he fell in a hole. And as he was going down, he called, "Lord, save me. I'm perishing!"

The Lord pulled him up, and you can be sure Peter walked back to the boat very close to the Savior. Peter had the courage of faith. The others didn't. His problem was that he did things on the spur of the moment without thinking. "Lord, if that's really You, let me come out to You." And Peter was safer when he walked on the water with the one word, "Come," under his feet, than when he was in the boat with two planks between him and the water. A believer is safest when he dares to trust what God says.

The Lord didn't think it was an awful thing for Peter to say, "Let me come to You." I think He was thrilled that Peter wanted to come. Jesus says, "Come unto me, all ye that labour and are heavy laden, and I will give you rest" (Matthew 11:28). "Him that cometh to me I will in no wise cast out" (John 6:37).

So many people feel pressed down by the weight of disappointments, troubles, sorrows, afflictions, and problems. They've prayed and prayed, but there does not seem to be any deliverance. My friend, sometimes the Lord permits us to sink just like Peter. He wants us to get to the end of ourselves. The Lord desires to have people trust Him to meet their every need.

Confession of Peter

Both in Matthew 16 and John 6 we have Peter's great confession. In Matthew 16:16 Peter says, "Thou art the Christ, the Son of the living God." In John 6 Peter says, "Thou hast the words of eternal life. And we believe and are sure that thou art that Christ, the Son of the living God."

Peter learned that truth by revelation. It wasn't revelation given to the Pharisees, the Sadducees, or the priests. Instead, it was given to a humble fisherman, an impulsive man, but a man whose heart yearned for reality.

Wherever God finds a heart that means business with Him, He will meet that heart. The trouble is, many today don't desire the things of God. Truth is imparted only to open hearts, to hungry hearts.

In Matthew 16 Peter received three revelations: of Jesus' person (that He is the Christ, the Son of the living God), of His purpose (that He is going to build a church), and of His program (that He is going to suffer, die, be buried, and be raised again).

But then Peter breaks out and says, "Lord, You forgot something. I have just declared that You are the Christ, the Son of the living God, and now You tell me You are going to suffer and die. Get this out of Your head. This can't happen to You."

And the Lord said to Peter, "Get behind Me, Satan. You don't understand the things that be of God." Poor dear Peter. He is always the same. But for all his frailty and for all his torrent of words, right down in Peter's heart there is a great yearning and a great love for the Son of God. He has a genuine love for the Savior.

Confidence of Peter

In John 13, Judas went out to betray Jesus, and it was night. The Lord said to the disciples, "I am going to leave you."

Peter said, "Lord, where are you going?"

"Well, where I'm going you can't come now, but you will come afterwards."

"Lord, why can't I go with You now? I'll die for You. I'll go to prison for You. I'll suffer anything for You."

But Jesus said, "Peter, before the cock crows tonight, you will deny Me three times."

Peter didn't realize what the Lord was saying. He had meant every word when he said, "I'll die for You, Lord." But pride and self-confidence in a Christian's life are the first steps to denial.

Then in Luke 22:31-32, the Lord said, "Simon, behold, Satan hath desired to have you, that he may sift you as wheat: But I have prayed for thee, that thy faith fail not: and when thou art converted, strengthen thy brethren."

Peter said, "Lord, don't You worry about that. You can count on old Peter."

Please notice that when Jesus announced Peter would deny Him, He also said, "I have prayed for you, Peter, that your faith fail not." So many Christians never realize the wonder of our Lord's present ministry.

Do you remember 1 John 2:1? "My little children, these things write I unto you, that ye sin not. And if any man sin, we have an advocate with the Father, Jesus Christ the righteous." The Lord had already prayed for Peter before he ever thought of denying Him. He didn't pray that Peter wouldn't sin, but that his faith would not fail.

There's no question about what happened. Even when he was denying his Lord with oaths and curses, Peter's faith did not fail. Faith is never destroyed by tests or by frailty. Peter's love didn't fail. Peter failed.

"Simon, when you're converted, strengthen your brethren." The very man who denied the Lord with oaths and curses was chosen to be the mouthpiece of the Spirit of God on the day of Pentecost. Three thousand were saved. It was the same man, transformed and indwelt by the Spirit.

What was Peter's original trouble? It was his pride and self-confidence. "Though all deny You, I will not deny You. I will die for You. I'll go to jail for You. Lord, you can sure count on me." This was his first step down.

Carelessness of Peter

Next, Peter became prayerless. The Lord brought the disciples across the brook, and took Peter, James and John apart and told them to watch and pray lest they enter into temptation. Then He went a little farther and prayed, "Father, if it be possible, let this cup pass from Me." When He returned, He found them asleep. They had found it easier to sleep than to pray.

Now Peter was a good sleeper. He slept on the Mount of Transfiguration in the Lord's glory (Luke 9:32). He slept here in the Garden in our Lord's agony. And in Acts 12:6 he slept in jail while Herod planned his execution. It seems to me, by the way, that there are quite a few Simon Peters in church every Sunday morning.

Peter's third step down was doing things in the energy of the flesh. This was the incident when he cut off the ear of the high priest's servant, which we had in verse 10 and 11.

And what was the next step down? Peter followed "afar off" after the soldiers bound the Lord and led Him away. Now Peter is still following. He is still in love with the Savior. But his love just drags its feet. He wants to run away, but his love keeps him following.

Compromise of Peter (18:16-18)

18:16. *But Peter stood at the door without. Then went out that other disciple, which was known unto the high priest, and spake unto her that kept the door, and brought in Peter.*

This is Peter's fifth step down. Peter stood outside the gate of the high priest's house. There are those who believe John was inside. How a commercial fisherman, a Galilean, should be a close friend of the high priest, is open to question. Whoever he was, I think he felt he was doing Peter a favor; but he wasn't. It would have been better if Peter had stayed outside.

18:17. *Then saith the damsel that kept the door unto Peter, Art not thou also one of this man's disciples? He saith, I am not.*

Here is Peter's first denial. This man, who took up a sword with courage and chopped off the ear of the high priest's servant, wilts before a girl, a servant girl.

18:18. *And the servants and officers stood there, who had made a fire of coals; for it was cold: and they warmed themselves: and Peter stood with them, and warmed himself.*

This is Peter's final step down. Here is a man who said he was going to die for the Savior, yet he is taking comfort from the enemies of Christ and warming himself at their fire. Peter compromised by being where the enemy was, doing what the enemy was doing. We will find Peter still warming himself by the fire when we come to verse 25. Many of God's people are like Peter today. We compromise by warming ourselves at the enemy's fire.

Trial Before Caiaphas (18:19-24)

18:19-24. *The high priest then asked Jesus of his disciples, and of his doctrine. Jesus answered him, I spake openly to the world; I ever taught in the synagogue, and in the temple, whither the Jews always resort: and in secret have I said nothing. Why asketh thou me? ask them which heard me, what I have said unto them: behold, they know what I said. And when he had thus spoken, one of the officers which stood by struck Jesus with the palm of his hand, saying, Answerest thou the high priest so? Jesus answered him, If I have spoken evil, bear witness of the evil: but if well, why smitest thou me? Now Annas had sent him bound unto Caiaphas the high priest.*

Matthew and Mark are very clear as to Jesus' trial before the religious court of Caiaphas (Matthew 26:57-68; Mark 14:53-65). John takes it for granted as he writes his Gospel many years later (18:24). This court was an illegal court. It was contrary to the law to try a man in the middle of the night and not give him an opportunity for defense. Furthermore, the sentence was passed before He was tried. The priests and the leaders of Israel had already determined to kill Jesus. When they brought Jesus before Pilate, they merely wanted Pilate to carry out their verdict. It was also illegal for the officer to smite the defendent during the trial.

"I have done nothing in secret," Jesus said. "My whole ministry has been above board. Ask those who heard Me." This was an open rebuke to the high priest.

I'm amazed at the longsuffering of the Lord of glory, to stand there to be buffeted, to be smitten, to be spat upon by these men who were supposed to be servants of God. In the other Gospels our Lord didn't answer his questions until they put Him under oath. The issue in this religious court concerns His person. It has nothing to do with His character. Our Lord had claimed to be the Son of God, equal with God in power and authority, He claimed to be the

Bread, the Light, the Deliverer, the Sinless One, El Shaddai, Abraham's God, the eternal One, One with the Father. The issue before the religious court is His Person. We have this in chapter 19, where the Jews tell Pilate, "We have a law, and by our law he ought to die, because he made himself the Son of God" (19:7).

Final Denials by Peter (18:25-27)

Here we have Peter again.

18:25-27. *And Simon Peter stood and warmed himself. They said therefore unto him, Art not thou also one of his disciples? He denied it, and said, I am not. One of the servants of the high priest, being his kinsman whose ear Peter cut off, saith, Did not I see thee in the garden with him? Peter then denied again: and immediately the cock crew.*

"Simon Peter stood and warmed himself." Many of God's people are like that, as I said before. We warm ourselves at the enemy fire, the fire of the world. We don't want to be separate. We want to be where the world is. We want to do what the world does. By doing this we compromise. I would rather stand for the person of our Savior and the authority of God's Word and stand alone, than warm myself at the enemy's fire and be one with the gang.

The logical sequence of Peter's steps downward ends in denial. Here we have the last two denials of Peter. But it started way back with pride and self-confidence, prayerlessness, demonstration of the flesh, following afar off, and compromise. That's why Peter denied the Lord with oaths and curses.

After Peter's third denial we read that "the Lord turned, and looked upon Peter" (Luke 22:61). I don't believe Jesus looked on him with a critical attitude or with a face that condemned him. Nor do I believe He looked with an expression of great disappointment. I think He looked on Peter with such love that it broke his heart. We read that he "went out, and wept bitterly" (Luke 22:62).

I love what happened after the resurrection. In Luke 24:34 we learn that "the Lord is risen indeed, and hath appeared to Simon." The Lord had a special meeting with Peter. And He wants to have special meetings with all such Simons who step away from the Lord and are out of fellowship with Him. The Lord sought out Simon. He is always the Seeker. No matter how many steps we take downward, He is the One who always says, "Come."

Trial Before Pilate Begun (18:28-40)

The Jews' Demand: "He Must Die" (18:28-32)

John does not discuss Christ's trial before the worldly court of Herod. But here he tells us quite a bit concerning His trial before the civil court of Pilate.

> **18:28-32.** *Then led they Jesus from Caiaphas unto the hall of judgment: and it was early; and they themselves went not into the judgment hall, lest they should be defiled; but that they might eat the passover. Pilate then went out unto them, and said, What accusation bring ye against this man? They answered and said unto him, If he were not a malefactor, we would not have delivered him up unto thee. Then said Pilate unto them, Take ye him, and judge him according to your law. The Jews therefore said unto him, It is not lawful for us to put any man to death: That the saying of Jesus might be fulfilled, which he spake, signifying what death he should die.*

The accusation of the Jews was spoken outside the judgment hall. You notice the empty profession, the false holiness, of these men whose hearts were full of murder against the holy Son of God. They said, "We can't come into the judgment hall lest we be defiled." You talk about empty religion. If they had gone into the judgment hall, Pilate wouldn't have defiled them. They would have defiled Pilate. They were full of murder and hate and envy against the Son of God.

"What accusation bring ye against this man?" Pilate asked them. The Jews dodged the issue. They said, "If he were not a malefactor, we would not have delivered him up unto thee. But we have tried him, and he must be put to death."

"Well, you take him, and judge him according to your law." Pilate is trying to get rid of this thing. And I want you to mark this man Pilate. I am of the persuasion he knew about Jesus. He was the governor, the ruler of Judaea, and he knew what was going on in his territory. Why, only a few days before, Lazarus had been raised from the dead. Pilate knew about these things. I have no doubt he had heard about Him.

And when Pilate saw them bring Jesus to him, he knew that they didn't want him to try Him. They wanted him to pronounce sentence and carry out the sentence they had already passed. Again, I say, Pilate is trying to get out of this.

Jesus' Response: "I Am Not This World's King" (18:33-37)

18:33. *Then Pilate entered into the judgment hall again, and called Jesus, and said unto him, Art thou the King of the Jews?*

Mark what the issue is with Pilate. It is a political thing. "Art thou the king of the Jews?" In the Jewish proceedings it was a question of the person of Christ. But in the Gentile court it is a question of the character of Christ.

18:34-36. *Jesus answered him, Sayest thou this thing of thyself, or did others tell it thee of me? Pilate answered, Am I a Jew? Thine own nation and the chief priests have delivered thee unto me: what hast thou done? Jesus answered, My kingdom is not of this world: if my kingdom were of this world, then would my servants fight, that I should not be delivered to the Jews: but now is my kingdom not from hence.*

Jesus is saying, "My kingdom is not of the earth. It is not run by soldiers and power and authority as the Roman government is." Again Pilate asks whether Jesus is a king or not.

> **18:37. Pilate therefore said unto him, Art thou a king then? Jesus answered, Thou sayest that I am a king. To this end was I born, and for this cause came I into the world, that I should bear witness unto the truth. Every one that is of the truth heareth my voice.**

You see, as you look into this scene, Jesus is not on trial. He puts Pilate on trial. The conscience of Pilate is becoming stirred. Pilate is confused. The issue is Christ, and Pilate doesn't know what to do with this man. He is obviously not a malefactor, and He isn't a criminal. He stands in dignity as a king would. Pilate is accustomed to having prisoners grovel before him, trying to get out of punishment. But here is a man already condemned to death by his own people.

Pilate's First Appeal: "Jesus or Barabbas?" (18:38-40)

> **18:38. Pilate saith unto him, What is truth? And when he had said this, he went out again unto the Jews, and saith unto them, I find in him no fault at all.**

Now the scene is outside the judgment hall again. This is the first of three attempts by Pilate to release Jesus. Notice his testimony: "I find no fault in him, no fault at all."

> **18:39. But ye have a custom, that I should release unto you one at the passover: will ye therefore that I release unto you the King of the Jews?**

"Ah," he is thinking, "now I'll get out of this thing. I'll find the worst man in my prison, and stand him against Jesus, and make them choose."

> **18:40. Then cried they all again, saying, Not this**

man, but Barabbas. Now Barabbas was a robber.

Pilate has made a decision. He brings out Barabbas on one side, and puts Jesus on the other. The very fact that he put them up for a choice indicates he has already passed sentence, although he said, "I find no fault in him." If Pilate found no fault in Jesus, why did he bring Christ out as a criminal to be chosen as one of two? How unreal it seems that the One whom we know as the altogether lovely One was "despised and rejected of men." Indeed, "he was despised and we esteemed him not" (Isaiah 53:3).

John 19

Christ, The Faithful One
(Part 2)

Trial Before Pilate Concluded (19:1-15)

Pilate's Final Appeals: "What Fault Is in Him?" (19:1-6)

Pilate has already failed once to release Jesus. Now he decides to
try another scheme. He wants to release Him, and he thinks he can
appease the Jews at the same time, but he simply doesn't understand them.

> **19:1-4.** *Then Pilate therefore took Jesus, and
> scourged him. And the soldiers platted a crown of
> thorns, and put it on his head, and they put on him a
> purple robe, And said, Hail, King of the Jews! and
> they smote him with their hands. Pilate therefore went
> forth again, and saith unto them, Behold, I bring him
> forth to you, that ye may know that I find no fault in
> him.*

The soldiers scourged Jesus in the presence of Pilate. They tore
His clothes off, and hung Him up with His feet off the ground, tied
and spread-eagled. They whipped Him until His body and His face
were marred more than any man's. Then they platted a crown of
thorns and jammed it down on His head. In mockery they put an
old robe on His back and a reed in His hand. "Hail, King of the
Jews!" they shouted. And then they snatched the reed out of His
hand and smote Him with it.

After this, Pilate took Him out to the Jews. Pilate must have thought their human sympathy for a mutilated Man would move them. He stood Jesus before them, blood and spittle running down His face. But Pilate didn't know these Jews. They couldn't care less that he found no fault in Him.

> **19:5. Then came Jesus forth, wearing the crown of thorns, and the purple robe. And Pilate saith unto them, Behold the man!**

"Behold the man!" I would love to spend an hour here. Here was the only real Man that ever walked the earth. He was God's Man. We are just poor imitations.

> **19:6. When the chief priests therefore and officers saw him, they cried out, saying, Crucify him, crucify him. Pilate saith unto them, Take ye him, and crucify him: for I find no fault in him.**

When Pilate said this, he knew they couldn't actually crucify Jesus. The Roman law forbade it. But mark this is the third time Pilate has said, "I find no fault in him."

Questioning of Jesus (19:7-12)

> **19:7-9. The Jews answered him, We have a law, and by our law he ought to die, because he made himself the Son of God. When Pilate therefore heard that saying, he was the more afraid; And went again into the judgment hall, and saith unto Jesus, Whence art thou? But Jesus gave him no answer.**

I am sure that Pilate was thinking of all the miracles he had heard about. "Who are you? Where did you come from?" Pilate is scared. He knew he had gone too far to have this Man scourged, and the Lord knew it as well. "Whence art thou?" Pilate asked, but Jesus gave no response.

Pilate questioned Jesus again.

> **19:10-12.** *Then saith Pilate unto him, Speakest thou not unto me? knowest thou not that I have power to crucify thee, and have power to release thee? Jesus answered, Thou couldest have no power at all against me, except it were given thee from above: therefore he that delivered me unto thee hath the greater sin. And from thenceforth Pilate sought to release him: but the Jews cried out, saying, If thou let this man go, thou art not Caesar's friend: whosoever maketh himself a king speaketh against Caesar.*

The Jews first of all chose Barabbas. Now they choose Caesar, and as a nation they turn their back on God. They have turned their back on the King, and have acknowledged their servitude to Rome. I remember the prophecy of Jacob in Genesis 49:10, where he says, "The sceptre shall not depart from Judah . . . until Shiloh come." Shiloh has come. The sceptre has departed. Openly before the Roman governor, they declared their allegiance to Rome. They preferred Caesar to Christ. Their decision is made.

The Final Decision: "Crucify" (19:13-15)

After questioning Jesus, Pilate made one more futile attempt to release the Savior.

> **19:13-15.** *When Pilate therefore heard that saying, he brought Jesus forth, and sat down in the judgment seat in a place that is called the Pavement, but in the Hebrew, Gabbatha. And it was the preparation of the passover, and about the sixth hour: and he saith unto the Jews, Behold you King! But they cried out, Away with him, away with him, crucify him. Pilate saith unto them, Shall I crucify your King? The chief priests answered, We have no king but Caesar.*

Notice that Pilate was being tried by the Son of God. Pilate was being forced to answer the question as to what he would do with

Jesus who is called the Christ. In the end, the cries of the Jews moved Pilate to deliver Jesus to be crucified. The Jews crucified One who claimed to be God. The Gentiles crucified One in whom they found no fault. Both are equally guilty of the crucifixion of Christ.

Peter picked this up in his sermon in Acts 2, where he said, "You men of Israel: you took Jesus, and by wicked hands you crucified Him." He accused them in Acts 4 and 5 of killing the Prince of life, the Savior of man. In 1 Corinthians 2:8 the apostle Paul wrote of the princes of this world who, "had they known it, would not have crucified the Lord of glory." Jew and Gentile are equally guilty of the crucifixion of Christ.

Crucifixion of Christ (19:16-24)

The Suffering, the Shame of Christ (19:16-17)

19:16. *Then delivered he him therefore unto them to be crucified. And they took Jesus, and led him away.*

Although John was an eyewitness of the crucifixion, he gives us few details of what took place. Matthew and Mark record Jesus' words, "My God, my God, why hast thou forsaken me?" They also note that there were three hours of darkness while Jesus hung on the cross. Matthew and Mark are dealing with Jesus Christ as the trespass offering and as the sin offering. For this reason they emphasize the separation of the Father and the Son during crucifixion.

John is dealing with the work of Christ at the cross as the burnt offering, as the One who is wholly satisfactory to God. Nothing is said about this separation here.

Very little is said in any Gospel concerning the sufferings of Christ. One has to go to Psalms 22 and 69, as well as Isaiah 50, 52, and 53. The scourging, the beating, the maligning, the scoffing, the mocking, the smiting, the crown of thorns—this has all taken place. Jesus has come before the religious court of the Jews, and they have given Him over to the civil court of Pilate to be crucified.

Pilate realized they had done this for envy. There was no justice being done.

> **19:17.** *And he bearing his cross went forth into a place called the place of a skull, which is called in the Hebrew Golgotha.*

Did you ever stop to think of the shame Jesus experienced? The Romans called those who were crucified, "the bearers of the cross." It was a special word of contempt that plumbed the depths of derision. "Bearers of the cross" became an accursed name. Our precious Savior, the holy One of God, after being scourged, beaten, abused, despised, spat upon, and crowned with thorns, became a "bearer of the cross."

None of us can even begin to realize the depths of this. But when our Savior in Gethsemane cried out, "My Father, if it be possible, let this cup pass from me: nevertheless not my will, but thine, be done," He knew what the cross meant. He knew. Beaten, bleeding, bearing His cross, He went forth to a place called, "The Place of the Skull," outside the city of Jerusalem. The crucifixion couldn't take place in the city. Wasn't it called "the holy city"? But He was crucified as an accursed thing, as we read in Galatians 3:13.

The Preeminence of Christ (19:18)

> **19:18.** *Where they crucified him, and two other with him, on either side one, and Jesus in the midst.*

John doesn't say a word about the thieves. Matthew and Mark declare they both railed on Christ. Luke tells us one turned to Jesus and said, "Lord, remember me when thou comest into thy kingdom." Jesus said to him, "To day shalt thou be with me in paradise" (Luke 23:42-43). Notice, the Lord sets the time when they will be in paradise.

When our Savior was crucified on the center cross, He was recognized as the preeminent criminal. The two thieves were dying because of their own crimes, but Jesus died for the sins of the world. If we want to see ourselves as we really are, we must look at Christ hanging on the cross. He became an accursed thing and was nailed to a cross in our place. "He humbled himself, and became obedient unto death, even the death of the cross" (Philippians 2:8).

The cross carries a curse, an anathema, a stigma. Paul wrote to the Galatian church, "God forbid that I should glory, save in the cross of our Lord Jesus Christ, by whom the world is crucified unto me, and I unto the world" (6:14). Paul could also say, "Why do I suffer persecution? If I were to have the rite of circumcision, or add any ordinance to what Christ did on the cross, I wouldn't suffer persecution. But then would the stigma, the offense, of the cross cease" (see Galatians 5:11).

Jesus was crucified "in the midst." He was the center. The Lord Jesus Christ is always, and always will be, in the center. When He was born in Bethlehem, He was the center of attraction to the shepherds and the wise men. When He was a lad twelve years of age, He was in the center of the leaders of Israel in the temple, confounding them with His questions and with His answers. When He was baptized by John in Jordan, He was the center, for the voice from heaven said, "This is my beloved Son, in whom I am well pleased" (Matthew 3:17).

On the Mount of Transfiguration with Moses and Elijah, Peter said, "Lord, let's make three tabernacles: one for You, and one for Moses, and one for Elijah." A voice came out of the excellent glory, saying, "This is my beloved Son, in whom I am well pleased. Listen to Him. Never mind Moses. Never mind Elijah. My Son has come."

On the way to Jerusalem Jesus was the center of attraction. At the feast He was the center. And now on the cross He is the center. They put Him on the center cross, making Him the preeminent criminal. And today in the glory at the very right hand of the Majesty on high He is the center of attraction. And may I add this, my friends? When He ceases to be the center of attraction in our worship, then we degenerate into a mere religious ceremony.

Kingship of Christ (19:19-22)

19:19-22. *And Pilate wrote a title, and put it on the cross. And the writing was, JESUS OF NAZARETH THE KING OF THE JEWS. This title then read many of the Jews: for the place where Jesus was crucified was nigh to the city: and it was written in Hebrew, and Greek, and Latin. Then said the chief priests of the Jews to Pilate, Write not, The King of the Jews; but that he said, I am King of the Jews. Pilate answered, What I have written I have written.*

Notice the anger of Pilate here. He was angry at the Jews! With deep cynicism he said, "What I have written, I have written. I am not going to change anything else for you Jews." So the sign, "JESUS OF NAZARETH THE KING OF THE JEWS," crowned the cross in three languages. Everyone could read it. It was as if Pilate were saying, "You've chosen Caesar, but here is your king. This is your king. This accursed one is your king.

They said, "We don't want Him. Change it."

Pilate refused. He had written that under the authority of God. He could not have changed it had he wanted to.

My friend, Jesus is the King of the Jews. He was born the King of the Jews. "Where is he that is born King of the Jews?" the wise men asked when they came to Herod in Matthew 2. Jesus also lived as the King of the Jews. He stood before Pilate as a King. He said, "My kingdom is not of this world." And here Jesus dies as the King of the Jews.

The day is going to come when the Lord Jesus Christ is going to be gloriously manifested before all nations, all kindreds, all tongues. He will be manifested as the Lord of Lords and King of Kings. He is going to shepherd the nations with a rod of iron. He came once in lowliness, in humiliation. But Jesus is coming again to reign with authority and to put the nations under His feet.

We read about Christ's reign in Isaiah 11. There we are told that righteousness will gird His loins, and that the poor man will have justice. The knowledge of the Lord shall cover the earth as the waters cover the sea. No wonder, when you come to the last verses in the Bible, we read that after the Lord Jesus says, "Surely I come quickly," John responds, "Even so, come, Lord Jesus" (Revelation 22:20). My, what a time that is going to be!

Raiment of Christ (19:23-24)

Here we see the authority of Scripture.

> **19:23-24.** *Then the soldiers, when they had crucified Jesus, took his garments, and made four parts, to every soldier a part; and also his coat: now the coat was without seam, woven from the top throughout. They said therefore among themselves, Let us not rend it, but cast lots for it, whose it shall be: that the scripture might be fulfilled, which saith, They parted my raiment among them, and for my vesture they did cast lots. These things therefore the soldiers did.*

These verses prove the inerrancy of Scripture. Some people tell me that the Bible is not worthy of our trust or belief, that our Lord as a Jew knew the Old Testament prophecies and tried to fulfill them. But did Jesus manipulate these Roman soldiers into buffeting Him, scourging Him, spitting in His face, beating and maligning Him, putting a crown of thorns on His head, and mocking Him? And now they sit by the cross and gamble over His garments, indifferent to the death of the Son of God, indifferent to the Jews around them. There they are, casting their dice for His garment. Who told them to gamble over His garments?

Why should the prophet, a thousand years before this, write of this very fact, that in the hour of His being crucified, they should gamble over His garments? If you doubt the Word of God, its authority, its inspiration, its inerrancy, think of this. Approximately one thousand years before Christ it was written that He would experience crucifixion, and that they would gamble over His garments, and give Him vinegar to drink.

Here it is. These were Gentiles. More than likely, they were idolaters with a great deal of contempt for the Jewish people among whom they lived. Cold, indifferent to His death, they gambled over His garments. And may I say this with sadness? Many people today are just as indifferent, just as cold, just as insensitive to the death of Jesus, the Son of God. Oh, the tragedy of that fact!

No wonder the prophet cried out, "Is it nothing to you, all you that pass by," that Jesus, the Son of God, the holy One, the sinless One, should die such a death as an accursed thing? The physical sufferings, terrible as they were, were not as dreadful as His spiritual sufferings. This is God's way of redeeming men and women. Every other way is a false way. I say that dogmatically. He, as the slain Lamb, satisfied divine holiness. He made it possible for us to be redeemed. This is the divine way.

Last Words of Christ (19:25-30)

"Woman, Behold Thy Son" (19:25-27)

Mark Christ's care for His own, even while He hung on the cross.

19:25-27. *Now there stood by the cross of Jesus his mother, and his mother's sister, Mary the wife of Cleophas, and Mary Magdalene. When Jesus therefore saw his mother, and the disciple standing by, whom he loved, he saith unto his mother, Woman, behold thy son! Then saith he to the disciple, Behold thy mother! And from that hour that disciple took her unto his own home.*

As far as I know in the record, Jesus never called Mary His mother. In John 2, when they had no wine, He called her "Woman." The other Gospels record that when Mary and the relatives came to see Jesus and couldn't get through the crowd, someone said to Him, "Your mother and Your brothers are outside waiting to see You."

Jesus replied, "Who is My mother, and who are My brothers, but those who do the will of My Father who is in heaven?"

Now, I don't want to minimize Mary's place as the mother of our Lord, the channel through whom our Savior should come. But it is rather remarkable that the Lord Jesus, as far as the record goes, never said, "Mother." Even on the cross, even though He was in intense suffering, He said, "Woman, behold thy son!" His care for His own was wonderful.

"I Thirst" (19:28-29)

Notice Jesus' cry as He hangs on the tree.

> **19:28-29.** *After this, Jesus knowing that all things were now accomplished, that the scripture might be fulfilled, saith, I thirst. Now there was set a vessel full of vinegar: and they filled a spunge with vinegar, and put it upon hyssop, and put it to his mouth.*

We read in chapter 13 that Jesus knew "that his hour was come that he should depart out of this world unto the Father." He also knew who should betray Him. And now on the cross He knew that "all things were accomplished."

Jesus didn't say, "I thirst," just that the Scripture might be fulfilled. He was actually thirsty. In Psalm 22:15 we read, "My tongue cleaveth to my jaws; and thou hast brought me into the dust of death." The process of crucifixion produces great thirst.

But may I say that every Scripture in the Old Testament, every detail concerning the first advent of our Savior among men, was fulfilled. If every detail of the first advent of Christ was completed, we can be sure that every detail of the second coming of Christ will be completed. If He came the first time to be a Savior, He is going to come the next time to be a Judge. If He came the first time in humiliation, He is going to come the next time in glory. If He came the first time to be maltreated, He is going to come the next time to be honored, and to reign as Lord of Lord and King of Kings.

"It Is Finished" (19:30)

19:30. *When Jesus therefore had received the vinegar, he said, It is finished: and he bowed his head, and gave up the ghost.*

When everything was completed, Jesus cried out, "It is finished!" Then He bowed his head. His head didn't drop. He bowed it in resignation and "gave up the ghost."

When our Lord Jesus said, "It is finished," He finished the work of redemption. He not only put away the sins of men, but He also made it possible to take sinners who believe in Him and fit them for the presence of God. This was eternally God's plan. Christ appeared once in the end of the age "to put away sin by the sacrifice of himself" (Hebrews 9:26). "This man, after he had offered one sacrifice for sins for ever, sat down on the right hand of God" (Hebrews 10:12).

We also have this in 1 John 3:5, where we read, "Ye know that he was manifested to take away our sins." And John the Baptist could say, "Behold the Lamb of God, which taketh away the sin of the world" (1:29).

Peter could write that Jesus bore "our sins in his own body on the tree" (1 Peter 2:24). Isaiah declared, "All we like sheep have gone astray; we have turned every one to his own way; and the Lord hath laid on him the iniquity of us all" (53:6).

Christ died to put away your sin and my sin, and He finished the work. Romans 5:9 says, "Much more then, being now justified by his blood, we shall be saved from wrath through him." In Him we have not only redemption, not only forgiveness, not only justification, not only life eternal, but we are covered with all the merit and beauty and glory of the Son of God. This He accomplished at the cross. This is God's way of redemption.

"Knowing that all things were now accomplished . . . he bowed his head, and gave up the ghost." You can't do that. I can't do that. No person can do that. Our times are in His hands. He's the One who settles the time of our death.

May you and I be delivered from all the coldness and indifference of these days concerning our Savior. How easy it is for God's people to be so occupied with things here that we miss out in our appreciation of the wonderful Savior we have, and what He has accomplished for mankind.

As you speak to the unsaved, tell them that He finished the work. Redemption is completed. He asks them to accept Him as Savior and as Lord. We sometimes sing, "Nothing in my hands I bring, Simply to thy cross I cling." He is the Savior, the complete Savior. He has finished the work. Blessed be His name.

Now you and I go free. You and I have become the children of God by faith in Him. Our sin question has been settled once, for all, forever. He has destroyed the evidence, and you and I now stand before Him dressed in His righteousness alone, in all the merit and beauty of our Savior. May the Lord make this real to you. The price of our redemption has been paid!

Death of Christ Confirmed (19:31-37)

Execution Completed by Soldiers (19:31-35)

19:31. *The Jews therefore, because it was the preparation, that the bodies should not remain upon the cross on the sabbath day, (for that sabbath day was an high day,) besought Pilate that their legs might be broken, and that they might be taken away.*

The Jews were very keen about keeping every detail of their religious rites. In Deuteronomy 21:22-23 we read that if a malefactor should be hung, his body should not be allowed to hang on the sabbath day. So the Jews came on that account to Pilate. They said, "We would like you to have the bodies taken down from the crosses and put away. Let them be tossed on the ash heap where criminals are tossed." That is what "taken away" means here.

Now the Romans let the victims hang on the cross until they died. Often this took two or three days. Then they were taken from the cross and thrown on the heap. But you see, it was the preparation for the Passover, and these who slew the Lord of glory were more concerned about some little religious rite than they were about Him. Pilate didn't care, but he did want to be sure that Jesus was dead. I do not know what was in his mind, but I think he was still a very scared man. He seemed relieved when the centurion declared that Christ was dead.

19:32. *Then came the soldiers, and brake the legs of the first, and of the other which was crucified with him.*

This word "to brake" is an interesting word. It means "to smash or break in pieces." In other words, when they broke the legs of malefactors, they had to be sure that when they were through that the victims were dead. As you remember, Jesus and the thieves were crucified in the middle of the day, between the third and the sixth hour. The soldiers took their mallets and smashed the bones of the two thieves.

But it was unnecessary to break Jesus' legs.

19:33-35. *But when they came to Jesus, and saw that he was dead already, they brake not his legs: But one of the soldiers with a spear pierced his side, and forthwith came there out blood and water. And he that saw it bare record, and his record is true: and he knoweth that he saith true, that ye might believe.*

Some say that Jesus really never did die, that He was only in a swoon, that He was not dead when they took Him from the cross the same day He was crucified. They say that in the coolness of the tomb He was resuscitated, and that when the stone was rolled away He merely came out of the tomb. They say that there is no need to believe in any resurrection because He never died.

But the Jews made sure He was dead. The Roman soldiers, who were accustomed to dealing with death, made sure He was dead. To confirm it, they pierced His side. Out came blood and water. The centurion knew He was dead. John, who saw all these things, knew He was dead. Joseph of Arimathaea and Nicodemus, two men who took His body from the cross, wrapped it in spices and linen cloths, and put it in the tomb, knew He was dead. There is no question as to the death of Jesus Christ. The Jews made sure of it. The Romans made sure of it. And the disciples knew it.

Scripture Fulfilled by Soldiers (19:36-37)

19:36. *For these things were done, that the scripture should be fulfilled, A bone of him shall not be broken.*

You remember in Exodus 12, where it speaks of the Passover lamb, it says, "neither shall ye break a bone thereof" (12:46). In the book of Psalms it speaks of the fact that "he keepeth all his bones: not one of them is broken" (34:20). God saw to that.

I want you to see the sovereign power of God in fulfilling His purposes. Jesus said, "I thirst," that the Scriptures might be fulfilled. Knowing that everything was accomplished, He cried out, "It is finished." Then He bowed His head in resignation, and He gave up the spirit. God even fulfilled His purposes though the actions of the Jews and the soldiers. They fulfilled every prophecy to the letter.

19:37. *And again another scripture saith, They shall look on him who they pierced.*

Zechariah 12:10, written between 500 and 600 B.C., gives this prophecy concerning the return of our Lord to the earth. Revelation 1:7 says, "Behold, he cometh with clouds; and every eye shall see him, and they also which pierced him: and all kindreds of the earth shall wail because of him." They won't rejoice, but wail when they see Him whom they pierced.

Now that Christ has died according to the Scriptures, what was His experience after His death? Someone has asked me what took place when our Lord died. Where did He go? May I suggest several Scriptures here? In Psalm 16 we read: "Therefore my heart is glad, and my glory rejoiceth: my flesh also shall rest in hope. For thou

wilt not leave my soul in hell; neither wilt thou suffer thine Holy
One to see corruption" (16:9-10). The apostle Peter in Acts 2 says
this refers not to David, but to our Savior, for he said that we have
David's sepulchre with us to this day.

In Psalm 69, which also has to do with the death and burial of our
Savior, we read these words: "Deliver me out of the mire, and let
me not sink: let me be delivered from them that hate me, and out of
the deep waters. Let not the waterflood overflow me, neither let the
deep swallow me up, and let not the pit shut her mouth upon me"
(69:14-15).

You remember our Lord mentioned the fact that as Jonah was
three days and three nights in the belly of the fish, "so shall the Son
of man be three days and three nights in the heart of the earth"
(Matthew 12:40). We have in Jonah 2 these verses concerning the
prophet's experience in the fish: "I cried by reason of mine affliction unto the Lord, and he heard me; out of the belly of hell cried I,
and thou heardest my voice. For thou hadst cast me into the deep,
in the midst of the seas; and the flood compassed me about: all thy
billows and thy waves passed over me. Then I said, I am cast out of
thy sight; yet I will look again toward thy holy temple. The waters
compassed me about, even to the soul: the depth closed me round
about, the weeds were wrapped about my head. I went down to the
bottoms of the mountains; the earth with her bars was about me for
ever: yet hast thou brought up my life from corruption, O Lord my
God" (Jonah 2:2-6).

And then if I might read from one more passage: "Wherefore he
saith, When he ascended up on high, he led captivity captive, and
gave gifts unto men. (Now that he ascended, what is it but that he
also descended first into the lower parts of the earth? He that descended is the same also that ascended up far above all heavens,
that he might fill all things)" (Ephesians 4:8-10).

Burial of Christ (19:38-42)

19:38-42. *And after this Joseph of Arimathaea,*

being a disciple of Jesus, but secretly for fear of the
Jews, besought Pilate that he might take away the
body of Jesus: and Pilate gave him leave. He came
therefore, and took the body of Jesus. And there came
also Nicodemus, which at the first came to Jesus by
night, and brought a mixture of myrrh and aloes,
about an hundred pound weight. Then took they the
body of Jesus, and wound it in linen clothes with the
spices, as the manner of the Jews is to bury. Now in
the place where he was crucified there was a garden;
and in the garden a new sepulchre, wherein was never
man yet laid. There laid they Jesus therefore because
of the Jews' preparation day; for the sepulchre was
nigh at hand.

Up to this time, you've had wicked hands at work. Wicked
hands scourged the Lord Jesus, took off His garments, put a purple
robe on Him, and beat Him. Wicked hands nailed Him to a cross.
But once He cried, "It is finished," Jesus was no longer in the
hands of wicked men. Now loving hands take over. All four Gospels mention Joseph of Arimathaea. Only John mentions that
Joseph did not agree with the decision of the council when it declared that our Savior must die. He was a secret disciple, a rich
man, the one who brought the linen.

Nicodemus came with him. Both men were members of the
Sanhedrin. Both were rulers of Israel. Both were possibly there
when our Savior was on trial. Only John mentions Nicodemus's
visit to the Lord Jesus by night. He came then, not because he was a
coward, but because he wanted a personal and private talk with the
Savior. What better time than at night? In chapter 7 of John he was
the one who said, "Doth our law judge a man before it hear him?"

Both men are like Elijah's seven thousand who would not bow
the knee to Baal. Nobody knew about them but God. And yet,
when Christ died, something got hold of these men. Notice, they
didn't go to the chief priests. They didn't go to the soldiers. They
went to Pilate for permission to take the body of Jesus. Joseph was

taking a stand against the Jews, against the leaders, and against the Romans. He took a stand for the Savior, even though his Savior was dead. He hadn't lost his love for Him, or his faith in Him. But he lost his hope, like the two disciples in Luke who said, "We trusted that it had been he which should have redeemed Israel" (24:21).

Joseph and Nicodemus gently took the body of our Savior down from the cross. Nearby was a garden in which was a tomb, "wherein was never man yet laid." I sat one time on a bench in front of that garden tomb. It was dug right out of the solid rock. And as you go into the entrance of the tomb, you stand in a short passageway. To the right, you can see where these two men put the body of Jesus after wrapping Him in spices. In that tomb someone had planned to put three persons, but only one crypt was finished and ready to receive a body. You see, no one else could have come out of that tomb because no one else was in the tomb. It was a new tomb. Scripture is very specific about this. It wasn't just anyone's tomb. It was a new tomb where no one had ever lain. Note how God in His sovereignty guards this thing. If there is a resurrection, it has to be that of Jesus.

Now, there was something about the death of our Savior that transformed these men from weak, secret believers into outspoken, courageous men. And believe me, they did a courageous thing. If they hadn't, what would have become of the body of Jesus? The disciples were not there. But God arranged that these men should take care of this, as was foretold in Isaiah 53:9. Oh, the marvel of it all! Our Savior was born in someone else's manger, and He was buried in someone else's tomb. He didn't have a place to lay His head. And this One became our Savior.

Remember, Jesus is no longer in the tomb. He who died, and was buried, and was raised from the dead, is going to come back to raise His people from the dead, and to fit us to enjoy eternal glory. Then the whole man—body, soul, and spirit—will be transformed and glorified, and made "like unto His glorious body" (Philippians 3:21).

John 20

Christ, The Victorious One

Introduction to John 20

Now we come upon the final testimony to the authority of Jesus Christ, the Son of God. All that our Savior has done, all that He has said, all the claims He has made, will go for nothing (as far as authority is concerned) if He is not raised from the dead. The very foundation of our Christian faith is wrapped up in the resurrection of our Savior.

"If Christ be not raised," wrote the apostle Paul in 1 Corinthians 15:17, "your faith is vain; ye are yet in your sins." Indeed, the great witness that God has given the world concerning the Person of His Son and the efficacy of His work at the cross is given to us in the resurrection from the dead, which marked Jesus Christ out from all others (Romans 1:4).

When the Jews asked the Lord for a sign in chapter 2, He answered, "Destroy this temple, and in three days I will raise it again."

In the book of Matthew, chapter 12, the Jews again asked for a sign. The Lord said, "There will be no sign given to this wicked and adulterous generation, but the sign of the prophet Jonah: for as Jonah was three days and three nights in the belly of the fish: so shall the Son of man be three days and three nights in the heart of the earth" (12:39-40).

It is still God's witness to the world concerning Jesus Christ.

Paul in Acts 17 on Mars Hill preached that God has set apart "a day, in the which he will judge the world in righteousness by that man whom he hath ordained; whereof he hath given assurance unto all men, in that he hath raised him from the dead" (17:31). More than twenty times in the book of Acts the apostles spoke of the resurrection of the Lord Jesus. Paul said to Agrippa, "Why should it be thought a thing incredible with you, that God should raise the dead?" (Acts 26:8).

And lest I be misunderstood, when we speak of the resurrection of Jesus Christ, we're speaking of the physical resurrection. There's no such thing in the Bible as a spiritual resurrection. The word "resurrection" doesn't mean a thing if that which died is not raised again. The spirit doesn't die; the body dies. It is the body that is raised. And all hell was determined to keep the body of Jesus in the tomb.

Discovery of the Empty Tomb (20:1-10)

20:1. *The first day of the week cometh Mary Magdalene early, when it was yet dark, unto the sepulchre, and seeth the stone taken away from the sepulchre.*

The Jews told Pilate, "That deceiver said, while he was yet alive, After three days I will rise again. Command therefore that the sepulchre be made sure until the third day" (Matthew 27:63-64). So Pilate gave them permission to make the sepulchre as sure as they could. They sealed the heavy stone and set a watch. It would have been impossible for anyone, especially one woman all by herself, to roll away the stone. I question if Mary or the other woman who came later even knew about the seal or the Roman guard. They were good Jews. They would have stayed home on the sabbath day.

20:2-6. *Then she runneth, and cometh to Simon Peter, and to the other disciple, whom Jesus loved, and saith unto them, They have taken away the Lord*

*out of the sepulchre, and we know not where they have
laid him. Peter therefore went forth, and that other
disciple, and came to the sepulchre. So they ran both
together: and the other disciple did outrun Peter, and
came first to the sepulchre. And he stooping down,
and looking in, saw the linen clothes lying; yet went he
not in.* (John, like Mary, just looked.) *Then cometh
Simon Peter following him, and went into the sepulchre, and seeth the linen clothes lie.*

Whether it be Mary, John, or Peter, you will notice how human
they are and what different personalities they have. It was so typical of Peter to dash in; so typical of John, "that other disciple," to
stay behind; so typical of Mary to be standing there sobbing. Each
acts according to his own personality.

Peter, just like Peter, went right into the sepulchre "and seeth the
linen clothes lie."

20:7. *And the napkin, that was about his head, not
lying with the linen clothes, but wrapped together in a
place by itself.*

Peter stood there bewildered by what he saw. He was con-
founded, confused. Read Mark 16 and Luke 24. He didn't know
what to make of it. There was no body there. Here were the linen
clothes that had been wrapped around the body of Jesus. And there
was the napkin which had been wrapped around His head. How
could a robber take the body and leave the linen?

If Jesus Christ were not dead when He was put in the tomb, how
could he have torn the linen wrappings off Himself? He was in a
linen straitjacket. God absolutely guarded this thing. The grave
was not robbed, and the Lord did not get out of the tomb except the
way the Scriptures say.

20:8. *Then went in also that other disciple, which
came first to the sepulchre, and he saw, and believed.*

This word "saw" here means "to see with the intellect, with assurance, with understanding." When John saw the clothes he believed.

John found the clothes as they had been on the body, with the napkin laid down in perfect order. In other words, the resurrection of Jesus Christ was a deliberate thing. God is the God of order. You wouldn't expect to find any chaos. You wouldn't expect to find things tossed around. When the Son of God was raised from the dead, He was raised supernaturally. He defeated death and the grave. He had robbed the grave of its prey. He came forth in resurrection and left the clothes just as they were. John saw and believed. His Savior was alive. He had been raised from the dead.

Personally, I will never forget the day that I looked into the tomb. It changed my whole ministry. It came to me that my Savior was really alive, that His work on the cross for sinners so satisfied divine justice and divine character and divine righteousness, that I would never see my sins again. God raised Him from the dead as a guarantee to me personally that death has no more authority over the man in Christ. It has been shorn of its power, "that through death he might destroy him that had the power of death, that is, the devil; And deliver them who through fear of death were all their lifetime subject to bondage" (Hebrews 2:14-15). At the cross we see His love, but in resurrection we see His power.

To grasp the meaning of Jesus' resurrection there at the tomb changed my whole outlook on life. God made it real to me that the One who had died on the cross of shame was no longer on the cross, no longer in the tomb. We've been joined to a risen Savior. That is why the apostles gave witness with such great power in the book of Acts. Paul stood before Felix, before Festus, before Agrippa, before the Sanhedrin, before the philosophers of Athens, and before the corrupt Corinthians with only one message. He preached the risen Christ.

Buy why is the resurrection of Christ one of the rarest messages you ever hear today? Even among evangelicals, where is this wonderful truth? You can go to evangelistic meetings week after week, and you hear about the cross and about Christ's death for our sins. And that's true. I wouldn't want to diminish that for one moment.

But I say, the cross is a tragedy if there is no resurrection. Would to God that His people would continually rejoice that our Savior is alive forevermore.

John looked in and he saw and believed.

> **20:9-10.** *For as yet they knew not the scripture, that he must rise again from the dead. Then the disciples went away again unto their own home.*

Nothing more is said about John and Peter at the tomb. The chances are good they went right back to Mary, the Lord's mother (since John had now taken her into his own home), and told her.

Christ's Appearance to Mary (20:11-18)

Mary Searches for Christ's Body (20:11-13)

> **20:11-12.** *But Mary stood without at the sepulchre weeping: and as she wept, she stooped down, and looked into the sepulchre, And seeth two angels in white sitting, the one at the head, and the other at the feet, where the body of Jesus had lain.*

I want you to mark the marvelous devotion of this woman. Mary Magdalene was the one out of whom the Lord had cast seven demons. He had become her Teacher and Lord. Her whole life was wrapped up in Him. She was not looking now for a living Christ. She was looking for a dead Christ. It was not in her thinking that He was raised from the dead.

> **20:13.** *And they say unto her, Woman, why weepest thou? She saith unto them, Because they have taken away my Lord, and I know not where they have laid him.*

She said to the disciples, "They have taken away the Lord." She said to the angels, "They have taken away my Lord, and I know not where they have laid Him."

They had asked, "Why are you weeping?" This word "to weep"

here is more than just crying. She was sobbing out her heart. Not even the angels could distract her. She had every right to weep if Jesus were dead. I wish you and I had half the devotion for Christ that Mary had. If He is raised from the dead, she has no ground for weeping. But she didn't know He was risen from the dead.

You know, as I have read this over and over again, and tried to put myself there in the garden, I couldn't help but ask myself, "Well, if I had seen two angels, what would I have done?" I would have become occupied with the angels. Here are two heavenly beings. I have never seen one in my life, either in my dreams or while awake.

But here are two angels, and they are sitting in the place where the Lord had lain. A vision of angels is not going to stop this woman from finding her Lord. Her life, her devotion, her love are all wrapped up in a dead Christ. "Where have you laid Him?" she asked. "If I only knew where they have laid Him."

Mary Meets the Risen Christ (20:14-16)

It may be that these angels somehow indicated that they saw someone outside, for the next verse tells us Mary turned around.

> **20:14-15.** *And when she had thus said, she turned herself back, and saw Jesus standing, and knew not that it was Jesus. Jesus saith unto her, Woman, why weepest thou? whom seekest thou? She, supposing him to be the gardener, saith unto him, Sir, if thou have borne him hence, tell me where thou hast laid him, and I will take him away.*

Mary's heart is wrapped up in the Savior. Is yours? Do you permit things to come into your life that distract you from Christ? Is this not true of all of us? We allow material things, friends, circumstances—anything under heaven—to come between us and searching and seeking the Lord.

Absolutely nothing, however, not even the vision of angelic beings, is going to hinder this dear woman from seeking her Savior.

You would think if she were so devoted to Him, and knew Him so well from having accompanied Him so long, surely she should have recognized Him. But remember, she is sobbing. She is not expecting to meet a risen Savior. She is occupied with her sorrow. It is very natural that she came to the conclusion that the person she saw there was the caretaker of the garden.

"Sir, if thou have borne him hence, tell me where thou hast laid him, and I will take him away." How she was going to carry the body away, I don't know. But she was determined to find Him. Let me say it again. I can't read this passage without being convicted in my own heart. How much devotion do you and I have for Him? We do so little for Him. We give so little. We say so little. We serve so little. God give us some of this devotion to Christ personally—a devotion that will not be sidetracked by anything in this world.

> **20:16.** *Jesus saith unto her, Mary. She turned herself, and saith unto him, Rabboni; which is to say, Master.*

That one little word, "Mary," transformed deep sorrow to joy. That one word transformed hopelessness into hope. It transformed Mary from a sobbing woman into a joyous woman. "Rabboni . . . Master!" Only He could meet such a heart's need. What did you say when you heard His voice for the first time? What is this risen Christ to you, believer? Is He your Lord? Is He your Master?

Mary Goes to the Disciples (20:17-18)

> **20:17.** *Jesus saith unto her, Touch me not; for I am not yet ascended to my Father: but go to my brethren, and say unto them, I ascend unto my Father, and your Father; and to my God, and your God.*

Now it is true in Matthew's Gospel that the Lord revealed Himself to the women who came together to the sepulchre, and they touched Him. They thus found it to be really true that He had been raised from the dead. But with Mary there was no such need. Once

He had said, "Mary," and she had said, "Rabboni," there was no unbelief here.

Jesus is saying, "Don't touch Me now, Mary. Don't lay hold of Me. I have something far better for you. I have a ministry for you. Go and tell My brethren that I am alive." The revelation of His person to her brought her an opportunity for immediate service.

Now there is also a new relationship. In the first fifteen chapters of John's Gospel, His followers were called "disciples." In John 15:15 He calls them "friends." "I no longer call you servants; . . . but I have called you friends; for all things that I have heard of my Father I have made known unto you." But now, after the resurrection, the new relationship with Him is as "brethren." That's why we read in Hebrews 2:11-12, "He that sanctifieth and they who are sanctified are all of one: for which cause he is not ashamed to call them brethren, Saying, I will declare thy name unto my brethren, in the midst of the church will I sing praise."

Jesus is determined that we shall be "conformed to the image of his Son, that he might be the firstborn among many brethren" (Romans 8:29). We are brought into a wonderful intimacy of relationship. "I ascend unto my Father, and your Father; and to my God, and your God." But let us be careful never to call Jesus our "brother." He's not our brother; He's our Lord.

> **20:18. Mary Magdalene came and told the disciples that she had seen the Lord, and that he had spoken these things unto her.**

The very first witness of the resurrection of Christ was a woman. Her message concerned His words, and His first words after the resurrection were personal words—words of comfort, words of love, words of instruction and inspiration.

Christ's Appearance to the Disciples (20:19-23)

The Disciples Receive Peace (20:19)

> **20:19. Then the same day at evening, being the first**

day of the week, when the doors were shut where the
disciples were assembled for fear of the Jews, came
Jesus and stood in the midst, and saith unto them,
Peace be unto you.

You remember the message of the heavenly host in Luke 2 was,
"On earth peace, good will toward men," or "Peace on earth to men
of good will." The testimony of the angels was for peace. And the
first word of our Lord to His assembled disciples after the resurrection was, "Peace."

Now, there is no question but that it was natural for these disciples to be in a room with the doors and windows shut. Just a few
days before this, our Savior had been crucified. I believe they were
together because they had heard the testimony of the women and of
the two who had seen the Lord on the road to Emmaus that Jesus
was alive. You can well imagine the consternation in their hearts
and minds. And how like the Lord to zero in on their essential
needs with His first words, "Peace be unto you."

Notice, Jesus didn't say, "Peace," and then call them down for
leaving Him. He didn't remind them of their cowardice. He didn't
remind them of their boasts, when they said, "Though all forsake
You, I'll never forsake You." They all had said that. And He didn't
remind them of their frailty. He didn't remind them of their failure.
He simply said, "Peace." What they needed was not a rebuke.
They needed to have their hearts comforted. They needed certainty
and assurance of the redemption He had accomplished.

His last words to them in the upper room had been, "These
things have I spoken unto you, that in me ye might have peace. In
the world ye shall have tribulation: but be of good cheer; I have
overcome the world" (16:33). God wants men and women to experience peace. Paul reinforces this by saying, "Therefore being
justified by faith, we have peace with God" (Romans 5:1).

The first experience for a person who accepts the Savior is
peace. His sins are forgiven. Condemnation is past. Eternal life has
been given as a free gift. He has been transformed from a child of
wrath into a child of God. This brings peace. "Peace I leave with

you, my peace I give unto you: not as the world giveth, give I unto you. Let not your heart be troubled, neither let it be afraid" (14:27). All through His ministry He has ever brought peace to troubled hearts.

The Disciples Receive a Commission (20:20-21)

20:20-21. And when he had so said, he shewed unto them his hands and his side. Then were the disciples glad, when they saw the Lord. Then said Jesus to them again, Peace be unto you: as my Father hath sent me, even so send I you.

It is the same Jesus they knew and loved, the same Lord they had seen crucified. "Then were the disciples glad." What an understatement! Death had been conquered. Life and immortality had been brought to light. Their Savior had burst the bonds of the tomb. He had finished the work of redemption. He proved His deity, being marked out from everyone else as "the Son of God . . . by the resurrection from the dead" (Romans 1:4).

"As my Father hath sent me, even so send I you." He is saying to them, "I have finished My work which the Father has sent Me to do. It is completed. I came with authority. I came with power. I demonstrated that authority. I have proved to the world, and to My people Israel, that I am the Messiah, that I am the Son of God as well as the Son of Man. I have finished the work of redemption, a work that will bring peace to troubled hearts.

"But I'm going back home to glory. And as My Father sent Me with authority to do a work, so send I you." He changes the word here. "I have the authority to send you with My power to finish the job that is to be done. I send you now as My representatives. I send you in union with Myself to do the job of bringing men to God."

What was the purpose of God when He sent His Son? He "sent His Son to be the propitiation for our sins" (1 John 4:10). What is His purpose now? To gather out "a people for his name" (Acts 15:14).

One isn't surprised to find in the first chapter of Acts that He gathers His disciples together just before His ascension and says, "But ye shall receive power, after that the Holy Ghost is come upon you: and ye shall be witnesses unto me both in Jerusalem, and in all Judaea, and in Samaria, and unto the uttermost part of the earth" (Acts 1:8). His final words then are the same as we have here: "My Father sent Me. Now I am sending you." He has given them the ministry of reconciliation. We are "ambassadors for Christ" (2 Corinthians 5:20).

The Disciples Receive Authority (20:22-23)

20:22-23. *And when he had said this, he breathed on them, and saith unto them, Receive ye the Holy Ghost. Whose soever sins ye remit, they are remitted unto them; and whose soever sins ye retain, they are retained.*

This is the only time in the New Testament where this word is used, "He breathed on them." It was used in the Old Testament in Genesis 2:7, where God breathed into man's nostrils "the breath of life; and man became a living soul." Man was nothing. There was a body without life, without a soul, until God breathed into him. The same thought is in Ezekiel 37, regarding the valley of dry bones. There Ezekiel said to the Spirit of God, "Breathe upon these slain, that they may live" (37:9). And life came.

Here Jesus breathed on these disciples and said, "Receive ye the Holy Ghost." This is something new. He's been raised from the dead, and He's going to send them into the world. They are to be His representatives. But they can't go as they are. They must have authority.

Now, I'm well aware that there are certain theological groups that believe that when Jesus breathed on the ten disciples (Thomas was not there, as we shall see), they received apostolic authority, and were given power to forgive or not forgive sins. I question if God ever gave any man the authority to remit sin. This is His own prerogative. In the other Gospels you read that Jesus said to the man with the palsy, "Son, be of good cheer; thy sins be forgiven thee." The Jews said in their hearts, "Who is this man that He can forgive sin? Only God can take away sin."

You and I may forgive each other, but we don't put away, give away, or take away sin. Nor is this something that is handed down from generation to generation in an apostolic succession. There is no such thing in the Book. If these men received something at this time, it would possibly be apostolic authority in the early church. Peter in Acts 5 pronounced judgment upon Ananias and Sapphira. He exercised apostolic authority. So did Paul with the Corinthian church when he talked of delivering "such an one over unto Satan for the destruction of the flesh, that the spirit may be saved" at the coming of the Lord (1 Corinthians 5:5). But I question whether this has to do so much with that, as it has to do with the fact that we have a new responsibility. Now only these ten men, but every believer has a responsibility.

What about the authority? What about the power to do this job? I believe here He has given to us the authority to bear testimony to men in sin that their sins can be remitted by their faith in the risen Son of God. He has given us the authority to declare nothing short of judgment for those who refuse the Savior (2 Corinthians 2:15-16).

Thomas Is Absent (20:24-25)

20:24. But Thomas, one of the twelve, called Didymus, was not with them when Jesus came.

I do not know why Thomas was not there. I take it, from the context, that Thomas came after the Lord had left them, the same evening. I gather that either Thomas had loitered on the way, or was concerned about his own sorrow.

Thomas loved the Savior. You remember in chapter 11 when the Lord spoke about going to the resurrection of Lazarus, that Thomas said, "Let us go with Him, that we also may die with

Him." He believed that if Jesus went into the environs of Jerusalem, that the Jews would take Him and kill Him. And he was willing to pay the ultimate sacrifice for Him. He was also the one in chapter 14 who said, when the Lord told them He was going to His Father's house, "We don't know where You are going, so how can we know the way?"

This is the third mention of Thomas in John's Gospel. Did you ever stop to think what Thomas missed? He missed the peace the Lord had brought. He missed meeting Jesus face to face. He missed the gladness and joy the other disciples had. He missed those wonderful words of responsibility: "As My Father hath sent me, even so send I you." He missed this marvelous commission to be His living representative.

Thomas was the loser. For a whole week following this, the disciples were filled with joy and blessing. They had seen the Lord. He had appeared to them. He had challenged them. And they were living in the joyous thrill of meeting a risen Savior. Thomas for that whole week was so far down that he challenged their statement.

20:25. *The other disciples therefore said unto him, We have seen the Lord. But he said unto them, Except I shall see in his hands the print of the nails, and put my finger into the print of the nails, and thrust my hand into his side, I will not believe.*

"I know you fellows have given a testimony, and I know you're my friends, and I know the woman brought the same testimony, but I will not believe unless I see Him, unless I touch Him. I won't believe."

Notice that Thomas lay down the terms for his belief. I've had people say the same thing to me. "Unless I can see God do something, unless I feel it, unless God answers my prayers, I won't believe." They are lying down their terms for faith instead of believing what He has declared. This is not ignorance or even honest doubt. It is nothing other than intellectual pride.

My friend, there's not a day that you don't live by faith. You don't sit down and examine everything. We take the word of people in many things. Teachers, salesmen, mechanics, referees—we trust them to know their business. Is faith dependent upon feeling, or does faith depend on the Word of God?

I'm not holding anything against Thomas. I can understand his position. But the people who are this way do not carry that doubt through in every sphere of life; they wouldn't be living if they did.

Thomas Receives Proof (20:26-29)

How did the Lord meet Thomas in his doubt? If ever there were a picture of the tenderness and understanding and love of the Savior, it is right here.

> **20:26-27.** *And after eight days again his disciples were within, and Thomas with them: then came Jesus, the doors being shut, and stood in the midst, and said, Peace be unto you. Then saith he to Thomas, Reach hither thy finger, and behold my hands; and reach hither thy hand, and thrust it into my side: and be not faithless, but believing.*

The Lord didn't come this time because of the ten. He came especially for one person. He came especially to see Thomas. He didn't rebuke him. He didn't call him down for running away. He didn't even criticize him for not being at the last meeting. But the Lord, ever omniscient, did pick him right up on his challenge. He gave him unmistakable proof that He was indeed alive from the dead.

My Christian friend, you may be weak and stumbling. You may not know very much about the power and presence and fellowship of the Lord. You may be one of the lame sheep, or one of the dull students, or one of the wayward children. He'll come especially, just for you. He understands you. If you really mean business, He'll even meet you on your terms. I say, He came especially for Thomas.

> **20:28.** *And Thomas answered and said unto him,*

My Lord, and my God.

Did you ever realize that Thomas was a pious Jew who had been trained all his life in these words: "Hear, O Israel: The Lord our God is one Lord" (Deuteronomy 6:4)? Now he stands before Jesus, before His face, and says to Him, "My Lord and my God." You talk about a testimony to the deity of our Savior! And the Lord didn't say, "Stop it, Thomas, stop it!" He accepted his worship.

Oh, how wonderful that we can say, "He is my Lord and my God." And He is a real Man. He is touched with the feeling of my infirmities. He is able to succor those of us who are tested and tried. As God, "he is able also to save them to the uttermost that come unto God by him" (Hebrews 7:25). Truly we can say, "My Lord and my God."

20:29. *Jesus saith unto him, Thomas, because thou hast seen me, thou hast believed: blessed are they that have not seen, and yet have believed.*

In Isaiah 53:1 we read, "Who hath believed our report? and to whom is the arm of the Lord revealed?" The Lord is revealed to the man or woman who believes the report.

"Thomas, you have seen Me, and you are blessed because you have. You have cried out, 'My Lord and my God.' In that one little statement you have manifested your repentance and your faith, love, and devotion. That's because you have seen Me. More blessed are they who have not seen, and yet have believed." My friend, you and I are more blessed than Thomas.

"Ah," you say, "I would like to have had what Thomas had. He saw the Son of God with his eyes. He saw the body that had been nailed to the cross and was now in resurrection. If I could see that, my faith would be strong."

My friend, listen. Your faith is far stronger, and your blessing is far richer, because you have believed even though you haven't seen. The world says, "I'll believe it if I see it." The Word of God says to the believer, "Believe and you will see."

The Challenge of Christ's Appearances (20:30-31)

Let me close with these last two verses.

20:30-31. *And many other signs truly did Jesus in the presence of his disciples, which are not written in this book: But these are written, that ye might believe that Jesus is the Christ, the Son of God: and that believing ye might have life through his name.*

Many believe that when John wrote these two verses he had reference to all the four Gospels, or to the whole Gospel through John. And that may be true. It is true that in these four Gospels there is not a record of all that Jesus did. But may I suggest that John here is specifically referring to this one chapter? The Lord had appeared to Mary, to the apostles, to Thomas, and there are many other signs which He did to prove the certainty of His resurrection. But, says John, "I have chosen just these three instances (of Mary Magdalene, of the apostles, and of Thomas) to prove to you that the resurrection of our Lord is God's testimony to the world (and to you personally) that this Jesus of Nazareth is the Christ, the Son of God. By believing in Him, you will have everlasting life. I am writing these things that you might believe, and in believing you might have life in His name."

This Gospel starts by declaring that "in him was life" (1:4). And all the way through we have the revelation that Christ is life. Now the book closes with the evidence of the resurrection. "I have picked these things out for you to see that Jesus is the Messiah, the Son of God. By believing you can have life through His name."

John 21

Christ, The Chief Shepherd

Christ Again Appears to the Disciples (21:1-14)

The Disciples Join Peter to Go Fishing (21:1-3)

It almost seems as if John closes his Gospel at the end of the last chapter. But he selects another incident to add to this book. It is one of the eleven recorded post-resurrection appearances of the Lord Jesus.

> **21:1-2.** *After these things Jesus shewed himself again to the disciples at the sea of Tiberias; and on this wise shewed he himself. There were together Simon Peter, and Thomas called Didymus, and Nathanael of Cana in Galilee, and the sons of Zebedee, and two other of his disciples.*

You remember the Lord had told Mary Magdalene to tell the disciples He would meet them in Galilee. I'm sure these disciples were very happy to get out of Jerusalem and back to more friendly territory in Galilee. They waited in Galilee for the coming of the Lord.

> **21:3.** *Simon Peter saith unto them, I go a fishing. They say unto him, We also go with thee. They went forth, and entered into a ship immediately; and that night they caught nothing.*

"That night they caught nothing." Now, you may blame Peter for this. You may say, "Well, in Matthew 4 the Lord called Peter to catch men, not to catch fish." You can analyze it all you want, but it was quite a natural and normal thing for these men to do. They were fishermen. Here's a lake, a boat, a net. What's the logical thing to do? Go out and fish, of course. I can appreciate Peter, whether you do or not. I'm a fisherman, too.

One of the hardest things believers have to do is to wait for God's time. It is so hard to wait. King Saul couldn't wait for God's timing, and it was his downfall. This caused Elijah to fail, as well. We want to go our own way. But the Lord is so wonderful with us. He understands, even when no one else does.

Christ Produces a Miraculous Catch (21:4-6)

Mark how the Lord reveals Himself to these disciples.

> **21:4-6.** *But when the morning was now come, Jesus stood on the shore: but the disciples knew not that it was Jesus. Then Jesus saith unto them, Children, have ye any meat? They answered him, No. And he said unto them, Cast the net on the right side of the ship, and ye shall find. They cast therefore, and now they were not able to draw it for the multitude of fishes.*

We have two cases of fishing where the Lord told the men to let down a net. One is at the beginning of His ministry, and one is here. Peter was the outstanding character among the disciples in both incidents. In Luke 5 they were in Peter's boat. It was to him the Lord said, "Launch out into the deep, and let down your nets for the draught." And it was Peter who said, "Lord, we have toiled all night and caught nothing; nevertheless, at Your word I will let down the net. I acknowledge You as the captain of the boat. I will obey orders from You."

So Peter let down the net. And you remember the net was so full of fish it broke. His partners in the other ship had to come help him. Peter fell down before the Lord and said, "Depart from me; for I am a sinful man, O Lord."

Then the Lord Jesus said to Peter and the disciples, "Follow Me, and you will catch men alive."

But now they are at the lake without the Lord. They have fished all night and have caught nothing. And if you have gone out fishing all night, you're cold, you're discouraged, you're tired. There's no fish, and it is a gloomy outlook when you row toward shore.

But morning was coming, Jesus appeared on the shore and told them to cast their nets on the right side. The disciples didn't recognize Him at first, but they obeyed. Obedience brought a harvest just as it did in Luke 5. Obedience to Christ always brings a harvest. He knows where the fish are. He knows where to put the net. He knows what to do.

We talk about soul-winning. We talk about personal work. We talk about Christian service. All He asks is obedience; and when we obey Him, He guarantees a harvest.

The Disciples Follow Peter to Go Ashore (21:7-14)

21:7. *Therefore that disciple whom Jesus loved saith unto Peter, It is the Lord. Now when Simon Peter heard that it was the Lord, he girt his fisher's coat unto him, (for he was naked,) and did cast himself into the sea.*

When the nets became full of fish, John is the one who has the eyes to see, and Peter is the one who acts. You notice that with these two friends. They are as different as night and day. John is the man of vision. Peter is the man of action. John says, "It is the Lord." Peter jumps overboard. He forgets the boat, he forgets the fish, he forgets John. The Lord is there.

How eager are we as Christians to come into the presence of the Lord? You and I may find fault with Peter. He denies the Lord with oaths and curses. He makes the biggest brag and falls the lowest of

the eleven. But there is love there. There's a yearning for the
Savior.

When the disciples came to shore, the Lord had their breakfast
all ready for them.

> **21:8-11.** *And the other disciples came in a little
> ship; (for they were not far from land, but as it were
> two hundred cubits,) dragging the net with fishes. As
> soon then as they were come to land, they saw a fire of
> coals there, and fish laid thereon, and bread. Jesus
> saith unto them, Bring of the fish which ye have now
> caught. Simon Peter went up, and drew the net to land
> full of great fishes, an hundred and fifty and three:
> and for all there were so many, yet was not the net
> broken.*

You can see the Lord there on His knees, blowing the charcoal
and getting the flame up. I tell you it is a wonderful thing when you
go out fishing all day, especially when you catch nothing and
you're hungry and you're cold, and you come home and find the
pot's on the fire and the meal is ready. You've missed something if
you've never had that experience.

Notice the Lord doesn't go right after Peter here. He just fed
these men.

> **21:12-14.** *Jesus saith unto them, Come and dine.
> And none of the disciples durst ask him, Who art
> thou? knowing that it was the Lord. Jesus then
> cometh, and taketh bread, and giveth them, and fish
> likewise. This is now the third time that Jesus shewed
> himself to his disciples, after that he was risen from
> the dead.*

Here was their resurrected Lord on the beach with their breakfast, waiting on them. They just sat there. They didn't ask a question. They were full of awe. But they were perfectly content, full of
peace, full of satisfaction.

They were at the very place where the Lord had preached to the people from the boat. It was on this lake He had done it. It was here they had seen Him still the storm and muzzle the wind. It was on the edge of this lake He had fed the five thousand with five loaves and two fishes. From here He had gone to Jerusalem, had been crucified, had been buried, and had been raised again. And now He is feeding them. What a Savior!

Christ Speaks With Peter (21:15-23)

Christ Calls Peter to Love and Service (21.:15-17)

21:15-17. *So when they had dined, Jesus saith to Simon Peter, Simon, son of Jonas, lovest thou me more than these? He saith unto him, Yea, Lord; thou knowest that I love thee. He saith unto him, Feed my lambs. He saith to him again the second time, Simon, son of Jonas, lovest thou me? He saith unto him, Yea, Lord; thou knowest that I love thee. He saith unto him, Feed my sheep. He saith unto him the third time, Simon, son of Jonas, lovest thou me? Peter was grieved because he said unto him the third time, Lovest thou me? And he saith unto him, Lord, thou knowest all things; thou knowest that I love thee. Jesus saith unto him, Feed my sheep.*

Three times Peter before an open fire had denied his Lord (compare Luke 22 with John 18). And now three times before an open fire Christ gives him an opportunity to reverse that declaration. He says to Peter, "Do you love Me? Feed My lambs."

When these six men heard the Lord give Peter this responsibility, they may have thought, "Why Peter? He hasn't any right to be a leading apostle after he denied the Lord." Yet Jesus picked him out, and in front of the others said, "Peter, I give you responsibility to feed My lambs, to shepherd My sheep, and to feed My sheep." Why Peter? Because he had the prerequisite for service, which is wholehearted devotion to the Person of Christ Himself.

The Lord didn't say, "Simon, son of Jonas, will you preach for Me? Will you suffer for Me? Will you evangelize for Me? Will you sacrifice for Me? Will you believe in Me?" He didn't say that. Instead Christ asked, "Simon, son of Jonas, do you love Me more than these? Do you really love Me?" That is what He is after.

If I am to be a servant of the Lord, if I am to be one who is to feed the lambs and to shepherd the sheep and feed them, the first thing He asks of me is wholehearted devotion to Him personally. There are a great many bruised, wayward sheep that do need to be guarded and shepherded. Now you might not be able to preach or teach, or to be an evangelist or pastor. But you can guard and guide and feed some of the little lambs, these newborn babes in Christ. You can shepherd some of these dear wayward sheep back into the fold of fellowship. You can take the Word of God and give it to someone else in the best way you know how. All He asks is love.

And may I say, our service will be the expression of our love for Him. Christianity is not a dead thing, not a passive thing. It is an active thing. Life is always active. That doesn't mean I am going to shout from the housetops, but it does mean that I will reach out to the weak, the wayward, and the stumbling. Shepherds must have concern for the little lost ones and be willing to search for the sheep that get lost.

What did the Lord mean when He said, "Do you love Me more than these?"? Did He mean these fish, these boats, these other disciples? Jesus wanted to be first in Peter's affections before both things and others.

Now, I'm not going to take up these two words for "love" that are used here except to say that the Lord Jesus used the word *agape* in his first two questions. This is a high, intensive form of love. "Peter, do you love Me more than anything else in the world? Am I first in your devotion, in your affection? Do you love Me more than these?" Actually you can take this question two ways. Either He meant, "Am I first in your affection before all others?" or "Do you love Me more than these fellows love Me?"

Peter answered with *phileo.* "Lord, I have affection for You. But the love You're asking of me, Lord, is so beyond me. But yes, Lord. You know that I love You." Peter didn't say, "I love You more than any of these other fellows." He couldn't say that. One time he did boast and say, "Though all forsake You, though these other fellows run away, Lord, You can sure count on old Peter. I'm the one You can bank on, Lord." He doesn't say that now.

Love is the greatest experience in the world, but it carries the greatest responsibilities. It is the prerequisite for service. If your service is not an outflow of your love for the Lord personally, it will become a chore. You will soon give it up. And conversely, the less I love Him, the less I'll serve Him, and the less I'll talk about Him.

One of the greatest needs among Christians is for shepherds. Little is said in the Bible about praying for the unsaved. But my, there is much said about praying for the saved. But I won't pray for the saved, or the unsaved for that matter, unless I'm really devoted to the Lord and unless His love floods my heart. We need more intercessors. We need more shepherds. We need folk whose love for the Savior overflows to feed and shepherd others. But loving Christ and serving Him can bring suffering, as we shall see.

Christ Calls Peter to Suffering and Death (21:18-23)

21:18-19. *Verily, verily, I say unto thee, When thou wast young, thou girdedst thyself, and walkedst whither thou wouldest: but when thou shalt be old, thou shalt stretch forth thy hands, and another shall gird thee, and carry thee whither thou wouldest not. This spake he, signifying by what death he should glorify God. And when he had spoken this, he saith unto him, Follow me.*

Here the Lord told Peter that he would suffer and die. There are three reasons for death among Christians, as I've mentioned before. One can die because his work is finished here on earth. Paul could say, "The time of my departure is at hand. I have fought a good fight, I have finished my course, I have kept the faith" (2 Timothy 4:6-7).

One can also die prematurely under the chastisement of God. We have this in 1 Corinthians 11:30, where we read, "For this cause many are weak and sickly among you, and many sleep." We also have this in 1 Corinthians 5, 1 John 5, and Acts 5. In these passages death was caused by a moral problem. In 1 Timothy 1 we find that death can also be caused by a doctrinal problem.

Or one can die for the glory of God, which we have here in this chapter. It is not for you and me to judge the cause when one dies. We can well afford to leave that with the Lord. Suffice it to say that death can be for the glory of God, and it can come when our work is finished. Actually, a believer living in the will of God cannot die until his job is finished.

Notice what Peter does when the Lord tells him he will die for the glory of God.

21:20-23. *Then Peter, turning about, seeeth the disciple whom Jesus loved following; which also leaned on his breast at supper, and said, Lord, which is he that betrayeth thee? Peter seeing him saith to Jesus, Lord, and what shall this man do? Jesus saith unto him, If I will that he tarry till I come, what is that to thee? follow thou me. Then went this saying abroad among the brethren, that that disciple should not die: yet Jesus said not unto him, He shall not die; but, If I will that he tarry till I come, what is that to thee?*

Dear Peter did a very normal thing when he asked the Lord about John. Jesus' answer was abrupt. "What is that to thee? Peter, your responsibility is to follow Me. Never mind John. Never mind Thomas. Never mind the rest of them. Follow *Me.*"

Many of us say, "If I follow the Lord, He may lead me in a certain way that includes suffering. Why do I have to suffer when another believer doesn't? Is that fair?" Jesus says, "It doesn't matter what happens to the other believer. Follow Me."

Do you really love the Savior? Are you ready to follow Him? That is what He wants. But remember that love brings responsibility. His call to follow may mean suffering. But it is enough that He calls. And it is enough for us to rise and follow Him.

This may be the year when our Lord shall come. Look at the tremendous needs of the hour: the need for undershepherds, the need for people who love the Savior. We need to follow Him and manifest our love for Him by caring for His sheep and feeding His lambs.

Responding to the Claims of Christ (21:24-25)

21:24-25. *This is the disciple which testifieth of these things, and wrote these things: and we know that his testimony is true. And there are also many other things which Jesus did, the which, if they should be written every one, I suppose that even the world itself could not contain the books that should be written. Amen.*

In other words, if the world were filled with the books of what Jesus accomplished and what He did and said, it still would not receive the truth. My friend, have you received the truth? Have you read this far and realized that all is not right with your soul? You may be religious, you may be moral, you may be a wonderful person. But, and I say this very frankly, simply, and honestly, unless you are in right relationship with Christ, you have no life. Unless you put your trust in this One who is the Son of God, the Savior, the Lord, you have no life in you.

"Why," you say, "That's drawing a pretty fine line, is it not?"

That's true. The Word of God draws it very fine. Broad is the way that leads to destruction. Narrow is the way that leads to life. If life is in Christ, if these claims of His are true (and He proved these claims by rising from the dead), then it is required of you to turn to Him and be saved. Without the shedding of blood there is no remission of sin (Hebrews 9:22). He is your sacrificial Lamb, slain at Calvary, to pay the penalty that you deserve. He died so that you would not have to die eternally in punishment for your sins. Receive Him. "But as many as received him, to them gave he power to become the sons of God, even to them that believe on his name" (1:12).

But supposing you don't believe. What then? Then, my friend, you shall die in your sins. Hebrews 9:27 says, "It is appointed unto men once to die, but after this the judgment." The difference between life and death is Jesus Christ. He is the difference between heaven and hell. He is the difference between entering the presence of God with joy, or standing before Him in your sins. "These things are written that you might believe that Jesus is the Christ, the son of God; and that by believing you might have life through his name."

And my Christian friend, may I say a word to you? If you believe this to be true, then it is your responsibility to impart this truth to others. I question if there is much time left to us. It has pleased the Father to use men and women like you and me. He doesn't use angels. He doesn't use the great of this world. He uses redeemed sinners like you and me. Let us be wise Christians, understanding the will of the Lord, redeeming the time, being filled with the Spirit, walking carefully lest we fall along the way.

I would plead with you, men and women. I would plead with you, young people. If you believe that Jesus is the Christ, the Son of God, pass the good news on to sinners that they may also know the Savior.

Our Savior has said to all men, "Come unto me . . . and I will give you rest." He is ever the Seeker. He is the One who was lifted up so that He might draw all men unto the Father. He is the altogether lovely One.

Scripture Index

Scripture Index

Scripture Index

Scripture Index

Scripture Index

Scripture Index